RELIGION, CONFLICT
AND COEXISTENCE IN IRELAND

Essays presented to
Monsignor Patrick J. Corish

Right Reverend Monsignor Patrick J. Corish, M.A., D.D., M.R.I.A.

Religion, Conflict and Coexistence in Ireland

ESSAYS PRESENTED TO
MONSIGNOR PATRICK J. CORISH

Edited by R. V. Comerford,
Mary Cullen, Jacqueline R. Hill
and Colm Lennon

GILL AND MACMILLAN

Published in Ireland by
Gill and Macmillan Ltd
Goldenbridge
Dublin 8
with associated companies in
Auckland, Delhi, Gaborone, Hamburg, Harare,
Hong Kong, Johannesburg, Kuala Lumpur, Lagos, London,
Manzini, Melbourne, Mexico City, Nairobi,
New York, Singapore, Tokyo
© The Contributors, 1990
Index by Priscilla O'Connor
Print origination by Irish Typesetting and Publishing Ltd, Galway
Printed by Billing & Sons Ltd, Worcester

British Library Cataloguing in Publication Data

Religion, conflict and coexistence in Ireland: essays
presented to Monsignor Patrick J. Corish.
1. Ireland. Christian church, history
I. Comerford, R.V. (Richard Vincent) II. Corish, Patrick J.
(Patrick Joseph), *1921–*
274.15

ISBN 0-7171-1736-7

Contents

Contents continued

Contributors

Candy, Catherine: MA (NUI Maynooth), 1987

Cummins, Seamus: MA (NUI Maynooth), 1977

Dooley, Terence: MA (NUI Maynooth), 1986

Gahan, Daniel: BA (NUI Maynooth), 1976; MA (Loyola, Chicago), 1979; PhD (Kansas), 1986

Griffin, Brian: MA (NUI Maynooth), 1983

Henry, Ann Gráinne: MA (NUI Maynooth), 1986

Leighton, C . D. A.: MA (NUI Maynooth), 1985

Lennon, Colm: MA (NUI University College Dublin), 1975; PhD (NUI Maynooth), 1987

Liechty, Joseph: PhD (NUI Maynooth), 1987

Mooney, Desmond: MA (NUI Maynooth), 1986

Murphy, Celestine: BA (NUI Maynooth), 1977

Walshe, Helen Coburn: MA (NUI Maynooth), 1985

Woods, C. J.: PhD (Nottingham), 1969

Editors

Comerford, Richard Vincent: *Professor of Modern History, Maynooth*
Cullen, Mary: *Lecturer in Modern History, Maynooth*
Hill, Jacqueline R.: *Lecturer in Modern History, Maynooth*
Lennon, Colm: *Lecturer in Modern History, Maynooth*

Preface

PATRICK Joseph Corish was born at Ballycullane, County Wexford, on 17 March 1921. Following secondary education at St Peter's College, Wexford, he entered Maynooth in 1938 and was ordained in 1945 for the diocese of Ferns, to the past, present and future of whose people he has remained devoted. In 1947, having received a doctorate from the Pontifical University of Maynooth, he was appointed Professor of Ecclesiastical History, a position which he held until 1975, except for the academic year 1967–68 when he was President of the College.

Every student of Theology in Maynooth during that period — of whom almost eighteen hundred became priests — attended his courses. Priests or laymen, most of them recall Professor Corish's lecturing as one of the highlights of their student days. Two lectures per week for four years in an era when attendance at lectures was mandatory provided fairly thorough acquaintance with a lecturer's style and substance. Erudition alone would not have secured the interest and attention that Professor Corish's lectures commanded in an audience consisting entirely of students who had already graduated in Arts, Science or Philosophy. His learning was presented with an unforgettable, infectious enthusiasm. That in its turn was based not only on the scholar's delight in his subject but on strong conviction about the centrality of history to the study of theology.

Numerous students in those years also benefited from Professor Corish's advice and counsel on an individual basis. He was one of those who led the Maynooth teaching staff away from an older attitude of aloofness towards students and their problems.

In 1975 Professor Corish was translated to the chair of Modern History in the Faculty of Arts, a post that he held until his retirement in 1988. During that time over two thousand undergraduates took courses in Modern History and experienced the scholarship and sparkle that continued to characterise his teaching. In addition he brought to his tenure an outstanding contribution on many other fronts, of which two may be selected for special mention.

The first of these was his combination of concern for the maintenance of the highest standards of academic excellence with an ability both to encourage those who at times fell short of these and to empathise with the problems faced by individual students, lay and seminarian, men and women. This combination will be vouched for with gratitude and respect by the many past and present students who have had personal experience of it.

The second was his commitment to the development of a vigorous postgraduate school as an essential component of a dynamic department of History. This involved him in painstaking and untiring academic guidance as well as continual efforts to increase financial provision for postgraduate study at Maynooth, to improve the facilities available to the students, and to seek out opportunities for their further study abroad. During most of his tenure economic conditions made the achievement of some of these objectives very difficult. The degree of success he achieved is a reflection of his energy in their pursuit. In acknowledgment of this success the present volume contains essays by twelve former students of his in the department of Modern History.

While the chronological range of this collection—from the sixteenth to the twentieth centuries—reflects the work of the department, it falls far short of the span of Monsignor Corish's own expertise. He is one of the very few scholars who is an authority in his field over the entire course of Irish history from the Patrician period to the present.

It may surprise some scholars of a younger generation to realise that when Patrick J. Corish began teaching in the 1940s ecclesiastical history was still regarded by many as a branch of Catholic apologetics in which, for example, the Spanish Inquisition might have to be defended. Church history as taught by Professor Corish was an incomparably richer enterprise. Instead of a polemical, desiccated and essentially fearful and defensive exercise, it was an intellectual exploration which had nothing to fear from the wider world of scholarship. The objective was not to provide ammunition for argument but to achieve understanding. If church history in Ireland now stands confidently in the mainstream of historical scholarship, credit is due to many people, but to nobody more than Patrick J. Corish. It is a change that can easily be taken for granted by those who are unaware of the barriers that had to be crossed. Comparison of the various contributions to the *History of Irish Catholicism*, edited by Professor Corish himself in the 1960s, illustrates the transition in progress.

Patrick J. Corish's role as a pioneer must be seen in the context of the wider developments in Irish historiography associated with the names of R. Dudley Edwards and T. W. Moody. He enjoyed warm professional and personal relations with both, and worked with them on various bodies including the Royal Irish Academy and the Irish Manuscripts Commission.

The work of the latter body has absorbed over the years a great quantity of Monsignor Corish's time. His attention to this side of the historian's task—rescuing and making generally available the raw materials of the trade—is further evidenced by his prodigious efforts as editor of *Archivium Hibernicum* for almost thirty years.

An essential aspect of Patrick J. Corish's contribution to Irish ecclesiastical studies reflected in his later works, particularly *The Catholic community in the seventeenth and eighteenth centuries* and *The Irish Catholic experience*, is his promotion of a wider view of the church as an institution. This recognises that 'the church' is not the same as 'the clergy', and that the history of the laity as members of the church is an essential part of any attempt to understand the nature of ecclesiastical structures and forms. Professor Corish has been keenly concerned with establishing the place of religion within the community, studying facets of daily Christian life and the impact of social and cultural factors upon pious practice. In this pursuit he has introduced models drawn from European religious studies and has thereby enhanced the standing of ecclesiastical history as a scholarly discipline.

The integration of Irish ecclesiastical history into the totality of historical experience in which Monsignor Corish has played so important a part has involved broadening the definition of the 'church' to incorporate the idea of the Christian community and it has also depended on the adoption of a rigorous scholarly apparatus which has been brought to bear on the entire subject matter, institutional church as well as the laity. At the same time, running through his work is a strand that is identifiable as the outlook of a committed Christian and pastor. It used to be contended by some in the heyday of scientific certainty that sound scholarship in any field could proceed only on the basis of complete scepticism and detachment. Today, when scientists themselves have drawn back from the claim that science can explain everything, and have admitted to possessing attitudes towards their own work which sound very like 'faith', the virtues of a religious belief in one who studies ecclesiastical history are more immediately apparent. The notion that the religiously committed are *ipso facto* disqualified from the scholarly study of religious history is at this stage as indefensible as the proposition that they alone are so qualified.

It goes without saying that Patrick J. Corish's combination of scholarly rigour and religious commitment has been employed for the most part in the field of Catholic ecclesiastical history. But the combination leads naturally to appreciation of the history of other churches. It may perhaps be said that one of the obstacles to a deeper understanding of the religious history of Ireland has been a tendency (not confined to the members of any one denomination) to regard the traditions of others as political systems, means of attaining or clinging to power, or as simply the product of ignorance and perversity. A major result of the transformation of the historiography of religion in Ireland has been the possibility of approaching one another's traditions as religions (whatever else they may also have been) and of moving from that perception to an appreciation of the difficulties posed by the presence of different religious traditions in Ireland. As a matter of deliberate policy students in the department of Modern History under Patrick J. Corish's chairmanship have been provided with special courses focusing on the history of Protestant as well as Catholic communities in Ireland and elsewhere. That dimension of the department's work is reflected in this collection.

Also in reflection of the department's work, these essays are not confined to any strict notion of what constitutes religious or ecclesiastical history. Some treat of the inner life of churches or religious individuals, while others at the opposite end of the spectrum deal with religious affiliations as a source of contention in areas of national or local life not themselves essentially religious. But even in Ireland religious differences do not always have to be a source of conflict and several contributions to this volume bring to light a measure of practical coexistence in every century from the sixteenth to the twentieth.

This volume is offered as a token of gratitude and respect by the editors and the contributors on behalf of themselves and many others: those others who offered contributions which for reasons of space it was not possible to include; all those students past and present who have benefited from the teaching and counsel of Patrick J. Corish; and the various admirers inside and outside Maynooth who have been urging that he be offered this form of tribute at this stage in a distinguished career from which so much more is still expected.

The editors are grateful to the contributors and would-be contributors for their co-operation and patience. We thank the Maynooth Scholastic Trust for a generous grant in aid of publication. We are indebted to Dr C. J. Woods and Elma Collins, as also to Una Jordan, Breeda Behan, Catherine Heslin, Bridget Lunn and Priscilla O'Connor.

R. V. Comerford
Mary Cullen
Jacqueline Hill
Colm Lennon

Maynooth, December 1989

COLM LENNON

1. The chantries in the Irish Reformation: the case of St Anne's Guild, Dublin, 1550-1630

> For as much as the chantries there [in Ireland] are yet undissolved, and that the incumbents thereof make spoil of the same as in giving leases of them for so many years, as in time neither the king shall have any profit whereof, nor yet any godliness thereby maintained, for avoiding whereof, and for the maintenance of [a] university, it may please his majesty to direct his highness's commission for dissolution of the said chantries, and the revenues thereof to be applied to the use of the university . . . and sundry free schools [to] be erected upon the same for education of youth there.
>
> (Archbishop George Browne's plan for a university of Dublin, late 1547, P.R.O., S.P. 61/1/10)

ARCHBISHOP Browne drew up his proposals for the founding of a university and free schools in his diocese of Dublin while on a visit to England in late 1547. He was aware that the process of abolition of the chantries and lay fraternities in that country was under way as part of the new phase of the Reformation under King Edward VI. As the pattern of change in ecclesiastical management in Ireland in the 1530s was almost a replica of that established in England, Browne would have expected the dismantling of the Irish chantries to have taken place under the supervision of a royal commission such as was being set up for England and Wales.[1] Among the benefits envisaged as flowing from the change of use of chantry buildings and revenues were opportunities for advancing education. Such a consequence was deemed to be particularly auspicious, and perhaps necessary, as, besides fulfilling their primary function of providing for priests to say or chant masses for the repose of souls of deceased members and benefactors, some chantries and guilds had schools or colleges attached to them.[2] Although Archbishop Browne had a low opinion of the chantries as maintainers of 'godliness' he was at one with those who believed that their resources could be applied effectively to the fostering of second- and third-level education.

Browne's hopes for the foundation of a university at Dublin were eventually realised almost fifty years later with the opening of Trinity College, but the chantries remained undissolved in Ireland. Another effort to appropriate the income from these institutions for academic purposes was made by Luke Challoner, the leading fellow of the college in its first decade and a half of existence. He drew up a lengthy catalogue of the 'concealed' lands of the chantries and fraternities and secured the approval of King James I for the conversion of the properties to the use of the university.[3] As the chantries had not been vested in the crown, however, it was necessary to take measures to ensure royal possession of the lands and properties. Proceedings undertaken by state agents against individual religious corporations in the court of king's bench served to prove that the fraternities at least had the protection of their charters of incorporation.[4] In 1614 the heads of a bill for acquiring royal possession of the chantry lands were drawn up for presentation to the parliament then sitting in Dublin but the legislation was not proceeded with.[5] Various attempts were made by lay and ecclesiastical figures in the succeeding century to resolve the issue of the status of these pre-Reformation foundations, but without success. There were at least a couple of cases of chantries in Dublin surviving through the eighteenth century and one, that of the Blessed Virgin in the church of St Nicholas Within, was in existence at the time of the disestablishment of the Church of Ireland in 1869, over three hundred years after the act for the dissolution of the chantries was passed in England.[6]

A good deal of scholarly attention has been devoted to the subject of the English chantries and fraternities and the impact of their dissolution upon society.[7] The general consensus is that the religious guilds played a significant part in the lives of the laity in the fifteenth and early sixteenth centuries. In England and Wales, as in Ireland, there were three kinds of institution under lay supervision or endowment which provided the spiritual benefit of services for the repose of souls of the deceased. The trade and craft guilds normally had chapels in

parish churches in which specially appointed priests said or
chanted mass for dead members. Chantries were endowed by
private individuals to support priests to pray for their relatives
and themselves in perpetuity. Religious guilds or fraternities
were established by royal charter specifically for the purpose of
providing obituarial masses for members. To a greater extent
than the chantries themselves (which tended to be founded by
the wealthiest in the community), the religious guilds, their
membership drawn from all orders and ranks, were central to
the affirmation of Christian kinship in town and county through
the rituals and privileges associated with those institutions.
Poor brothers and sisters as well as rich could be assured of
future spiritual aid through the keeping of their obits, while
sharing in the fellowship of patron's day festivities and the
practical benefits offered by many, such as schooling, financial
assistance and medical care. Loyalty to the fraternities is attested
by the evidence of the wills of many individuals in the decades
before the 1530s and 1540s who bequeathed sums, large and
small, and objects to the religious guilds.[8] There is less agreement among scholars as to the effects of the dismantling of the
system of obituarial prayer and intercession. Some see the
English chantries and fraternities as having been ripe for
dissolution because of the widespread prevalence of decay
through indifference and loss of zeal. Furthermore the Protestant attack on belief in Purgatory, combined with the vitiation
of devotion to patron saints (to whom guilds were always
dedicated) as intercessors may have led to a weakening of the
perception of religious corporations as efficacious in the achievement of salvation.[9] Others, however, have represented as
deleterious in religious and social terms the disappearance of
this form of pious practice. In particular the 'spoliation' of the
religious guilds and chantries deprived the lay members and
benefactors of the opportunities for appointing chaplains and
chantry priests, thereby facilitating a marked shift in the ecclesiastical balance of power in favour of the clergy.[10]

By contrast the Irish chantries and guilds have not been
studied to any great extent. It has been pointed out that the
strength of kinship institutions among the Gaelic population in
the late middle ages may have rendered fraternities inapplicable

in many parts of the island.[11] There is ample evidence to suggest, however, that lay associations were popular in parishes throughout the English areas during the period.[12] In the absence of an exhaustive visitation register such as emanated from the work of the commissions in Edwardian England, however, (and such as exist for the monasteries at the time of their dissolution in Ireland) the exact number of institutions is not known. We do know that several guilds and chantries survived the promulgation of reformed doctrines in mid-Tudor Ireland and thereafter,[13] but little or no research has been carried out into the effects of social and political, as well as religious, changes of the latter half of the Tudor era upon these remnants of the devotional corporateness of the late middle ages. Were the Irish fraternities similar to their English counterparts in having lost their *raison d'être* by the mid-sixteenth century? To what extent does the history of the surviving institutions after 1550 reveal the *terminus ad quem* of those changes which have been diagnosed as setting in in the case of the English guilds? Or did they, as Mgr Corish has suggested, prove to be vital enough to provide a source of assurance for the key urban patrician element as its members changed from nominal conformity to the state religion to commitment to Tridentine Catholicism?[14]

We are fortunate that in the case of one Dublin fraternity, that of St Anne in the parish of St Audoen, there is extant, uniquely for England or Ireland, a mass of ordered documentation spanning the centuries from the fifteenth to the nineteenth, and allowing for a close scrutiny to be made of the decades immediately after the introduction of the Reformation into Ireland.[15] In essaying this task I wish to raise the questions posed above in relation to the history of St Anne's guild in the period from the 1550s to the 1620s, by which time the pattern of religious allegiances had stabilised. Because of the absence of comparative documentation it is impossible to say whether the guild was typical or not, but the very survival of such detailed records from a time of great upheaval may enable us to understand the part played by the guild membership. It will be useful to set the study in the context of a very brief review of the growth of the Dublin fraternities and chantries down to the 1530s, and to assess the changes of that time which may have altered the purpose of the lay religious foundations and most particularly that of the institution chosen for examination here.

The religious guild of St Anne was one of at least six urban and five rural lay confraternities in the Dublin area in the early sixteenth century.[16] Besides several private chantries, such as that of the Eustace family in the Portlester chapel in St Audoen's and the St Lawrence family in Kilbarrack, the trade guilds also provided facilities for the celebration of masses for the dead by chaplains who served the guild chapels in the parish churches and monasteries.[17] In all there were up to thirty institutions of varying size and with a range of devotions in Dublin and environs which had as one of their functions the benefiting of deceased members or individuals by remitting the sojourn of their souls in Purgatory. While some offered secular advantages such as schooling or poor relief, all of the fraternities, guilds and chantries shared the characteristic of being lay-run with lay prerogative in the appointment of clergy. Apart from a couple of fraternities which catered for special interests, such as that of the Blessed Virgin Mary comprising English merchants resident in Dublin and based in the chapel of Mary of Grace at the end of the great bridge,[18] the religious guilds embraced men and women of humble and middling station as well as members of the mercantile élite. Testimony to the attractiveness of the fraternities for persons of modest means may be found in many wills dating from the late fifteenth century. Among the bequests which most testators left to the church, including their parishes and the religious orders, were several for the maintenance of guild personnel and property. For example, in his will, dated 1476, Nicholas Delaber of Balrothery, County Dublin, left the sum of two nobles for the fraternity of the Blessed Virgin in his parish, and also in that year Richard Whitaker bequeathed 3s. 4d to the same institution.[19] In 1471 John Kempe willed that two acres of rye be set aside to benefit the fraternity of St Canice in Hollywood.[20] Sums were also appointed for supporting devotional rites associated with fraternities and chantries, such as the keeping of lights before chapel altars in Crumlin, Swords and Clondalkin, for example, and the maintenance of images such as that of St Katherine in Lusk.[21] Most of the bequests simply went towards the support of guild chaplains of whom there could be several ministering at certain times in some foundations. Very wealthy citizens sometimes left large amounts of money or property in their wills for the specific purpose of maintaining priests to chant anniversary masses for themselves and their families, but within the framework of existing guilds. Thus, for example, Sir Robert Dowdall gave 100 marks for the living expenses of two priests to be supernumerary to the six chaplains of St Anne's guild with the duty of keeping his mind day.[22] The endowment of obits through the guilds and chantries continued to be a feature of the testaments of men and women up to the eve of the Elizabethan religious settlement in 1560, showing the appeal of the belief in the propitiary role of masses for the dead.[23]

With the implementation of state-sponsored religious reforms in the period beginning with the later 1530s, the prevailing environment became alien if not lethal for the carrying on of guild devotions. Although members of the Irish church were not exposed to the full force of the Henrician *Injunctions* which required an English Bible to be placed in every parish church and the extinguishing of lights before altars and removal of images,[24] the regime of Archbishop Browne in Dublin from 1537 onwards revealed the official disapprobation of 'superstitious' practices such as pilgrimages and veneration of shrines and images. Thus many of the rituals attached to the practices of fraternities were called into question, although not formally quashed. While major shrines such as those of Our Lady of Trim, the Baculus Iesu in Christ Church and the crucifix at Ballyboggan were suppressed, many of the minor cults appear to have escaped the attention of the commissioners for destroying images.[25] The fate of the cycle of the Dublin mystery plays performed at Corpus Christi annually with members of the guild of Corpus Christi as leading participants is not known, but there is a reference to a performance as late as 1553.[26] Archbishop Browne complained about the holding of stations of the cross and a play of the passion on Palm Sunday in 1538 at St John's well at Kilmainham, but at that stage had no control over the Hospital of St John of Jerusalem there which supported the pious enactments.[27] We have seen that Browne supported the suppression of the Irish chantries and fraternities in the Edwardian period and he gave his backing to the rigorous campaign for abolishing many older practices such as pilgrimages, veneration of saints and sacramentals such as holy water and candles.[28] Clearly such guild rituals as processions to places of worship, the keeping holy of patronal days and the very celebration of mass for the deceased were imperilled, if not ended, at least temporarily. A revival of these practices would have been possible in the reign of Queen Mary as would their continuation in the early phase of lenience in the enforcement of the Elizabethan settlement. There are signs, however, that some atrophying of quasi-religious customs of the trade guilds was taking place under the aegis of changing official attitudes. The guild merchant or Trinity guild, which had its chapel in Christ Church, took the opportunity to change the symbol of a crucifix on the seal of the corporation to that of a ship under sail.[29] In July 1563 the guild of butchers were alleged to have refused to 'keep their light' on the eve of the feast of St John the Baptist in the Fleshambles for four or five years, while the fishmongers had dispensed with their fire and light in Fish Street on the eve of St Peter's feast-day.[30] The city council, which remained circumspectly aloof from religious controversy, insisted that these practices should be maintained on pain of fines, declaring that 'their wilfull attempts if they be not reformed will give boldness to outhers to disorder themselfs in higher points'.[31] Civic order rather than piety lay behind the council's concern but the guildsmen's recalcitrance may point to a fading of enthusiasm for traditional customs.

While there was no formal suppression of the religious guilds, the system of lay-sponsored arrangement of services for the dead did suffer a blow from official action in the dissolution of the religious orders. The obits endowed through chantries and the religious services of trade guilds which were entrusted to monks and friars were swept away with the closure of the religious houses after 1539. The chantry established by John Chever in the abbey of St Mary in 1474 would have been abolished with the suppression of that institution in 1539.[32] Among the trade guilds, those of the barber-surgeons (dedicated to St Mary Magdalen), the carpenters, millers, masons and heliers (dedicated to the Blessed Virgin and St Thomas), and the weavers (dedicated to the Blessed Virgin and All Saints) would have lost their guild chapels and altars in St John's, Newgate, St

Thomas's abbey and the White Friars, respectively.[33] Severe curtailment of the religious practices associated with the trade guilds may have hastened the disappearance of this dimension altogether. Although they had their chapels in the parish churches, the religious guilds could be adversely affected by the monastic suppressions. The guild of St Anne, for example, was threatened with the loss of some of the properties which it held of the religious orders or had leased to them. Thus the tenements in the parish of St Audoen, which were parcels of the land of St Mary's abbey, were probably relinquished by the guild as tenants, but the two valuable properties to the west of the city, the great and little farms of Kilmainham, were salvaged, despite their being claimed by the occupier at the time, the prior of the Hospital of St John.[34] By and large the religious guilds and the chantries survived the upheavals of the mid-Tudor period with their real property intact, their chapels still standing and their devotions unsuppressed.

It was against this background that the masters, wardens and members of the guild of St Anne sustained a corporate existence in the Elizabethan and early Stuart periods. The leadership showed great skill in adapting the operations of the fraternity to the circumstances of the time. A roll of prestigious members and valuable assets of land and buildings aided the resilience which was evident on many occasions, especially in the face of government inquiries and legal proceedings. A resuscitation of lost religious purpose was fostered by the defensiveness and solidarity which outside pressures brought into being, and it was in this context that the guild may have played its part in the establishment of a Counter-Reformation church in the Dublin area.

For three decades after the passage of the Reformation laws in parliament in 1560 the officers of the guild of St Anne concentrated on secular matters, especially the shepherding of the possessions which had accumulated in the century and more since the guild's foundation charter, December 1430.[35] There was, however, a period of transition during which long-standing customs were acknowledged if in restrained fashion. The last recorded obit for which provision was made was in 1545 at the behest of Alexander Beswick and his wife, Alison Fitzsimon.[36] Certainly the traditional rituals were to be followed in this mind:

a *dirige* by note on the vigil with five 'pryketts' of wax burning, and a requiem mass by note on the anniversary with the same sacramentals.[37] No further reference occurs to the keeping of anniversaries of deceased members but chaplains were appointed to minister at the altars of the guild in St Audoen's down to 1564. Four appointments were made in the period from 1549 to that date, those of Sir John Rochford, Sir Nicholas Corr, Thomas Caddell and, ironically, one George Browne, all for life, and, in the case of the first three, at a salary of eight marks with board and accommodation in the college of Blakeney's Inns.[38] None of the deeds of appointment mentions the names of the altars at which the chaplains were to officiate as had been customary, and only in the case of the first, that of Rochford on 26 August 1549, was the customary duty of the guild in the matter of finding 'all ornaments for service, with bread, wine and wax, and other necessaries' alluded to.[39] The principal responsibility of the chaplains was to 'sing at all divine service' in St Audoen's, scarcely different from the usual formula.[40] Two clerks were also provided for out of the revenues of St Anne's guild, possibly on foot of bequests from members. The appointees in the 1540s, William Fynnyn and Robert Fitzsimon, were to be engaged generally in the worship and pastoral affairs of St Audoen's parish. Among Fynnyn's duties, for which he received seven marks per annum, were singing and reading daily in the choir and attending the parish priest on his sick calls.[41] Fitzsimon's annuity was £8 for which he was expected to play the organ at all services, principal feasts and holy days.[42] In the case of Fynnyn's appointment the guild and the proctors and parishioners of St Audoen's were joint nominators, though the salary came from guild funds. Co-operation between the officers of St Anne's guild and the representatives of the parish continued until the early seventeenth century.

Circumspect management of the affairs of the guild by the masters and wardens for much of the Elizabethan period facilitated this concordance between fraternal and parochial interests. Elected for terms of three years, the officers swore to maintain the revenues and rights of the guild, according to the terms of the oaths which survive from 1584.[43] Gone were the promise of homage to the patron saint and the reference to religious practices which were contained in the oaths of entry of the fifteenth century.[44] The masters continued to be drawn from the mercantile élite, all of those elected from the early sixteenth century to the end of the 1620s being aldermen of the corporation.[45] Usually the master came to the office in the year immediately following his mayoralty and thus had garnered much experience in the fields of administration and commerce. The wardens assisted the masters closely, there being two elected at a time. From the 1540s onwards one of the wardens serving at any time was a merchant and the other, following a long-standing custom up to 1571, was one of the chaplains who were evidently full members of the guild.[46] With the death of George Browne in 1571 after a wardenship of several years, his place as long-serving official was taken by Laurence Enose who was clerk of St Audoen's parish in the early 1560s.[47] With his retirement in 1594 both wardenships came to be held by merchants.[48]

Until the decision was taken by the members in 1597 to vote funds for the restoration of St Anne's chapel in St Audoen's, at that time 'old and ruynous', there had been no vestige of the special religious function of the guild since the appointment of the chantry priest in 1564.[49] The records are devoted almost entirely to the leasing of the properties in town and county and the collection of revenues from lessees. The educational role of the guild appears to have lapsed completely in the later sixteenth century but its social and charitable concerns were manifested in the 1590s.[50] In 1593 £10 was awarded from guild funds to the proctors of the parish for general repairs and another £10 for the restoration of the north-western battlement of St Audoen's.[51] In the same year the members donated £6 for the relief of poverty, and four years later, in a time of dearth, they attempted to relieve the burden on parishioners by lending £50 to the proctors for the repair of the steeple and the replacement of a clock, damaged by the great gunpowder explosion in March 1597.[52] The records of guild meetings from the 1570s preserve a silence about the activities of the priests, and whether they continued their ministry. The college premises where they had had their chambers were ruinous in 1588 and major repair work was undertaken in 1597.[53] Within the church building only the altar of St Anne among the original six guild chapels survived and it may have been out of use for many years before its restoration began in 1597. In 1619 the stipendiaries appeared in a new guise. The chantry priests were termed singing men (of whom there were six), the clerks became choristers and an organist played on Sundays and holy days. All were paid by the guild: the singing men received 6 marks, the choristers £2.13.4 and the organist £10 per annum. In addition the parson of St Audoen's was granted twenty marks a year from guild funds.[54]

A survey of the membership over a period of eight decades from the 1540s reveals certain characteristics which strengthened the guild and sustained its sense of purpose. Continuity of family associations with St Anne's fraternity among the patriciate of Dublin is a significant feature. The descendants of several gentry and merchant foundation members were active participants in guild affairs in the period under review. Walter Tyrell was among those listed in the royal charter of 1430, for example, and a namesake was master of the guild in the mid-1540s.[55] The latter Walter's son, John Tyrell, was warden for some years at the turn of the century.[56] Also represented among the membership were the Barnewall, White and Cusack families, all of which shared in the setting up of the guild.[57] The majority of those admitted to membership within the three-generational span after 1550 were closely related to deceased or living members. There are at least three examples of succession of membership directly through three generations: fathers, sons and grandsons of the Malone family (John, Edmund and William), the Plunket family (Henry, Thomas and Robert) and the Sedgrave family (Christopher, Walter and James).[58] The presence of wealthy bakers among the early members and benefactors suggests that there may have been an association with that trade, many practitioners of which lived and worked in Cook Street at the back of St Audoen's.[59] The link was maintained in the later sixteenth century through the membership of the prosperous Browne family of bakers in the guild. In the early seventeenth century the assembly hall of the guild members in Blakeney's Inns was described as the 'bakers' hall in the college of St Anne's guild', indicating that the autonomous fraternity of bakers had been using the premises for some time previously.[60] The connection between trade and religious guild (both dating from the fifteenth century) may have afforded some protection from official scrutiny in the later Tudor period for St Anne's fraternity, if the interests of the two associations appeared to be intertwined. One further source of reinforcement for the membership was the admission of women, three of whom are listed as sisters in the early seventeenth century, viz. Anna Sedgrave, Margaret Stephens and Katherine Barnewall.[61]

Of great importance for the survival of St Anne's guild was its operation under the aegis of the civic corporation. As in the case of some religious fraternities in England such as St George's in Norwich, for example,[62] St Anne's may have succeeded in adapting to the post-Reformation circumstances by stressing its role as adjunct to the city council in providing members with opportunities for investment in property and for socialising in convivial conditions. The membership was heavily representative of the influential coterie of twenty-four aldermen who were a force in civic administration and in city-state relations.[63] It has been noted already that the position of master was always held by an alderman and ex-mayor, and the vast majority of the non-clerical wardens elected between 1550 and 1630 were of that elevated rank. In that same period there were over seventy known enrolments of new members into the fraternity. Of these at least forty, or 57 per cent, were members of the aldermen's bench of the corporation. In 1584, fifteen of the bench of twenty-four aldermen were brethren of the guild of St Anne and in 1600 twelve had been enrolled.[64] Thus the fraternity was a kind of shadow body to the corporation. Possessed in itself of full corporate powers through its charter, it had at least half of its membership in common with the municipal body. It had a similar headship, the master and two wardens reflecting the leadership of the corporation by the mayor and two sheriffs. As with the greater body there were close ties of marriage and business partnership among the members with strong traditions of participation within individual families (with the notable addition of women). Tied in with the commercial and trading network of the city through the involvement of merchants, bakers and other tradesmen, the guild, like the civic corporation, was entitled to hold and lease lands, houses, shops and other premises which came into its possession. As the umbrella body, through the tightly-knit group of aldermen, built an impressive edifice of municipal privilege and autonomy in the latter half of the sixteenth century, a subsidiary association such as St Anne's guild could enjoy protection and scope for its activities.[65] It was the most conspicuous activity of the guild after the 1550s — the leasing of property — which proved to be an incentive for so many eminent citizens to become involved.

At its incorporation in 1430 the guild of St Anne was permitted to hold lands and premises to the value of 100 marks yearly to allow for the maintenance of six chantry priests. Pious testators in the succeeding century donated properties to ensure that that income would be available without the necessity of purchase of lands on the part of the guild's officers. The surviving collection of leases (of which there are 841) shows that there was a lively pattern of transactions involving guild property during the fifteenth and sixteenth centuries, and thereafter. For the 1560s to the 1590s the records do not have any reference to the disbursement of income from guild rents. As is clear from the account book begun in 1584 the principal concern of the guild's members at that time was to 'reform the neckligence and abusses' which had for a long time affected the collection of revenues and the enforcement of guild rights.[66] Backdated to 1555 are the accounts of the three auditors appointed on 25 February 1584,[67] and there follow a series of regular accountings which continue into the nineteenth century.

Over fifty properties in the city and surrounding district were in the possession of the guild in the later sixteenth century. Of these the preponderance were in the vicinity of St Audoen's church and the surrounding streets and lanes. Central to the guild's activities was the college of Blakeney's Inns, made over to the guild by the Blakeney family in 1534 in return for lands in Saucerstown in the county of Dublin.[68] Besides containing several chambers which had accommodated the six chantry priests, there was a large hall in the building where guild meetings were held, as well as lofts and cellars. From 1568 the guild made leases of parts of Blakeney's Inns as well as the surrounding gardens to local merchants and businessmen.[69] There were several houses to which the guild had title in Cook Street including substantial stone residences returning up to £4 per annum.[70] Many other tenements were held by the guild in the major streets of the city and suburbs and all of these were the subject of detailed leases before, during and after the

Elizabethan period. They included a tavern and loft in High Street, a garden at White Friars, a cellar in Winetavern Street and a shop with garden in St Francis Street. Of the rural lands, those at Kilmainham were the most extensive. The great farm there contained fifty-eight acres, and the small one twenty-six. Other farms in Carpenterstown, Crumlin, Nutstown, Bally-dowd and Boyarstown made up the complement of agrarian holdings. When the accounts were ordered in 1584, it was found necessary to trace the record of leaseholding and income back to 1555, and a total of £229.19.9 was found to be outstanding.[71] When a full account was drawn up for the year 1585 the total revenue from all properties was £65.18.0, a mere 15s. 4d under the permitted figure of 100 marks (£66.13.4).[72] The next full accounting period was for the years from 1605 to 1615 and the auditors found that the income from rents due was £737.1.11 for ten and a half years, or an average of £70.4.0 per annum.[73] Thus the stipulated maximum value of landed income was surpassed by an average of £3.12.0 per annum. In the years after 1585 some adjustments upwards were made when the leases of properties were being renewed[74] but an increase of $6\frac{1}{2}$ per cent in rents over a thirty-year period seems to be modest enough given the inflation of prices and the monetary dislocation which marked the *fin de siècle* period.[75] It seems clear that the level of rents for the guild properties was considerably below that obtaining generally because of the constraint of the allowance of 100 marks per annum for income, which had been ordained by the charter. Many properties were rented out to tenants in the early seventeenth century for the same rents that had been appointed a century earlier.[76] Accordingly leases of the guild of St Anne represented very attractive investments for city merchants and traders, and the value of the fraternity as a landholding corpora-tion was enhanced as prices and rents elsewhere rose during the sixteenth century. This was a very sound reason for the members and supporters to stand to the defence of the guild when external pressures mounted upon the fraternity to explain its activities and to show cause why it should continue in existence.

The series of challenges to the guild, beginning in 1593-4, came from officials of church and state. The clergy of St Audoen's parish conducted a long-running campaign in the seventeenth century, beginning with John Richardson, parson in 1605, for the major share of the revenue of St Anne's guild to benefit themselves and the parish.[77] Richardson demanded a stipend of £40 per annum, but the guild's officers granted £13.6.8, protesting that the sum requested almost amounted to 'the uttermost of our guild revenue'.[78] The leading Protestant churchmen and academics were affronted by the continued existence of a chantry and desired to have the possessions and those of the other surviving fraternities converted under the crown to the advancement of the Reformation, and specifically to the use of the new university college. In 1593 and 1603 commissioners for ecclesiastical causes probed the affairs of the guild as part of a determined policy on the part of the authorities to enforce conformity to the established church.[79] The campaign of an individual Protestant luminary, Luke Challoner, was initially successful in that the king granted the possessions of the guild to the provost and fellows of Trinity College about 1611 but legal proceedings in pursuance of this grant failed to alienate the properties.[80] State officials in the early Stuart period, most notably Sir John Davies, were anxious to proceed against the guild as part of a policy of questioning of the chartered rights of corporations.[81] The officers and members of the guild pleaded their charter in the case of *quo warranto* brought against them in the court of King's Bench.[82] The failure of all of these inquiries and suits against St Anne's guild is seen by the renewed campaign of both church and state officials in the 1630s to bring that body to account. Eventually a commission issued by the chief governor, Thomas Wentworth, in 1635 under the great seal led to a complete overhaul of the guild's membership and activities, pending a decision on its closure.[83] Thirty political, judicial and ecclesiastical leaders were elected on the order of the Irish council on 16 July 1638 and this majority of the membership set about recovering the revenues and properties for the Church of Ireland parish of St Audoen's.[84] After the turbulent decades of the 1640s and 1650s the control of the guild reverted to local merchants and civic dignitaries.[85]

The response of the guild's members to the 'troublesome persons that daily lette not to speke as they would (if they could) over throw' the institution[86] entailed the securing of the fraternity's records, the hiring of legal counsel and the making of special arrangements in respect of many of the lands and houses in their possession. The fact that the minutes of meetings were recorded with great meticulousness from 1584 may be indicative of a desire on the part of members to safeguard their interests.[87] In 1591 measures were taken to secure the archives in a stout chest with three locks, the keys to be held by the two wardens and Alderman Christopher Fagan, a senior member.[88] Two years later it was decided that the muniments would be safer in the home of Fagan, named Fagan's Castle, near Cook Street.[89] On Fagan's death the chest with its contents was transferred to the care of Alderman Nicholas Ball and thence to that of Alderman Matthew Handcock.[90] State officials were to complain regularly of their failure to gain access to the records of the guild of St Anne. Among the learned counsel consulted by the officers of the guild in the period from 1594 to 1609 were Henry Burnell, Peter Delahide, Richard Bealing and William Talbot.[91] These were distinguished lawyers from the Pale area and had much experience of defending the interests of local corporations and individuals against the encroachment of state interests. Their advice was obviously most useful as the guild fended off all the legal challenges of the first decade and a half of the seventeenth century. The burden of defending the position of the fraternity, however, was a heavy one, and on 1 March 1620 it was decided to defray the costs by granting fee-farms of selected premises to guild brothers and sisters, and other lessees as they and the master and wardens 'shall thinke fitt'.[92] An entry fine and increase of $16\frac{2}{3}$ per cent in rent were demanded of those favoured and by 1623 average yearly income had increased to £105.2.0. At least fifteen fee-farms of guild property were granted in the three years after 1620.[93]

It was the issuing of the fee-farms which focused attention on the question of the surplus funds of the guild of St Anne in the 1620s and 1630s. While the members might argue as they did later that fee-farms were granted to selected persons to encourage them to improve some of the holdings of the guild which had become waste, state and church officials saw the transactions as the culmination of a pattern of concealment and subterfuge.[94] On foot of the charges of impropriety laid by Archbishop Bulkeley and some of his metropolitan clergy, the conciliar investigation of the guild's affairs examined the rent-rolls and muniments of the corporation and found a large number of houses in the city and suburbs as well as farms in counties Dublin and Meath which had been concealed, not being accounted for in the records of the auditors.[95] The commission reported also that the annual rents were £289.1.7, and not £74.14.0 as claimed by the guild.[96] Even if the lower figure was accurate there was still a healthy excess of income over expenditure: the commitments of the guild to the stipendiaries, including parson, organist, two choristers and six singing men, amounted to £54 in 1619.[97] The 'pious uses' to which the guild claimed to devote its extra resources were never accounted for in the minuted proceedings after 1605. Archbishop Bulkeley and the parochial clergy sought the benefits for the parish of St Audoen. In 1630 Bulkeley had found in his visitation that the church of St Audoen's was 'out of repairacon'.[98] A quarter of the homes in the parish at that time had Protestant households while the rest, about fifty, were described as recusant. Bulkeley declared that the guild of St Anne 'hath swallowed upp all the church means which should be for the minister and repairation of the church'.[99] Rev. Thomas Lowe voiced the suspicion in the minds of many that the profits of the guild were being divided up between its own members and Catholic priests and friars.[100]

The principal item of evidence adduced by Lowe for his allegation was a copy of a papal bull from the pontificate of Pius V, dated 1569, which was found among the muniments of Christopher Fagan, the guardian of the papers in the 1590s.[101] The document enjoined members of religious guilds and confraternities to rent out their properties only to Catholics, and to contribute their revenues to the maintenance of priests.[102] An analysis of the list of leaseholders of the guild from 1585 to 1623 reveals that, of the number whose religious orientation can be known with certainty, 70 per cent were Catholic and 30 per cent Protestant.[103] While the guild membership itself contained Protestants such as Walter, Robert and Edward Ball, and John Cusack, the proportion was small, being less than a fifth.[104] Perhaps of greater significance is the character of the leadership of the guild in the period when a decisive shift towards Catholicism was taking place among the civic patriciate at large. Walter Sedgrave (1592-8), Michael Chamberlain (1598-1606),

Matthew Handcock (1606-18) and Thomas Plunket (1618-26) were masters in successive terms and each was noted for recusancy. Sedgrave had been arrested for supporting the rebellion of Viscount Baltinglass in the early 1580s and, being released, was known to be a protector of priests in his home.[105] Chamberlain and Handcock, along with Sedgrave, were imprisoned for their recusancy in 1605-6, having refused to obey the mandates ordering them to accompany the governor to divine service.[106] Plunket also spent time in jail for his beliefs and left the sum of £1,000 in his will for the Irish college at Douai.[107] In the period from 1605 to 1622 the wardenships were held by Edmund Malone and Nicholas Stephens, both staunch Catholics. Stephens's execution was ordered in 1613 for his leading role in the riot in Dublin after the overturning of the parliamentary election but he was subsequently reprieved.[108] During the years of greatest threat to the guild, then, the officers charged with directing its affairs were under pressure as individuals for their Catholic beliefs. As with the civic corporation the pattern of office-holding was severely disrupted in the guild, with Handcock, Malone and Stephens serving for abnormally lengthy periods. All three spent the early months of 1606 in prison in Dublin Castle, the administration of the guild being thereby hindered.[109] Also notably recusant were the lawyers hired by the guild to defend its privileges. Burnell, for example, a veteran of many campaigns against the curtailment of communal rights by the government, was heavily involved in the petition of protest against the mandates in 1605-6, and William Talbot lost his position as recorder of Dublin in 1605 because of his refusal to take the oath of supremacy.[110]

While the preponderance of members and lessees, and all of the officers and advisors of the guild, were manifestly recusant in the early seventeenth century, the evidence for their support for a system of Catholic worship and ministry in the Dublin region is circumstantial. Taken together, though, the indications make for a compelling case. The decision to refurbish the altar and chapel of St Anne in St Audoen in 1597, reaffirmed in 1605,[111] was significant as the shrine had been the centrepiece of guild ritual since the early fifteenth century. As a place of worship it was apparently superseded in the early seventeenth century by the hall of the guild's college, adjoining the church, and newly restored at guild expense. The walls had been wainscotted and the windows glazed, and the building reroofed with tiles.[112] The hall was one of several places where mass was said to be celebrated in the city and suburbs about 1618.[113] Among the other locations were the private residences of three guild members: those of Patrick Browne, Nicholas Queytrot and John Carey.[114] Funding for the living costs of priests may have been channelled through the guild. It is possible that some or all of the six singing men who received six marks each per annum in 1619 were priests but more likely that the subsidies for Catholic clerics did not appear in the books of the guild at all. Some of the members were closely related to seminary-trained missionaries and therefore may have been able to arrange financial support on their behalf. Anna Sedgrave, who was widow of Nicholas Fitzsimon and mother of Rev. Henry Fitz-simon, S.J., was a sister of the guild from 1608.[115] Henry had spent some years in Dublin, setting up the framework for a Catholic alternative to the state church. Members of the Sed-grave, Browne and Malone families were among those who worked as priests in the Dublin area in the first three decades of the century, and all had kinsfolk in St Anne's guild.[116]

The fostering of the confirmed Catholicism associated with the Counter-Reformation by the guild of St Anne came about in response to the crystallising of the political and religious issues in the years around the turn of the century. While the momentum of the late medieval devotional system was strong enough to continue through the guild into the early years of the Elizabethan period it was not maintained long after that as ecclesiastical structures gradually changed. For a time the fraternity concentrated almost exclusively on land transactions and the gathering of revenues, though some vestiges of its charitable functions were evident in the donations to the poor and to the parish proctors. When, in common with the major corporation of Dublin and other ancillary bodies, the guild began to experience a withdrawal of trust and a questioning of its privileges by officials in government and church, a rallying to the defence of chartered rights and hallowed traditions ensued. This phenomenon drew strength from the solidarity and unity of purpose displayed by the leading city councillors, many of whom had dual membership of guild and aldermen's bench.[117]

Protestant as well as recusant guildsmen could identify with the struggle to maintain an old civic institution which had the great attraction of providing lucrative investment opportunities. Linked by marital and commercial ties, complemented by the entry of representatives of the more militantly Catholic women-folk and steeled by the resistance to anti-recusancy measures in the tribunals of the years from 1603 to 1606, the leading members were emboldened to commit the resources of the fraternity once again to religious purposes. In time the new devotions sponsored by the Tridentine priests would replace those which had flourished in the lay-run guild of the late middle ages.[118]

Unlike the other Irish chantries which survived the imposition of Protestant reforms in the mid-sixteenth century the guild of St Anne was strong enough by virtue of its élite membership to play an important part in the delayed Catholic response of the early seventeenth century. There may have been a period of discontinuity in terms of religious practice but it is surely noteworthy that the focus of the old devotion, the chapel of St Anne, was restored at a time of crisis for the guild members. Also important perhaps is the fact that the only late medieval fresco in a Dublin church to have survived the Reformation period was discovered, lightly whitewashed over, in the church of St Audoen in the late nineteenth century. Depicted in it were St Anne and her daughter, Mary.[119] The late seventeenth-century writer who spoke of the guild of St Anne as having a 'charm' which enabled it to resist all hostile inquiries was probably unaware of the presence of this icon which, though partially hidden, represented for generations of guild members a patronal link with the faith which gave birth to the fraternity in 1430.[120]

2. The rebellion
of William Nugent, 1581

BY THE last quarter of the sixteenth century the outer reaches of the English Pale, including the lands of Westmeath where the Nugent family were dominant, were still far from being amenable to the queen's law. The Dublin administration was still forced to rely on powerful individuals to maintain order in these districts. Though the trustworthiness of such men might be in doubt, their power to keep their kinsmen reasonably quiet, if they so desired, had to be acknowledged. Thus, for example, despite their reservations as to his reliability, the administration conceded considerable local power to the earl of Kildare, up to and including military authority, until the events of 1580 convinced Dublin that the earl under arms was doing more to undermine the security of the realm than to augment it. Baron Delvin, the head of the Nugent family, was adjudged to have even more influence over his kinsmen than Kildare had over his. He was, it was said, 'the shrewdest man in Leinster, able to do more than Kildare'.[1] Delvin's uncle, James Nugent, also enjoyed considerable prestige in the district of Westmeath: it was said that he could 'do great service there if he be so disposed, the only man that can keepe those parts in quietness'.[2]

The rebellions in the English Pale during 1580 and 1581 involved both Kildare and Delvin, as well as other individuals upon whom the government had been forced to rely as outer bulwarks of its power. This convinced the administration, if it had needed convincing, that its security in the long run depended on its escape from reliance upon local leaders to maintain order in their districts. Ultimately, of course, this could not be done without far greater financial and military resources than the Irish Elizabethan regime normally possessed. Nevertheless, the Elizabethan conquest, of which the crushing of the rebellions in the Pale may be seen as a part, dealt the power of the Anglo-Irish lords, as well as that of the Gaelic chieftains, a near-mortal blow. By the end of the sixteenth century, local leaders, of whatever persuasion, who maintained a band of military retainers, were seen as a threat to the administration and not as a support.

This was not a phenomenon confined to Ireland. Even in England the revolt of the northern lords indicated that local military power could still pose a serious threat to central government. Nonetheless, that revolt, like the rebellions in Ireland, was decisively defeated and central authority reasserted. All over Europe at this period monarchs were struggling to establish central power over local military networks. By the early seventeenth century, it was clear in England, as in France and Spain, that central authority would prevail. It had done so not only by military means but also by the use of increasingly sophisticated bureaucracies.[3]

This did not mean that local lords and gentry were left totally powerless. They simply began to exert their power in a different way. One possible way was through estates or parliaments. Another was to become themselves an important part of the new style of government. Kings could not rule alone and the nobility and gentry were ideally placed to help them. The nobility could take their places in the royal councils and at court, the gentry in the ever increasing bureaucracy. In Ireland, however, the reduction in the military power of the Anglo-Irish élite was not compensated for by such consolidation of their civil power. The process of replacing the Anglo-Irish in official posts by men of English birth, begun by the Henrician regime, continued apace under Elizabeth. Thus, the Elizabethan conquest of Ireland could be said to be a true conquest and not, as with the assertion of royal power elsewhere in Europe, simply a re-alignment of influence.

The Nugent family straddled the borders of the Pale both geographically and culturally. Significantly, they were often referred to by the Dublin administration as a 'sept' and it seems clear that some of them practised child fosterage. Both the English and Irish languages were in use among them. Delvin, a man of extensive learning, presented a primer of the Irish language to the queen, containing text in English, Irish and Latin.[4] His younger brother William, leader of the rebellion in

1581, was a student at Hart College, Oxford, and wrote poetry in both the English and Irish tongues.[5]

It is not surprising, therefore, that the rebellion which William Nugent led in 1581 was a two-pronged one in that it drew its support from both the English Pale and the Gaelic Irish. It was not, as the Dublin administration for a time supposed, part of the Baltinglass revolt which had begun in July 1580 although it was linked to this revolt through certain machinations of Nugent's brother Delvin and the earl of Kildare. There were also contacts with the followers of Desmond, the Burkes of Sligo and Turlough Luineach O'Neill, but the aims of William Nugent were by no means identical to those of any of these groups.

The élite of the English Pale had, by 1580, some reason to feel aggrieved with the queen's government. The conflict between the Palesmen and the Dublin administration over the question of cess has been extensively documented.[6] It was admitted by the administration itself that 'cesse and the oppresyon of the soldyer' were the 'chief orygynall' of unrest in the Pale during 1580 and 1581.[7] The Nugents had been associated with the campaign against the cess during the 1570s and in 1575 Delvin and William Nugent were, with others, suspected of carrying the struggle against the queen's government further than was tolerable. Having arrested the earl of Kildare on a charge of treason, Sir William Fitzwilliam, the lord deputy, 'layd an easy restraynt of lyberty' upon Delvin, Lord Louth and William Nugent.[8] In 1577 Delvin and his uncle Nicholas Nugent, an eminent lawyer and second baron of the exchequer, with other gentlemen of the Pale, including Lords Trimleston and Howth, found themselves in Dublin Castle for attempts to prove cess contrary to law. By July all these gentlemen had presented their submissions to the lord deputy, claiming that they had 'heard more of the queen's prerogative than before we understood'.[9] They secured their freedom but the Nugents continued to be mistrusted by the administration; Delvin was considered by it to be the ring-leader of the 1577 protest.

Lord Deputy Sidney was recalled in 1578. His departure led to a profound change in the relationship between the Dublin administration and the Pale. By the late 1570s the administration had come increasingly to include those who advocated physical force as the only means of bringing the Irish to 'civilitie' and who leaned, to a greater or lesser degree, towards Puritan forms of Protestantism. Their view was succinctly summed up by Sir Edward Waterhouse when he declared that there could be 'no room for justice till the sword hath made a way for the law'.[10] The new lords justices, Pelham and Drury, endorsed such sentiments, and Pelham, in particular, became known for the violence of his policies. Before 1578 Sidney had succeeded in holding back the zeal of men such as these. But with his departure from Ireland and the gradual replacement of Burghley by Walsingham at the centre of Irish affairs in London, the stage was set for confrontation between the Dublin administration and the Pale gentry. Walsingham shared the views of men such as Wallop, Waterhouse, Pelham and Drury both on religion and coercion, and it was inevitable that the Dublin officials should, after 1578, move towards extremes of policy which Sidney would never have initiated nor Burghley endorsed.[11]

The Nugent rebellion, while not part of the Baltinglass revolt, came about chiefly because of it. There is sufficient evidence to be certain that Baron Delvin and the earl of Kildare, who was his father-in-law, were deeply implicated in the plans of Viscount Baltinglass from an early date. This revolt, which broke out in the summer of 1580, involved both Gaelic Irish and Palesmen, as did the Nugent revolt. Delvin, whose cousin was married to the viscount, met with Baltinglass during Easter 1580 at Baltinglass's house at Monkstown. Baltinglass had, at this time, sent his brother 'beyond the seas' for foreign aid, and it seems clear that the meeting was held to discuss plans for future military action.[12] Along with Fiach MacHugh O'Byrne, chief of the O'Byrnes of Wicklow, who was seeking revenge for the killing by the seneschal of Wexford of some of his allies among the Kavanaghs, Delvin was 'sworn to ioyne with the viscount' at that meeting.[13] Delvin furthermore 'brought a letter from the earl of Kildare withe his oathe that he would take their parte' and protect the rebels from those who might oppose them.[14] It is clear that both Kildare and Delvin at a muster in Tara in July 1580 protected Baltinglass from the eyes of Archbishop Loftus and that Delvin had ridden in the viscount's company that day.[15] There was at least one other meeting between Delvin and Baltinglass that July, at Bolton.[16] It is also clear that Delvin was in close communication with Turlough Luineach O'Neill.[17]

It is certain that William Nugent was at the meeting at Monkstown but the extent of his involvement in Baltinglass's plots is uncertain. There is no evidence of his presence at the muster at Tara nor at Delvin's meeting with Baltinglass at Bolton. It is true that he was sufficiently under the suspicion of the administration for Delvin to have been obliged to offer sureties for his good behaviour around August 1580, when Baltinglass's revolt broke out.[18] There may have been some irony here, however, in that it seems likely that Delvin himself was far more deeply implicated in Baltinglass's conspiracy than was his younger brother. Although he may have toyed with the idea of rebellion before 1581, there is no evidence that William Nugent actively participated in the Baltinglass revolt. Those questioned later about the revolt made no mention of his involvement: these include the wife of Fiach MacHugh O'Byrne, who appears to have been privy to most of the plans of her husband and of Baltinglass.[19] In fact, the evidence points rather to the conclusion that having apprised himself of the plans of Baltinglass, Delvin, Kildare and O'Byrne, William Nugent decided to have no further part in them. Why this was so is uncertain: it may be that he considered their schemes impractical, or the high-toned Catholic fervour of Baltinglass may not have appealed to him.

By December 1580 Delvin was well aware that the administration viewed him with suspicion, and on or around the twentieth of that month he was warned by a retainer named Walter Beloo that he would be apprehended.[20] Perversely, perhaps tiring of the fencing between himself and the administration, he decided upon the following day to bring matters to a head. Challenging the council, he 'desired if any man could charge him, he might answer and clear himself or ells rest condemned'.[21] Immediately his bluff was called as 'all the boord universally, the earl of Kildare being one, ordered his commitment to the castle'.[22] The council then rounded upon Kildare, however, accusing him of foreknowledge of Baltinglass's rebellion and of guarding the viscount from apprehension. Adjudged to be 'a principal comforter of the viscount to enter into this action', he too was imprisoned.[23] By 23 December the administration could hazard a guess as to what each man was worth: Kildare's lands alone were said to be worth £3000 while the value of Delvin, Baltinglass and others that were to be proved traytors' was also estimated at £3000.[24]

William Nugent's reaction to the news of the arrests was swift. The administration had intended to place him also under arrest but when the sheriff's company came in search of him he succeeded in eluding them.[25] By 23 December Wallop had heard that 'William Nugent, the baron's brother, and therewith diverse others of their sept . . . be gathered together to the number of three or four score horsemen and some footmen and mynd to join with O'Rourke and O'Donnell and others of the Irishry and say they will have the baron of Delvin owt'.[26] Nugent appealed to his uncle James Fitzchristopher Nugent for support but this was not forthcoming despite the fact that he and his brother Oliver seem to have been much to the fore in encouraging their nephew to rebellious action.[27] Nicholas Nugent, now chief justice of the common pleas, was despatched to the countryside to persuade William to go to Dublin 'but he would not because he had bin committed before'.[28] By Christmas Day William Nugent had assembled 'about 200 persons who as yett did no other harme but take their meate and drinke appe the country'.[29] Clearly most of these men were members of the Nugent sept; some, probably, were of the Gaelic Irish. It would not seem that any of the gentlemen of the Pale later arrested for conspiracy with Nugent were yet involved, although Robert Scurlock met with him on Christmas Day.

Disappointed, no doubt, that his modest show of force had not encouraged Dublin to release his brother, William Nugent retired to his tower house at Lough Sheelin, which he prepared to defend against attack.[30] His 'base brother' Edmund accompanied him and some of the O'Reillys continued to show support. Of his more important kinsmen, only Richard Nugent of Dunowre was prepared to rally to him 'with as many men as he could muster'.[31] Others, who toyed with the idea of joining him, were by 'the good exhortation' of Sir Lucas Dillon and Nicholas Nugent 'bridled and stayed'.[32] Nonetheless, William had by no means given up hope of having his brother released. He made contact with Turlough Luineach O'Neill who made promises of support but would do nothing until Nugent made the first move. Maguire, too, promised aid in the form of 'xxiii shott and targettmen upon his owne proper charges', but again would wait to see that Nugent 'woulde attempt to doe any harme to the English pale'.[33] It is unlikely that Nugent relished exposing himself to the risks of initiating a rebellion on his own. Since it was clear to him that no substantial help could be expected from the Irish chiefs unless he did so, however, he set about assembling forces. By February 1581 he could boast of '190 swords' and stood assured of O'Reilly support. Joining with an old ally, Brian MacGeoghegan, together with a number of O'Connors, he moved, in March, to Robinstown in Co. Westmeath where he succeeded in gathering some 300 men.[34] He appears, during this time, to have been in regular correspondence with his brother Delvin who freely encouraged him to rebel and proposed to him various schemes which, the baron hoped, would secure his release.[35]

Dublin was made aware of Nugent's movements almost immediately. At Dublin Castle, Delvin was induced to write to his brother to persuade him 'to give over his enterprise' and a messenger was sent in the hope of encouraging him to come in to Dublin.[36] Upon Nugent's refusal to submit, Sir Edward Moore, Sir John Plunkett and 'two bandes of footmen' entered Westmeath with the intention of capturing him. The rebels decided to disperse. William Nugent, Brian MacGeoghegan, Nicholas Eustace and others elected to go north through the Brenney where the O'Reillys were friendly, while Edmund Nugent and his company would go into O'Rourke's country. The O'Connors were to remain in the district so that they might 'draw the Irish lords to come and disturb the English Pale'.[37]

It was during the following months, while William Nugent was in the north, that the conspiracy in the Pale took shape. The central figure in these schemes was John Cusack of Ellistonrede, who appears to have been a tenant of the Scurlocks of Scurlockstown. The professed aim of Cusack in involving himself in subversion was for 'the cause of religion'; it would appear that William Nugent had been declared by Sir John of Desmond, invoking papal authority, to be 'general of the Pale'.[38] Nonetheless, it is clear that private grievance supplied a motive at least as powerful as that of religion.

It would appear that trends in the distribution of government rewards and offices during the decades preceding the Pale revolts of 1580-1 had a bearing upon the disposition of some young Palesmen to become involved in subversion. That even relatively humble posts in the Dublin government were being increasingly occupied by Englishmen from the reign of Henry VIII onwards has been noted by recent historians.[39] Not all of these officials were of high calibre. Sir Henry Wallop complained that 'soche hongrey men be sent owt of England which either have nothing or have spent that they had'.[40] These men, not unnaturally, were anxious to exploit their tenure in Ireland to the best material advantage, before moving, as they frequently did, to fresher fields in the New World or the continent. It was Burghley's view that 'thinges of benefitt sholde be not delivered to them that be but persons transitorie', but this view was often not shared in Dublin.[41] While it is widely recognised that the exclusion of the Anglo-Irish gentry from a growing number of rewards and offices resulted in a significant decline in their political influence, what is sometimes overlooked is that this trend had important social and economic consequences as well.

The fact was that rewards for official posts often provided the only opportunity for younger sons to acquire lands and upward social mobility. Nicholas Nugent, a younger son of a baron of Delvin, accumulated considerable wealth during his years of legal office; at his death his lands alone were worth at least £140 a year.[42] In contrast, his brother James Fitzchristopher, who held no official post, owned no lands as of natural right: 'the lands which he holdeth he had from his brother the baron of Delvin's father, appe condicion to serve him and his heires in their honest affairs'.[43] It would appear that his property status was dependant upon the good nature of a brother. William Nugent himself had modest properties at Ross, on Lough Sheelin, but his real wealth derived from the properties of his wife at Skreen, Navan and Santry.[44] A generation earlier he might have expected an official post in Dublin to augment his income. The wealth of Sir Thomas Cusack, that supreme office-holder, may be guessed at from the resources possessed by his son, Edward of Lismullin, who had wide property and business interests and was wealthy enough to own a ship and nine

hundred pounds worth of personal goods.[45] Edward Cusack
did not need an official post to boost his income but his young
relative, John Cusack of Cosington, who became involved in
Nugent's conspiracy, would no doubt have welcomed such an
opportunity, having a more modest income of £50 a year.[46]

While several older members of the Netterville family of Co.
Meath were eminent lawyers, George Netterville, later executed
for his part in the Nugent conspiracy, had no such advantage. In
1581 he was 'thirty-one years old and having neither land nor
living'.[47] Another young rebel, Ferral O'Reilly, who had been
brought up in the Pale, and served the Viscount Gormanston
against his own name' also had 'neither land nor living', though
after such service he might have expected better.[48] With other
conspirators, such as Robert Scurlock and William and Marcus
Clinch, it was the longevity of their fathers which deprived
them of independent resources but here too access to official
posts was denied.[49] Not only may contracting outlets for young
gentry in officialdom have resulted in a strong sense of grievance but it also, one suspects, left many of these young men
without occupation. It would be wrong to suppose that all who
were involved in rebellion in the Pale from 1580 to 1581 were
idle men of little means: David Sutton who was executed for his
part in the Baltinglass rebellion, for example, 'might dispose of
£300 of good land', while his personal goods were worth at least
£110.[50] Nonetheless, very many of the young gentry who
became rebels were men who might formerly have looked to
official posts as a means of either making their way in the world
or of keeping them solvent till they should inherit family lands.

While lack of means and occupation may have propelled
many of the young gentry towards rebellion, their immediate
motivations in joining the Nugent conspiracy were varied.
William Clinch, for example, declared that 'nothing else moved
him but the persuasions of Richard and John Cusack of Ellistonrede'.[51] George Netterville claimed that their cause was 'for
religion', and Christopher Bathe, too, understood that their
intent was to secure 'lyberty of conscience'.[52] William Nugent's
own motive was primarily to 'set at lyberty the earl, baron
Delvin and others the prisoners at Dublin', and John Cusack of
Cosington believed that their 'first purpose' was to release

Delvin and Kildare.[53] According to John Cusack of Ellistonrede, this was to be done by launching a surprise attack upon Dublin Castle.[54] However, William Clinch understood that Sir Nicholas Malby and the chief baron were to be kidnapped and held till Kildare and Delvin were released and there is evidence that Delvin had encouraged his brother to adopt such a scheme.[55] Patrick Cusack of Drakestown claimed that he had been drawn by Richard Cusack to join 'all the rest of the Cusacks to make a prey for the revenge of the death of the said Richard's father'. He further declared that their 'full entente and purpose' was to burn a number of towns in County Meath as well as the homes of Sir Lucas and Sir Robert Dillon and Sir Edward Moore. The rebels also planned to 'have away the bishop of Meath his kyne owt of Ardbraccan', an exploit which clearly had little to do with plans to release Kildare and Delvin or to secure 'lyberty of conscience'.[56] What is clear is that elements of private vendetta loomed as large in the minds of the conspirators of the Pale as did hopes for the lords' release or the restoration of the Catholic religion.

John Cusack of Ellistonrede made his first approaches to the gentlemen of the Pale in January 1581. At that time George Netterville and Christopher Bathe had discussions with him during which he encouraged them to 'go to William Nugent'.[57] However, it was between July and September of that year that most of the recruiting within the Pale was done. Not all the recruits were of gentry status. Of a list compiled in October 1581 of twenty-six young men believed to have participated in the conspiracy, twenty-one were of good family. Of the others, three were retainers of the Baron Delvin and two his servants.[58] It is clear that others were involved who were of humbler degree — some of whom were executed — but, unfortunately, the authorities did not consider it worth while to record their names and status.[59] Exactly how many conspirators there were is difficult to say. Wallop referred to the conspiracy's being known to 'more than one hundred gentlemen of the Pale but not one of them would reveal it'.[60] Clearly, however, many of those who had heard of the conspiracy took no active part in it. On the other hand, many of those who did take part drew others, often humbler kinsmen or retainers, with them. Evidence elicited by the administration in October 1581 suggests that the number of Palesmen involved amounted to little more than one hundred men.[61]

A number of those recruited by John Cusack who were not of gentry status were soldiers in the queen's pay. Lucas Dillon wrote that the 'more parte of the countrye soldyers have been practised withal by Cusack to revolte and yet none of them discovered the same' to the authorities.[62] It seems to have been his hope not only to acquire men but also to secure additional arms for the proposed attack upon Dublin Castle. There was widespread disaffection among the crown soldiery during 1580 and 1581. Wages were irregularly paid. The supply of military provisions was woefully inadequate and it was freely admitted 'that the want thereof hindreth much the service and bryngeth the souldiarie to many miseries'.[63] Clothing, too, was unsuitable and irregularly supplied.[64] There was a constant stream of deserters. According to Robert Dillon, writing in the autumn of 1581, 'her majesty is in charge of 6000 men, many reporte and affirme in private speaches there are not indeede above three thousand'.[65] John Cusack seems to have had extensive contacts among these discontented soldiers and to have persuaded a number of them to go over to William Nugent.[66] It was also noticed that numbers of cassed (discharged) soldiers were joining rebel forces.[67] Not surprisingly, many of these men were raiding her majesty's ordnance before their departure. One of these was a Captain Garrett who before joining the earl of Kildare's force 'took the queen's wages and furniture owt of the store'.[68] So great were these depredations of the army's re-sources that before long it was proposed that a new code of regulations governing the removal of supplies from army stores should be drawn up.[69]

In July 1581 William Nugent invaded Longford with O'Rourke. This invasion was part of a grand scheme devised by O'Neill and O'Rourke for a two-pronged attack on the outer edges of the Pale.[70] At about the same time Turlough Luineach O'Neill clashed with O'Donnell's pro-English forces and although O'Donnell's losses were substantial he 'had the better at the last' and succeeded in fighting an effective holding action.[71] By 23 July it was believed that 'William Nugent hath 400 Scots appointed by Turlough Luineach and O'Rourke to invade Westmeath'.[72] The O'Connors were making ready to go to the assistance of this force.

It is probable that it was at about this time that Nugent and John Cusack laid their final plans for combining a revolt in the Pale with the Irish attack from the outside. From July onwards Nugent was regularly slipping in and out of the Pale, making contact with his supporters there. Not a great deal, he believed, could be achieved before harvest time but he had hopes that after that, sufficient force could be gathered within the Pale in order to launch an attack upon Dublin Castle and secure the release of the prisoners.[73] In August, accompanied by some thirty kerne of the Nugents and O'Reillys, Nugent moved about the Pale conducting meetings with supporters there. John Cusack travelled the countryside whipping up enthusiasm for revolt; to William Nugent he spoke expansively of the numbers that were certain to join them.[74] No doubt he exaggerated the degree of support forthcoming. To every man whom he encouraged to join the conspiracy he made assurances that all his neighbours were already firmly committed although in many cases that commitment extended no further than a willingness to talk about the matter. When George Netterville, for example, agreed to join the conspiracy along with Robert Scurlock and Christopher Bathe, he did so in the belief that dozens of his neighbours were sworn to revolt.[75]

By August Lord Deputy Grey had moved northwards to counter the threat of Nugent's Scots and the forces of O'Neill. The weather was particularly cold and wet and disease was rife throughout the army. The lord deputy had already found several bands 'utterly consumed by a plague growen upon colde and evil diet'.[76] In July he had written that 'God's hand is still heavily uppon us in sickness' and by the time he reached the north he was finding his efforts greatly hampered by fever, which killed many of his soldiers, and by frequent desertions, many to the enemy.[77] The rebels were able to derive temporary benefit at least from these circumstances. Despite being encamped at the Blackwater, Lord Grey was unable to secure by force his demand that O'Neill should yield up William Nugent to him. In truth, O'Neill's defiance may have been inspired by the fact that Nugent was not at that time in the north. It seems that as soon as Nugent was made aware of the deputy's approach, he 'came up from there because he stoode in doute of O'Neill and he dispersed his people and went but a few in company'.[78]

By September, 'about a fortnight befor Michaelmas', Nugent was known to be with the O'Connors. During that month he took part, with his Irish allies, in the burning of some properties of Archbishop Loftus.[79] Meetings with the conspirators of the Pale were held and efforts to recruit additional support were continued until the end of September.[80] Nonetheless, as his primary objective of releasing his brother seemed no nearer, it appears that Nugent had begun to weary of the struggle. O'Neill's 400 Scots seem to have no longer been available to him and by early September he was toying with the idea of submission. However, the summary hanging of a young messenger whom he had sent to Dublin caused him to decide to attempt to link effectively his supporters among the Irishry with the conspirators recruited by John Cusack within the Pale. At a meeting arranged between the Palesmen and Nugent's friends among the O'Connors at a place known as the 'Great More' John Cusack administered oaths to the gentlemen that they would support 'William Nugent, their general, in whatever enterprise he would take in hand'.[81]

Despite their oaths, Nugent was to find that the friendship of the Palesmen was but a tenuous thing. A meeting with Ferrall O'Reilly fell through when O'Reilly failed to appear at the arranged spot, despite Nugent's waiting twenty-four hours in the hope of his arrival.[82] By the closing days of September he was reduced to lurking in barns and was begging the servant of Nicholas Nugent to bring him 'a tent to lie in at night'.[83] In Dublin, the administration had begun to unravel the threads of the conspiracy in the Pale. On 4 October Sir Lucas Dillon arrested William Clinch who then implicated John Cusack and others. Cusack slipped through Dillon's fingers and returned to William Nugent but Sir Lucas succeeded in arresting Nicholas Cusack of Drakestown and imprisoning him at Trim. The following days saw the arrests of Christopher Bathe and George Netterville, followed by Marcus Clinch, Ferrall O'Reilly and Richard Cusack of the Grange. These were accused of having gathered together about one hundred men, including members of the Garland, Drake and Clinton families, who had all promised 'to be with the said William to ayde and assyst him'.[84] Confessions of those arrested and questioned universally implicated John Cusack of Ellistonrede as the main instigator of the conspiracy. George Netterville also implicated Simon Barnewall of Kilbride, Edward Penteney of Cabragh, James Tankarde of Castleton and John Plunkett, brother to the baron of Louth.[85]

In the meantime William Nugent and his remaining supporters found themselves in desperate straits as the queen's soldiers pressed them ever more closely. Anxiously, Nugent made contact with his brother Delvin, imploring his advice as to 'what shall I do, whether I should burn or spoil or lie still'.[86] The reply was somewhat callous: 'I care not', wrote Delvin, 'let him do what he will so he spare my lands.' Another letter sent to William by means of his wife, however, 'bid him get as many pikemen as he could lest horsemen harme him'.[87] It is clear that William Nugent was strongly under the influence of his brother. The nature of the correspondence between the brothers during 1581 must belie any idea that Delvin attempted to forestall rebellion; on the contrary, as he had earlier done in regard to Baltinglass, he encouraged it at every turn.[88] By now, however, neither Nugent nor his allies were in any position to benefit from the baron's advice. At the end of October the O'Connors, it was said, dared not 'stay two nights together in eny place', while the O'Mores were 'greatly dymynished by slaughter'.[89] By 23 November it would appear that Nugent, with Phelim O'Toole, made some offer of submission. It was Secretary Fenton's opinion that O'Toole's submission should be accepted as he was a 'daingerous enymye'; Nugent, on the other hand, 'being left to a fewe horsemen and wandering ... from wood to wood is not to be reckoned in the tytle of an enymye hable to mayteine hostilite but as an owtlawe and robber'.[90]

The administration had by now apprehended twenty-five gentlemen alleged to have been involved in Nugent's conspiracy. One, William Garland, had died in custody, while the rest were to be tried by 'judges and jurors with others of the privey counsell'.[91] By the end of November 1581, seven had been executed. There was little difficulty in securing guilty verdicts despite the fact that the juries were comprised of Palesmen; for the time being, at least, the majority of these had been effectively 'staied and terryfyed'.[92] The future Protestant bishop of

Meath, Thomas Jones, witnessed the executions, on 18 November, of Robert Scurlock, George Netterville, John Scurlock (a servant who did not belong to the more prominent family of Robert Scurlock) and Christopher Eustace, the last being ex-ecuted for his part in the Baltinglass revolt. Their manner of death was that of Catholic martyrs; certainly Mr Jones, whose task it was to escort them to the gallows and, if possible, to secure a last-minute conversion of their souls, could make no incursions upon their faith. His efforts met cries of 'Vade Satana' and the saying of 'pater nosters, salves and misericordias'. It is clear from Jones's account that it was George Netterville who was the chief inspiration of the group: John Scurlock had earlier conformed to Protestantism, although he now recanted, but Netterville appears to have been among the few followers of William Nugent who sincerely believed that their cause was a religious one. The four met their end with considerable courage, proclaiming the fact that it was for their religion they died: 'moved to pray for the queen's majesty they obstinately refused to do so, saying bothe that they died for him which had died for them'.[93]

Nine gentlemen were executed for their part in the Baltinglass revolt; in addition a number of men of 'mean calling' who had supported the conspiracies were 'executed by marshall lawe'.[94] With these, the bloodletting ended and the administration turned its attention to the more profitable side of the rebellion. Comprehensive lists of the monetary worth of the attainted rebels were drawn up and by early November their properties had already begun to be distributed. The distribution of these properties aroused immediate and intense bitterness as the clique of Dublin officials who had served there since the 1570s saw themselves passed over and the most valuable properties given to Lord Grey's close associates and military men. It was alleged that even the humbler servants of the lord deputy were profiting by the attainted goods more than were men like Fenton, Waterhouse and Wallop, although the latter did receive Baltinglass's house at Monkstown worth £14.5.8. Wallop and others protested indignantly and, indeed, there seemed to be some foundation for their grievance. Wallop might have Monkstown but the lord deputy's steward had a custody of Barry's land worth £30, one of Grey's gentleman ushers had a custody of Brian MacGeoghegan's land while another servant of the deputy, John Savage, received the custody of the lands of Richard Nugent of Dunowre.[95] Captain Denny received the property of John Cusack of Cosington. The list, it seemed, was endless and the Dublin officials lost no time in apprising London of the fact that properties were being given 'only by the lord deputy at his pleasure without advice or consent of any other of the counsell that is knowne'.[96]

In January 1582 events took an unexpected turn. William Nugent with Brian MacGeoghegan and others had moved out of the Pale towards the security of Turlough Luineach's country but John Cusack, who had intended to join them, was apprehended by Hugh O'Neill, the baron of Dungannon. Cusack decided to turn queen's evidence in return for a pardon. He made statements which purported to implicate in rebellion more than twenty persons, including more than a dozen members of the Nugent family as well as Edward Cusack of Lismullin, the son of the late lord chancellor. Ultimately, the evidence against many of these proved scant. Lavallen Nugent, for example, was said to be a 'confederate' of rebels and nothing stronger could be proved against him than that he had supplied some food to rebels on the run.[97] Edward Delahide of Maghaler was 'charged only by supposition'.[98] More serious charges were made against Lord and Lady Delvin and Lord Dunsany. Lord Dunsany and Lady Delvin were in England but the charges against Delvin himself lent weight to a proposal, already several times mooted, to send him and Kildare into England to be dealt with more effectively. Most sensational of all, however, were the charges made by John Cusack against Nicholas Nugent, the chief justice, and Edward Cusack of Lismullin. Nicholas Nugent had become chief justice of the common pleas in the previous year, much to the dismay of certain of the Dublin officials. It was alleged that Nugent had bribed the then lord chancellor, William Gerrard, with £100 to grant him the office. Nugent's support of the Palesmen in their campaign against cess had, of course, alienated him from many of these officials. None, however, detested him as much as Sir Robert Dillon, who had sought the chief justiceship for himself. There is evidence that a bargain was struck between Dillon and John Cusack at the time of Cusack's apprehension that if Cusack would 'accuse the Justice Nugent, he should have a pardon and a living'.[99] This may not have been known to the administration at the time of Nugent's trial.

Cusack's motives in denouncing Edward Cusack were a little more personal. Before breaking out at the beginning of 1581 Ellistonrede had mortgaged his land to Edward Cusack in order to raise money for the rebellion.[100] It would appear that Cusack of Lismullin later intimated to him that he would put difficulties in the way of John Cusack's getting his properties back. In November 1581 Edward had acted as foreman of the jury which had convicted Robert Scurlock; this seems to have made him highly unpopular with his neighbours, including John Cusack, whose wife was cousin to Scurlock's wife.[101] Edward Cusack had more powerful enemies too. Over a number of preceding years, Cusack had become embroiled in a property dispute with Sir John Plunkett of Dunsoghly, who claimed that a large proportion of Edward Cusack's land should revert to Jennet Sarsfield who had been Sir Thomas Cusack's third wife and who was now married to Plunkett. Unfortunately for Cusack, Jennet Sarsfield was also kin to the powerful Dillon family. There is little doubt that Cusack's great wealth made him a highly attractive target for his enemies.

The evidence against Edward Cusack and Nicholas Nugent was tenuous at best. It was John Cusack's claim that Edward of Lismullin had given him a token to buy a calliver from a smith named John Norris.[102] Edward Cusack refuted this by pointing out that since he was himself the owner of several callivers it was unlikely that he would take the risk of sending such a token should he have wished to supply a calliver to rebels.[103] Indeed little could be produced against him beyond the fact that he had had some advance knowledge of the rebellion. The main point of the evidence against Nicholas Nugent was the claim of John Cusack that he had revealed the conspiracy to Nugent. He said that Nugent had urged him to 'make force enough, to give them large pay . . . to spare no man's goods'.[104] Against this, Nugent could point to the fact that at Christmas 1580 he himself had advised many of the young Palesmen to stay out of the rebellion and that he had urged William Nugent to give himself up.[105] There is no evidence that Nicholas Nugent had any other contact with William save on one occasion in September 1581, when he was sent by the administration itself to secure William's infant son, Christopher, who was being held by William lest he should be taken hostage by the lord deputy. It is uncertain whether William Nugent yielded up the child: an entry in the 'Calendar of the Irish Council Book' suggests that he may have done so but one John Nugent, a servant of Nicholas Nugent, who was present at the negotiations for the child, declared that the child had been sent north and was still there in February 1582.[106] Nicholas Nugent's orders had been to present the infant at Dublin or else surrender himself or his own son to the lord deputy. The 'Master Nugent' presented to the lord chancellor in September 1581 may have been Nicholas Nugent's own son, Richard.[107]

Nugent and Cusack were tried at Trim on 4 and 5 April 1582. It would appear that Sir Robert Dillon brought pressure upon the jury to find Nugent guilty when they appeared ready to acquit him.[108] It seems that Dillon further exerted himself to work against a pardon for Nugent.[109] Edward Cusack, too, believed that Dillon had had a hand in his own guilty verdict.[110] Pardons were eventually offered to the two men if confessions were made. Cusack's female relatives were brought into his cell to persuade him to admit to the charges 'who put me in such a passion that I was content to write what John Cusack laid to my charge was treiw'.[111] Nugent 'denyed in forme most of what John Cusack charged him with' and he also denied some admissions which he had apparently made earlier to Lucas Dillon and Geoffrey Fenton.[112] Cusack was reprieved but Nugent was executed the following day. In the lord deputy's own words, Nugent was convicted not so much on the evidence as on the supposition of treason. Referring to Nugent's 'disposition to repine at and impugne her majesty's prerogative' and 'his aptnes to be of the combynacyon', Grey wrote of 'howe easilie a man of thies properties and kindred maie be drawn to consent' to rebellion.[113] In short, the Dublin administration had succeeded in ridding itself of one of the Palesmen's most articulate spokesmen in the most effective way possible.

This was the last of the executions for the Nugent conspiracy. The properties of both Edward Cusack and Nicholas Nugent were 'given awaie and their lands disposed by waie of custodie' by 13 April. This was before their value was known and despite the fact that they were in theory 'fullie and whollie escheated to her majesty'.[114] Sir Henry Wallop was outraged at this proceeding of the lord deputy. 'All Nugent's goods and lands', he wrote, 'are given to Sir Edward Moore, a man of small desert for making his owne profyt . . . Cusack's goods are also given to two of my L. Deputy's men . . . Cusack's lands are worth yerely £300.'[115] Wallop was not, in fact, quite correct: while Edward Moore had Nugent's goods, Sir Robert Dillon had his land and soon would have his place upon the bench.[116]

By 1 April the clique of officials led by Wallop had succeeded in making their weight felt in London. It was considered that the lord deputy had been precipitate in distributing the attainted properties and Dublin learned that her majesty was displeased, 'considering her charge ought to have bene first considered before rewards had bene disposed'.[117] A restraint was placed upon Grey, preventing him from bestowing any further rewards. Despite this, the victory was felt by Wallop to be a hollow one; he was chagrined to discover that his request for a lease of £60 worth of rebels' lands had been rejected. It was London's view that lands should be bestowed only upon prospective planters.

It had also been decided in London to extend a general pardon to the rebels. The Dublin administration, including Grey, were generally against the pardons, but the privy council in London, having weighed up the cost of continued forceful prosecution of the rebels, had decided to cass, or discharge, large numbers of soldiers. Cassing began in earnest in February 1582 and, indeed, may have had an extremely unsettling effect upon the city of Dublin as hundreds of soldiers were cassed with little in their pockets to sustain them. Grey wrote that 'troopes of poure soules . . . dispending of all they receaved or having rested goode have nothing to pay for theyre passages, dayly heere do flock about me and crye owte for relief'.[118] By April the garrison was reduced to 2000 men and it seems that Dublin was swarming with cassed soldiers, destitute, bitter and violent. This situation made pardons for the rebels inevitable, however much the administration might cavil at them.

In the end sixteen persons, including William Nugent, were excluded from the pardon but many erstwhile rebels were able to benefit at a price.[119] Fines were extracted and, in effect, pardons had to be paid for. At least forty-five gentlemen of the Pale received their pardons within the next few months. Some of them had to pay up to one hundred pounds for the privilege.[120] It would appear that these fines were assessed according to the means of those pardoned; typically, the fine paid amounted to approximately one year's income. Lavallen Nugent, for example, who was worth about £100 a year, paid that sum as a fine, as did Edmund Delahide of Maghaler whose annual income was just above £100.[121] Just into whose pockets these sums finally found their way is difficult to ascertain. Most fines were collected by the local sheriff or under-sheriff; John Kearnan, the under-sheriff of Co. Westmeath, received fines totalling 'many hundred pounds'.[122] It is probably fairly safe to assume that much of this money failed to reach the Dublin exchequer. Certainly, there does not appear to be any full record of the amounts received in such fines. The Dillons were instrumental in obtaining pardons for many of their kin; both Sir Lucas and Sir Robert had a reputation for taking bribes and it is hard to avoid the conclusion that they found the distribution of these pardons a profitable affair. It is likely that other Dublin officials found themselves in a position to benefit from the collection of these fines. Sir Henry Wallop condemned the practice whereby 'very many names passe in one pardon without fyne for the most parte to the benefit of some particular persons that procure the same'.[123]

Despite the restraint placed on the lord deputy's disposal of attainted lands, it is clear that many of the Dublin officials did not share in the spoils of the rebellion to the extent that they had hoped. Much of the available land seems to have been distributed before the restraint was imposed; by the early months of 1582 it was plain that royal policy was going to be one of fines and the restoration of many of the rebels to much of their property. Apart from Lord Grey's close associates and staff it was the army captains that benefited most from the distribution of attainted lands.[124] Discontent with Grey's distribution policies caused a good deal of tension between himself and his subordinates and made his government increasingly difficult to sustain. Some of the officials had already begun to work for Grey's recall but few of them could have been as anxious for him to go as he was himself. The work of suppressing rebellion with limited resources and in abominable weather had taxed both his health and his temper. He begged for release from his post and in July 1582 he was recalled to London.

For the families of the Pale who had members involved in the Nugent conspiracy the repercussions were, in fact, less than might be supposed. They were mistrusted by the administration but scarcely more than they had long since been. Financially, the aftermath of the rebellion was a painful blow but it was partially cushioned by the fact that many of the rebels were younger sons or sons yet to inherit. Most families escaped with a fine and although some of these were substantial, they were not devastating. Those who had been attainted ultimately had their lands restored to them in the main. John Cusack of Cosington was restored in February 1583 although there was some delay before he was actually returned to the property.[125] For him the fine was heavy—£200—but it was to be paid in five instalments.[126] William Nugent's wife received in April 1584 a lease of her lands for the life of her husband while a fine of £500 was remitted.[127] In January Edward Cusack was formally pardoned and the following year was restored to much of his property.[128] In April 1584, also, Nicholas Nugent's widow and son were returned to the 'profitte' of Nugent's lands.[129] His goods do not appear to have been returned.

It is clear that a certain proportion of attainted lands were not returned to their former owners and here the Baltinglass conspirators seem to have fared rather worse than those involved with Nugent. It was also difficult, especially in the case of goods and chattels, to secure their return from those who had benefited from the dispersal of attainted property. There does not appear to have been any compensation system for those who had so benefited when the properties had to be returned. Sir Warham St Leger received nothing when his custody of William Nugent's land came to an end. Unavailingly, he sought that the proposed fine of £500 which Nugent's wife had been ordered to pay should come to him instead of the queen.[130] As has been seen, this fine was ultimately remitted and it would seem that St Leger was not the only one who felt that the benefits of the attainted lands had, in the long run, proved somewhat chimerical and brought more cost than gain.

It has often been said that the violence of Lord Deputy Grey's reaction to the Pale rebellions was such that it served to fling the gentry into the arms of the Counter-Reformation.[131] While there is no doubt of the vigour with which the Munster rebellions were suppressed, the reaction of the administration to the Pale rebellions was a great deal more moderate than has sometimes been appreciated. While it is true than an unascertainable number of men of humble degree were executed for involvement with conspiracy, only seventeen of the gentry met this fate.[132] It could be said that this was a modest enough tally by the standards of those times. Although Sir Henry Wallop demanded that a rack be sent from London, none was despatched and there is no evidence that any form of torture was used on any of those arrested for conspiracy.[133] Nor were they kept in solitary confinement or denied visitors. Wallop loudly berated the level of communication that the prisoners kept up between one another, while Delvin was allowed to dine with his sister-in-law while both were detained at Dublin castle.[134] In the countryside of the Pale, where the deputy was capable of exerting control over the military, he was quick to temper the excesses of the soldiers. In Co. Westmeath, where the populace had complained of the behaviour of soldiers billeted upon the district, the deputy himself travelled to Mullingar to hear grievances and to administer justice.[135] He ordered that anyone who had had provisions unlawfully seized should be 'repayde by the treasurer'.[136] It is likely that the deputy's fair dealing and judicious use of armed force within the Pale served to narrow the base of support for rebellion there.

The adherence of the Pale gentry to Catholicism was due less to the violence of the administration than to the fact that, especially from the 1590s, the Counter-Reformation in Ireland became highly dynamic while the Protestant missionary effort was dilatory in the extreme, with few, if any, churches being built and almost no clergy of quality being appointed.[137] It seems clear that the Pale gentry did feel attracted to the Counter-Reformation as a means of forging a communal identity to act as a counterpoise to the growing influence of those who were soon to be known as the New English.[138] In this regard the Nugent conspiracy, like the Baltinglass revolt, had a political message. It was that against the queen's government, physical force was even less likely to bolster the gentry's declining political influence than the constitutional methods employed by the 'countrymen' during the 1570s. Perrot's parliament saw a return to these methods and a comparatively successful opposition to the new deputy's administration was mounted. No doubt one of the attractions of the Counter-Reformation for politically conscious members of the Pale gentry was the manner in which the movement put them in touch with foreign powers whose influence could perhaps be used to increase the political strength of the gentry.

Between 1582 and 1584 William Nugent was mainly in France and Rome, usually in the company of his close friend and ally, Brian MacGeoghegan. Leaving Ireland in January 1582, they travelled to Scotland and from thence to Paris. At Paris MacGeoghegan entered into negotiations with the English ambassador in the hope of obtaining a pardon and permission to return home. He later joined Nugent at Rome, claiming that the conditions of submission had been 'too hard'.[139] However, it would appear that MacGeoghegan had made some kind of arrangement with the English authorities. In October 1582, Sir Henry Cobham, the English ambassador to Paris, wrote to Walsingham that 'he [MacGeoghegan] promised to write to me and wherever he becomes to remain true to her majesty'.[140] On 24 October, Nugent and MacGeoghegan left Paris for Rome. Presumably, Cobham was in full possession of their plans and circumstances; on 1 November he wrote to Walsingham that 'I judged it the best means to discover the pack and to weaken the party . . . whereof I have plucked "Maghogan" from thence, so that he rests at her majesty's devotion, ready to discover what has passed and their intents'.[141]

The following months were spent by Nugent and the other Irish in the usual dispiriting state experienced by such exiles. Hovering at the edge of Roman society, dependant for money on the uncertain bounty of such as the dukes of Guise, Savoy and Florence, their lot cannot have been a particularly happy one.[142] Nonetheless, contacts were made with sources close to the papacy; it would appear that it was Nugent's hope to persuade the pope to supply 10,000 men 'to keep Ireland against the forces of the Prince'.[143] Around Easter 1584 Nugent and MacGeoghegan were informed that they should return to France. On arrival they made contact with the duke of Guise who instructed them to accompany certain Scottish lairds to the court of Scotland.[144] The nuncio at Paris undertook to pay their passage and they arrived in Edinburgh by the middle of June

1584. The two were also in receipt of a papal pension of some 200 escudos a month but this ceased in about August 1584.[145]

Walsingham was well aware of their movements and it may be that MacGeoghegan had passed information to the embassy at Paris. By 22 June Walsingham was able to inform Davison, the queen's representative at Edinburgh, that Nugent and MacGeoghegan were sent 'hither to practice that some Scots may be permitted to go out of the islands to Ireland'.[146] By July 12 it is clear that the crown, in the hope of avoiding 'some new trouble in Ireland', was willing to grant Nugent a pardon if he submitted himself.[147]

In fact, Nugent and MacGeoghegan did not find the situation in Edinburgh to be quite as favourable to them as they had expected. When they had been in Scotland in early 1582 power had been in the hands of the Sieur D'Aubigny, Esmé Stuart, newly created duke of Lennox. Lennox had been a Catholic but had conformed to Protestantism. Nevertheless, he was widely suspected of Catholic sympathies and the Catholic powers abroad hoped to be able to make use of him. But by 1584 the situation had changed. The government of Scotland was now in the hands of James Stewart of Ochiltree, earl of Arran. Arran had made himself the enemy of the Presbyterians by supporting the authority of the episcopacy. On the other hand, he was not favoured by Walsingham or by the queen's agents in Scotland. Moreover, Arran's immediate predecessor in power, the earl of Gowrie, had been a radical Protestant and despite his overthrow still retained the support of Protestant lords such as the earls of Mar and Angus. Thus up to the early months of 1584 Arran was forced to flirt with the continental powers in order to strengthen his own hand against the more radical Protestants and Presbyterians. But with the execution of Gowrie in May, Arran found his position less vulnerable. His preferred policy of moderate Protestantism became more tenable and he had less need of continental support. In August 1584, Queen Elizabeth made a rapprochment with him through her new agent, Hunsdon, and it began to look increasingly unlikely that Arran or the young king would promote an enterprise in Ireland.

Another close associate of the king from whom Nugent had expected a great deal was Patrick, Master of Gray. Gray had been a friend of Esmé Stuart and deeply embroiled in continental intrigues. He entertained Nugent and told him he could not conceive of how an Irish enterprise could fail.[148] However, Nugent's suspicions of Gray were aroused and he formed the impression that Gray's hopes were for an invasion of England rather than Ireland.[149] That Gray was playing a deep game was true, but his objectives were somewhat different to what Nugent imagined. It was Gray's hope to strengthen the position of King James by securing, if possible, the execution of the Queen of Scots and the formation of an Anglo-Scottish alliance. He had no intention of jeopardising these plans by encouraging a large-scale invasion of Ireland.

The expedition which William Nugent finally accompanied to Ireland in August 1584 was more of a private adventure than a royal enterprise. It was comprised of 800 men led by Maclean of Duart with the objective of securing some part of the patrimony of Shane O' Neill's sons, Maclean's cousins. Some men of the Isles were with them, perhaps as many as two thousand.[150] Turlough Luineach, though suspicious of the Scots' purpose, did not oppose them and soon they had launched an attack on MacSweeney's country. Brian MacGeoghegan had elected to remain behind for reasons which are unclear but it is possible that, in view of his hopes for a pardon, he had no wish to involve himself again in overt rebellion.

By September Nugent had made contact with Maguire and O'Rourke and was apparently travelling the outer Pale dressed as a friar in order to muster support.[151] By November he was in the Glynns in the company of Sorley Boy MacDonnell. It was here, on about 1 December, after a clash between the Scots and the queen's forces, that William Nugent finally decided to submit himself to Lord Deputy Perrot, who gave him hope of a pardon in return for 'something that may be serviceable to the state'.[152] On 4 December, at Dublin, Nugent made a formal submission, in a rather elegantly worded document which succeeded in being humble, yet not craven. This was accompanied by a declaration giving a brief account of his and MacGeoghegan's activities abroad.[153]

William Nugent's formal restoration to his property did not take place until 1608 but he clearly had the use of much of his lands long before that.[154] During the 1590s he and Delvin made attempts to avenge the death of their uncle by pursuing Robert

Dillon through the courts on charges of corruption and subversion. In the end their efforts failed and Dillon was declared innocent of the charges.[155] After this time, William Nugent retired, as it were, from public life and never, although he lived on until 1625, became involved in subversive activities again. When his son Richard joined Hugh O'Neill in 1600, it would appear that he did so without family approval.[156]

Essentially, the elements which brought together the Nugent rebels were local and private. Yet in some ways the revolt can, very tentatively, be compared with uprisings elsewhere in Europe during the sixteenth century. J. H. Elliott has noted that a recurring feature of popular revolt in the early modern period was an antipathy to outsiders, and certainly hostility to the New English élite was present among some of the conspirators of the Pale.[157] The revolt can be seen, too, against a background of resistance to change in that it had links with the campaign against cess which was frequently based upon appeals to old forms of common law.[158] It shared with other continental rebellions such as those in Corsica or the Netherlands the dimension of rebellion against a foreign power; that this power incorporated an equally alien religion added weight to feelings of disaffection. Like the Scots in the 1560s and William of Orange in the Netherlands, the Irish rebels looked to foreign governments for assistance. However, to draw too many parallels between the Nugent revolt and those which occurred beyond Irish shores or to imagine that it fell into some pattern of international revolt would be misleading and would tend to exaggerate the significance of Nugent's conspiracy. It may be that such comparisons could be fruitful in relation to the Baltinglass rebellion, at least in the sense that Baltinglass himself, possessed of the fervour of the Counter-Reformation, appealed to a wider European dimension beyond the Irish scene. But William Nugent's supporters were few in number and, as we have seen, their outlook was narrow in scope. It is certain that William Nugent, while in continental exile, saw the advantages of allying himself with the forces of the Counter-Reformation. But during 1581, unlike Baltinglass, he made scant appeal to religious feeling. It had been Baltinglass's original intention that he and the Nugents should combine forces with the Munster rebels and the Gaelic Irish in order to launch a

Catholic crusade.[159] Nugent ultimately rejected this idea and like the O'Connors and the O'Reillys who provided the greater part of his support among the Gaelic Irish, his foray into rebellion was primarily a response to local events. To believe that he or his fellow-conspirators had some clear notion of 'patria' or were possessed of a well-developed ideology, religious or social, would be to run the risk of imposing upon them modern perceptions of the revolutionary.

3. The emerging identity of an Irish military group in the Spanish Netherlands, 1586–1610

I
'A la guerra me lleva, mi necesidad:
Si tuviera dineros, no fuera en verdad'
(I was driven to the wars by my necessity
If I had money truly I would never go).
                              Cervantes, *Don Quixote*, ii

THE quotation from *Don Quixote* is singularly apt in relation to all military groups, and the Irish military group in Flanders[1] from 1586 to 1610 was no exception. Undoubtedly, the Irish who fought in the Spanish armies in Flanders were there because fundamentally there was little option of going anywhere else. Here men could use their fighting skills which they had perfected during the many wars in late sixteenth century Ireland and here, above all, they could earn money and be reasonably sure of a constant supply of food and basic medical attention. To provide a definition of this group, however, is somewhat more complex than giving this explanation and must involve an analysis of it within the context of continuing colonisation and social change in Ireland and the political and religious ideology of Counter-Reformation Europe. It is the aim of this essay firstly to outline the circumstances which precipitated migration from Ireland to the Netherlands, secondly to examine the social and structural organisation of the Irish military group in Flanders and thirdly to assess the emergence of a religious and political identity within this group.

The period from 1586 to 1610 witnessed the first generation of Irish military service in Flanders and forms a convenient unit of study, consisting of three distinct phases of Irish service in the Army of Flanders (the name given to the Spanish forces in Flanders). From 1585 to 1586 Sir William Stanley organised the levy and transport of over 1,000 troops from Ireland as part of an English expedition sent by Queen Elizabeth to assist the Northern States in the Low Countries, then in rebellion against Spain. In January 1587, however, Stanley surrendered the garrison of Deventer to Spanish forces and Irish military service with Spain in Flanders began from this date. The first phase of Irish service with Spain, then, was from 1587 to 1595 when most Irish troops in Flanders served under Stanley as part of his regiment of English, Irish and Scots troops. The second phase lasted from 1596 to 1604 during which time independent Irish companies under Irish captains were established, while a third phase from 1605 to 1610 witnessed the consolidation of all Irish companies into a regiment under Colonel Henry O'Neill.

In seeking to answer the question as to the number of people in that military group, one is handicapped by lack of accurate information on demographic patterns during the sixteenth century. Records of the Army of Flanders are incomplete and Irish names were often mistakenly listed as English or Scottish. From English sources, however, we know that in the two official levies for the Low Countries—one carried out by Stanley and the other by several Irish captains commissioned by the Spanish government, for Flanders in 1605—the numbers of Irish going to serve in Europe were high. Sir William Stanley brought over 1,000 troops with him to the Low Countries, recruited both from the ranks of the English army in Ireland and the Irish rebel camps.[2] In the period from 1605 to 1606 most of the six captains—William Walshe, Walter Delahide, Christopher St Lawrence, Thomas Preston, William Darcy and Maurice Fitzgerald[3]—managed to recruit their quota of 200 men each for the Archduke.

Of equal significance to this response to official levies was the fact that independent departure for foreign service in Ireland was a continuous process that coincided with the twenty-five years of our study. The records of the Army of Flanders as well as the reports of English agents show evidence of Irishmen arriving for army service right through the period from 1586 to 1610. Some names such as John Stanihurst and Thomas Butler appear in the records of the Army of Flanders before the Stanley expedition took place at all in 1586[4] and such freelance departures were not confined to isolated cases or to the upper levels of society. The correspondence of the banker, Von Fugger, in 1597 noted that 'wild Irish troops' joined the Archduke's service 'in great numbers daily'[5] and between 1597 and April 1605 the numbers of independent Irish companies rose from two to five.[6] These were mainly formed to accommodate those who left Munster and Connaught towards the end of the Nine Years War, and, after the flight of the earls in 1607, the number of Irish companies in Henry O'Neill's regiment was fifteen with a total of between 1,600 and 1,700 men.[7]

Two calculations about the overall numbers of Irish soldiers in question over a twenty-five year period can be made. Firstly there was a definite growth in the numbers of Irish serving in Flanders between the years 1586 and 1610. Estimating that about 700 of the 1,000 or so soldiers in Stanley's expedition of 1586 were actually Irish,[8] this can be compared with 1,700 Irish soldiers in Henry O'Neill's regiment before the Twelve Year Truce in April 1609.[9] This represented an increase of roughly 1,000 troops and the growth appears to have been a steady one although this is difficult to calculate as Irish companies were often segregated, some being deployed, for example, in France in the 1590s and some in Spain after 1605.[10]

Secondly, the number of Irish fighting in the Army of Flanders was maintained at a level of at least 500 a year.[11] Given Geoffrey Parker's estimation that between two and seven per cent of 'wastage' occurred amongst foreign troops in the army per month,[12] this would imply that over a twenty-five-year period a total of roughly 20,000 Irish soldiers saw service in Flanders. A certain percentage of this figure would be made up of those who came and went from Flanders a few times and it is difficult to know how far the Irish group was involved in heavy campaigning. It is noteworthy, however, that the numbers of Irish were at their highest (about 900) during two of the most intense periods of fighting in Flanders i.e. 1586–88 and 1600–1602[13] and a figure of 15,000 is probably a conservative estimate of the numbers of Irish soldiers in question.

Essentially, then, departure to foreign service was a form of migration. Whether with a contractor, an expedition, or by private means, a continuous stream of people voluntarily chose to enter military service in Flanders. Moreover it was a process almost certainly linked to periods of political upheaval and economic stress in Ireland.

For many of the poorer classes, military service in Flanders seemed to be an alternative to starvation or at least tremendous economic misery at home. The devastation of Ireland after the Desmond rebellion and the Nine Years War has been well documented and, significantly, the highest numbers to enter foreign service were in the period after the Desmond rebellion and at the culmination of the Nine Years War. These were also the periods which saw a mass exodus from Ireland of beggars and those seeking pensions in Spain, and there was certainly a close link between the migration of this group and those leaving for foreign service. The lords of the Council in England, in both the late 1580s and the early 1600s, complained consistently about the 'poore Irish people' or the 'great nombers of vagrant and masterless persons of the Irish byrthe' who passed through England begging on their way to Europe.[14] In 1606 Charles Wilmot noted that since his time in Ireland 'he saw no passage that had been for Spain but had been stuffed with Irishmen to seek for pensions of the Spanish King'.[15]

Not only did the migration of soldiers and beggars occur at a parallel period but many of those who went to beg or seek Spanish pensions in Europe almost certainly ended up in the rank and file of the Irish companies in Flanders or Spain. Many Irish beggars were encouraged to enter the service of the Archduke either by Spanish civil and military authorities, to whom they posed a social problem, or by interested parties within the Irish companies themselves. In July 1606, Arthur Chichester wrote to Salisbury about some Irish 'beggars' who, on their return to Munster from Flanders, told him they had been 'commanded to resort to the service of the Archduke' by Spanish authorities.[16] Similarly, captains from Henry O'Neill's regiment in 1608 were sent specifically 'into France to make a collection of all the Irish beggars who are there, and to reduce them into companies'.[17]

With the officer corps of the Irish in Flanders a similar parallel is obvious between the growing numbers in the military group and economic and political circumstances at home. Biographical details about the captains and officers of Irish companies indicate that they were either younger sons of the Pale gentry seeking a career or the sons of Gaelic and Anglo-Irish lords whose estates had been confiscated or hopelessly encumbered. Walter Delahide, Thomas Stanihurst and Thomas St Lawrence, for example, were all younger sons who later became captains under Henry O'Neill.[18] The estates of Captain Maurice Fitzgerald had been, according to his wife, 'confiscated by the English'[19] while Cormac Ros O'Connor and Cornelius O'Reilly in the Archduke's service were both younger brothers of those who held land under crown titles within Gaelic lordships.[20]

Migration to European armies from 1586 to 1610 was, then, closely linked to a wider pattern of migration from Ireland during this period. Service in Flanders was becoming to an increasingly wider group a temporary or long-term solution to their problems at home, attracting 'poore Irish' beggars and kerne as well as 'idle swordsmen', younger sons in pursuit of a career and heirs to estates severely in debt. It represented for many, if not a better way of life, at least an opportunity to make a better life for themselves. As a consequence the military group we are defining did not just consist of fighting men but also of their women and families.

Within the upper ranks of the Irish military circle in Flanders, specific mention is made in letters of wives or female relatives of a number of officers. Captain Thomas Finglas requested a passport in 1591 for himself and his wife to come from Antwerp to London,[21] while a report on Owen O'Loughye MacSweeney noted that he had brothers in the Irish regiment as well as 'a mother and sisters in Spain'.[22]

These women were not exceptional. It may be thought that family migration would be confined to those of the military class with wealth enough to pay their families' passages. In fact it was certainly common amongst the lower ranks as well as the higher. Reports from both the English and Spanish administrations make it clear that women and children formed a part of the constant stream of Irish coming to work in the Spanish armies. In 1605, William Ward, lieutenant of the Tower of London, noted that amongst the Irish levies on their way through London to Flanders, there were 'many women'[23] while in October of that year the lords of Council in England issued a formal complaint to the English administration in Dublin that those seeking 'employment' under foreign Princes and the 'poor and miserable inhabitants of Ireland . . . with their wives and children' had put the towns of England 'to continual charges' augmenting the threat of plague.[24]

Those in charge of the Irish troops on the field of battle in Flanders regularly referred to the wives and families of the troops. The earl of Leicester's disciplinary code in 1586 — formulated for the benefit of the Irish and English recruits newly arrived in the Low Countries — indicated that these women in fact could cause problems. Rule 5 of this code stated clearly that due to the 'sundry disorders and horrible abuses' caused by the existence of 'many vagrant idle women in an armie':

> . . . no man shall carrie into the fielde or deteine with him in the place of his garrison any woman whatsoever other than such as be known to be his lawful wife or such other women to tende the sicke and to serve for launders.[25]

Women and children, then, formed an important part of the Irish military group in Flanders, and, whether as wives or 'unlawful' companions, women in the lower ranks of the army certainly played an important supplementary economic role in 'the warrs'. The pay of the soldier in the Army of Flanders was both poor and irregular and, as the earl of Leicester implied, women could earn money in the army by nursing or doing the laundry. Von Grimmelshausen, a contemporary writer, noted that the list of women's jobs in the army could in fact include anything from selling tobacco and Branntwein to collecting snails and birds' nests.[26] However it seems from Spanish documentation that begging was the chief occupation of the Irish women in Flanders and Spain.[27]

Of course many soldiers who went to Flanders left their families in Ireland. This is clear from the small amount of correspondence which survives between husbands and wives in the two countries.[28] A number of soldiers in the twenty-five-year period 1586–1610, also received licences from the Spanish authorities to return to Ireland 'on business relating to their family'.[29] The proportion of those soldiers who did or did not bring their families to Europe is impossible to determine. What is evident is that the presence of women and children in the Army of Flanders was customary.

A further aspect to this practice of family migration to foreign service was the fact that soldiers serving in the Low Countries went themselves in family groupings. There are a few sources of information for this. Firstly family groupings are indicated by evidence we have on soldiers' surnames in the records of the Army of Flanders. Out of approximately twelve names of old Irish stock that we have from the rank and file of Stanley's regiment, there are two O'Doynes, three O'Moroghoes, two O'Shaughnessys and two O'Brynes.[30] Significantly, in Henry O'Neill's regiment, for which more detailed information is available, this pattern becomes even more pronounced. Fifty-four 'groups' of soldiers under the same surname emerge out of a total of 250 soldiers receiving ordinary pay.

Apart from the evidence of surnames in the records of the Army of Flanders, recruiting of 'servants and retainers' of the captain or recruiting officers appears to have been one of the cornerstones of both the 1586 and 1605–6 levies for the Low Countries. Florence MacCarthy, who had fought with William Stanley in Ireland, was reported in 1600 to have 'five of his kinsmen and servants fighting in Europe for Spain'.[31] Christopher St Lawrence recruited most of his quota of men from the Monaghan, Fermanagh and Cavan area where he was governor in about 1602 and was, according to Sir Arthur Chichester, 'well beloved' in these counties. In a letter to the Infanta Isabella in 1617, one Charles O'Daly, referring to a period probably prior to the truce with Holland in 1609, noted:

> After I had been for a long time a prisoner and persecuted by the heretics of my own country, I found a means of escape and fled with two hundred of my relations, kinsmen and friends, to France where I left them all, and came here myself with the purpose of bringing them into the service of his Majesty and . . . obtaining a commission as their captain.[32]

While O'Daly's reason for entering foreign military service may not have applied to all recruiting officers, it seems reasonable to assume that the composition of his levy was typical of those of the levies conducted by many captains.

Finally, within the upper ranks of the Irish companies for which more information is available, examples abound of family and kin relationships. The numbers of brothers, uncles and cousins serving together in the Irish military group is quite amazing. In 1588 a report in the records of the Army of Flanders described five members of the Burke family, viz. William, David, John, Richard and Walter as 'five Irish gentlemen, all brothers who have left their own country and possessions to come and serve his Majesty in these States'.[33] George and Walter Delahide, captains of independent Irish companies, were both sons of Lawrence Delahide of Moyglare, Co. Kildare,[34] while the most obvious example of these close family ties in Gaelic circles was that of Captains Owen Roe and Art MacBaron O'Neill who were brothers serving in the Irish regiment under their cousin.

Overall, then, the organisational pattern, both amongst the officer corps and the rank and file of the Irish in the Army of Flanders, consisted basically of an amalgamation of cohesive kin groups. Many soldiers were of course adventurers and wanderers but the majority appear almost certainly to have been bound up in some form of kin or family group.

II

The implications of this family and kin group migration to the Spanish army in Flanders were enormous. The Army of Flanders remained at an average strength of 65,000 men throughout the Eighty Years War between Spain and the United Provinces. It consisted of units from six different 'nations' — Spain, Italy, Burgundy, Germany, the British Isles and the local Walloons — although the commander corps was predominantly Spanish. Within this multi-racial and multi-lingual conglomerate, there is, however, substantial evidence that the Irish soldiers did conceive of themselves as a separate unit.

This can be explained partly by a brief examination of the army organisation of the Irish troops in Flanders. Up to 1596 the Irish troops did not serve under a distinctly Irish command. Within the officer corps of Colonel William Stanley's regiment from 1587 to 1596 there were only three Irish captains, Lawrence Fielan (Phelan?), Thomas Finglas and Oliver Eustace. Amongst the 'inferior officers' only eleven names which could have been Irish appear in the army records for this regiment.[35] This was to change between 1596 and 1605. The detailed 'Reformacion' or reorganisation of the Army of Flanders in 1596 by the newly installed Archduke Albert favoured the segregation of the six 'nations' of the army into 'national' and, therefore, more manageable units. Two Irish companies were formed under the command of Irish captains John de Claramonte and Edward Fitzgerald. For the first time the Irish had been recognised as a group distinct from the English and Scottish. Although many Irish appear to have continued to serve in Stanley's regiment after 1596, and Scottish and English names appear in the ranks of Irish companies right up to 1610[36]—these new Irish companies had an Irish officer corps and a rank and file membership that was mainly Irish while all new Irish arrivals to the Army of Flanders appear to have gone into them. Between 1597 and 1605, at least three other Irish companies were established under George and Lawrence Barnwall and Alexander Eustace.[37] In September 1605 when Henry O'Neill was given a commission to form an Irish regiment of 2,000 men, this was merely the logical culmination of a trend towards Irish consolidation established between 1596 and 1605.

Apart from the military organisation of the Irish group, perhaps the greatest significance of family and kin-migration to the wars in Flanders lay in the implication it had for the emergence of Irish military settlements or communities there. An examination of the parochial records of Flanders shows that Irish names existed in the parish registers of certain churches, indicating the emergence of Irish communities in these areas. Examples of these for the period up to 1610 seem to occur only in Brussels from 1587 (in the parishes of St Michel et Gudule and St Catherine) and Bruges from 1605 (in the parishes of St Giles and Notre Dame). However, such clusters of Irish names appear in an ever-increasing number of parishes up to 1700.[38]

Marriages certainly took place between Irish soldiers and Irish women suggesting that there was close interaction between the Irish military families in Flanders. Fifteen marriage certificates of Irish interest survive in parish records of Brussels while many more weddings almost certainly took place in military garrisons conducted by army chaplains.[39]

Baptismal records of Irish interest also indicate that Irish families had settled in the areas of Bruges and Brussels. Six baptismal certificates for the parish of St Catherine in Brussels between 1594 and 1609 show the birth of six Irish children, Peter O'Neill, William Burke, Nicholas and Jeanne Barry and Josse and Jeanne O'Donnell. The parents of these were associated with the Irish regiment and the records of the parishes in both Bruges and Brussels show an ever-increasing number of Irish baptismal certificates up to 1700.[40]

Apart from the close interactions of Irish families, other factors also indicated an introverted Irish military community. Language was one element. Although some officers like Maurice Fitzgibbon or Thomas Stanihurst were able to speak Spanish or French,[41] many Irish soldiers appear to have been unable to speak any language other than their own. A contemporary at Deventer garrison in the late 1580s noted that the Irish soldiers 'spoke an unintelligible language and could not have any intercourse with the inhabitants'[42] while in 1610 after three years at Louvain, neither the young earl of Tyrconnell's tutor, Hugo O'Gallagher, nor his wife Cecilia 'could speak one word of Flemish'.[43]

There was also a preoccupation, particularly amongst the upper circles of Irish military society, with genealogy and ancestry. The inscription on the memorial cabinet of Jean Antoine Preston, son of Thomas Preston, for example, bore not only the Preston arms but also the arms of the Fitzwilliams, Fitzgerald and Finglas families to whom the Preston family in Ireland were related.[44] Amongst old Irish circles, chroniclers such as Tuileagna MacTerna Conry, O.F.M., or Thomas O'Gorman were employed up to the end of the eighteenth century, to trace back the genealogies of their clients.[45] Perhaps of greatest significance was the practice by soldiers at all levels of military service of identifying themselves with the birthplace of their fathers. Dorothy Molloy, in a study of the personal details of the sick and wounded Irish soldiers at the hospital of Santa Cruz from the mid-seventeenth to the mid-eighteenth century, noted that even Irish soldiers who had obviously been born on the continent gave their fathers' birthplace in Ireland as their own.[46] The practice was also common in Flanders in the early seventeenth century as is evident from the letters of men like Dermot Mallun (O'Malley) or Thomas de Burgo (Burke) who also gave their Irish titles on any correspondence.[47]

While obviously the preoccupation with lands and lineage was one confined mainly to the upper circles of the Irish military group in Flanders and indeed is a feature of the period up to 1610, by 1610 there are signs of an emerging Irish military community in Flanders not only in terms of organisation and structure but also in terms of self-identity. There was a growing awareness of the 'separateness' of the Irish soldier from the English or Scottish, there was close interaction between families with military connections while certain areas of Brussels and Bruges can be identified as 'Irish quarters' with Irish the language almost certainly spoken there.

This Irish military community, however, should not be identified with our modern-day perceptions of an Irish community in England or the United States. Records of Irish interest may appear to be clustered in certain parish registers but Irish names were listed among many others including the local Walloon or French-speaking population and these parishes or quarters were by no means exclusively Irish. There were in fact surprisingly close links between the Irish military group and the local Netherland population.

Intermarriage certainly occurred between the two groups. Of the sixteen marriage records of Irish interest surviving in the parish registers of Brussels, at least ten seem to have been mixed marriages between Irish and Flemish or Walloon, while of the baptismal certificates where both parents' names are mentioned, four of the six children were of mixed marriages. Those named in these registers, however, were most likely from the upper levels of Irish society in Flanders while family migration from Ireland was probably most common amongst the poorer sections. However, even amongst the rank and file such marriages were common. From an army list of widows' pensions in 1635, which included the wives of both soldiers and officers, one-third of the marriages were mixed and it is noticeable that most of the rank and file widows were of Netherland extraction.[48]

Even closer links between the Irish military and the Walloons and Flemings can be established from Irish baptismal certificates for this period. In accordance with the Council of Trent decrees only two godparents were named for each child and these often appear to have been either Flemish or Walloon. From sixteen fairly complete baptismal certificates only three in fact have not at least one Flemish or Walloon godparent even where both parents were Irish. Given the important role of the godparent in European kin groups, even as late as the beginning of the seventeenth century, this particular link signified a degree of intimacy and mutual acceptance between two groups that was remarkable.

Family ties were of course not the only links established between the Irish military and their new environment. Many of those who went to serve in the Army of Flanders forged important military and political careers for themselves. Thomas Preston was eventually appointed governor of Geneppe in North Brabant in 1641. Even before 1612 John Bal, Dermot O'Mallun, Edward Fitzgerald and Walter Delahide were given positions 'cerca la persona' in the Archduke's service—the highest position a non-Spaniard could attain in the Army of Flanders.[49] Unlike English subjects, the Irish in Spanish territories were accorded the same legal privileges as Spanish subjects. Hence Irish traders flourished and military commanders like Thomas Preston and John Kennedy acquired estates in Flanders.[50]

The integration of the Irish military community into the local environment should not, of course, be exaggerated. We have already seen that this community was in many ways introverted and conscious of its links with Ireland. Moreover relations between the soldier and the civilian populations, particularly at the level of rank and file, were often far from harmonious.

The Irish, particularly in the sixteenth century, had a reputation for barbarity and wildness. Grotius called the Irish soldiers 'strangers both to humanity and civility' while Le Clerc described them as 'half naked and extraordinarily savage'.[51] This reputation was often merited though it was much less justified by the early 1600s. The very nature of a soldier's career, particularly in the Army of Flanders, was transient and unstable. Apart from the huge death rates during campaigns, pay was often years in arrears and food in short supply for such a huge army while Irish soldiers seem to have been particularly affected by a fever illness. The Irish regiment in 1607 was, for example, down to two-thirds its force due to illness.[52]

Between 1580 and 1601 no less than twenty-three mutinies occurred within the Army of Flanders. Most of them lasted well over six months and the Irish were involved in at least some of these. Not surprisingly, many Irish soldiers sought licences to return home. Between 1588 and 1610, 130 licences were granted to Irishmen to travel back to Ireland. As licences could only be granted in cases of sickness or family deaths, one can assume many more Irish deserted. Even amongst the captains of companies, we know that of the forty who had companies between 1587 and 1610, four died in service, twenty remained for ten years or more while six, we can conclude from English sources, almost certainly went home after less than three years of service.[53]

Transience and movement, then, were constant factors in a soldier's life and form part of any definition of the Irish military community in Flanders—and the term 'Irish military community' needs careful definition. Certainly the years, 1586 to 1610, saw increasing numbers of Irish families migrating, a growth in the size and spread of Irish settlements, and links established with the local Netherlanders. Ultimately, however, these twenty-five years witnessed only the first generation of an Irish military presence in Flanders and the number of Irish soldiers who settled in Flanders by 1610 was probably a great deal smaller than the number of those who were temporary migrants. The importance of the social cohesion of this military group lay in its sense of community or belonging. The traditional view of the soldier in exile, which saw him purely in terms of a dispossessed wanderer from camp to camp was wholly inaccurate. Not only did he form a part of a cohesive collection of kin groups and family units, but he was also establishing certain links with his new world in the Netherlands.

III

The 'new world' of the Irish soldier was that of Counter-Reformation Europe. The southern provinces of the Netherlands were dominated by Catholic Spain. Not only did these provinces owe political allegiance to Spain but they were characterised by an emerging Catholic identity and the flowering of a Counter-Reformation movement that was directed largely by the Habsburg government. From the patronage of traditional shrines and new religious orders to the implementation of regulations regarding discipline and education for the laity and the clergy, Philip II and the Archdukes Albert and Isabella (1598–1633) consciously reshaped the Catholic church of the Spanish Netherlands in the Tridentine fashion.[54] From the 1590s then, the Archdukes, and to some extent the Nunciature at Brussels,[55] created in the Spanish Netherlands a spirit of Catholic reform as well as a political asylum for recusant Catholics which attracted English and later Irish religious and emigré groups to these provinces. An essential part of the soldiers' world was a wider circle of Irish, English and Scottish Catholic Counter-Reformation groups in the Low Countries. The values and ideals which were to bind this military group together can only be examined in the context of the wider Irish community in the Spanish Netherlands.

For convenience, those who formed part of the soldiers' 'wider world' can be divided into two categories. There were those students in Catholic seminaries and Catholic clergy who made up the Irish religious community of the Low Countries; and there was the exile group, who, while also embracing Catholicism as their religion, had left Ireland for a variety of complex motives and settled on the continent.[56] The links established between these groups and the military community were close both in terms of personal contacts and the influence exerted by religious and exile groups in military domains.

English reports clearly emphasised a close association between Irish soldiers and 'popish priests' in Flanders right through the period from 1586 to 1610. Sir William Stanley's defection to Spain gave rise to much speculation in English circles that this had been as a result of Jesuit influence both on Stanley and on his troops. Sir Ralph Sadler referred to Stanley's regiment after Deventer as 'a regiment of seminarie soldiers', while in the early 1600s administrators like Arthur Chichester and John Davies continued to regard Irish soldiers and Irish priests as a twin threat to the security of the Irish realm.[57]

To a large extent this association of the two groups was justified. The growth and consolidation of the Irish military group in the Low Countries had been parallelled in the 1580s and 1590s by a similar process amongst Irishmen and women going to the continent to study at Catholic colleges and convents. During the 1590s Irish colleges were established at Valladolid, Salamanca, Alcala de Henares and Lisbon in Spain and Portugal, while in the Spanish Netherlands an Irish college at Douai was founded in 1594 by Christopher Cusack, and St Anthony's of Louvain was founded by Florence Conry, O.F.M., in 1607.[58] Although lack of funds and constant changes of location were features of all religious houses and colleges until well into the 1620s, Louvain and Douai with its appendages at Lille, Tournai and Antwerp were to form the Irish centres of post-Tridentine Catholic learning.

Not surprisingly, close family ties existed between Irish religious and military groups. Although statistics are incomplete for both groups, the numerous examples of those serving in the Army of Flanders who had brothers or near kin in the colleges and religious institutions, must indicate that the percentage of such ties was high. Even a cursory examination of the registers of the religious houses and colleges in the Low Countries would seem to bear out this close family relationship between the religious and military groups. For example, of the twenty-eight Irish names listed as clerical students in the archdiocese of Malines (including Louvain) between 1600 and 1610,[59] there were only five who did not have either brothers or near kin serving during the same period in the Irish regiment. In 1625, although admittedly at a period later than our study, six of the seven founders of the Irish Poor Clare Order of nuns appear to have had brothers serving in the Army of Flanders.[60]

A formal channel of communication between the religious and military groups was initiated by the Spanish army officials. It was the usual practice in the Army of Flanders to appoint a chaplain to each company of soldiers, and accordingly chaplains were appointed to Irish companies a few months after the surrender of Deventer. According to a report by Salisbury in 1592 there seem to have been '8 priests and Jesuits' receiving some sort of pay in Stanley's regiment.[61] They all appear to have been from the English Catholic emigré community with the exception of James Archer who was almost certainly charged with the specific task of working with the Irish kerne in

Stanley's regiment. In 1593 Walter Talbot, S.J., was reported to be serving the needs of the Irish in Stanley's regiment and since Fr David Sutton was officially appointed as chaplain to Alexander Eustace's company some time before 1605 it can be assumed that chaplains must have served the other Irish companies as well.

The formation of the Irish regiment undoubtedly stimulated a more regulated approach to the appointment of priests to minister to these soldiers' needs. Nicholas Brae, William Barry, Edmund O'Donoghue, John White, Dermot O'Hullacayn and John Delahide were appointed by the Spanish authorities as chaplains to six of the fifteen companies established by 1608, while those listed as 'sacerdotes' were obviously employed in the specific capacity of preachers or confessors to the soldiers. There were thirteen and possibly fifteen appointees that were know of, and all were Irish with the possible exception of Rodrigo Magel.[62]

What function did chaplains have amongst the soldiers and what kind of influences did they exert over them? A. Poncelet's study of the Society of Jesus in the Low Countries outlined the nature of a chaplain's work in the Army of Flanders. He wrote:

> They preached, catechised, heard confessions and celebrated mass in the presence of the army. On campaign they accompanied the soldiers, living under tent, following them unto the field of battle, animating them before combat and thereafter comforting the wounded and dying under enemy fire.[63]

In times of peace, he wrote, chaplains visited hospitals, settled quarrels amongst the men and encouraged them to become members of confraternities and sodalities. This is a somewhat idealistic picture perhaps, especially when some Irish Jesuits such as Henry Fitzsimons had a notorious reputation for gambling and fighting.[64] On the whole, however, eye-witness accounts bear out the picture as being accurate, at least in terms of what the Jesuits, in particular, hoped to achieve. The curate and echevins (aldermen) of Zichiem in 1598 noted that Walter Talbot worked regularly amongst the Irish soldiers as their 'preacher and ghostlie' father and went with them on pilgrimage to Montague.[65] Nicholas Brae heard confessions and administered the last rites to both Irish and English soldiers at the military hospital at Malines[66] while Henry Fitzsimons, S.J., worked with the victims of the plague in 1611–12 until he contracted it himself.[67]

Nor were religious instruction and ministration among soldiers confined to the chaplains or priests appointed by the army authorities. In the Jesuits' Annual Letters of Tournai in 1606 a report related the activities of 'two Jesuits from the Novice House of Tournay' who went to the Irish soldiers in winter quarters in Mildeburg. There, it claims 'they converted thirty-eight heretics, taught soldiers to say the Angelus on their knees', and encouraged soldiers to give up swearing, observe fast days and do penances.[68] Such a report indicated the close relations established between the soldiers and the religious houses in their proximity. Likewise in the case of Louvain, Hugh MacCaughwell's dual appointment as chief chaplain of the Irish regiment in 1606 and guardian at St Anthony's, Louvain in 1607 ensured that there was frequent contact between the Franciscan friars and the soldiers. In fact the friars were granted special leave by the archbishop of Malines to carry out religious duties within the Irish regiment and it was no coincidence that Bonaventure O'Hussey's catechism was produced at Louvain, to cater 'for the instruction of Irish soldiers in the doctrine of Trent'.[69] Based on Bellarmine's *Copiosa Explicatio*, and the teachings of Trent, the essential articles of faith in verse form and the simple presentation of the catechism were ideal for the instruction of the predominantly Irish-speaking soldiers.

The extent to which Counter-Reformation doctrine was being openly preached amongst the Irish soldiers in Flanders was probably best exemplified by the wrath of Sir Thomas Edmondes, English ambassador at Brussels. He complained consistently about the 'meddling by Jesuits' amongst the Irish serving in Flanders. On 5 April 1606, he demanded of Salisbury that 'the practising with any for change of their religion be forbidden' in the service of the Archduke, and 'that order be taken for the affording of charitable burials to the Protestants' who volunteered for service there.[70]

The chaplain's role was by no means restricted to religious instruction and devotional work. He had also a wide role in administering the sacraments in accordance with the rules laid down by Trent. He heard confessions, administered the last rites and almost certainly officiated at marriages for the soldiers of ordinary ranks whose names do not appear in the parish records of Brussels and Bruges.[71] The chaplain or priest, being literate, also had considerable responsibility in practice for various financial and business transactions within the military circle. Chaplains in the Army of Flanders were until 1596 wholly responsible for the wills and testaments of soldiers and even after this date continued to assist with them. Religious authorities sometimes gave loans to soldiers, and in return for such services and the duties carried out in general by the religious, regular collections were made amongst the soldiers for the religious houses. Henry O'Neill organised a collection within the regiment towards the building of St Anthony's College and chapel at Louvain.[72] James Gernon organised a similar collection in his company in 1616. In this latter collection 850 escudos was the total contributed by 122 men. Most of the soldiers gave four to eight escudos, the equivalent of a month's salary,[73] which may have reflected somewhat the extent to which the priest had already established himself as a figure of authority within the Irish military group at this time.

Another factor that linked the religious and military communities was the number of clerical students who appear to have served as soldiers in Irish companies in order to finance their studies. Edmund O'Kelly, for example, got special permission in 1606 to transfer 'his army grant to assist him in his studies at Louvain', while in May 1608 Florence Carty received a grant of fifteen escudos monthly on the Citadel at Cambrai 'without obligation to serve while studying at the university of Douai'.[74] There is no specific information to indicate that these men carried out religious duties in the Army of Flanders but their presence amongst the Irish soldiers must have represented some type of religious influence.

In fact a measure of the extent to which the Spanish authorities identified the religious and military groups can be seen in the number of contributions made frequently to religious institutions from army funds. In 1596 the money allotted to the Irish infantry included a grant 'to the fifty-three students at Douai', while in 1614 nine Irish and English institutions, including the college of Douai, lost all or part of their annual allowance due to the last 'reformacion' of the army.[75]

The official appointment of chaplains and priests to cater for the soldiers' spiritual needs, the family ties between the two groups and the close association between clerical students and the army camp represented a deep bond between the army and religious personnel. It was a bond that was probably strengthened in relation to the growth in the number of Irish colleges and the number of Irish students going to study in the Low Countries. The shift from a corps of army chaplains and priests who were predominantly English to an all-Irish one was in itself an indication of this. Closer contacts undoubtedly existed between the religious and military groups in the period after 1600 than in Stanley's time, when, in the first instance, language problems would have created a tremendous barrier between the English chaplains and the Irish soldiers.

Apart from the close links established between army and religious personnel, the clergy exerted a considerable degree of influence on the promotion and recruitment of the Irish soldiers in the Army of Flanders. From 1587 those Irish priests and religious with influence at the duke of Parma or the Archduke's court consistently used this influence to get military grants or positions for those favoured by them. A letter believed to have been written by O'Connor Sligo to the archbishop of Tuam at Antwerp in 1591 commended the son of Robert More and requested that the Archduke procure a good position for him in 'the service of the Spanish King'.[76] Similarly, from the time of his appointment as one of the chief advisers to the Spanish Council on Irish affairs, Florence Conry vouched for several of the Irish then entering Spain.[77]

Charles Wilmot, joint-commissioner for Munster, claimed in 1606 that 'all Irish' had pensions or military positions allotted to them by 'religious men of the Irish nation',[78] but this was an exaggeration. The control which priests exerted depended on the position or influence they had with the king of Spain or the archdukes. The archbishop of Tuam in 1581 and Florence Conry after 1607 were exceptional in the political authority they had. Not even these men, however, were likely to have allotted positions and pensions to 'all Irish' coming to Spain. This was the business of Spanish army and state officials. The authority of the Irish priests lay in their literacy and their intimate knowledge of genealogies and social divisions in Ireland. Within a military context their role was almost certainly to advise Spanish authorities in the granting of *entretenimientos*, promotions and honorary titles.

Priests had also by 1606 come to exert considerable influence on recruitment in Ireland for foreign armies. While there seems to be no evidence of clerical opposition to Stanley's levy in 1586, one complaint of interference by priests during the 1605–6 levies was very significant. Captain William Nuse wrote in January 1606 that it was almost impossible to recruit a company in Ireland for the United Provinces because the Irish under the influence of the priests would 'not serve against the King of Spain'. On the other hand, if he were to recruit for the Archduke he would have 'not only choice of as many men as he desired, but the lords of the countries would arm them and give them cess till their embarking . . . at the procurement of the priests'.[79]

It is difficult to know how true this statement was but it seems that there is no reason to doubt its validity especially in the light of documentary evidence on priests' activities during the state-sponsored Swedish expedition of 1609–10. Organised to rid the country of its 'worst sort', this expedition of troops, mainly from Ulster, to the Swedish king was opposed by both friars and Jesuits. Furious reports were sent to England by Arthur Chichester and John Davies about 'seminary priests' who 'persuaded the people that it was altogether unlawful to go to such a war where they should fight for a heretic and an usurper against a Catholic and rightful king'.[80] Moreover the priests seem to have made some impact. In September 1610 Chichester wrote to the Privy Council that 'the priests and other ill spirits which govern them, spread false tales and . . . have caused idle and able men to run into the woods or to stand upon their keeping for the time'.[81] Some of those who did set out for Sweden appear to have ended up serving Spain anyhow. Oghy Og O'Hanlon (Tyrone's nephew) and Art Og O'Neill, driven by storms onto the coast of England, escaped and made their way to the Spanish armies on the continent, while some who did arrive in Sweden were drawn by Cornelius O'Reilly and 'a couple of friars in the habits of soldiers' to the Polish or Imperial armies.[82]

The Irish clergy in Flanders, then, exerted a significant degree of control not only over the religious practices of the Irish soldier but over the organisation and structure of the Irish military group. Given the growth in both the religious and military communities, the overall pattern during the years from 1586 to 1610 was one of increasing influence by the religious group on those following a military career in Flanders. A similar pattern of influence was to emerge in the military group's connection with the wider circle of Irish exiles on the continent.

The term 'exile group' needs careful examination. Although the term obviously applied to Irish who, in this case, had settled in Spain and the Low Countries, the word 'exile' could have many connotations. J. J. Silke defined the different categories of Irish going abroad as exiles of conscience or recusants, those who went abroad for political and economic reasons and those who sought help from foreign Catholic rulers in the struggle against the English crown. Although such categories are of necessity artificial they probably represented adequately the different strands identifiable within the exile group, and while the word 'exile' implies enforced asylum in a foreign country, the decision for many of this group to go to the continent was, at least in part, opportunist.

The 'exile group' incorporated people who had gone to the continent for a variety of complex reasons and saw their position in relation to Ireland in many different ways. However, an emphasis on the distinctions within the Irish exile group could be misleading. The term 'exile' had certain political connotations. During the 1580s and 1590s the exile group, whether for religious ideals or a desire to regain the social and political status they had enjoyed before Tudor encroachment, sided with Spain in her war against England and Protestantism and became increasingly associated with Spanish aggression and Counter-Reformation Catholicism.

The exile group had from the late 1580s close associations with the emerging military community in Flanders. Many of the exiles like Walter Talbot, Terence MacSweeney, Denis Fitzgerald and Cormac O'Connor received an *entretenimiento* or monthly salary from the army funds allotted to the Irish infantry in Flanders.[83] While most of the leaders in the Geraldine and Baltinglass revolts fled to Spain and were identified chiefly with the Spanish court at Madrid, many of the leading members of these exile groups actually spent time in Flanders. Thomas

Fitzgerald, cousin of Maurice Fitzgerald, was noted in the Army of Flanders records of 1589 to have 'served his Majesty in the royal armada' where he was lost off Scotland whence recently he came to these states'.[84] John Lacey, described as an 'entretenido' in the Army of Flanders, received a passport for Spain 'on personal business' in 1589.[85] Gaelic Irish, who had been associated with revolts in Ireland, were also the recipients of such grants. O'Connor Faly, claimant to the lordship of Offaly, 'served in the Army of Flanders for 28 years', while Cormac Ros O'Connor, Dowling O'Byrne and Hugh O'Reilly all appear to have spent a number of years attached to the army in the capacity of gentlemen soldiers.[86]

It would be a mistake, moreover, to regard the interests of the 'exile group' as being confined to a small élite old English and old Irish corps who were determined to regain their property or the social and political status they had enjoyed in Ireland before the extension of New English authority. Their position in Ireland affected a whole range of people, not only within their own family circles or extended kin, but also their former dependants and the 'idle swordsmen' who had been employed by the Anglo-Irish and Gaelic lords. In this context the vested interests of the exile group were well represented at every level within the ranks of the Irish military group. Not only did the Anglo-Irish families involved in the Geraldine and Baltinglass revolts predominate within the officer corps of the Irish companies, both under Stanley and the independent Irish captains,[87] but the bulk of the rank and file also appear to have consisted mostly of the vassals and dependants of these families. Moreover this was also a pattern that continued clearly from 1601 to 1610 with the arrival on the continent of the Gaelic lords and their dependants, and the second phase in the development of the exile group. Apart from the fact that the dependants of Hugh O'Neill, Teig MacCarthy and Connor O'Driscoll were accommodated both within the officer corps and the rank and file of the Irish infantry, the presence of the 'exile' group was clearly evident in the impressive list of 'entretenidos' in Henry O'Neill's regiment, the majority of whom had left Ireland after the battle of Kinsale. The influence of the community of exiles was not only growing in relation to the military group, but its members were increasingly becoming an inherent part of the latter's structure.

There is no doubt that the external pressure put on the Spanish government, particularly by the northern exile group after 1607, did affect the organisation of the Irish military group. This was particularly true in the case of Hugh O'Neill, earl of Tyrone. In the first instance, Henry O'Neill undoubtedly owed his own appointment as colonel of the Irish regiment in Flanders to Hugh O'Neill's prestige in Ireland and well-established diplomatic network at the Madrid court.[88] Henry, at eighteen years of age, had less than two years' military experience before his appointment as colonel in 1605.

Hugh O'Neill's arrival with O'Donnell and Maguire and their dependants on the continent further enhanced Hugh's influence within the Irish regiment. Not only were many of Hugh O'Neill's 'company . . . disposed into the regiment' in 1608,[89] but in the following years he consistently used his influence to recommend his allies for positions in the Irish regiment. In October 1608 he wrote to Henry directing him 'to procure for the bearer James O'Gallacher, the late earl of Tyrconnell's servant, a safe passage through England, if possible, or else the place of a soldier in his regiment',[90] while in 1612 he made a special request to the Archduke that Cornelius O'Reilly receive the payment he had previously enjoyed in the Army of Flanders.[91] In both these cases O'Neill's suit seems to have been successful, and at times his requests could be more ambitious. In 1613 he asked Philip III that seven Irish companies, which had been dismissed by the King of Poland, be incorporated into the Irish regiment. These men had been part of an expedition originally sent by Chichester, 'to serve the heretics of Moscow and Sweden in their wars against the King of Poland', but had 'passed over to the Catholic army'.[92] The circumstances of this plea made by Hugh O'Neill on their behalf were interesting. The Spanish Ambassador at Rome, Conde de Castro, noted:

> . . . the poor men go begging from door to door and many of them have come to the Earl for they feel that he has an obligation towards them; this is true for, in his cause, they were exiled. The hardship they suffer is a cause of great sorrow to the Earl, all the more as he kows that, if they return to their country, all of them will be beheaded.[93]

These soldiers had obviously been dependants of either Hugh

O'Neill or Rory O'Donnell in Ulster, and O'Neill's desire to see them enlisted in the Irish regiment was undoubtedly related to this factor. It was a measure of O'Neill's determination that these men be established 'as soldiers among those of their nation' in Flanders, that he turned to Philip III after a flat refusal from the Archduke.[94] Significantly O'Neill achieved partial if not total success with this request. Philip III promised to persuade the Archduke and the Marquess Espinola to 'examine what could be done with them and the manner of admitting them'.[95]

Sir Arthur Chichester was convinced of Hugh O'Neill's all-powerful influence over the Irish regiment. In 1608 he wrote to Salisbury that the regiment 'would disband of themselves if the fugitive Earls had not come amongst them and dealt with the Archduke for their stay and better usage'.[96] This, however, was an exaggeration. The Archduke had always wished to maintain a strong military force in what he saw as a vulnerable Spanish Netherlands between France, England and Holland, and he had shown this to be his priority when he refused to allow Irish companies to go to Ireland in 1600. At least until the Truce with Holland in April 1609 he showed himself continually averse to losing any part of his force.

There was, however, no doubt that Hugh O'Neill's ambition, with regard to the Irish regiment, was to preserve it intact. In expressing concern to Philip III in 1608 on the numbers of Irish either sick or leaving the regiment, he made his position clear. He wrote: 'It is of great importance to the service of Your Majesty and to the benefit of our country that the Irish Regiment should be preserved' and further begged his Majesty to 'ensure that the soldiers remain in their regiment.[97] Already by July 1608 there were several references in discussions in the Spanish Council of State to 'The Regiment of Tirone' in place of the Irish regiment, and in October 1610 the Conde de Castro wrote to Philip III on the occasion of Henry O'Neill's death, that

> . . . at the end of his days, Colonel Don Enrique Onel begged Your Majesty not to allow his appointment as Colonel to be filled by any other than a person nominated by the Earl of Tirone his father.[98]

It was a measure of Hugh O'Neill's success in identifying his interests with the Irish regiment that this request made by

Henry O'Neill was granted. Against both the wishes of the English ambassador at Brussels and such an influential person as Florence Conry, who favoured Owen Roe O'Neill[99] it was Hugh O'Neill's own son John[100] who was appointed as Henry O'Neill's successor as colonel of the Irish regiment in 1610. There can be no doubt that Hugh O'Neill saw the Irish regiment as a body over which he intended to have complete control and his ambitions appear to have been accepted by Spain.

By 1610 the military community had become thoroughly immersed in the ideological world of the Counter Reformation. It had not only become an inherent part of such a wider community in the Low Countries through a network of family ties, social interaction and financial interdependence; it was also increasingly becoming part of this wider community's religious and political ambitions in Ireland. The precise role which Hugh O'Neill envisaged for the regiment was made clear in a 'Memorial of Hugh O'Neill to the King of Spain' in 1610. In requesting Philip to send 'an army secretly and in the name of His Holiness' to Ireland, O'Neill assured Philip that this army 'with the help of the Irish who are in these parts, especially . . . the Irish Regiment of one thousand, five hundred men serving Your Majesty in Flanders . . . would be sufficient to take Ireland with speed'.[101] The Irish regiment was obviously to be used as a vanguard in the military overthrow of the English administration in Ireland.

The military community in Flanders has for too long been assessed in terms of its members being mercenaries or militant nationalists. The political identity of the Irish regiment in 1610 was a complex and developing one. There were certainly regional and cultural differences, individual aspirations and political loyalties amongst the soldiers within it. However, by 1610 this identity had come to include an identification with Counter-Reformation Catholicism and a growing sense of national consciousness. In 1626 Captain Sorley MacDonnell of the Irish regiment commissioned the friars at Louvain to collect and transcribe certain old Irish manuscripts. Significantly the manuscripts in question recounted the story of the epic of the Fianna,[102] the protectors of Ireland against outside forces and Fionn, the personification of perfection both in body and soul.

4. *The Wexford Catholic community in the later seventeenth century*

IN a recent survey of Catholicism in Wexford in the early modern period Patrick J. Corish has shown how the agents of the Counter-Reformation achieved a fair measure of success in establishing a diocesan church in the county despite major military and political upheavals. There were, according to this account, three separate attempts to stabilise Catholic church organisation, each coinciding with the career of a notable bishop of Ferns and each following a period of disruption and discontinuity: that of Bishop John Roche (1627-36) after the rapid social and religious changes of the Tudor and early Stuart period; that of Bishop Luke Wadding (coadjutor bishop and then bishop, 1671-91) following the Cromwellian overthrowing of Catholic structures; and that of Bishop Nicholas Sweetman (1745-86) in the wake of the imposition and early implementation of the penal laws. The picture of Catholic life in County Wexford which emerges in the late eighteenth century is a favourable one on the whole. Allowing for local variations, one can discern a pattern of well-organised parishes, closely supervised by the bishop and served by well-educated parish priests who provided the sacramental and catechetical ministry decreed by the Council of Trent.[1]

In this essay I wish to examine the history of the Catholic community of the town of Wexford during the crucial phase of recovery after the dislocation caused by massacre and its consequences in the 1650s. The general developments which Mgr Corish has perceived as characterising the history of the Catholic church in the county may be scrutinised at work among the Catholic population of the town. In particular the size of that population will be discussed as a prelude to the assessment of the nature of religious practice which emerged under the supervision of Bishop Wadding. A most significant aspect of the

subject is the extent to which Catholics accommodated themselves to some of the requirements of the state church within the
context of fairly harmonious relations between members of the
Protestant and Catholic élites. Besides the records from Catholic
sources such as the earliest surviving Catholic register and the
writings of Bishop Wadding, the state records preserved in the
papers of H. F. Hore are indispensable for the researcher of the
ecclesiastical and local history of Wexford.[2]

On the question of the number of people in the Catholic
community of Wexford town in the later seventeenth century
there is an extreme shortage of statistical information and of
population estimates for similar towns which might provide
comparisons.[3] Catholic baptismal records do exist for part of the
period, begun by Luke Wadding as parish priest in compliance
with synodal regulations.[4] Although there is no record of death-
rates within the Catholic community or of the overall birth-rate,
an examination of the baptismal register for the years 1695-9
may be taken as providing a reasonably reliable estimate of the
number of Catholics in Wexford at the end of the century. The
following are the relevant data:

Year	Number baptised
1695	68
1696	76
1697	65
1698	58
1699	66
Total	333

Assuming a birth-rate of 1 in 30, or 33 per 1,000,[5] we may
multiply the average yearly figure of 66.6 by 30 divided by 2,
and the result is 999. This figure seems to square with evidence
from other sources. Writing in 1682 Solomon Richards had
remarked that Wexford town 'was in good order and very
populous since the last rebellion, but much depopulated in its
taking by Oliver Cromwell'.[6] Wadding wrote that of the large

number of Catholics in the five parishes of the town, 'scarcely 400 survived', an estimate made on his first coming to Wexford about 1674.[7] Obviously the population had not by any means returned to its pre-Cromwellian level but Wadding's estimate of 1674, and the 1659 'census' figure of 562 'Irish' within the town, seem to justify the estimate of 1,000 Catholics in Wexford town in 1699.

What then were the characteristics of this community? Its small numbers suggest that it was probably very close-knit. Intermarriage between Old Irish and Old English was not prevalent between 1672 and 1690. Although the Old Irish appear frequently in the register it is still obvious that the Old English form the majority group. After 1690, however, intermarriage between the two groups becomes more frequent but it is by no means an established fact of life even as late as 1720. This is borne out by a contemporary account: '[the inhabitants] seldom dispose of their children in marriage but unto natives, or such as will determine to reside in the barony. So that generally they are in consanguinity or affinity nearly related.'[8] This last reference to consanguinity ties in with the evidence of the parish register: the majority of dispensations recorded are concerned with impediments of consanguinity or affinity, the degree being mostly of the third and fourth grade, i.e. second and third cousins.[9] Besides this intermarriage, the parish records also show that the community was bound together by other forms of 'kinship': members frequently acted as godparents to each other's children and we can identify various circles of friends by the frequency with which they did so. The children were most often named after a sponsor and the naming of children after their parents was extremely rare.

It is customary in the twentieth century to consider participation in the sacraments of one church to be exclusive of that in those of other churches. Church authorities insist that the faithful should be baptised, married and confirmed within certain traditionally prescribed rites. Certain accommodations have been made in the matter of mixed marriages which allow the partners to marry in the rites of both churches concerned, but partners of the same religion are required to marry in their own rite only. The Catholic church authorities, for example, would take a very dim view if two of its members, married within a Catholic rite, should suddenly feel the need to go through a Protestant service as well, and it is doubtful if the Catholic laity would understand the thinking behind such a move either. In the seventeenth century, however, though church regulations were basically the same as present-day ones, the mentality of the Catholic laity was somewhat different. The Irish provincial synods found it necessary to condemn the practice of Catholics contracting marriage before a Protestant minister and presenting their children to be baptised, and, in some cases, rebaptised, by a non-Catholic minister.[10] Social conditions in Wexford during the 1670s and 1680s exercised a particular pressure on the Catholic laity in this regard. Certain accommodations were necessary if a Catholic wished to protect his economic and social status, and a practice of 'playing it safe', particularly in the contracting of marriages, seems to have become fairly widespread.

A comparison of the details in the Catholic parish register with those in the Protestant marriage licences in the diocese of Ferns reveals an interesting state of affairs.[11] At least twelve couples are found to have sought registration in both sets of records.[12] At first sight these appear to have been marriages between partners of differing denominations but further examination proves that in all cases except one both partners were Catholic. This conclusion is adduced from a study of the lists of godparents of Catholic children. By checking the names of those involved in the doubly-registered marriages against these lists one may establish which of them were Catholic, as godparents of Catholic children had to be Catholics themselves. Thus, for example, the marriage of John Shapland and Ellen Bond: Ellen Bond is listed as godparent in the Catholic register on several occasions while her husband, who never acted as sponsor to a Catholic child, was clearly Protestant, as shown below. Another interesting feature of all of these marriages is that even in those which were mixed, the children were baptised as Catholics. Also the couples seem to have known each other well, for one or both partners of one marriage often appear as godparents to the children of another such marriage.[13] The inference would appear to be that the Catholicism of these individuals, though genuine, was being concealed from the authorities for some reason, and that these couples felt it necessary to obtain the protection of a Protestant marriage licence to ensure that their religion remained undiscovered.

The successful operation of this policy of double registration must at some stage have required the co-operation of both Protestant and Catholic authorities: the registrar of the Ferns diocesan marriage licences and the Catholic parochial registrar in Wexford. While the identity of the Protestant official remains uncertain, there is considerable evidence for the conclusion that the Catholic recorder was Luke Wadding, later bishop of Ferns. There is a very close similarity between the handwriting in Wadding's *Notebook* and that in the Parochial Register, which between 1671 and 1686 is all in the one hand.[14] A study of the twenty-nine pages of the parish register for this period would sustain the following interpretation. The character of both handwriting and layout in these pages has a uniformity which suggests very strongly that these entries were made not only by the same person but at the same time. This indicates that the recorder was either putting down on paper for the first time material informally retained, possibly in his memory, or that he was transferring from another source. Whatever the explanation of this uniformity it is clear that a new and more rigorous organisation of Catholic records was being instituted. This is in keeping with the known character of Luke Wadding whose *Notebook*, so full of lists and catalogues, reveals an engagingly meticulous personality. Furthermore we know that Wadding was in Wexford town in 1674, the year in which he established a chapel there. It is likely, then, that the Catholic register was begun at that time and that as many marriages and dispensations as could be remembered for the previous three years were set out in the first few pages.

It is unlikely that Wadding did not know that some of the people entered in his marriage records were also listed in the Protestant register.[15] It seems too that Wadding had more than just a passing acquaintance with these families. His relationship with the Shapland family in particular seems to have been one of considerable mutual trust. In his will he bequeathed to Mrs Shapland his 'stil, watering-pot and sheres' on condition that she give the use of them to the future Catholic priest in Wexford and to his successors.[16] This presupposes two things which are not perhaps of equal importance to our inquiry: that Mrs Shapland would be on friendly terms with the future Catholic priest and that the bishop expected that priest to have an interest in gardening! Wadding also entrusted many other items of property to at least one of the partners in some of these doubly-registered marriages.[17]

Having established that these couples were genuinely Catholic and having discovered that Wadding's acquaintance with them was more than casual, we must now find a reason why the individuals concerned felt it necessary to conceal their religion by such a stratagem. A check through the civil records for the time reveals that in nearly all cases these families were either merchants or seamen and that the members were also among the leading citizens of the town.[18] Thus they had a certain social status and economic interest to protect, both of which would quickly dissolve if the government were to discover that they were Catholics. While the question of how exactly the families managed to maintain this deception will be examined below, it is obvious that within the town at least the real religion of the parties must have been a rather open secret. The Protestants there could not have failed to realise that these fellow-citizens were not in any sense genuine Protestants and they must have had better reason than simply friendly relations with these Catholics to prevent them from informing the authorities of the subterfuge. It seems likely then that the adherents of the different sects in Wexford had reached some form of *modus vivendi* and that this understanding had some connection with a growing prosperity based on trade within the town.[19]

According to Wadding, the achievement of this prosperity was a slow process which had not begun in 1672. Writing to Bishop French who was still abroad in that year he explained the reasons for his reluctance to accept consecration as coadjutor bishop of the diocese of Ferns:

> I am little inclined to it because of the state of our people, because of the extreme poverty of everyone here, the uncertainty of the times and a hundred other things. I have no means to support a servant or anyone else. Up to the present I have existed on my own resources and the help of a few friends who, as I know too well, are everyday getting fewer and fainter.[20]

His caution was well founded for the government was still particularly interested in apprehending Catholic bishops for exercising foreign jurisdiction.[21] Moreover his decision to defer consecration left him free to perform his pastoral duties among his flock without endangering them or incurring the ill-will of the otherwise friendly Protestants in the area. Wadding appears to have been a particularly astute reader of the circumstances of his time and to have realised the difficulty in implementing reformed Catholicism and organising the diocese along Tridentine lines. From his first coming to Wexford he fostered friendly relations with the Protestant community. So successful was he that in 1674, the year in which all popish convents, friaries and schools were ordered to be suppressed in Wexford,[22] Wadding was permitted to build a public chapel within the walls of the town.[23] In his *Notebook* he recorded the details of its building, ceiling and thatching, and the making of the altar, pulpit, confessional, seats and other items. It cost him £53.14.9 and was apparently subscribed to by several Protestants in the town.[24]

In this thatched chapel, the Catholic community of Wexford began to experience for the first time since the confederate wars something akin to the parochial life enjoined by the Tridentine decrees. Wadding was ably assisted in his mission by a dedicated clergy, the majority of whom were educated abroad.[25] Following the example of Bishop John Roche, Wadding fostered friendly relations with members of the religious orders in the town. In his will he bequeathed to the Franciscans some black vestments, with an alb and missal, 'to pray for me'.[26] It is clear too from references in the parish register[27] that the administration of the diocese involved co-operation between secular and religious clergy.[28] With the aid of both groups Wadding set about familiarising his flock with the basics of the Tridentine reforms but the work was to be interrupted in late 1678 when Ireland was affected by the popish plot.

On 16 October 1678 a proclamation was issued commanding archbishops, bishops, vicars-general and all regular clergy to depart the kingdom by 20 November.[29] It seems that Wadding was detained for a while by the authorities but he evaded banishment by a curious defence. In August 1678 Bishop French had died in Ghent. Wadding now ceased to be vicar-general but was elected vicar-capitular by twenty-one priests of the diocese. Thus he could plead that he was neither bishop nor vicar-general.[30] It is pertinent to point out here that a vicar-capitular exercised jurisdiction from the papacy but the authorities did not know or chose not to know that fact. Bearing in mind that Wadding's wide circle of friends included some well-disposed Protestants, not to mention those Catholics who were posing as Protestants, it is likely that not inconsiderable influence was brought to bear in the matter of Wadding's interrogation and subsequent release uncharged.[31]

The upheaval caused by the popish plot seems to have been reflected in the marriage and baptismal register kept by Wadding. In 1678, the year of the plot, it lists only four baptisms and one marriage, a contrast with both 1677 when there were seventeen baptisms and two marriages, and 1679, when there were twenty-four baptisms and eight marriages. It is difficult to decide whether this sharp decline was due to an interruption in the records occasioned by Wadding's detention and inability to record or to the reluctance of the community to risk seeking Catholic sacraments at a time of persecution. If the latter is held to be the true reason for the decline it is worth noting that one of the baptisms listed for 1678 is that of Christine Shapland, daughter of John Shapland and Ellen Bond. The decline or interruption, whichever be the case, was not lasting and the entries were resumed in April and May of 1679. To Wadding, directly affected himself by the ramifications of the plot, it may have seemed that the aim of reform was rendered unattainable. His carol, 'On Christmass-day in the year 1678, when the clergy were banished in the time of the plot', reflects the deep depression which he felt at the loss of the privilege of saying Mass on Christmas Day:

> This is our Christmass-day, the day of Christ's birth,
> Yet we are far from joy and far from Christmass mirth;
> On Christmass to have no Mass is our greatest discontent,
> That without Mass this day should pass doth cause us to lament,

> The name of Christ-mass must changed and altered be,
> For since we have no Mass no Christmass have we;
> It's therefore we do mourn, with grief our hearts are prest,
> With tears our eyes do run, our minds and thoughts want rest.[32]

Wadding appears to have kept himself well informed on the controversy surrounding the plot. His library contains many contemporary pamphlets including Oates's *Narrative of the horrid plot*, and Catholic refutations of the conspiracy and the intrigues of the Jesuits.[33] Also included were accounts of the trial, condemnation and last speeches of Oliver Plunkett and other alleged conspirators. What exactly Wadding's private opinions were on the matter we have no idea. There is an apparently hearty condemnation of Jesuits and their plots in the verses on Christmas Day, 1678:

> Some news each post doth bring of Jesuits and their plots,
> Against our sacred king, discovered first by Oates;
> Such plotters we may curse, with bell and book at Mass.[34]

If this is really what Wadding felt it is hard to reconcile these lines with the fact that he had great respect and affection for at least one Jesuit of his acquaintance, Stephen Gelosse.[35] It is worth mentioning too that Gelosse himself had succeeded in establishing a large college in New Ross which was attended by Protestants as well as Catholics. When the college was finally suppressed in 1670, Wadding expressed his grief at the closure in a poem entitled 'The lamentation of the scholars presented to the Master, S.G., at the dissolving of the school in Ross'.[36] Wadding obviously felt deep sympathy for the Jesuit's attempts not only to establish and maintain a Catholic school but to do so by establishing cordial relations with the Protestants of the area. In this venture Gelosse was a man after Wadding's own heart, both men realising that nothing could be achieved for Catholics by alienating Protestant opinion in the matter of Catholic education and religious practice. At the time of the plot Wadding probably felt that, to defend the Jesuits, who were in any case established as skilled intriguers in the eyes of many Protestants, would not have served the interests of Catholicism to the same extent that condemnation of the plot and protestations of continuing loyalty to the king would have. His poetical condemnation, then, was motivated more by needs of diplomacy than by any serious belief that the plot was anything more than a hoax.[37]

In any case, as soon as the hysteria generated by the plot had subsided, there was a return in Wexford to the *modus vivendi* which had operated in the years leading up to it. In 1683 we find that the jury at an inquisition relating to the appointment and functions of incumbents, or holders of Protestant ecclesiastical benefices, was composed of twelve Wexford citizens, of whom at least five are revealed by the parish register to have been Catholic.[38] Clearly these five were passing themselves off as upstanding Protestants; it is unlikely that the authorities would be overtly enthusiastic about permitting Catholics to appoint Protestant clergymen.

Besides seeking registration in the Protestant marriage register, there were other ways for Wexford Catholics to maintain the pretence of being true Protestants. Not all Catholics posing as Protestants took the precaution of obtaining a Protestant licence and in any case such a practice appears to have waned in Wexford after 1685.[39] The case of Anthony Talbot, one of the jurymen at the inquisition mentioned above, will serve to illustrate this point. In his *Notebook* Wadding refers to Talbot as his 'cossen' or cousin.[40] This does not necessarily mean, however, that Talbot was related to the bishop. Wadding refers to several 'cossens' but it is clear that he uses the word in a very wide sense as meaning anything from very close friend to the modern meaning of a blood relation.[41] Talbot married Mary Lampord some time before 1683 but he did not seek a Protestant marriage licence. Neither does the marriage appear to have been recorded by Wadding in the Catholic register. The children of the marriage, of whom there were at least two between 1683 and 1690, were baptised Catholics and registered as such. Talbot himself is listed as godfather to several Catholic children, the inference being that he was a Catholic. In common with those who did seek a Protestant marriage licence, Talbot was a merchant and came into possession of a considerable amount of property during his lifetime.[42] It does not appear to have worried Wadding that 'cossen' Anthony Talbot was posing as a Protestant. In fact the bishop benefited from the deception in 1684 when he leased a house in Talbot's name.[43]

With the accession of the Catholic James II in 1685, the lot of Catholics improved.[44] Under the new charter issued to Wexford by James, Talbot was made an alderman of the town.[45] We cannot say with certainty whether the authorities believed Talbot to be a Protestant alderman or a Catholic one. There are several genuine non-Catholics among the twenty-four aldermen appointed under the charter, so that Catholicism does not appear to have been a criterion of appointment.[46] In any event Talbot's guise of Protestantism – if he continued it – did not save him after the Williamite possession of the town. From 1694 there appeared a notice of his attainder on a charge of treason and his subsequent death.[47] The conclusion from the facts of Talbot's career seems to be that Catholics could quite easily, though not without some risk, pose as Protestants, acquire property and use their influence to assist fellow-Catholics without taking any precautions to convince the government that they were genuinely Protestant.

It will be noted that Talbot's success in this venture depended not only on the good offices of Protestants within the town but on the continued acquiescence of Wadding. His experience among the people of Wexford had taught Wadding that the Tridentine decree that Catholics should at all times publicly declare their religion, which had been enthusiastically complied with by the Catholics in Wexford during the 1640s, could no longer be rigidly enforced without entailing the destruction of Catholic livelihoods. Wadding had at all times an understanding of the difficulties in which Catholics found themselves during these years. It was nevertheless his mission to ensure that his flock would be as familiar as possible with the dictates of Trent. The bishop, in implementing the counter-reforms, was always mindful of the condition of his people and the need for the utmost caution if his mission was to be successful.[48]

In 1683 the Holy See had ordered Wadding to proceed immediately with his conseration. Ever cautious, Wadding continued to argue that he could work more efficiently as a priest, and pleaded once again the poverty of his people and the uncertainty of the times.[49] But this argument was apparently not as convincing as it had been some years earlier and Rome insisted that he comply. There is no information about when and where his consecration took place but it had certainly occurred before 20 June 1684.[50] The Wexford Catholic community now had a resident bishop for the first time since 1649.

If we investigate the lives of several other leading citizens in the town we shall see the part that Wadding played in safeguarding the spiritual and temporal affairs of his flock. The fate of Anthony Talbot after 1691 was not necessarily shared by others who found themselves in circumstances similar to his. This point is illustrated by the career of Edward Wiseman. Like Talbot, Wiseman was a merchant and also one of Wadding's 'cossens'.[51] On his first coming to the town about 1674 Wadding lodged at Wiseman's house and was still there in 1684 when he leased a house convenient to his chapel in Talbot's house.[52] Some time before 1672 Wiseman married Joan Whitty ('cossen Gowan')[53] but, as in the case of Talbot's marriage, there is no trace of this one in either Catholic or Protestant records. The Wiseman children were baptised Catholics and, like the Talbots, the Wisemans are often named as godparents to Catholic children.

In 1687 Wiseman was appointed an alderman of the borough and two years later he became mayor of the town. In that year too (1689) the so-called Patriot Parliament met in Dublin. This parliament was almost exclusively Roman Catholic and Old English. Among its enactments was one which removed all civil disabilities on account of religion. This act for liberty of conscience is referred to in a proclamation issued late in 1689, in which it is cited as the grounds for allowing Protestants the free right of worship and forbidding the seizure of their churches, of which there had been a number of instances.[54] One such seizure was carried out in Wexford town by Edward Wiseman. The petition of the Protestant minister of the time relates the manner of that seizure:

The humble petition of Alexander Allen, of Wexford, most humbly sheweth:

That your petitioner, being minister of the parish of St. Iberius in the town of Wexford, has therein for several years past daily celebrated divine service . . . yet your petitioner on the 25th October last was dispossessed of his said church, contrary to the late act of liberty of conscience by Edward Wiseman, mayor of Wexford, who a few days after, did not only, by the rabble introduced by him, break down and demolish all the pews and altar of the said church, but did seize, and unjustly deny your petitioner's vestments, church book, and other ornaments thereof, to the great prejudice of your petitioner and his parishioners, although your Majesty's Roman Catholic subjects have several chapels fit for the free exercise of their religion both within and without the walls of the said town, and where unto several Protestant inhabitants have given liberal contributions.[55]

What is of interest in this passage is that the import of the minister's grievance seems to lie in his indignation that the harmony in which Protestant and Catholic communities had existed until then was now seriously disrupted by the mayor's action.

Wiseman was to pay for his hastiness, however, for, not only was the church restored to the minister, but after the occupation of the town by the Williamite forces Wiseman's property, which included a sizeable house, shop, yard, malt house, garden and brewery, was confiscated.[56] One would expect that this marked the end of Edward Wiseman's career as a leading citizen of the town. Indeed it might also be expected that any co-operation which had existed between Catholics and Protestants was now at an end, and that there was little possibility of re-establishing the *modus vivendi* which had operated before the accession of James II. In the long term, however, both expectations proved groundless. Many Catholic merchants fled the town in 1691 but the parish registers show that they had started to return by 1694. As in Edward Wiseman's case their property had probably been declared forfeit to the crown and there followed in 1695 a wave of enactments which sought to deprive them of any property, education facilities and political power they might have retained.[57] For the remaining years of the century we do not find any Catholics among the officials of the town and only one couple sought registration of their marriage in both Catholic and Protestant records. Initially the Penal Laws were to prove effective in excluding Catholics from local government. In the first decade of the eighteenth century, however, some Wexford Catholics appear to have found a way around this problem. A document, signed by the mayor and two aldermen, was drawn up and published on 21 February 1708, testifying to the treachery of Captain James Stafford in surrendering Wexford castle to Cromwell in October 1649.[58] The signatures on this document are extremely interesting. By them we discover that the mayor was one Leonard Bolan who, according to the Catholic register, married Anstas Sinnott in 1684, according to Catholic rites. One of the aldermen is David St John who was also an alderman under the charter of James II, and whose marriage to Cata Carny produced at least four children, all of whom are listed in the Catholic baptismal record, St John himself being godfather to at least two Catholic children. But the most astonishing signature to this document is that of the second alderman, Edward Wiseman. Several facts indicate that this can be taken to be the Edward Wiseman under discussion. In the first place there is no mention in any record of another man of this name. Edward Wiseman did not apparently ever have a son named after him. Also his inclusion with the two other signatories of this document whose Catholic associations I have indicated suggests that Wiseman shared a similar background and is thus the Wiseman of our investigation.

It will be recalled that Bishop Wadding in his will bequeathed his gardening tools to one Ellen Shapland, née Bond, with the proviso that she give the use of them to the future parish priest of Wexford. The career of this lady's husband, John Shapland, is the subject of our third examination of the lives of Wexford citizens of this time. Although there is considerable evidence concerning the career of this man, he himself remains very much a mystery.[59] The marriage of John Shapland to Ellen Bond in 1675 is recorded in both Protestant and Catholic records. The Catholic register reveals further that a dispensation, inexplicably on grounds of blood *and* cult ('consanguinitate cultuque') was required before this marriage could take place.[60] The children of the marriage (there were at least six) are listed as baptised Catholics. John Shapland is never listed as godfather to any Catholic child and this fact, coupled with the grounds for dispensation, suggests that Shapland was most likely a Protestant.

It seems that, unlike Talbot and Wiseman, Shapland was not a merchant but he was obviously a prominent and influential citizen. The charter of James II referred to him as 'John Shapland, Esq.,' and appointed him alderman of the borough.[61] In 1683 he sat with Anthony Talbot on the jury which appointed Protestant clergymen.[62] Through his wife, Ellen, Shapland came into close association with Wadding: the bishop even appears to have lent money to him![63] It seems reasonable to assume then that Shapland was one of those well-disposed Protestants whose co-operation permitted Catholics to acquire property and power locally. He was acquainted also with Anthony Talbot, Edward Wiseman and other Catholic merchants such as Luke Bryan, Thomas Esmonde, Paul Turner and David St John, and these men and their wives often acted as godparents to the Shapland children. Shapland's wife, Ellen, returned this favour by acting as sponsor at the baptisms of several of the merchants' children.

Such associations do not explain, however, why Shapland permitted his children and heirs to be baptised into the proscribed Catholic religion—if indeed he did permit it. It is possible that the baptisms were clandestine, though it is difficult to see any point in this if the children could not be brought up as practising Catholics. We are left then with a portrait which may appear to be strange from a modern perspective: that of a wealthy Protestant, whose wife and heirs were Catholic, who was a close associate of the Roman Catholic bishop of the area and also of certain Catholic merchants in the town, and who colluded with these Catholics, certainly at some risk to his own position and property, for *their* advancement. Despite this situation Shapland managed to remain acceptable to the establishment throughout his lifetime. Even after the Williamite Wars during which the disguise of Protestantism had been removed from his associates, Talbot and Wiseman, Shapland continued to hold an official post. In 1696 we discover him to be the recorder of the poll tax returns for the town.[64] For his children too, nothing much had changed. In 1697 his daughter, Christine, married William Swiney, a marriage which, like Shapland's own, was registered in both Catholic and Protestant records. Like her parents, all Christine's children received a Catholic baptism.

If Anthony Talbot, Edward Wiseman, John Shapland and their families have one thing in common it is surely their friendship with Luke Wadding. Indeed this association may well have been the basis on which the *modus vivendi* of these years was established. The arrangement which allowed Catholics to feign Protestantism in Wexford during these years could certainly not have existed without the co-operation of the Catholic Bishop Wadding in the matter of performing secret, or at least discreet, Catholic marriages and baptisms. On the other hand, it was necessary too that the Protestants of the town be well disposed towards their Catholic neighbours, agreeing to assist in the deception. The friendship which Wadding established with the influential Shapland family and with other Protestant families may well have created an atmosphere in which mutual good will between the different sects in the town could be fostered.

It must be stressed, however, that the Wexford Catholics did not waive their religious principles for the sake of this settlement. In this sense the *modus vivendi* was not a compromise in religion *per se*, but in politics. The reasons why it was necessary that this settlement be arrived at were not primarily religious but economic and social. A political situation had arisen in which a majority group, which happened to be Catholic, was believed to hold political views detrimental to effective government and the economic interests of a ruling minority group which happened to espouse Protestantism. From their insecure minority position, the Protestant authorities felt it necessary to enact laws which were designed to curb the political, economic and social activities of the dissenting majority. But the law was one thing: how people lived was an entirely different matter as the experience of the Wexford inhabitants was to show. The Protestant element within the town had been introduced by the government primarily to ensure that local government was kept out of Catholic hands.[65] It was also hoped that Protestants would successfully replace Catholics in matters of trade and commerce and thus make the town not only politically but also economically viable. In this second hope, however, the government was to be disappointed. Catholic merchants could never be successfully excluded from the trade of the port. The reason for this was twofold: in the first place Catholics could not survive without deriving their livelihood from their original occupation. Accordingly they continued to use every means available to continue the exercise of trade for themselves.[66] In the second place, experience had shown the Protestant traders that the Catholics' long tradition of commercial contacts with the continent was indispensable. During the interregnum an important group of Catholic sea captains and traders had removed themselves and their ships to the continent.[67] The effect on trade in Wexford was catastophic. New Protestant settlers were few and in any case lacked the resources for extensive trading. Trade in Wexford and in other port towns went into serious decline. After 1660 Charles II took measures to ameliorate this situation by restoring the position of Catholics in the trade of the towns.[68] This seriously disturbed the upholders of the Protestant interest. The admission of Catholics to the trade of towns would mean an automatic increase in their power and influence since they would now form the mainstay of the economic life of the towns.[69] Protestants were alarmed lest Catholics, seizing on this opportunity of gaining local power, should use it as a foothold for attaining national dominance and regaining land now in Protestant hands. Accordingly many boroughs refused to admit Catholics to trade but Wexford does not appear to have been among them.

As early as 1662 Catholics are listed in the subsidy rolls which give us the names of all the principal proprietors, householders and merchants in the town at the time.[70] It should be added, however, that at no time before 1685 do Catholics form a majority on any jury, nor does any Catholic become mayor or alderman of the borough. One wonders why Wexford should be the exception in this matter. The answer appears to lie in the fact that these Catholics were not regarded as such by the government and were in fact the first of those nominal Protestants who have been described above. Set out logically, the facts of this situation seem to offer such an explanation. The experience of Catholic merchants was needed to revitalise trade in Wexford. Catholics would have been only too glad to return to this trade. But to readmit Catholics to the borough was to endanger the overall Protestant interest. Therefore Catholics, if they were to be readmitted to the town, must not be seen to be Catholic. Control of the town must remain, and be seen to remain, in Protestant hands.

It is difficult to say whether Catholics, faced with this dilemma, assumed the guise of Protestantism voluntarily or were obliged to do so by the Protestant population. In any case the co-operation of both sides was a prerequisite for the successful operation of this arrangement and the resulting recovery of trade within the town was, from an economic point of view, mutually beneficial.[71] It will be seen too that any benefit to the Catholic religion was incidental to this arrangement and came as a natural consequence of the friendly relations established by it between the two communities. Catholics were sufficiently clear-minded to distinguish between a compromise with Protestantism and a working arrangement with Protestants. This distinction, born of the Catholic experience of these years, was also recognised as a genuine one by the representative of Rome in Wexford, Luke Wadding. The bishop endeavoured at all times to be on friendly terms with the Protestant community and tried not to jeopardise the situation or antagonise either Catholic or Protestant interests by enforcing strict regulations on his people or attempting too much too soon. Thus by his reluctance, for example, to accept consecration as bishop of the diocese, he showed a sensible caution in not pressing Tridentine reforms too far and an understanding of the delicate and new-found arrangement between Catholics and Protestants, which they had established for their mutual benefit. The result was, as we have seen, that Wadding was allowed to do far more than perhaps any other bishop in the country in the matter of reorganising the Catholic church in his diocese. The building of his chapel in 1674 is probably the most outstanding example of this fact.

However, Wadding never compromised his Catholicism nor was he lax in permitting his clergy or laity to do so. Schooled in the tenets of Counter-Reformation Catholicism, he tried at all times to bring the directives of Trent to bear on the Wexford Catholic community. Realising that here, as elsewhere, the barrier to the progress of Counter-Reformation Catholicism was caused by lack of education and instruction, he distributed popular books of doctrine and devotion among relations, friends, benefactors, gentry and widows as well as among their children. These gifts included six dozen Christian diurnals by Nicholas Caussin, author of the *Holy Court*; eighteen copies of *An Introduction to the devout life* by St Francis de Sales; 100 dozen small Christian doctrines by Bellarmine, Ledesma and others.[72] These, together with objects of piety such as rosary beads and medals, he imported from England and the continent, principally Bristol, Rouen, St Malo and Rotterdam, making use of the re-entry into trade of Catholics such as Anthony Talbot and Thomas Esmonde to do so.[73] The reason for the distribution of these books, Wadding tells us himself, was that those who had them should make good use of them.[74] Whether the sentiments expressed in these spiritual works made an imprint on the hearts of the Wexford Catholics is a matter for conjecture. The only description of the religious behaviour of Catholics in Wexford is in an anonymous account of the barony of Forth, written about 1670:

> The native inhabitants celebrate with singularlie pious devotion the yearlie festivities, or patron dayes, as they term them, in the several parishes, in honour of God and his saints, esteeming him profane (if a constant inhabitant) who doth not on such dayes penitently (by confession to his spiritual pastor) purge his conscience from mortall sinne, be reconciled to his neighbours, and reverently receive the sacred Eucharist. Of such festivals, they mutually invite theire neighbouring friends and alliance unto their howses, whom they cheerfully, piouslie, and civily intertaine, with variety of the best accommodation the country can afford; not without incentive facetiousness and Musical Instruments . . . [75] They are very precise and exact in the observacion of Ecclesiasticallie injoined fasts, never eate flesh on Fridayes or Saturdayes, few use eggs, butter or milk on Fridayes, abstained always from flesh on Wednesday, and untill about the yeare 1670 they were dispensed with all (or rather commanded the contrary). They are not inclined to debauchery, nor excessively addicted to the use of any liquor.[76]

The inhabitants, then, displayed at least outwardly strong devotion to Catholic religious practice and beliefs. On this point, however, the opinion of G. Le Bras is worth quoting:

> We must insist on this frequently neglected truth: the fulfilment of periodic duties does not constitute genuine, deep-rooted Christianity. The man who believes in the divinity of Christ and eternal life, the man who observes the commandments even by habit is better than the regular mass-goer who observes the law by habit but does not practice the virtues.[77]

What then are we to conclude about the Wexford Catholics? They certainly seem to have placed great emphasis on the externals of their religion, at least among themselves. A clergy, schooled in Tridentine formulas, should, perhaps, have attempted to purge the community of some of their less worthy 'devotions' but this was not always the case. In 1682 Colonel Solomon Richards was remarking on the townspeople's devotion to 'a wooden idol in the shape of a man, called St. Iberian' before which they used to settle disputes by swearing an oath. An amused Richards continues:

> some idle fellows who love not wooden gods, have twice or thrice stolen St. Iberian away, and cleft him out and burned him—once to roast a pig; but still, Phoenix-like, another rises out of the ashes, and is placed there again, and the silly people are persuaded that it's restored by a miracle . . . and a living priest goes over now and then to fetch the silly people's offerings, to keep them for St. Iberian, no doubt on't.[78]

In contrast to such open display we have the town merchants' attempts to conceal their religion from the authorities. Yet it was this Old English element which seems to have had a more inherent tendency to obey the moral dictates of the church. Of the twelve illegitimate children presented for baptism 1685-1699 not one is the product of a totally Old English union, and only two have one Old English parent. In distinct contrast, all the others are of Old Irish parentage.[79] This is partly explained by the circumstances in which the two groups found themselves socially. The Old English had regained some kind of social status and financially they were considerably better off than the native Irish who probably formed the lowest and least educated stratum of Wexford society. In the slum conditions in which they lived it was inevitable that the illegitimacy rate among the native Irish should be considerably higher than that of the Old English who, if the circumstances of Edward Wiseman and Anthony Talbot are representative of their class, must have had something approaching middle-class living conditions.

We must add to this the fact of the Old English close association with Wadding. This is not to suggest that the bishop did not care to be associated with the native Irish members of his flock; the point is that Wadding was himself of Old English stock and extremely proud of that fact.[80] His affinity was more naturally with the Wisemans and Talbots of the town than it was with the Murphys and Connors. With historical hindsight we can see that he was witnessing the demise of his class as an identifiable group, culturally and socially distinct from the native Irish. Caught between his sense of mission as a Counter-Reformation bishop and his sense of loyalty to his ethnic origins, Wadding tried to remain faithful to both without compromising either: thus his acquiescence in the matter of the merchants' nominal Protestantism, their only hope of survival as a group, and his insistence, at the same time, on instilling something of the spirit of reformed Catholicism into them. Wadding's contribution to the development of the Wexford community then was twofold: firstly he gave the Old English an opportunity to establish the basis of trade, a factor which was to be instrumental in their becoming the urban middle-class of the eighteenth century,[81] and which was also to ensure that in the future merging of Old Irish and Old English cultures, the latter would be the dominant strain—a fact which is still recognisable in modern Wexford society. Secondly, by establishing something of the spirit of the Counter-Reformation among them, Wadding unconsciously prepared the ground for the fusion of the two groups in the common bond of Catholicism. At this point I can do little better than to conclude by quoting the opinion of John Bossy on the formation of a Catholic community:

> While the history of a Catholic community is in the first place the history of a laity, and the history of a laity is something which has meaning and structure in itself, nonetheless the source of its dynamics must, given the general character of the Counter-Reformation Church, mainly be looked for in its clergy. The mission did not by itself suffice to create the community, but without the mission no community could have been created.[82]

5. Religion and land tenure in eighteenth-century Ireland: tenancy in the southeast

SECTARIAN rivalry has always been closely related to economic competition among the adherents of different religions in Ireland. This competition has occurred in all spheres of economic activity but has been especially intense in the area of the ownership and control of land. Historians have now carefully documented the extent to which landownership became almost the exclusive preserve of members of the established church during the eighteenth century. The story of the gradual undermining of this Anglican monopoly and the ultimate displacement of the entire landlord class has also been given considerable attention. The related story of the religious/sectarian dimension of land tenancy has been largely ignored, however. For example, we have long assumed that middleman tenants dominated the Irish rural scene for most of the eighteenth century. Apart from a few recent efforts, scholars have not attempted to assess the exact importance of the middleman in rural Ireland during that century or to determine the religious composition of the middleman population.[1] Historians have worked largely on the assumption that middlemen were prevalent in most of the country and that the majority of them were Protestants.[2] It is imperative that quantitative studies of the nature of the 'tenant class'[3] of eighteenth-century Ireland be conducted to provide more evidence to confirm these assumptions. Such studies are especially vital if we are to understand the socio-economic background to the sectarian bitterness which characterised the country in the eighteenth century, a phase of Irish sectarianism which has been given careful treatment by L. M. Cullen.[4]

The objective of this study is to examine the tenurial system operating in the southeast of Ireland in the middle of the eighteenth century. We will look at the composition of the tenant population on seven estates in Counties Wexford, Carlow and Wicklow in the period 1745–58 to assess (a) the precise extent to which the middleman dominated the tenant classes of the area at this time, (b) the degree to which Protestants dominated the middleman class and (c) the extent to which middlemen were resident tenants rather than mere 'paper tenants' or absentees. From these findings we can form an opinion as to whether or not the eventual abandonment of this middleman system in favour of direct leasing to former subtenants would have seriously undermined the overall position of the local Protestant community, a development central to Cullen's discussion of the causes of the 1798 rebellion in this area.[5]

Rentals comprise the major source consulted for this study although materials from the Registry of Deeds such as abstracts of mortgage deeds and leases have also provided important data.[6] These sources yield reliable information on the location and sizes of farms held by tenants and the annual rents paid; some of them also indicate the addresses and social status of tenants. Unfortunately, rental records from Irish estates seldom specify the religions of the individuals they list. Consequently, we are obliged to use 'terms of tenure' and surnames as indicators of religious affiliation. In the case of the former it is usually possible to distinguish between Catholics and Protestants since it was illegal for Catholics to hold land for terms based on length of life or for terms of years longer than thirty-one.[7] Where terms of tenure are not specified, we can use surnames as a less reliable but nonetheless useful indicator of religious background. Naturally, this is a dangerous exercise, especially in an area such as the southeast where English colonisation had occurred both before and after the Reformation. Several scholars, especially historical geographers, have resorted to this technique in recent years, however, and it is acceptable as at least a partial solution to a difficult problem.[8] Most of the estates to be studied in this essay were located in areas of the southeast which did not in fact have English settlers before the Reformation and it seems reasonable to assume in this instance that tenants with Gaelic surnames were Catholic and those with Anglo-Saxon surnames were Protestant.

Key
1 Rockingham
2 Anglesey
3 Ram
4 Donovan
5 Kavanagh
6 Carew
7 Colclough

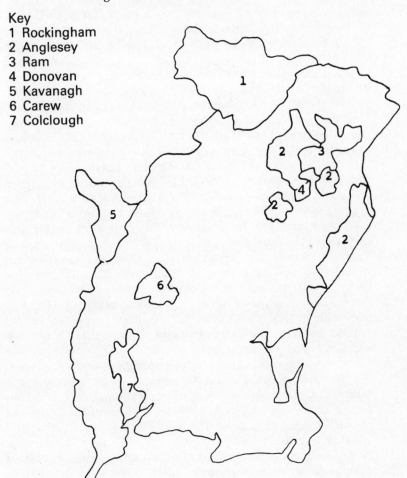

Map 1. Location of Estates Discussed
 Note: Small scattered fragments of some of these estates are not included in
       this map.

The seven estates which provide the basis for this study are
those owned by the Rockingham, Anglesey, Kavanagh, Carew,
Ram, Colclough (Tintern branch) and Donovan families. These

estates represent a wide variety of properties (See Map 1). One of them, the Rockingham (later Fitzwilliam)[9] property was owned by an absentee member of the English aristocracy while all of the others were residential. The Rockingham estate spread over a large area of Co. Wicklow from its southwestern extremity to Rathdrum. For our purposes here the section of the property within the half-barony of Shillelagh will be studied. This tract accounted for about half of the estate's acreage, contained its best land and also held its demesne (at Coolattin). In all, the Shillelagh section of the estate contained about 25,000 acres.[10] The Anglesey estate in Wexford consisted of several widely scattered tracts, as Map 1 shows. The entire property in the county accounted for about 24,000 acres but most of the data in this paper are drawn from the sections of the estate along the east coast and around Camolin. The Carew property, also extensive but more compact than the Anglesey, consisted of about 7,000 acres. The Kavanagh and Colclough estates were of about the same size as the Carew, although it should be noted here that the data from the Colclough property come from lands immediately around Tintern, representing about one-third of the estate's total area. The two smallest properties in the sample, the Ram and Donovan lands, amounted to about 5,500 and 2,500 acres respectively.

The religious composition of the populations of these properties also varied considerably (see Map 2). Five estates in the sample, the Donovan, Ram, Rockingham, Anglesey and Colclough lands, were located in areas with substantial Protestant populations by the standards of the south of Ireland; the Kavanagh and Carew properties, on the other hand, were located in areas which probably had extremely small Protestant communities by comparison.[11] Finally, there is the question of the religion of the proprietors; while six of these estates were owned by Protestants, one, the Kavanagh lands, occupying the southern part of Carlow, was owned by a Catholic family.[12] The Kavanaghs were unusual in this respect and the presence of this property in the sample provides an added opportunity to test some important assumptions about the sectarian dimension of Irish land ownership and land tenure in the eighteenth century. In addition to this, we can use the data from these units to look at the connection between the nature of the tenure system and

Key

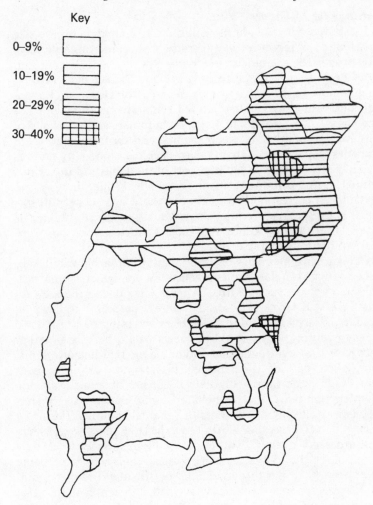

0–9%

10–19%

20–29%

30–40%

Map 2. Distribution of Protestant Population in Co. Wexford, 1861.
  Source: Census of Ireland, 1861
  Note: This pattern has probably not changed radically since the 1750s.

such factors as estate size, presence or absence of large Protestant populations, and absenteeism.

Extent of the Middleman System

Estate records provide us with quite reliable data on the size distribution of tenancies in our study area. In the case of four of the properties examined, the Ram, Rockingham, Carew and Colclough estates, rental records provide the acreages held by each tenant. In the remaining three cases, the Donovan, Kavanagh and Anglesey estates, annual rents are recorded but not acreages. Therefore, Table 1, which summarises the results of this analysis of the data, treats the first and second categories of statistics separately. Tenants have been assigned to various tenancy size-ranges in the first part of the table and to various annual rent size-ranges in the second. While there is no certainty of correspondence between these two sets of categories, it is likely, given rent levels prevailing in the county at this time,[13] that the four cohorts in Table 1a correspond approximately to the four in Table 1b.

Categorising members of a population into arbitrarily established ranges is a dangerous practice but one which is unavoidable in a project such as this. Tenants have been grouped into what we will term 'very large', 'large', 'medium' and 'small' holdings. Very large holdings, (those containing more than 300 acres or renting for over £30 per year) would have been either extensive pastoral operations and/or classic middleman 'farms' (on which part of the land is sub-let and part is worked directly).[14] Such farms might well consist of more than one townland and thereby be held by what David Dickson has labelled 'multi-townland' tenants.[15] Large holdings, (farms of from 120 to 300 acres, or worth £16 to £30 per year), would have encompassed most if not all of a townland; in Dickson's terminology the individual leasing these units would probably have been a 'farmer of a townland' or 'townland rentier'[16] and such 'large' tenants would also have had sufficient land to sublet much of their holding. Arbitrary though it may seem, we will assume that the majority of tenants holding over 120 acres and practically all of the tenants holding more than 300 acres were middlemen. 'Medium' tenants (21-120 acres or £6 to £15 per year) might have been subletting some land but the likelihood is that the majority of them were working most of their holdings directly. This would certainly have been true of 'small' tenants (less than 20 acres or less than £5 per year) many of whom were probably working all of their holdings directly, using family or wage labour or both.

Table 1

a. Tenancy Size Distribution (Acreage), c. 1750

Estate	0–20	21–120	121–300	300 plus	Total	Date
Ram	–	47(60%)	32(40%)	–	79	1758
Rockingham	1(2%)	10(16%)	24(38%)	28(44%)	63	1745
Carew	–	12(35%)	18(55%)	3(10%)	33	1748
Colclough	41(62%)	18(27%)	6(10%)	1(1%)	66	1755
Totals	42(17%)	87(36%)	80(33%)	32(13%)	241	

b. Tenancy Size Distribution (Annual rent in pounds), c.1750

Estate	0–5	6–15	16–30	30 plus	Total	Date
Donovan	21(46%)	16(35%)	7(15%)	2(4%)	46	1745
Anglesey	–	9(19%)	14(29%)	25(52%)	48	1758
Kavanagh	4(12%)	3(10%)	11(33%)	15(45%)	33	1746
Totals	25(20%)	28(22%)	32(25%)	42(33%)	127	

Comb. Totals 67(18%)   115(31%) 112(31%) 74(20%) 368

Sources: Registry of Deeds, 187–366–12550 and 194–55–128607; Rockingham, Colclough, Donovan and Kavanagh papers (N.L.I.); A. K. Longfield (ed.), *The Shapland-Carew papers* (Dublin, 1948).

The evidence presented in Table 1 demonstrates the prominence of the large leaseholder in the region. The seven estates sampled for the study contained a total of 368 tenants, 74 of whom held farms of more than 300 acres or more than £30 per year annual rental value. A further 112 tenants held between 120 and 300 acres or paid between £16 and £30 per year in rent. Of the 182 tenants who were not in either of these large categories, 115 held 21–120 acres (or paid £6 to £15 per year) and only 67 held less than 21 acres (or paid less than £6 per year).

These figures suggest a number of important general observations. First, if our assumptions about the internal structure of large tenancies is correct, then at least half of the tenant population on these seven estates were middlemen; of those remaining most were in the medium category and so may also have been sub-letting. Middlemen did not monopolise the ranks of the tenant classes by any means, of course, but the middleman was, without question, the dominant figure in the economic life of the region since tenants holding over 120 acres were obviously in possession of most of the rented land on all of the estates in question. It is reasonable to assume, therefore, that small tenants who leased land directly from the landowners represented only a minority of the entire 'peasant' population and the majority of that population were in fact sub-tenants. Thus, arguably, it was the middleman class, not the landlords, who directly controlled the economic destiny of the vast majority of the rural population of this area.[17]

Not surprisingly, the importance of the large and very large tenant varied considerably from one estate to another. These types of tenants were especially common on the Rockingham, Anglesey and Kavanagh lands. As Table 1 shows, leaseholders with over 120 acres accounted for 52 out of a total of 63 tenants on the Rockingham estate and the prevalence of such leaseholders seems to have been almost as marked in the Kavanagh and Anglesey cases where tenants paying over £16 per year accounted for 26 out of 33 and 39 out of 48 tenants respectively. The position of the large leaseholder on the Carew and Ram estates was also important but slightly less so than in the preceding examples: on the Carew estate 21 out of 33 tenants held more than 120 acres (although a far smaller number held over 300 acres than in the Rockingham case), and 32 of the 79 tenants on the Ram estate held over 120 acres (although, significantly, none of them held more than 300).[18] The Donovan and Colclough properties were the only ones in the sample whose tenurial structures were truly exceptional. Small tenants were almost entirely absent from the records of the five estates discussed so far, yet tenants of 20 acres or less accounted for 41 out of 65 tenants on the Colclough lands and tenants paying less than £5 per year in rent accounted for 21 out of 44 tenants on the Donovan lands. Of course very large and large leaseholders still accounted for 19 per cent of the tenants on the Donovan estate and, while we can assume that a large majority of the tenancies were being worked directly by their lessors and were not being sublet to any significant degree, we must also note that a disproportionate share of these estates was in the hands of middlemen; for example, tenants of 120 acres and over held 51 per cent of the sampled section of the Colclough estate and tenants paying £16 or more in annual rent were responsible for 54 per cent of the Donovan rental.

The data summarised above show that middlemen were to be found on all types of properties in the southeast in the mid-eighteenth century and that, generally speaking, the middle-man was the dominant figure in the countryside of the region. The system was especially well established on the large estates in the sample and was weakest on its smallest property (the Donovan) and on the section of the Colclough lands examined here where a community of Protestant artisans had been settled by the proprietor.[19] This pattern suggests that the middleman system was created in part for management purposes; in other words, to simplify the task of collecting rent and the develop-ment of land on extensive or fragmented properties. In this connection, however, it is significant that the system developed independently of the presence or absence of the individual proprietor from the region; thus, the middleman was almost as important on large residential estates as he was on the sole absentee property, the Rockingham lands.[20]

The data in Table 1 also lead to the significant conclusion that there was little connection between the religion of the proprietor or the religious composition of the general population of an estate and the presence or absence of a middleman system on that estate. Thus, the system was as well developed on the one Catholic property in the sample, the Kavanagh lands, as it was on the five large Protestant properties. Also, while the system was to be found in areas which had large Protestant communit-ies by the general standards of the southeast (e.g. the Rock-ingham lands) it was also to be found in areas where there were very few Protestants (e.g. the Kavanagh and Carew estates). Conversely, it was only moderately or poorly developed on some estates which had fairly large Protestant populations (e.g. on the Colclough and Donovan lands).

Religious Composition of the Middleman Class

The apparent unimportance of the religion of the proprietor as a factor in the development of the middleman system would seem to negate the argument that the system was a prop to the Protestant community in the southeast. However, the evidence at our disposal also shows that on most estates in our sample the

Table 2   [Sources: As in Table 1.]

a. Position of Catholic Tenants (Acreages), 1750

Estates	Tenants	Cath. tenants	Land held	Avg. Catholic tenant	Avg. Protestant tenant
Ram	60	9(15%)	805(14%)	89	96
Rock'm	63	5(8%)	1,470(6%)	298	421
Carew	39	28(72%)	5,947(60%)	212	365
Colcl.	71	11(15%)	738(27%)	67	33
Totals	233	53	8,960		

b. Position of Catholic Tenants (Annual rents in £s), 1750

Estates	Tenants	Cath. tenants	Rent Paid	Avg. Catholic tenant	Avg. Protestant tenant
Donovan	46	22(48%)	167(35%)	7	12
Anglesey	55	14(25%)	443(23%)	32	35
Kavanagh	34	27(79%)	831(78%)	31	30
Totals	135	63	1441		
Comb. tot.	368	116			

tenant population, and especially the large and very large tenant population, was overwhelmingly Protestant in the mid-eighteenth century in spite of the fact that in no part of our study area, except perhaps the Ram estate, were Protestants a majority of the local population.[21]

Table 2, based on an analysis of terms of tenure and tenant surnames, illustrates the degree to which the total leaseholder population of these seven estates in the southeast was dominated by Protestants. Thus, of the 368 tenants on these properties, only 116 (or 32 per cent) were Catholics, according to our measure. Furthermore, as a group the Catholic tenants on the Rockingham, Ram, Carew and Colclough estates combined held only 8,960 acres out of a total of 44,762 (or 20 per cent) and those on the Donovan, Anglesey, and Kavanagh lands were assessed at only £1,441 (42 per cent) out of a total annual rental of £3,429. It is reasonable to assume therefore that even though they constituted a substantial majority of the population in the sampled area, Catholics held no more than about one third of the land which was rented directly from the proprietorial class.

As one would expect, the Protestant middlemen tended to be far more important on estates in areas with large Protestant populations than on those with small ones. They were in a stronger position on the Rockingham estate than on any other property; in this case tenants with Anglo-Saxon surnames accounted for 92 per cent of the tenant population and held 94 per cent of the rented land. On the Ram lands tenants with Anglo-Saxon surnames accounted for 85 per cent of the tenantry and held 86 per cent of the land; in the Anglesey case the proportions were 73 per cent and 77 per cent respectively and in the Colclough case 85 per cent and 73 per cent. On the Donovan estate the position of Protestants was not quite so dominant; here they accounted for only 52 per cent of the tenantry. However, since these Protestant tenants paid 65 per cent of all the annual rent, their economic position was obviously much stronger than their numbers would suggest. Indeed, the fact that the average rental of Protestant-held tenancies on the Donovan estate was almost twice as large as Catholic-held ones indicates that most of the large tenants on this property were Protestant. Only on the Carew and Kavanagh estates were Protestants clearly a minority of the direct tenant population; in the former case they accounted for 28 per cent of this population and in the latter for 21 per cent. Since both of these properties were dominated by large tenants, these were clearly properties on which the Catholic middleman was an important figure. Nonetheless, on the Carew property Protestant-held farms were significantly larger than Catholic-held ones and even on the Catholic-owned Kavanagh estate, Protestant tenancies were as large as Catholic ones. The Colclough 'estate' presents us with a somewhat unusual situation. Here, while Protestant tenants outnumbered Catholics, Catholic tenancies tended to be much larger than Protestant ones. In this case the Protestant population was apparently centred around the demesne, holding small farms directly from the proprietor, while in the outlying sections of the property large farms, many possibly held by Catholic middlemen, were more important. In general, Protestant tenants almost completely dominated three estates in our sample (Rockingham, Ram, and Anglesey), in both numerical and economic terms; they were slightly superior in both these terms on one (the Donovan); they were in a numerical majority but in a less favoured economic position than Catholics on one (the Colclough); they were in a numerical minority but in a more favoured economic position on one (the Carew) and they were in a less advantaged position than Catholics in numerical and perhaps economic terms on only one property (the Kavanagh).

Based on this evidence, there was a direct connection between the religious composition of the general population on an estate and the religious composition of that estate's middle-man population.[22] Protestant middlemen tended to be dominant in areas with unusually large Protestant populations and Catholics tended to be more favoured in areas with small Protestant populations. The Rockingham estate is the best example of the first situation. Here, in the half-barony of Shillelagh, the Protestant population was large and, it seems, almost all leaseholders were Protestant.[23] Conversely but exceptionally, on the Kavanagh estate, located in a heavily Catholic section of Carlow, the exact opposite pattern prevailed. Here the proprietor was Catholic, the local Protestant population was small (probably less than 10 per cent) and the Catholic middle-man was the dominant figure in the countryside.[24] So, while Protestants by no means monopolised the middleman class in the southeast, they certainly dominated it and that domination appears to have been most pronounced in the north Wexford/south Wicklow area. In light of this finding Miles Byrne's embittered complaint that landowners discriminated systematically against Catholics in granting leases and that 'descendants of Cromwell . . . professing the protestant religion got leases of nine hundred and ninety nine years or ninety nine years renewable forever, they thus became the middlemen and cruel task masters of the Irish serfs' seems justified.[25] While such 'perpetuity leases'[26] were not in fact as common as Byrne implies,[27] the data discussed above would appear to justify the tone of this particular Catholic middleman from the north of the county.

Residential Patterns of Middlemen

It is essential that we confirm that the middlemen we have

described thus far were permanent residents of the region and so fully part of its social and political life. An investigation of the residential patterns of Irish tenants in the eighteenth century faces the problem that few rentals give background information about the tenants they list. Abstracts of leases in the Registry of Deeds, however, frequently provide valuable information on the tenants' backgrounds (both residential and 'occupational'), and are relatively easy to trace for a given estate or locality. Sixty leases drawn up between 1745 and 1755 on various sections of the Anglesey lands in Wexford have been examined.[28] This group of abstracts may not represent all of the leases made on the Anglesey property over this time-period, as landlords were not obliged to register leases and probably did so only on a very irregular basis. The sample does provide us with valuable data on the tenantry of this property, however, since most of the leases in question specify the address and status (gent, farmer, merchant etc.) of the lessee and indicate place of residence. As we have seen, the Anglesey estate was dominated by middlemen, the majority of whom were Protestants, at this time in its history and therefore it is probably representative of the situation on many larger estates in the southeast in the mid-eighteenth century.

Table 3 summarises an analysis of the information on tenants' backgrounds given in the sixty Anglesey leases mentioned above. Table 3a classifies tenants according to place of residence, depending on whether they lived (a) in the townland being leased, (b) outside the townland being leased but on the Anglesey estate, (c) outside the Anglesey estate but within Co. Wexford, or (d) outside the county altogether. Tenants in the last of these categories could certainly be regarded as absentees since they cannot have been an important factor in the social and political life of the area. Tenants who held land outside the estate but did live in Co. Wexford can only be regarded as absentees in a limited way; although not living on their tenancy, they would have been very much part of the society of the county. Tenants living on the Anglesey property or living on the land being leased were probably fully part of the community of the estate and the area.

The figures in Table 3a show that the vast majority of tenants in the Anglesey case were residents on or near the land they

Table 3

a. Addresses of Tenants Named in Leases of Anglesey Property in Co. Wexford, 1745–1755

Addresses	Number of Tenants
Townland leased	33(55%)
Elsewhere on estate	19(32%)
Elsewhere in County	4 (7%)
Outside County	4 (7%)
Total	60(100%)

b. Status of Anglesey Leaseholders

Title	Number of Tenancies
Farmer	19(32%)
Gent	22(37%)
Esquire	5 (8%)
Clerk	1 (2%)
Artisan	2 (3%)
Merchant	5 (8%)
Unknown	6(10%)
Total	60(100%)

Sources: see note 28.

rented. Thirty-three of the leases granted in this sample of 60 were to tenants who were living in the townland being leased. If this sample is representative, then over half the tenants of the region were resident in the strictest sense and held over half (51 per cent) the land covered by the sample. (Since these leases all involved entire townlands, we can assume that these 33 men held at least one—and perhaps several more than one—townland). A further 19 tenants, or 32 per cent of the total, had residences on the Anglesey estate in Co. Wexford although they did not live on the land being leased in this case. These tenants held roughly one-third (or 35 per cent) of the land covered by the sixty leases in our sample; presumably such tenants were renting at least two full townlands, the one covered by the lease in question and the one on which they resided. Four tenants, or 7 per cent of the total, resided outside the limits of the Anglesey estate but within Co. Wexford. These tenants held just over nine hundred acres altogether, or 7 per cent of the land covered by the leases. Like the previous category of tenants, such lessees can also be considered residents. They too would have been part of the social and political life of the area and must find a place in the sectarian equation. In all, therefore, 56 tenants (93 per cent), leasing 11,734 acres out of 12,700 (93 per cent) can be broadly classified as residents of the study area. The truly absentee tenantry was insignificant both in terms of numbers and in terms of the area of land they held.

Table 3b summarises the information on tenant 'status' provided by the leases in question. The terms 'esquire', 'gent' and 'farmer' are the most common labels used in these particular leases although occasionally lessees are also described as 'clerk', 'merchant' or 'artisan'. The term 'esquire' probably refers to a member of the landowning class. The term 'gent' might refer to a landowner, although usually one of modest means but could also be used in reference to a large tenant who did not himself work on his leasehold. 'Farmer' most likely refers to a man who, regardless of the size of his leasehold, worked some of the land he rented directly, using family or wage labour. The distinction between any two of these three grades of society was never clearly drawn but the hallmarks listed here provide a workable guide for our purposes.[29]

The data summarised in Table 3b indicate that the vast majority of these tenants were given either the title 'farmer' or 'gent'. Thus, 19 of the 60 leases (32 per cent) were to 'farmers'. Leases to 'gents' numbered 22 (37 per cent). These two categories together accounted for 75 per cent of the tenancies. Of the remaining categories, none was large enough to be of great significance. The most important of these, the 'esquires' or 'landowner tenants', and 'merchants' each accounted for only 8 per cent of the total, while 'clerks' and 'artisans' were even less important in terms of numbers.

The middleman was therefore a weighty feature of this area of rural Ireland in the mid-eighteenth century if the data cited above are at all typical of the region. Both the residential and occupational patterns are indicative of a group which was fully part of the life of the area and which had a fairly well-defined socio-economic status, intermediate between the large land-owners and the majority of the tillers of the soil. A genuinely rural population, middlemen were rarely local townsmen and the merchant and professional lease speculator was uncommon. There were different kinds of middlemen of course and, no doubt, this society would have distinguished carefully between those labelled 'gentlemen' and those described as 'farmers'. In reality, however, the two groups together occupied a privileged position which differed little in terms of function for either of them.

Conclusions

The evidence tends to confirm the impression we have of the Irish middleman. First, tenants who were probably middlemen of various kinds were a prominent feature of the southeast. Middlemen were particularly common on large estates, but they were present in significant numbers and controlled relatively large amounts of land even on most smaller properties. Second, the majority of all tenants, especially large tenants, were Protestants. A few estates were almost completely dominated by Protestant tenants and, on estates where both Catholic and Protestant tenants resided, Protestants were usually in the majority; only two properties out of the total of seven had Catholic majorities among their tenantry, and only one of these, the single Catholic-owned estate in the sample, had a Catholic majority whose tenancies were, on average, comparable in size to those of their Protestant neighbours. Third, the middleman tenants of the region were almost all permanent members of this general community. Absentee tenants seem to have been rare, and the vast majority of large tenants could be given no loftier title than gentleman and farmer. Speculator tenants, including merchants from nearby towns, were uncommon.

It is clear from these findings that any developments which would have tended to undermine the middleman system would threaten to shift the balance of economic power from the

Protestant to the Catholic community. L. M. Cullen's fascinating explanation for the 1798 rebellion in Wexford is based largely on the argument that this kind of tenurial change seriously upset an established equilibrium between the two religious communities of the southeast. Cullen concentrates especially on the accentuation of an ongoing rivalry between Catholic and Protestant gentry as an underlying cause of tension once the leasing system upon which both groups depended began to disintegrate, implying that previously the Catholic middleman had been almost as common as the Protestant middleman. For example, speaking of north Wexford in the 1790s, he argues that 'Catholics were numerous among the small gentry and rising middleman families in the north of the county—much more so than among the tenantry below'.[30] The evidence of this paper suggests that Cullen's argument is essentially correct in that the middleman class, the 'gentry' in other words, was indeed a mixture of Protestants and Catholics. It should be noted, however, that the numerical and economic preponderance of Protestant over Catholic middlemen in the north Wexford and south Wicklow estates examined here was quite striking. Thus Catholic middleman families such as the Byrnes of Ballymanus and Monaseed, used as examples by Cullen,[31] appear to have been very rare in the Wexford/Wicklow borderland, at least at the height of the middleman system in the mid-eighteenth century. So, in the north Wexford/south Wicklow area at least, the abandonment of the middleman system, beginning in the 1780s, would have dissipated, either by emigration or downward social mobility, an entire class which had been almost exclusively Protestant. The shift in power from the Protestant to the Catholic community may have been even more dramatic than Cullen implies, therefore. Of course this assumes that the estates sampled here are typical of the region; they may not be. It is significant, however, that the first truly brutal local violence of 1798, the Carnew massacre, took place on the Rockingham estate, a locality completely dominated by the middleman system in the mid-eighteenth century but where Catholic middlemen were practically unknown.

Clearly, the end of the middleman system and its replacement by direct leasing to former undertenants, sometimes Protestant, but more often Catholic, would have had serious consequences for the region's non-middleman Protestant community too. Not all Protestant tenants in the southeast were middlemen. A large number were probably sub-tenants or small direct tenants whose holdings were too small to be sub-let on a significant scale. But the Protestant middleman population would have functioned as a kind of shield for both these smaller Protestant tenants and the local landlords, since middlemen no doubt often played an important role as military as well as social and economic leaders in the region. It is likely that large lease-holders, like proprietors, were biased in favour of Protestants when adopting their own renting policy, thereby ensuring that Catholic sub-tenants occupied a position in the social hierarchy of the area that was markedly less favoured than their Protestant counterparts, a situation which would have embittered the Catholic population greatly.[32] Middleman emigration, which probably occurred both before and after 1798,[33] would obviously have affected the smaller Protestant tenants who depended on this group for protection and leadership. If this *scenario* is at all typical, then the development of increased sectarian tensions in the southeast in the late eighteenth and early nineteenth century is hardly surprising, nor is the apparent enthusiasm with which Protestant 'yeomen', often sub-tenants, waged war on their Catholic counter-parts during that period.

We shall need a large number of local studies before we can determine the general importance of the middleman tenant in eighteenth-century Ireland. Presumably the granting of large leaseholds was common everywhere but presumably also the religious composition of the class varied from one area of the country to another. The pattern of this variation will eventually allow us to speculate as to the influence this system of leasing had on local socio-political conflicts. In this connection it will be especially interesting to discover the extent to which the decline of the middleman system exacerbated agrarian tensions in areas where the middleman class was dominated by Catholics. Such studies will throw much needed light on what has, to this point, been a dimly perceived aspect of the eighteenth century. This work is especially vital since the time-period between the confiscations and the Napoleonic Wars marks the transition in much of rural Ireland from a pre-modern to a modern rural economy, in circumstances of colonialism. The role of tenurial institutions such as the middleman system in that modernisation process, and the preservation of a colonialist power structure, must have been central. Only by understanding the evolution of this institution on a national scale, therefore, can we hope to comprehend the conflicts, sectarian and social, which characterised this era.

6. Extra-parliamentary agitation in Dublin in the 1760s

THE 1760s, like many others in the eighteenth century, is a neglected decade in the history of Dublin popular politics. Following the politicisation of the Dublin guilds by Charles Lucas and James Digges La Touche during the 1740s, the 1750s had been a period when much of the energy generated by Lucas's campaign went into striving for a measure of municipal reform, which was finally obtained in 1760.[1] The Dublin city corporation act of 1760 (33 Geo. II, c. 16) represented a measure of partial democratisation along the lines urged by Lucas and La Touche in the 1740s; the lower house of Dublin corporation gained new rights in the election of the city magistrates, and the guilds gained full control over the selection of their representatives to the lower house. As if to set the seal on these gains, Lucas himself was elected as one of the city MPs in 1761 following his return from exile, having received a royal pardon on the accession of George III. The following decade proved to be a good one for the parliamentary opposition; ministries in Britain were short-lived and weak, so that there were frequent changes of viceroy, and this militated against the government taking firm control of the Irish parliamentary situation. Only during the administration of Lord Townshend (viceroy 1767–72; a politician who was prepared to adopt new methods) did the executive begin to gain greater control, through the formation of a 'castle' party.[2]

In Dublin the 1760s witnessed periodic bouts of political activity involving both guild and (less frequently) crowd action. In the background lay spells of commercial distress, which punctuated the overall experience of economic growth and demographic expansion in the city during the 1750s and 1760s; since the beginning of the century the population had doubled, rising to around 140,000 by 1760.[3] The commercial interests of Dublin chafed under a series of trade embargoes and restrictions which were the practical manifestation of Poynings' law during a period of war (the Seven Years' War with France, 1756–63) and expectations of war (Britain almost went to war over the Falkland islands in the winter of 1770–71). These grievances were articulated first and foremost by the Dublin guilds (twenty-five in all), which enjoyed many advantages in speaking out on such matters; they held regular meetings, they could pass resolutions in their guild halls, and they could give instructions to their representatives on the corporation. As chartered bodies, in which full membership was confined to Protestants, they formed part (even if a lowly part) of the political establishment, however much government spokesmen might dismiss all extra-parliamentary agitation as the work of a 'mob'. It was the guilds, particularly the large and prestigious guild of merchants, which took the lead in supporting the more flamboyant opposition personalities; which called for a septennial bill to increase their control over their representatives, and which drew attention to the detrimental effects of falling trade and public credit. The crowd, in a less decorous manner, could make the same or similar points; it was, moreover, an instrument open to manipulation by a 'crowd hero' — in Dublin this meant Lucas — who could play on its emotions in order to threaten an administration with popular demonstrations as a means of extra-parliamentary pressure.

A means of communication was essential if influence by opposition politicians over the public was to be exerted and maintained. The spoken word at meetings provided an immediate stimulus. Lucas was not only MP for Dublin from 1761 to 1771, he also served as a representative of the barber-surgeons' guild on the corporation from 1762–5, and thus had many opportunities to attend guild and corporation meetings.[4] In addition, pamphlets and newspapers provided ideas and helped to mould public opinion. Pamphlets in particular acted as a barometer of political activity during the eighteenth century; in times of social, economic and political stress their numbers multiplied. A new public was developing and gaining its knowledge from print. The commercial classes were among those who eagerly responded to opposition pamphlets, which contained a strain of anti-oligarchical sentiment that was part of the common political legacy in Britain, Ireland and America.

The glorious revolution of 1688 formed the touchstone and basis of contemporary political institutions, and was invariably referred to for guidance or support. Opposition pamphlets also reveal the influence of Enlightenment thought, the common law, and classical literature.

From 1759 onwards, opposition within and without parliament began to interact to form an increasingly cohesive alliance of interests which rendered the task of government more difficult. 'Patriotism' and an entrenched opposition had become synonymous, and could not easily be bought off. What made Lucas's influence in Dublin so strong was his evident sympathy with the commercial classes, the guilds and artisans; and he formed part of that public opinion which was occasionally critical of the aristocracy.

The point should also be made that popular agitation in Dublin cannot be seen in isolation from similar action during the same period in America and in England, particularly London. Lucas from time to time referred to events in London, and saw a close parallel between the rights and privileges of London, and those of Dublin.[5] The career of John Wilkes (the crowd hero of London) was followed closely in Dublin. Certainly, the Dublin disturbances were regarded by the authorities as part of a pattern, an indication of general social breakdown:

> A virulent spirit of licentiousness has broke out among us, threatening the destruction of all order and subordination . . . The situation of affairs in America and the late disturbances in England ought to be strong inducements to the friends of Ireland to exert themselves in supporting the King's measures . . .[6]

The issues which inspired popular action in Dublin during the 1760s fell into three main categories; the defence of the rights and privileges of the Irish parliament; civil liberties in general (especially the supremacy of civil over martial law), and matters which concerned trade. Contemporaries saw a close connection between these issues. As the guild of merchants put it in 1766,

> We know that Freedom and Commerce are nearly related, that the one cannot suffer and the other flourish; Trade must decrease with every Violation of Liberty . . .[7]

In addition, the perceived need for the defence of Irish rights in these areas frequently arose in consequence of action taken or proposed by the British government, over whose actions Dubliners had no control. It was this which helped make the guilds and the Dublin crowd supporters of Irish legislative rights.

The period under examination (1759–71) began and ended with economic depression. The year 1759 saw the collapse of the aristocratic bank run by Anthony Malone, Nathaniel Clements and John Gore, three politicians who had been identified with the successful parliamentary opposition during the money bill disputes of the mid-1750s.[8] This collapse had adverse effects on Dublin trade, commerce and employment, which permeated down to the lowest level of society. Public confidence was not helped by the various invasion scares which were rife throughout 1759, particularly in the latter half of the year. Trade was also affected by an embargo imposed in 1758, arising out of the war with France, on the export of provisions from Ireland. The embargo caused some embarrassment to the lord lieutenant, the duke of Bedford;[9] but what turned popular resentment into mob action was a measure intended to compensate for the difficulties caused by the embargo. In April 1759 an act of the British parliament (32 Geo. II, c. 11) removed the restrictions on the import of Irish cattle into Great Britain. Although this was a liberating measure, and doubtless welcome to farmers and landlords, it represented a serious blow to the butchers, cooks, tallow chandlers and associated tradesmen of the metropolis, all of whom stood to lose from the export of live cattle from Dublin. The Dublin butchers (who were notorious for their participation in the sectarian and recreational faction fighting which was endemic in the capital—they formed the backbone of the Catholic participants)[10] were not slow to defend their interests, and in May the lord lieutenant had reason to complain of 'the atrocious behaviour of the mob of Dublin towards those who came from England to buy cattle in Ireland'.[11]

The disturbances of May 1759 were only a foretaste of those which occurred later in that year. Again, it was British action (or fear of possible British action) which sparked off the trouble. In 1756, once more in the context of the war with France, a clause had been added to the English militia bill allowing parliament to be summoned in case of emergency (such as an invasion) by royal proclamation; and it was suggested that the clause should be extended to cover the Irish parliament.[12] (Through the declaratory act of 1720 (6 Geo. I, c. 5) the British parliament claimed the formal right to legislate for Ireland, although this right was exercised very sparingly.) Anticipating resistance in the Irish parliament to such a mode of proceeding, the Irish chief secretary, Richard Rigby, argued that the measure should be undertaken by the Irish parliament itself.

In early November leave was given to introduce the necessary legislation into the Irish parliament. Almost immediately the project ran into opposition. Unfortunately for Rigby, rumours of the possibility of a legislative union between Great Britain and Ireland had become rife in Dublin during the summer of 1759, arising chiefly from the publication of certain pamphlets a :vo-cating the measure, and the efforts of London booksellers to advertise such works. It appears that public opinion in Dublin misinterpreted the proposed legislation as a move to facilitate the introduction of a union, and this provoked a powerful response.[13] The effect on trade and employment of closing the Irish parliament for a prolonged or indefinite period would be disastrous. The parliamentary session with its influx of wealthy people into the capital represented an inflow of cash and employment, especially for the service industries, but also for Dublin trade and industry in general. The effect of the rumour on a population already angry and agitated as a result of the 1758 embargo and the live cattle exports was to make an overcharged situation much worse. Disturbances began on 22 November—the day the bill was to be introduced—and lasted on and off until 3 December. During that period:

> . . . there were public clamours through all the streets, whis-perings, cabals, murmurs, in every coffee house and place of resort; the parliament house was daily surrounded, & thronged with rioters; many of the representatives stopped and insulted by the rabble . . . letters publickly printed and directed to the Lords and Commons, with express threats of *graves*, and broad hints of assassinations; and lastly those threats put into execution, by dashing chairs and coaches to pieces, pulling the members out by violence, striking, wound-ing and casting some into the kennel, and compelling others

to swear allegiance, before a mob magistracy to a mob administration.[14]

Parliamentary connivance was suspected. Lord Chancellor Bowes declared that there was collusion between forces in parliament and elements outside. Opposition to Rigby's bill, he wrote,

> . . . by art gave rise to fears without doors that the disuse of Parliament was intended preparatory to an union with Britain, which produced tumults about the House and insults threatened to some of the members . . .[15]

A government supporter believed that

> . . . the malice of the mob is grown to such a height against the honourable House of Lords and Commons 'tis scarcely safe for a nobleman to venture himself in the city. Yesterday many thousands of them were collected by public beat of drum . . .[16]

On 3 December Bowes himself had travelled to parliament under the protection of the lord mayor of Dublin, but was refused entry to the house of lords by the crowd. He was eventually told by the lord mayor that he could no longer guarantee his protection. 'With difficulty we got to the coach, the mob calling out to swear that we were for the country against the union . . .'[17]

There is evidence of some organisation of the crowd. There was a tocsin in the form of a drum-beat, the rallying to the parliament buildings, and the policy of swearing MPs to be true to the country. The use of the drum-beat as a signal, and furthermore the reading of a proclamation as a means of assembling the crowd into a cohesive unit, indicates some planning and organisation behind the scenes.[18] Certain individuals came in for special abuse, particularly Rigby, whose role as sponsor of the offending legislation exposed him to the indignation of the crowd. Rigby certainly believed his life was threatened. 'When I stay out late at night, I make my servants carry firearms; and by God, if I am attacked, I will wait for no peace-officer to give the word of command.'[19] But what struck one of Bowes's English correspondents most forcefully was the religious composition of the crowd, which (it was generally agreed) was made up largely of Protestants from the weavers' quarter of the Liberties:

> . . . to see a Protestant multitude attack a Protestant Government, in a country where all together do not make a sixth of the whole, without any imaginable cause of complaint, but because it is Government . . . is to me a very striking and a very shocking picture . . .[20]

In fact, however, not only did Protestants compose almost half the population of Dublin, but (as noted above) membership of the body corporate—the corporation and guilds—was entirely confined to them, which naturally fostered the belief that the public good of Dublin was their responsibility.[21]

In the December riots the Castle administration complained bitterly of the lack of support shown by the city magistrates and the lord mayor.[22] These magistrates, with their guild background, would have shared popular fears about the implications of legislative union, and were little inclined to risk injury or public opprobrium by calling out the Dublin garrison. It was the lord lieutenant's decision to call out the troops which eventually dispersed the rioters. However, this decision did nothing to help the popularity of the administration, and probably reinforced the chauvinistic attitudes noted by Rigby:

> . . . there is a general indisposition to the people of England from those in Ireland . . . they are unwilling to acknowledge the dependency of this on the British L—sl—re; and . . . they are all bred up in a settled antipathy to the superiority of the latter . . .[23]

The proposed legislation which had sparked off the riots was dropped, practically as soon as the first popular demonstrations began.[24] The end result was therefore a victory for the opposition, in and out of parliament, and a weakening of the administration's prestige. Since the proposed legislation would have jeopardised the power of the undertakers (who managed the administration in the absence of the lord lieutenant) the result represented a victory for Irish rights and privileges. The riots also helped bring to a head the popular campaign for reform of Dublin corporation; the act passed in 1760 was intended, in part, to restore the authority of the city magistrates in order to help them maintain the public peace.[25]

Following these opposition successes, and the election of Lucas for the city in 1761, the 1760s saw the guilds from time to time taking up political issues, on the assumption that freedom of trade and legislative independence were complementary. One such issue related to the duration of parliaments, since regular elections gave the voters an opportunity to influence candidates. During the 1760s the parliamentary opposition repeatedly expressed its view that Irish legislation should be introduced similar to the English septennial act, and political advertisements on that theme became increasingly common in the press.[26] There was support for this campaign in the guilds.[27] From 1763 there was also much support in the guilds for John Wilkes, who had incurred the wrath of the British government for the tenor of his attacks on Lord Bute's administration. The *Freeman's Journal* (founded, with Lucas's help, in 1763) took up Wilkes's cause, with articles, poems, letters and advertisements in his honour. Even his supporters were honoured: in 1764 the Dublin guild of merchants unanimously voted the freedom of the guild to the English judge, Chief Justice Pratt (who had ruled in favour of Wilkes's release from prison).[28] Irish MPs who found favour with the guilds were similarly honoured. In 1766 Lucas received the public congratulations of the merchants' guild, in an address which encouraged him to work for a measure to limit the duration of parliaments as 'the only means of securing us against future Incroachments in our Constitution, and future Restraints upon a Trade already too much limited'.[29]

Meanwhile, from the mid-1760s public opinion was being aroused in relation to matters concerning the army. Two distinct, but evidently related, issues were involved: the administration's desire for an augmentation of the army, and the question of the perceived threat posed to civil liberties by the existence of a large garrison and the consequent prevalence of martial law. In this respect, it should be remembered that Dublin possessed nothing like a modern police force, and that citizens frequently found themselves at the mercy of the local garrison. Dislike of standing armies, therefore, had a foundation in day-to-day experience. As early as 1761, the lord lieutenant was advising the cabinet that he would have to tread carefully in the matter of an augmentation, as 'they [the Irish parliament] have always been averse to an increase of expense, and an augmentation of the army'.[30] The death in 1764 of Archbishop Stone upset the political equilibrium and gave new opportunities to the parliamentary opposition. At the same time, the conduct of soldiers presented opposition MPs with the opportunity to highlight constitutional problems to their own political advantage. Lucas had long shared the traditional whig attitude that a standing army represented a threat to liberty, as well as guaranteeing Ireland's commercial oppression, and he was to reiterate these views during the period of the augmentation debate.[31]

During August 1765 a series of military outrages took place in Dublin. The central episode concerned troops of the Dublin garrison who broke into Newgate gaol to release fellow soldiers who were in custody. A number of civil prisoners were also set free. Most of the participants were arrested within a short time, and punished severely after a general court martial.[32] Lucas took up the issue, in part as a means of embarrassing the administration, which stood by the action of the army officers. He and others stressed the supremacy of civil law and implied that the refusal to subordinate military to civil law constituted a grave danger to the civil liberties of a people already suffering from severe constitutional grievances.[33] One correspondent in the *Freeman's Journal* argued that the case established a dangerous precedent, 'by which the Military of all Degrees may be exempted from being amenable to the Common Law, within the Liberties of this City'.[34] The issue became mixed up with another dispute which broke out in 1765, and which concerned the operation of Poynings' law. The harvest of 1765 was poor, and grain was scarce. As a result, heads of a bill were introduced into the Irish house of commons for preventing the export of corn.[35] According to Lucas, when the bill returned from the English privy council it had been altered, thus bringing into focus the issue of Poynings' law and opening up a second front in his attack on government. A brief vituperative pamphlet war erupted, centring on a series of addresses to the lord mayor of Dublin from Lucas, in which the issues of military excesses, Poynings' law, and the threat to civil liberties were intermingled. Lucas came under attack for being a mob orator; he turned the tables by claiming that 'mob magistrates and mob administrations were produced from the same source, evil governors'. He defended his guild supporters:

It is the mode to abuse the citizen, to represent the loyal regular corporations of this city, legally convened in their halls and performing lawful deeds, as a rude uncivilised barbarous mob . . .[36]

The guilds rallied to Lucas's defence, culminating in an address of thanks at the quarterly meeting of the merchants' guild. This was passed despite the efforts of government supporters to block the move, pointing out the dangers 'of disobliging great men'.[37]

By 1768 the campaign to provide for regular elections for the Irish parliament had been successful. The octennial act (7 Geo. III, c. 3) was passed in February, to the satisfaction of the opposition in and out of parliament. The guild of merchants voted the lord lieutenant a congratulatory address; other guilds passed resolutions welcoming the act, and hundreds of journeymen from the Liberties, wearing Orange cockades, paraded to the Castle where they cheered the lord lieutenant for his support for the measure.[38] The prospective dissolution of parliament, and the prospect of a general election (which was to take place the following year), heightened public interest in parliamentary affairs. Meanwhile, the main political issue of the day was the proposed augmentation of the army. The attempts of the new lord lieutenant, Lord Townshend, to secure an army augmentation with the minimum of political trouble had run into difficulty. By January 1768 he was warning 'every art will be used to prejudice the minds of the people against this salutary measure'.[39] The passing of the octennial act had strengthened the parliamentary opposition, which disliked the augmentation proposal partly on constitutional grounds and partly because of the cost, and there now occurred an incident concerning the Dublin garrison which Lucas was able to exploit in the campaign against augmentation.

The matter came to public attention following the court martial of one David Blakeney, a 'matross' (gunner's assistant) in a Dublin artillery regiment. According to Lucas, who subsequently wrote a pamphlet on the subject, soldiers who served in such lowly capacities were particularly liable to exploitation and arbitrary treatment by their officers; and following a period in which Blakeney and his fellows had allegedly failed to receive their full pay and issues of clothing, Blakeney took it upon himself to raise the men's grievances with his commanding officer. Although (in Lucas's view) he was merely acting in accordance with his rights, to his own astonishment Blakeney was accused of malicious intentions in raising the matter. He himself became the subject of a court martial, which, despite finding most of his complaints to be justified, sentenced him to five hundred lashes. On the day appointed for the punishment to be carried out, Blakeney became distressed and stabbed himself, causing serious injuries.[40]

Lucas took up Blakeney's case, campaigning for a pardon (in this he was unsuccessful: the sentence was carried out in March 1768 when the soldier had recovered from his self-inflicted wounds). However, Lucas's pamphlet on the case ran into several editions and was undoubtedly a severe embarrassment to the administration, appearing as it did at a time when the augmentation issue was under parliamentary discussion. Lucas seized the opportunity to raise a whole range of issues relating to the army: its expense; the fact that soldiers were deprived of their rights under common law ('Officers are often the prosecutors and judges of those Soldiers, who are so much their inferiors');[41] the outrages committed from time to time by soldiers, especially in the capital. And naturally he expressed his opposition to any augmentation of the army. (It is noteworthy, however, that Lucas acknowledged the need for some military force in Ireland 'until the natives of Ireland become capable and qualified to defend their liberty and property, in the form of a militia').[42] The pamphlet became the vehicle for a strong defence of the supremacy of civil over military law: 'every inferior court is answerable for its conduct to some superior, and all, to the High Court of Parlement'. There was also a panegyric on 'the sacred fundamental institution of juries', and the duty of the 'good Citizen' to defend the innocent.[43] Lucas rehearsed his (unsuccessful) attempt to get the house of commons to take up the case, and his appeal to the lord lieutenant to show clemency. His account of Blakeney's stoic endurance of the sentence, when it was eventually carried out, was affecting, and public interest was considerable. Counter arguments were produced.

One pamphleteer argued that the real motivation behind the publicity given to the case was 'an attempt to raise dissension and animosities, to relax discipline and order, and make the private men of every regiment look with an evil eye on their officers . . .'[44]

For his part, Townshend affected an attitude of lofty detachment:

> Here is a Doctor Lucas, the Wilks [sic] of Ireland, who has been playing the devil here and poisoning all the soldiery with his harangues and writings, but I have treated this nonsensical demagogue as he deserves with his mob at his heels . . .[45]

Yet Townshend evidently feared the effect of all this on Dublin opinion, especially in the light of recent developments in London. There Wilkes had returned from the continent and had been elected MP for Middlesex in March 1768, amidst scenes of popular enthusiasm which threatened civic order. On 27 April Wilkes was committed to prison as an outlaw, but before reaching prison he was rescued by a crowd, which continued to congregate in St George's Fields until dispersed by troops (with some loss of life) two weeks later.[46] During this latter period Townshend wrote to Lord Granby, 'the mob of Dublin hath been talked of in imitation of what you new experienced, and that ungrateful demagogue Lucas, restored by the King's favour, hath done everything in his power to poison the minds of the garrison here'.[47] But although the lord lieutenant was able to boast that populist opposition had been muted ('that vile incendiary Lucas . . . harangued the citizens against us without success') when the augmentation issue came up in the house of commons in May, Townshend's request for an additional three thousand men was rejected by 105 votes to 101.[48]

The military question continued to be a sensitive one for the rest of 1768 and into 1769, for despite the setback Townshend had not given up hope of gaining support for augmentation. In these circumstances it was important to ensure that no further embarrassing episodes occurred, and the administration became stricter about allowing officers of the Dublin garrison to go on leave, since it might weaken a discipline already under attack.[49]

Nevertheless, in the spring of 1769 there was another controversial court martial, this time of two private soldiers of the 53rd regiment. They had been troublesome and insubordinate for some time previously. The administration certainly believed that outside forces had been at work in their case: 'There is a great probability that these men have been privately advised and supported by some persons in this country, one of whom is a member of Parliament'.[50]

The central issue in this particular case was the validity of army regulations in Ireland. The regiment concerned had just returned from Gibraltar, and (since Ireland was a separate kingdom with its own legislature and laws) there was a constitutional case to be made, championed by opposition MPs, that special legislation, in the form of an Irish army act, was necessary to give effect to army regulations in Ireland.[51] In the absence of such a measure, it appears, the men had become convinced that they were not subject to military law. Again, the administration was embarrassed: 'the utmost industry is used to throw reflections upon the conduct of Government, to kindle a flame against officers, and to render odious the good discipline and service of the army in this kingdom'.[52]

One result was that the administration adopted an uncharacteristic leniency in dealing with these soldiers, suggesting that the appeal to public opinion over the army question had had its effect.[53] In November 1769 the house of commons at last agreed to the proposed augmentation of the army, but that was followed only a week later by an opposition victory which robbed the administration of much of its satisfaction. On 21 November a money bill was defeated on the grounds that it did not take its rise in the house of commons. The whole issue of the role of local assemblies in relation to money bills had become a sensitive one as a result of American protests about taxes imposed by the imperial parliament, and the British government responded to this rejection of the money bill as a matter of principle. A month later, as an act of imperial displeasure, Townshend registered a protest in the journal of the house of lords, and prorogued parliament.[54]

It was a mark of the administration's new sensitivity to public opinion in Dublin that Townshend was aware that proroguing parliament would have an adverse effect on trade in the capital, and that he should have striven to compensate for this by the judicious use of public money.[55] In January 1770 he held a masquerade ball in the Castle. Entry was conditional upon guests dressing only in the manufacture of the country, thus providing an outlet for goods in stock, providing employment, and securing the administration from attack over the economic effects of the prorogation.[56] The opposition was also active, via a strong pamphlet campaign, so during 1770 both administration and opposition vied with each other to win popular support. While the government blamed what it called 'faction' for bringing about the prorogration, the opposition charged the viceroy with exceeding his powers and undermining the constitution. Lucas produced his last great printed outburst in defence of the privileges of the Irish parliament (he was to die in November 1771).[57] However, the parliamentary opposition had been thrown into disarray by the lord lieutenant's vigorous action, his close attention to parliamentary management, and by his distribution of official patronage to a wider circle of MPs than had gained access to it during the regime of the undertakers. The result was that during 1770 the administration steadily gained support in parliamentary circles.[58]

By March 1770 Townshend was claiming that Dublin was quiet and loyal, although signs of anxiety were evident in his request for instructions in advance of how to act 'upon the instant if the ambitious design of particular men should proceed to innovate upon the authority of the Crown and raise a ferment'.[59] The administration was not helped, however, by the state of the economy in Dublin. Rapid economic growth during the 1760s had brought about a speculative fever by the end of the decade. Bankruptcies were increasing, and were to take a severe toll of Dublin business between 1770 and 1772. On top of this came another embargo on the provision trade, imposed in December 1770 when it was expected that Britain might go to war with Spain over the Falkland islands.[60] During the months before the meeting of parliament in February 1771, the press was full of reports of the decay of trade and credit, and public bodies, including guilds and the corporation, took steps to alleviate distress among the tradesmen.[61] This helps explain why Dublin proved at least a partial exception to the general failure of the parliamentary opposition to whip up public opinion over the issue of the prorogation. Although Townshend was able to report that the lord mayor and aldermen had blocked the adoption by the corporation of an address in support of the opposition's constitutional stand, it is evident that there was considerable sympathy for the opposition in the guilds and in the lower house of the corporation.[62]

On 19 February, a week before parliament met, the *Freeman's Journal* printed a letter which contained an incitement to popular action: 'our Rights, and those of our Parliament, have been invaded: Who can with Patience bear another Attack?' The writer continued, 'The worst Oppression, is *arbitrary Taxation* . . . A *Precedent* once established of Privy-Council Taxation, the Irish Parliament must sink into the Condition of that of Paris . . . ' The members of the lower house of the corporation were exhorted 'to kindle the proper fire, they will see it blaze in every Corporation, and spread the Warmth of patriotic zeal all over the Kingdom'. In an attempt to orchestrate opposition inside and outside parliament, opposition MPs were urged by the *Freeman's Journal* to meet before parliament opened to coordinate their strategy.[63]

Parliament met on 26 February. The *Freeman's Journal* for that day declared, 'we must rouse, and exert those Powers which God and the Constitution have invested us with, to stop the rapacious Plunders of our Country'. And on the following day, as the opposition opposed a resolution of thanks to the lord lieutenant's opening address, the plea was answered:

> A desperate mob, armed with clubs, cutlasses, &c, surrounded the House of Commons in Ireland, and attempted to swear several Members, who very spiritedly refused the proposed oath. Upon which they insulted some, and beat others, selecting with great nicety the Supporters of Government from the Members in opposition . . .[64]

On this occasion it appears that the immediate cause of the crowd action was a rumour that the majority of MPs had been bought off by the government, and were willing to follow its dictates to such an extent as to abrogate the rights of the Irish parliament itself. According to the lord mayor and sheriffs, 'the cry amongst the mob was that the Lord Lieutenant had got a great majority, and was going to carry away their Parliament'.[65]

The fact that some at least of the crowd were armed worked against its dispersal by the civil power alone. Townshend had no hesitation in sending in the army, and the promptness with which he did so indicates a certain preparedness on his part, while the speed with which the streets were cleared shows resolute action by the troops also.[66] The opportunity provided by the disturbance was seized upon by a hard-pressed opposition to move for an adjournment, but to no avail.[67] Townshend had made much progress towards stabilising the executive's control over the Irish parliament. Yet, weeks later, he recognised that control was still precarious:

A well-timed and ample advancement of those who have distinguished themselves at this important crisis, will establish the authority and influence of English government upon a permanent basis. Otherwise, the stone will immediately roll back on English government here and all future faith in it will forever explode[68]

The appearance on the Irish political scene of a metropolitan public opinion, rivalling that of London in its political awareness and tenacious defence of its interests, proved to be a headache for governments, more especially because of links between the opposition inside and outside parliament. Although government spokesmen were often contemptuous of 'the mob', it is important not be misled into imagining that Dublin popular politics in the 1760s reflected mindless agitation. It has been shown that Dublin public opinion, whether expressed (legitimately) in guild halls and guild resolutions or (more dubiously) by the assembling of crowds, had rational aims, and that popular interest in constitutional issues arose from the real difficulties posed for Dublin tradesmen by the impact of decisions taken in Britain. Although the lead in defending the citizens' commercial and constitutional interests was inevitably taken by Protestants, who formed the body corporate of the city, even Catholics (despite the penal laws) were not without the means to express their resentment over measures which affected them as much as Protestants.

It was the absence of effective police forces in Britain and Ireland which afforded the citizens such scope in demonstrating their views, and the assembling of large crowds was a feature of metropolitan politics in both London and Dublin. Ministers could only fall back on calling out the troops—a blunt instrument, which could do more harm than good by alarming citizens about the danger to civil liberties. Reluctance to take such a step thus exposed ministers to physical danger from crowds to an extent which has no parallel today. The attempted intimidation of Lord Chancellor Bowes in Dublin in December 1759 was matched by that experienced by Lord North in London in March 1771, when he was assaulted, his coach demolished and his hat captured by the crowd. On both occasions the ministers had been on their way to a meeting of parliament where a controversial constitutional issue was on the agenda.[69] Despite such experiences, the consensus in favour of a civic system of self-policing, as opposed to the professional 'gendarmeries' of continental countries like France, remained so strong that governments made no serious attempts to reform the police before the 1780s, following the notorious Gordon riots in London.[70] By that time, the tradition of civic action in Dublin had merged with the tradition of self-defence in time of national danger to produce the Volunteer movement, which was to play a central part in the campaign for Irish legislative independence.

7. *Gallicanism and the veto controversy: church, state and Catholic community in early nineteenth-century Ireland*

IN the view of contemporary observers from the European mainland, the most singular characteristic of the political life of nineteenth-century Ireland was the firm alliance which existed in that country between Catholicism and the forces of liberalism and nationalism.[1] That the Irish church was predisposed to such an alliance is to be explained, fundamentally, by the extraordinary importance of religious affiliation in the constitution of the Irish *ancien régime* as it survived into the nineteenth century. That it was able to endorse that alliance to the extent that it did and with remarkably little reticence must be ascribed to the relationship which existed between the Irish church and, on the one hand, the British state and, on the other, the Irish Catholic community. These relationships certainly did not emerge directly from the era of legal proscription of Catholicism in their characteristic nineteenth-century forms. Playing a crucial role in their development and definition was the protracted dispute about the legitimacy and expediency of involvement by the civil power in ecclesiastical affairs, known as the veto controversy.[2] In the absence of a satisfactory account of this dispute,[3] which occupied such a prominent place in public debate for some two decades after 1808, the present study considers the issues involved and the terms in which they were debated.

A further determinant of the relationship between the nineteenth-century Irish church and the state and society in which it existed—that is, the emergence of a renewed, militant Catholicism, and a renewed and militant papacy, in post-revolutionary Europe—has not escaped the attention of historians. To this revival, as the nineteenth century advanced, the Irish church contributed very substantially throughout the English-speaking world; from it, it drew considerable strength. Its new position of strength, powerfully reinforced by the steadily increasing political influence of the Irish majority, opened to the church a much wider range of possible modes of relating to the state than it had hitherto known. The result, in the opinion of some, was a divergence of view within the church, which is best described in terms of a Gallican-Ultramontane dichotomy.[4] It is doubtful if the introduction of these terms is useful in disentangling the skein of nineteenth-century Irish ecclesiastical politics. The term 'Gallicanism' in particular has been used in reference to very varied phenomena observed in a number of countries and in almost every era from that of Philippe le Bel to the present. If the term is to be applied in speaking of nineteenth-century Ireland, some temporal and local specificity must be introduced into the use of it. The present study attempts to do so with reference to the early decades of the century, when an obviously Gallican issue exercised the public mind and when the designation of an individual or his views as 'Gallican' did not necessarily, even in ecclesiastical circles, signal disapproval.

A further objection to the description of mid-nineteenth century Irish ecclesiastical politics in terms of a Gallican-Ultramontane dichotomy lies in the apparent absence of a strong Gallican tradition in Ireland before that period. The frequent expression of Gallican sentiments among those concerned with advancing the cause of the Catholics in the eighteenth century has indeed been pointed out.[5] However, it is doubtful if this reflects much more than a willingness to utilise opinions not uncommon in the period to present the Catholics' case to Protestants in the most attractive form.[6] It is perhaps notable that the leading Catholic apologist of the eighteenth century, Charles O'Conor of Belanagare, was willing enough to commend a Gallican position in general terms, particularly in speaking of other countries, but was decidedly hesitant about expressing approval of specific proposals intended to diminish the dependence of the Irish church on the Holy See.[7]

In approaching the neglected history of the immediate post-union decades one is frequently thrown back on a substantially unrevised tradition of writing which suggests that Gallican views in that period were less widespread and less influential than in the eighteenth century. For in its explanation of the sustained popular hostility to the veto this tradition spoke not merely of the outrage to national sentiment which the proposal offered but also of the instinctive hostility of the Irish faithful to the heterodox views of the English Cisalpines, which were utilised in defending it. Initially it may be said that this view of the matter appears to confuse cause and effect.

The contemporary historians of the Catholic agitation, Francis Plowden and Thomas Wyse, upon whom many later writers were dependent, perceived the origins of the veto controversy in a spontaneous reaction among Irish Catholics to the 'extraordinary and till then unheard of proposition',[8] advanced by the parliamentary friends of the Catholics during the debates of May 1808 on the Catholic petition of that year, that the government might be granted rights in the appointment of Irish Catholic bishops.[9] In fact the proposition was not extraordinary or unheard of. It had been advanced as early as 1782 in association with the relief measures then before the Irish parliament and discussed, together with more extreme proposals to increase government involvement in Irish ecclesiastical affairs, intermittently throughout the following decades.[10] As recently as 1805, on the occasion of the presentation of the previous Catholic petition, the matter had been spoken of in parliament and about that time had been discussed in pamphlet literature and in the press. None of this provoked any considerable public agitation. Nor indeed did the revelation in February 1808 by the scurrilous and popular Dublin journalist, Watty Cox, that the matter was soon to be raised in parliament again. Not even the incautiously worded statements of the parliamentarians themselves in May did so, though Cox in his own journal, the *Irish Magazine*, and the writers of a number of letters published in the columns of the *Dublin Evening Herald* launched a violent attack on the proposals which had then been advanced. These writers, it is probably fair to say, were less concerned with defending the integrity of the Irish church than with attacking the so-called 'aristocratic party' within the Irish Catholic body, represented chiefly by the earl of Fingall and his friends, who had commended the veto proposal to the parliamentarians. However, it became clear that the weapon they had taken up was a useful one. Many others were hostile to the veto in itself. These included the majority of the episcopal bench who, in September 1808, reversed their nine-year-old decision to accept a veto, a decision taken when it appeared that the new union constitution would inaugurate a brighter era for Irish Catholics. Despite the intentions of some members of the hierarchy, public opinion was quick to interpret this action as a decisive lead and from this point onwards it was to be the constant ally of the anti-vetoists.[11]

It had, however, taken long to reach this point. Moreover even when a clear negative response to the veto proposals did emerge, its motivation was one which had its origins chiefly in convictions about contemporary Irish politics and not in a concern about ecclesiastical polity in itself. These circumstances are indicative of the lack of any extensive thematised reflection in Ireland in the period on the subject of church-state relations. Consequently, the question of how the Irish church was to relate to the British state which no longer persecuted it, or for that matter to the emergent Catholic political nation, had to be answered on an *ad hoc* basis in response to political circumstances, as it was in 1808. However, the question did not go away; for the answer given then was both unacceptable to the parliamentarians on whom the Catholics depended, and controverted by an influential part of the Catholic body itself. Further response was necessary. As this response was elaborated, themes which were characteristic of Catholicism's nineteenth-century assertiveness rather than its eighteenth-century timidity emerged and Gallican views were subject to violent attack from writers such as J. B. Clinch. Anti-Gallican sentiment certainly manifested itself in the course of the veto controversy, but it can hardly be held to have been its cause.

Still, whatever their reasons for doing so, Irish Catholics as a whole did become decidedly hostile to the veto and this, it is still commonly assumed, prohibited any very widespread adherence to Gallican views. However, this assumption is unwarranted and can only be justified by a severe restriction of what might be comprehended under the term 'Gallicanism'. The difficulty is one of definition.

In the matter of definition, as has already been suggested, the prime necessity is for the introduction of temporal and local

specificity. In speaking of the late eighteenth and early nineteenth century, an element of temporal specificity might be
introduced by relating Gallicanism to the decline of papal
authority in the period, which has been quite accurately described as constituting 'the nadir of the Tridentine papacy'.[12]
Gallicanism in this period might accordingly be described as that
response to the decline which welcomed it, or at least accepted it
with equanimity as the basis for reflection on questions pertain-
ing to the relationship between the Catholic church and the state
or the lay community. It is true that this preliminary description
pays little attention to the intellectual, particularly the theological, tradition, of which the articulators of the response made
use, and this may appear unacceptable. However, the description has considerable appeal when one attempts to introduce
local specificity by describing the Irish phenomenon in contrast
to the English one. Anglo-Gallicanism, even if it never attained a
very extensive intellectual development, possessed a coherence
as a body of thought, given to it chiefly by the existence of a
party within the Catholic body which perceived its *raison d'être*
as primarily the defence of certain intellectual, chiefly theological positions.[13] No such Gallican party existed in Ireland, and
Irish Gallicanism consequently lacked the coherence of the
corresponding English phenomenon. Irish Gallicanism existed
as a variable body of beliefs capable of influencing individuals
and groups whose primary concerns were more immediate
political and social issues. Indeed, the major distinctions which
might be drawn between the different strands of Gallican
opinion in Ireland are largely attributable to divergence on these
political and social questions. This generated the argumentation
which exposed Gallican presuppositions and called forth explicit
Gallican views.[14] In brief, the term 'Gallican' when used in
speaking of Ireland in this period refers neither to a party nor to
a fixed body of opinions, but rather to a mutable element in
ideological discourse.

If the descriptions of Irish Gallicanism offered above are
accepted, then Gallicanism is not to be regarded as the doctrine
of the pro-vetoists exclusively. Certainly their cause rested on it
more consistently than that of their opponents did. However, it
must be observed that, on the whole, anti-vetoists were no more

disposed than pro-vetoists to make exalted claims about the rights possessed by the Catholic church or the Holy See. Moreover, when in the course of the veto controversy attempts were made to find a compromise through schemes of domestic nomination, designed to diminish Roman involvement in Irish episcopal appointments without bestowing influence on the British government, such schemes found fervent advocates among the anti-vetoists, who freely cited the precedent for the arrangement they proposed in 'the liberties of the Gallican church'. The Gallican views of the anti-vetoists will be taken up at a later point. Meanwhile, however, to allow further comment on Gallicanism as a whole in the period, some of the characteristics of the Gallicanism espoused by the proponents of the veto must be pointed out.

By stressing the contradistinctive importance of the role of political and social considerations in the development of the various strands of Irish Gallicanism, it is not of course being suggested that the enlightened Catholicism of the English Cisalpines had its origins in exclusively theological considerations. Enlightenment ideas were adopted because they were obviously useful in arguing for greater toleration and because the criticisms of Catholic modes of expressing doctrine and of characteristically Catholic institutions, such as the Latin liturgy, conventual life, or clerical celibacy, which they engendered, tended to promote a rapprochement with liberally minded Protestants. In other words, Cisalpinism had as a fundamental motivation the desire to effect a conciliation between the English Catholic community and the Protestant English nation.[15] However, this should not be allowed to obscure the fact that the perennial theological desire to effect a conciliation between contemporary thought and Catholic practice and doctrine was also of considerable importance in creating the phenomenon of Cisalpinism.

Irish Gallicanism, on the other hand, may be said to have been marked by the almost complete dominance of political motivation. The point may be illustrated by looking briefly at what was probably the most substantial statement of the Gallican sentiments of the pro-vetoists, though, since it was published in 1805, it antedated the public controversy about the veto. Written by the Dublin lawyer, Theobald McKenna, the leading apologist for the views of the aristocratic party in the last years of the eighteenth century and the first decade of the nineteenth, the very title of the work, *Thoughts on the civil condition and relations of the Roman Catholic clergy, religion and people in Ireland*, reveals that ecclesiastical polity in its own right was not the primary concern of the author. Fundamentally, the work constitutes a development of the argumentation of McKenna's earlier writings, all of which were concerned to oppose the use of denominational affiliation as a principle of division in Irish society. By 1805 McKenna's confidence, like that of many Catholics, in the ability of legislation to effect the changes in society he desired had diminished considerably. Neither the substantial repeal of the penal code towards the end of the eighteenth century nor even the abolition of that bulwark of Protestant ascendancy, the Irish parliament, by the new union constitution had had the results desired by the Catholics.[16] Now he projected the integration of the Irish Catholic body into the British state by means of a change, partly in the attitude of the British establishment to Catholicism, but chiefly in the Catholic body itself. The problem to be dealt with, as perceived by McKenna, was the continuing identification of the Catholic body as an alien helot class, which, of course, conformed to the nature of such a class by periodically engaging in insurrection, as it had in 1798. To effect a change more was required than a mere legal declaration that its members were now fully included within the bounds of the constitution. There had to be a sustained effort on the part of the government to effect the moral and thus, indirectly, economic improvement of this section of the population.[17] It could only be effectively reached, however, by the Catholic church and consequently this would have to be refashioned to serve as an instrument of government, chiefly by providing an establishment for its clergy.

The views on properly religious topics which McKenna expresses in the course of the work display his substantial conformity to the mind of the English Gallicans. Central to his purpose was the drawing of a distinction between the religion espoused by enlightened members of his communion, by means of which the Irish church, if properly managed by government, might effect the desired amelioration of the Catholic masses, and the popular Catholicism of his day, so much influenced 'by foolish conceits, by pretended sanctities, by the illusions of superstition and the extravagancies of fanaticism'.[18] However, McKenna did not allow his hostility to that immanentist super-naturalism, which appealed to the Irish *profanum vulgus* but which was quite unintelligible to the enlightened mind with its deist tendencies, to develop into a critique, comparable to that of the English Gallicans, of contemporary Catholicism in general. Nor was he specific when he came to speak of the kind of religion which he wished to replace that which he found objectionable, preferring merely to point to a suitable model, which he found in 'the Gallican church, the most liberal and enlightened, without any question, that ever existed'.[19] These failures are probably attributable, fundamentally, to McKenna's lack of any deep interest in religion, which he repeatedly depicted as little more than a moral preceptor or, it might even be said, an effective instrument of social control.[20]

It is this perception of religion which accounts for McKenna's marked divergence from the mainstream at least, of English Cisalpine thought on the crucial matter of ecclesiastical auth-ority. Cisalpine hostility to Roman authority sprang of course from an anxiety to conciliate English Protestant opinion, influenced as it was by the anti-Catholic tradition which depicted Catholicism as literally Popery, a system of pseudo-religion elaborated for the subjugation of the laity to the clergy, perceived as mute instruments of their Roman master. How-ever, in this as in other matters, more purely theological motives for the Cisalpine stance ought to be noted. There was what might be called a democratic strand to their thought, a certain tendency to see the priest or the bishop as the representative of the faithful of the parish or the diocese, rather than as one who ruled over them in his own right. When this thinking was applied to the universal church, it produced a strong conciliar-ism, an inclination to see the pope almost as a constitutional monarch.[21] This was a motive for hostility to Roman power which McKenna could not possibly share. His advocacy of the creation of an establishment for the Catholic clergy sprang, he made clear, from a wish to render them independent of those over whom they were required to exercise authority,[22] and he was equally concerned to ensure that the clergy in turn were effectively 'under the control and peremptory jurisdiction' of their ordinaries.[23] If the Irish church were thus to be rendered an efficient instrument for the use of the civil power, it would only remain to place that instrument in the hands of the civil power by removing Roman influence.[24]

Of course, despite the existence of the new royal college at Maynooth, there were few grounds for believing that the creation of a subsidiary establishment for Popery could be seriously considered. Nevertheless, McKenna's work remains of interest, in that it reveals with clarity the somewhat Erastian cast of mind of many of the pro-vetoists, which distinguished them from the English Cisalpines, on whom, it has commonly been held, they were dependent for their opinions. An explanation of this can readily be offered. The almost universal eclipse of ecclesiastical power to be observed in continental Europe in the period did nothing to remove the habitual timidity of the Catholic clerical body in the British Isles. The climate of the times was hardly conducive to strident assertion of the rights of the church and its ministers. The inevitable consequence, the assertion of lay influence, was however, in Ireland, an ambiguous phenomenon. What laymen were to exercise the influence which the clerics seemed prepared to surrender? Such lay influence seemed more likely to come to reside with the democracy of the Catholics than with the respectability of their body, to use the contemporary expressions.[25] It is hardly surprising if many Catholics preferred to place the available influence in the hands of the government.

The fact that quite overtly Gallican views existed among anti-vetoists, though it has gone largely unnoticed and the nature of those views has hardly been discussed, need not perhaps occasion surprise. After all, contemporaries insisted that it was on political and not religious grounds that the veto was opposed by Irish Catholics and it is not at least immediately obvious why a divergence of views on political matters should have produced a divergence of views on ecclesiastical ones.

It should be remarked in passing that it would certainly be wrong wholly to disregard religious motivation in attempting to offer explanations for Irish hostility to the veto. For many anti-vetoists undoubtedly believed that this attempt to meddle in their ecclesiastical affairs was a covert assault upon their religion. Such fears had become habitual to Irish Catholics in the course of the campaigns over the previous sixty years and they had not always been without foundation. The Catholic relief measures of the late eighteenth century were to a considerable extent the product of a strain of apologetic for the Catholics' cause, which, like so much of the argumentation against élite privilege in Europe in this period, rested not on the claim of abstract right, but on an appeal to the élite's understanding of what was of general public utility.[26] Perhaps one might more simply say that the relief measures required the widest possible Protestant support. This circumstance rendered some of these measures profoundly ambiguous, particularly at an early period. Lord Limerick's proposals, for example, for a new registry of priests in the 1750s were depicted as 'calculated to do . . . [the Catholics] service, to better their state, to make them first useful and safe, and afterwards easy and happy',[27] and it is true that the proposals did offer the prospect of a legal recognition of their clergy. However, in the view of even the most liberal of Protestants, such as Bishop Clayton of Clogher, the best possible service that could be rendered to the Catholics was the effecting of their liberation from 'the slavery they are reduced to by their priests'.[28] Consequently Lord Limerick proposed not only to register the Catholic clergy but also to reduce their numbers drastically and place those remaining under the control of the government to a considerable extent. Catholics were undoubtedly alarmed. Charles O'Conor held that if the bill embodying Lord Limerick's proposals were to pass into law it would inflict far greater damage on Catholicism in Ireland than had any previous legislation.[29] The bill was in the event lost, but subsequent proposals for legislation shared its ambiguous character. As the years elapsed and the Catholics' cause advanced, the element which the Catholics perceived as threatening, in some relief proposals, became an expression of Protestant anxiety rather than of aggressive anti-Catholicism. By the early nineteenth century, of course, fears that Catholic relief proposals might in reality have been motivated by anti-Catholicism were quite groundless. However, the fears remained; for aggressive anti-Catholics there still were, and Catholics were ever ready to see their hand at work, attempting to subvert their religion.

When this has been said, the assertion that the motivation of Irish Catholics in opposing the veto was political remains essentially true. However, it would be desirable to state the nature of the political considerations involved with some precision. It has frequently been supposed that these amounted to little more than a nationalist hostility to English interference in the affairs of an important national institution, 'the cherished pride of Ireland, and the pledge of her resurrection into the rank of nations',[30] as one anti-vetoist put it. Indeed it can hardly be denied that nationalist sentiment did play a substantial part in provoking and developing the veto controversy. However, it should be noted that when contemporaries asserted that the veto was opposed on political grounds they generally intended to indicate that it was opposed on the grounds of hostility to the augmentation of ministerial power.

It is certainly true that anti-vetoist sentiment found a convenient expression in the radical, and previously country party tradition of complaint against a corrupt and venal ministry.[31] However, it is not easy to believe that a concern for the restoration of Britain's pristine constitution, or even, more credibly, nationalist zeal, was capable of sustaining the tenacious opposition of Irish Catholics to what seemed to others, and indeed to many members of their own body, a most reasonable concession. That opposition to the augmentation of ministerial power was not at the heart of anti-vetoism is revealed with some clarity by the history of the unsuccessful relief bill of 1813. Its proposal that the functions, which previous veto proposals would have assigned to the minister, be exercised by commissions composed predominantly of lay Catholics did nothing whatsoever to diminish anti-vetoist attacks on it.

An understanding of what was contended for by the anti-vetoists cannot be reached without an understanding of what was contended for in the Catholic agitation in general. This was clearly more than the mere passage of legislation. Indeed, it may be said that the demands for the removal of legally imposed disabilities were, for the majority of those making them at any rate, little more than the slogans of the campaigns of the early nineteenth century. Their object was the subversion of the position of Ireland's curiously constituted *ancien régime* élite, the Protestant ascendancy. Attaching as it did extraordinary import-ance to religious affiliation in the regulation of its membership, it was an élite which included a large number of persons whose lack of property rendered their position as members anomalous, rather in the manner of the 'poor nobles' of some eastern European countries.[32] It was the relationship between this privileged community, its members widely if unevenly distri-buted throughout the country, and the surrounding Catholic population, which constantly motivated the agitation for those political and social changes comprehended by the term 'Catholic emancipation'.

Thus for those who agitated it, particularly those whose property and eduaction gave them some claim to membership of a more acceptably constituted élite, the Catholic question could be seen as an immediate and local, even a personal one. McKenna was stating in a sentence the nature of the Catholic question, at least at one important level, when he remarked: 'There is a superiority asserted between men of the same rank— there is a jealousy which occurs in daily practice.' [33] It is to this level of motivation that it is profitable to look when seeking an understanding of Irish Catholic conduct in that part of the Catholic agitation known as the veto controversy. For the veto was feared not so much as a proposed extension of ministerial influence, but rather as a proposed extension, at a local as well as at a national level, into an area of Irish life regarded as free from it, of the power of the members of the Protestant ascend-ancy. That ascendancy, it was firmly believed, would be con-sulted and prove influential when ecclesiastical appointments were being made under any veto arrangement.

It was hardly possible for the anti-vetoists to discuss this perceived threat extensively in their writings without displaying a hostility to Protestants which would have run counter to the tenor of emancipationist literature. Such literature was, ostensi-bly at least, addressed to all Irishmen—for good reason in view of the Catholics' dependence on Protestant support to achieve change—and constantly maintained that the *raison d'être* of the emancipation campaigns was the ending of what was referred to as the conflict of parties in Ireland. Nor was it easy to oppose the veto on religious grounds. The proposals were moderate and neither Catholic principles governing church-state relations nor Catholic practice as it was to be observed in other countries spoke against them.[34] At any rate, there was a general aversion among the Catholics' apologists to religious argumentation, the preserve of their opponents who believed that religious considerations were important in politics, important enough to exclude their fellow countrymen from full participation in the constitution. Thus, alternatives not being readily to hand, much had to be made of the objection to the augmentation of ministerial power.

The theme of anxiety, then, about the extension of the power of Irish Protestants failed, in general, to achieve centrality in anti-vetoist writings. However, an understanding of its importance can be retrieved by reflection on the relationship between Irish Catholics and the members of the Protestant ascendancy and on the relationship of Irish Catholics to their church in the period. At any rate it should be noted that the theme does occur with very great frequency, indeed in almost every specimen of anti-vetoist literature that is taken up. An anonymous pamphleteer is worth quoting for a concise disclosure of the nature of the fear spoken of. He wrote in the wake of the issuing of the celebrated Quarantotti rescript, which gave Roman approval to the terms of the relief bill of 1813. This bill proposed to place the veto in the hands of those Catholics whom the writer considered, on account of their social station, most susceptible to Protestant influence. He maintained that those who accepted the rescript were declaring that they believed that

> It would be more dangerous to the interests of the Irish church, to have the election of bishops left to twelve or twenty conscientious priests, than to Dr. Duigenan [the most fervent and extreme parliamentary spokesman of the anti-Catholics in the period] and such fellows, the road jobbers of counties and the corrupt members of grand juries. For, as by the late bill, the crown would have an effectual and indefinite negative on the successful candidate, and as this negative would not be

exercised except through the medium and from the report of persons locally acquainted with the candidates' district; and as persons so acquainted would, for the most part, come under one or other of the denominations we have just described, it is the clearest inference, that in the event of the bill and the rescript having effect, the true and efficient electors of your future hierarchy would be the Protestant men of influence in the dioceses, communicating directly with government, and communicated with themselves, through all the intermediate and subordinate gradations of rank, and dependency and subserviency, from the dean and deacon— from the foreman of the grand jury to the turnpike man— from the Protestant rector to the clerk of the church.[35]

At this point it should be made clear what the extent of the threat offered by the veto proposals was perceived to be by those who opposed them. In the first place we may note that some proponents of the veto, such as Sir John Cox Hippesley, a member of parliament inclined to depict himself as a natural spokesman of the Catholics by virtue of an acquaintance with Pius VI, commended interference by the civil authorities not only in episcopal appointments, but also in the appointment of the parochial clergy.[36] Moreover, all the veto proposals seemed to threaten not merely periodic interference in Catholic affairs, on the occasions on which appointments were made, but constant interference; for it was not doubted that priests rendered dependent on Protestants for preferment would be inclined to pay constant attention to the sentiments and wishes of Protestants. In short, the veto appeared to threaten a constant interference, at all levels, in virtually all the affairs of the Catholic church, by those whom Catholics believed, frequently with justification, were most hostile to their religion.

In the context of the present discussion what should be noted is that this threatened augmentation of Protestant influence would have been directly at the expense of existing Catholic influence, the influence not only of the bishops,[37] but also of the lower clergy and of the laity. For if attention is directed away from formal ecclesiastical structures, as recognised by canon law, and towards the conduct of ecclesiastical affairs in early nineteenth-century Ireland, at both a national and a local level, it becomes clear that these latter groups possessed considerable power. With regard to the lower clergy, it may be said that the most obvious evidence, albeit circumstantial, for the existence of such power lies in the Richerism which was manifested in the campaign for domestic nomination, discussed at a later point in this essay. Their confident self-assertion and the willingness of their bishops to accommodate their views on the occasion of that campaign certainly suggest that the priests of Ireland regarded themselves as a body of men who had to be heeded and that they had justification for such an opinion.

However, it is local studies of early nineteenth-century church life which reveal most clearly the existence and the nature of the influence exercised by both the lower clergy and the laity in ecclesiastical affairs. These draw attention to the extremely widespread phenomenon of clerical and lay factionalism in the period. Minimally it may be claimed that such factionalism indicates that both the lower clergy and the laity believed themselves to be entitled to exercise and capable of exercising substantial influence in their local churches. In fact that belief was frequently justified. Clerical factions could and did influence the choice of bishops and were even capable, as the celebrated case of Bishop O'Finan of Killala demonstrated a little later in the century, of removing a bishop who had already entered into possession of his see.[38] Lay factions also were from time to time involved in disputes about episcopal appointments.[39] Generally, however, their concerns were more parochial. The appointment of a parish priest, of course, was a matter particularly liable to generate conflict, although almost any circumstance of parochial life was capable of calling a faction into existence.[40] These petty disputes serve to make clear that the conviction of Irish Catholics that they had a legitimate role in the affairs of their church existed down to almost the lowest levels of society, a fact which assists considerably in accounting for the genuinely popular nature of the reaction to proposals which were depicted as threatening to diminish that role.

Of course, we should not suppose that it was necessary for either the clergy or the laity to band together in order to influence the course of events in general or the actions of their bishops in particular. There were undoubtedly even less formal ways in which much could be effected. It is difficult, of course, to make general statements about the extent of the influence exercised in such ways. It obviously varied considerably from diocese to diocese and from time to time, depending, for the most part, on the character of the ordinary, the capabilities of his more influential subjects and, to speak in particular of lay influence, the degree to which Catholics were possessed of wealth and respectability. In some areas this lay influence was undoubtedly considerable, as in some districts in Connaught with a surviving Catholic gentry or in towns with a Catholic merchant élite, such as some of the more important seaports. Galway, where lay power in ecclesiastical affairs was uniquely institutionalised in the Wardenship,[41] can hardly be regarded as typical. Nevertheless, the social conditions which, together with historical accident, had ensured the survival of this medieval institution in Galway, existed in other towns, and we need not doubt that a degree of lay influence not much less than that exercised by the Galway Tribes, and indeed by other inhabitants of Galway, was exercised, in rather less conspicuous ways, in those other places.[42]

To summarise the discussion above, it may be said that in attempting to explicate the causes of the veto controversy, it is crucial to understand the perception among Irish Catholics of the veto as threatening to introduce another power, one viewed as generally hostile to Catholics and Catholicism, into the area of Catholic ecclesiastical affairs, certainly at a national level, but more importantly at a local level, where the interests of the laity, the lower clergy and the episcopate were often fairly delicately balanced. This observation relates directly to the central concern of this article, the definition of early nineteenth-century Irish Gallicanism.

In speaking of the phenomenon of Gallicanism in France itself, it is customary to distinguish, for example, royal, episco-pal and parlementary Gallicanism. By these distinctions it is intimated that Gallicanism *tout court*, at least as a phenomenon which is of interest to the historian rather than to the expounder of the *De ecclesia* tract, is best regarded as an abstraction from the actual positions constructed for the defence of interests within the French church or as a common ideological store from which argumentation might be drawn by the promoters of those interests as need arose. Indeed, the positions thus constructed clearly served, in some cases at least, not primarily for defence against the encroachments of the Roman See, but for defence against the encroachments of other French interests. It is suggested that this perception of Gallicanism as essentially fragmented, not as a single ideological position, but as a series of such positions in the service of often conflicting interest groups, is the most useful one in attempting to gain an understanding of the Irish Gallicanism of the period under discussion here. An examination of McKenna's Gallicanism, discussed earlier, a position wholly constructed as supportive of one Irish interest, the state, certainly gives some grounds for perceiving Irish Gallicanism in this way. However, so also does the understanding, offered above, of the motivation behind the anti-veto campaign.

Bearing in mind this understanding of Gallicanism as fragmented, when in the course of the anti-veto campaign we perceive a defence of their existing influence over ecclesiastical affairs by groups of Irishmen, clergy and laity, and that defence framed in terms of national rights, it seems that we have at least some grounds for a description of the campaign as Gallican. Still lacking, of course, are expressions of disregard, at least, for the rights claimed by the Roman See. These, however, did emerge in the course of the attacks on the veto, in the debate over domestic nomination. This debate is deserving of treatment in its own right. For, though hardly adverted to in studies of the period,[43] it in fact constituted a most important part of the veto controversy and reveals much about its nature. It may be added that an examination of the debate will justify further the perception of Irish Gallicanism as characterised by its dependence on the advancing of interests within the Irish church.

The idea of domestic nomination was brought forward very shortly after the emergence of the veto as a subject of public discussion. If indeed, it was argued, the reason for the demand for a government veto was the anxiety of Protestants about the exercise of foreign ecclesiastical power in the matter of the appointment of Irish bishops—and this the pro-vetoists generally maintained was the case—the veto would become unnecessary if these appointments became, to a much greater extent, a domestic Irish matter. The point was a good one, for, since the cessation of the Stuart nominations to Irish sees more than forty years previously,[44] the Holy See had exercised in Ireland a degree of influence over episcopal appointments which would have been regarded as totally unacceptable in most of Catholic Europe. The Holy See possessed everywhere the right of conferring the legal title by which episcopal power was held, i.e. the right of canonical institution. However, it did not by any means universally possess the right to nominate candidates for the episcopal office, this right most frequently being in the hands of the secular ruler, at least in Catholic countries.[45] In Ireland, since 1766, the entire process by which appointments were made, both nomination and canonical institution, had been in the hands of the Holy See.[46] However, the major beneficiaries of this situation were the Irish bishops. Propaganda (the Roman congregation in charge of Irish affairs) was prepared to consider almost any representations with regard to Irish episcopal appointments. However, the informality of the system tended to allow more weight to the opinions of the bishops than could have been the case otherwise. The bishops were, of course, particularly influential when coadjutors were being appointed in their own dioceses. Indeed, the supporters of domestic nomination complained that the practice of appointing coadjutors with the right of succession, under the existing arrangements for making appointments, virtually allowed the bishops to appoint their own successors.[47] Thus, while they were no doubt sincere in protesting their desire to defend the rights of the Holy See, the bishops had other reasons for the hostility they showed to proposals to change the existing methods of appointment.

However, it should be pointed out that the term 'domestic nomination' was used to describe a considerable number of different arrangements by which bishops might be appointed and not all were grossly offensive to the members of the episcopal bench. The matter may be stated in the following way. The various schemes, taken together, referred to the claims of three juridical persons to participate in, or even, in speaking of two of them, assume complete control over, the process of making appointments. The three juridical persons mentioned were the Roman pontiff, the Irish hierarchy and the clergy (though frequently only the dean and chapter) of the vacant see. Some schemes, it may be added, referred to the rights of the king, since some domestic nomination proposals included a veto proposal.[48] All the schemes were, of course, advanced with the intention of reducing the role of the Holy See in the process of appointment. The variation between the schemes arose essentially from the varying weight of influence which those who brought them forward wished to be accorded to each of the three juridicial persons. In some schemes reference to one or even two of them was omitted altogether. However, for the most part it was assumed that any scheme of domestic nomination adopted would give a considerable degree of influence to the diocesan clergy. It was precisely this that disturbed a number at least of the bishops. However, since it was possible to conceive of schemes of domestic nomination which minimised the involvement of the lower clergy or, indeed, institutionalised the existing power of the bishops, there was no need for total intransigence on the part of the hierarchy.

The matter came formally before the prelates at their meeting of February 1810. Consideration of it was necessitated by the enthusiasm which had been shown for the idea in the General Committee of the Catholics. Here a sub-committee had drawn up concrete proposals and hopes were high that these would be accepted by the bishops or, at least, that the bishops would commend the idea in principle. After all, they seemed to offer a solution to the veto dispute acceptable to vetoists and anti-vetoists, to Irish Catholics and their Protestant allies. Moreover, Pius VII was a prisoner at Savona and this circumstance appeared to make it necessary for the bishops to make some change in the arrangements for making episcopal appointments, in order to ensure that Irish sees which became vacant were filled. In fact, there was no real possibility that the bishops would approve the sub-committee's scheme for 'a mode of election [which] would not be English or Roman, but . . . Irish and national'. In the first place it proposed that a considerable degree of power be given to parish priests and the superiors of religious houses. More startlingly, it challenged the papal right of canonical institution when it was suggested that it would be sufficient to preserve ecclesial unity to require of 'the prelate elected, the transmission of letters of communion and canonical obedience to the Holy See'.[49] The scheme laid before them could thus be seen as verging on the schismatic and the bishops had excellent grounds for rejecting it. The resolutions which issued from their meeting expressed that rejection forcefully. However, they went further and declared their opposition to any change in the existing arrangements for making episcopal appointments. They also issued to the laity a dissuasive against any further agitation of the matter, by reminding them that the bishops and the Holy See were the sole competent authorities in such matters.[50]

The laymen of the Catholic Committee were not, however, cowed by this. For a few months later, in May 1810, the Committee met and passed a series of resolutions of its own, which declared 'that the privilege of exclusively and immediately appointing Catholic bishops forms no part of the primitive and essential rights inherent in the said [Roman] see'. Becoming more specific, they expressed opposition to the Holy See's nomination of Irish bishops, but made no proposal that could have been construed as threatening Rome's right of canonical institution.[51] After this declaration had been made, however, there was, it seems, little inclination to press the matter.[52] That the dispute did not become a serious one until considerably later is probably mostly attributable to the attitude of the parliamentary friends of the Catholic cause, who continued to be informed and continued to believe 'that it would be easy enough to gain them [the bishops] over to the wishes of the English government [in the matter of the veto] if the influence and means of government were properly and liberally applied for that purpose',[53] and consequently could see little point in investigating the compromise of domestic nomination, though it was mentioned occasionally.[54] Since the idea of domestic nomination was not influencing consideration of the Catholic question in parliament, it was hardly a matter of urgency for the Irish Catholic body to decide whether it supported it or not.

Nevertheless, domestic nomination was far from being simply forgotten in the years between 1810 and 1814. These years saw the publication of Charles O'Conor's *Columbanus letters*.[55]

O'Conor was a vetoist and his hostility to those whom he regarded as the major enemies of the veto, the Irish bishops, was frequently expressed in terms that can only be described as excessively violent. Consequently his views were considerably less influential in Ireland than they might have been. Nevertheless, there were many in Ireland who were prepared to give their erudite, expatriate countryman at least a selective hearing. Certainly the leading lay opponent of domestic nomination, James Clinch, regarded O'Conor's defence of the rights of the 'second order of priests', i.e. priests as opposed to bishops, as influential enough to warrant his writing a substantial refutation,[56] a project which was reputed to have been undertaken at the request of the bishops.[57]

The aspects of O'Conor's position which proved attractive to Irish Catholics and those which did not can be quickly distinguished by referring to the pages of the *Dublin Political Review*. Founded by the editor of the *Dublin Evening Post*, John Magee, in 1813, when the relief bill of that year was renewing the threat of the veto, the *Review* undertook the advocacy of the alternative of domestic nomination and discussed the matter at some length, in almost every issue for the duration of its short life. Of course O'Conor's vetoism had to be excised, but when this was done, the Gallican position he espoused was substantially acceptable to the *Review*, which insisted on the right of the Irish church to determine its own discipline, specifying what might be encompassed by the term 'discipline' by advocating the adoption in Ireland 'of that discipline which prevails in the church of France—'.[58] Despite this statement there was no intention of commending the imposition on Ireland of an ecclesiastical polity constructed on the lines indicated in the concordat of 1801. O'Conor's Richerist variety of Gallicanism was obviously preferred. It was insisted 'that the inferior clergy should be restored to their rank in Christian society', something that was to be brought about chiefly by restoring to deans and chapters the exclusive right of nominating candidates for bishoprics.[59] This view produced, of course, a degree of hostility to those who were usurping that right, the Irish bishops, although this hostility was expressed in more moderate terms than O'Conor's, and his quite accurate view of the matter was reversed when the *Review* rather absurdly attacked the bishops for conspiring to promote the acceptance of the veto in an effort to avoid domestic nomination.[60] In point of fact the bishops were not nearly so hostile to domestic nomination as Magee believed, a fact which became obvious when public dispute over the matter reached a climax in 1814.

In early May of that year news reached Ireland that a certain Monsignor Quarantotti, the vice-prefect of Propaganda, acting in the absence of the prefect, Cardinal di Pietro, who was still at Fontainebleau with the pope, issued a rescript commending acceptance of the terms of the bill of 1813.[61] The surge of popular hostility to the veto which Quarantotti's action produced has been frequently remarked upon. However, it should be added that this agitation largely took the form of support for the policy of domestic nomination and that the major effect of the rescript was to commit the Irish Catholic body as a whole to support of that policy. That a threat originating in Rome was capable of bringing about a resolution of the long debate over domestic nomination, while the threat which originated among British parliamentarians in the previous year was not, is to be explained in part, of course, by the former's removal of many inhibitions among Irish Catholics about adopting an anti-Roman stance. It was indeed the rescript affair which produced the most extreme and most widespread expressions to be observed in the period of the Richerist variety of Gallicanism we have been discussing.

However, it should also be noted that the Roman origin of this new threat appeared to render it a more serious one than had hitherto appeared. Not only would demands for a veto now be increased and resistance to those demands among Irish Catholics as a whole be reduced, but, more importantly, episcopal resistance, consistently the crucial factor since the bishops took the initiative in 1808, would, it was feared, be removed. This fear was, in fact, almost wholly without foundation. Troy's initial inclination to accept the rescript was not shared by his colleagues and the hierarchy had little hesitation in resolving to oppose it.[62] Before this, however, anxiety was considerable. Thus it seemed quite imperative that the alternative to the veto be offered.

Thus too the clergy were, for the first time in the history of the veto conflict, willing to take a decisive stand without waiting for the decision of their ordinaries. The Dublin clergy were the first to do so,[63] and the *Evening Post*, which was enthusiastically publishing the letters of numerous clerical correspondents pointing out the limits of Roman authority and commending domestic nomination, exclaimed delightedly:

> At length, thank God, it has come to this—the Catholic priests have joined the popular voice—the secretary of the Propaganda has brought the question to issue. Things cannot remain as they are; it has come to the veto or domestic nomination.[64]

The resolutions of the clerical meetings convened in dioceses throughout the country to oppose the rescript generally confirmed the *Post's* contention that the priests of Ireland were willing to come forward in support of 'domestic nomination in the good old way of deans and chapters', as the Ossory clergy, for example, put it.[65] The laity followed the clerical lead. In 1810 the Catholic Committee had hesitated to take a decisive stand by passing resolutions in favour of domestic nomination in advance of the episcopal conference. Now its successor, the Catholic Board, showed no such hesitation in calling on the bishops to consider 'the propriety of forever precluding any public danger of either *ministerial* or *foreign* influence in the appointment of our prelates'.[66]

The bishops yielded easily in the face of this renewed campaign. They did, after all, sympathise with its anti-vetoist motivation and, in view of the variety of meanings given to the term 'domestic nomination', a general declaration in favour of the idea was likely to cost little. Thus when Daniel Murray, the Dublin coadjutor, was dispatched to Rome to present the objections of the Irish bishops to the rescript, he was instructed to present also proposals for domestic nomination, though not 'in the good old way of deans and chapters'.[67]

Of course, the proponents of domestic nomination in forms unacceptable to the hierarchy were not unaware of the ambiguities of the term and the dispute was continued. However, its later history need not be commented on here,[68] enough having been said to establish its importance in attempting both to elucidate the history and nature of the veto controversy and to speak of the phenomenon of Gallicanism in the period. With regard to the latter, it can be said, certainly, that the domestic nomination dispute points to the importance of the phenomenon, to the widespread acceptability of Gallican views. However, it also points to its lack of importance. For the advancement of Gallican views was never the primary concern of those involved in the dispute. The protagonists of domestic nomination were preoccupied throughout with advancing a credible alternative to the veto proposals and, to a considerably lesser degree, with the extent of episcopal power. These were matters of real concern to the Irish Catholic laity and clergy. In the course of pursuing their objectives, many members of both these groups were willing to put forward Gallican opinions. Such opinions were no doubt sincerely held, but by themselves would hardly have induced those who held them to engage in public controversy. In other words, the domestic nomination dispute provides the most lucid illustration of the dependence of Irish Gallicanism in this period on political motivation for the formulation and advancement of its tenets, a circumstance which ensured that this Gallicanism would be a complex phenomenon, reflecting the presence of divergent interests.

8. The popular Reformation comes to Ireland: the case of John Walker and the foundation of the Church of God, 1804

THE turbulent Irish Protestant religious revival of the early nineteenth century, often remembered as a 'Protestant crusade' to convert Catholics, is commonly called the Second Reformation. The name is quite appropriate, for it had a wide currency at the time, and revival leaders frequently harkened back to Reformation doctrines and precedents. The term seems to have its origin in testimony given by William Magee, Church of Ireland archbishop of Dublin, before a select committee of the house of lords investigating the state of Ireland in 1825. Through the course of his interview Magee spoke with quiet optimism about the apparent increase in religious interest and seriousness among many Irish people, clergy and laity, upper classes and lower, Protestant and Catholic. At one point he asserted,

> there has been lately an excitement of attention to the subject of religion throughout the people, such as perhaps there has not been before at any period since the Reformation. In truth, with respect to Ireland, the Reformation may, strictly speaking, be truly said only now to have begun.[1]

Magee's testimony circulated widely in newspapers and in pamphlet form, the Reformation imagery apparently caught the public fancy, and the term Second Reformation was born. However, there is a case to be made for taking Magee quite literally and arguing that the events and currents he described were not a Second Reformation, they were for Ireland a first experience of Reformation. To be more precise, the evangelical revival in Ireland doubled as a long-delayed popular Reformation.

Of course Ireland participated in the sixteenth-century

Reformation along with the rest of Europe. But anyone coming to the study of the Irish Reformation with even a casual knowledge of the English or continental Reformations must be struck by the extent to which it simply did not happen in Ireland. It was embraced by only a small minority of the population, and many Irish people were for a long time entirely unaffected by it. It was for the most part a state-sponsored, top-down Reformation, strongly influenced by imperial considerations. Brendan Bradshaw, in his seminal article on 'Sword, word and strategy in the Reformation in Ireland', argued that the dominant question of the Irish Reformation was strategy, and the debate was conducted at the level of official and semi-official correspondence, as befits an issue of state policy. Pulpit controversy was rare, the pamphlet literature was insignificant, and the hot theological debates of the Reformation in England and on the continent had no apparent Irish parallel.[2] As for some equivalent to the continental Anabaptist groups, Ireland seems to have had none. The closest link to Anabaptism is obscure indeed, and it came through the person of John Bale, bishop of Ossory for a short spell in 1553. Bale was no Anabaptist, but he was sufficiently sympathetic to comment positively on the courage and faith of an Anabaptist executed in England, and he acknowledged the influence of Anabaptist leader Melchior Hofmann's eschatology on his own, although the two were not identical.[3] Ireland had no closer encounter with Anabaptist ideas, and presumably they would have met no more favourable a reception than did Bale, who fled Ireland after his aggressive and uncompromising Protestant preaching inspired altogether plausible death threats.

Nicholas Canny and Stephen Ellis are the historians who have made the boldest claims about the extent of a Reformation milieu and mentality in Ireland. In a summary of Bradshaw's work on the Irish Reformation, Canny says Bradshaw has uncovered 'evidence of an indigenous reform movement in Ireland clearly recognisable in European terms, concerned principally with political reform but also acknowledging the need to reform abuses in ecclesiastical matters', and he adds that the participants in this lay movement 'were intensely preoccupied with salvation'.[4] Certainly the indigenous reform movement is there in Bradshaw. But he emphasises the 'smallness of the reform *milieu*',[5] and it seems to have been overwhelmingly politically orientated, touching on ecclesiastical matters only when they were rather obviously politically or economically relevant. As for the intense preoccupation with salvation, it is simply not there in the sources to which Canny's notes direct us. Ellis takes John Bale's account of his brief episcopal career in Ireland, conventionally used to demonstrate the catastrophic failure of the Irish Reformation, and shows that in fact Bale did achieve some significant successes in a difficult situation. Ellis concludes that 'properly evaluated, Bale's *Vocacyon* suggests the government's need for many more preachers of Bale's calibre and convictions in order to capitalise on the innate loyalty of the Old English community and to provide, during a crucial transitional period, the intellectual underpinning for its reform movement'.[6] Canny and Ellis provide a helpful corrective to traditional assumptions that the failure of the Reformation in Ireland was necessary, complete, and immediate. But in the end they are still describing a meagre phenomenon. Ireland did have a sixteenth-century Reformation, but a severely truncated one.

The Reformation process can be usefully, if rather crudely, divided into three phases, or levels: state, church, and popular. In those places where the sixteenth-century Reformation was experienced most intensely, all three occurred simultaneously and influenced one another, which is neatly illustrated by the career of a man like the aforementioned Melchior Hofmann. Between 1527 and 1532 his spiritual journey included a position as a favourite court preacher in the employ of the Danish king Frederick X; a running dialogue (usually a dispute) with Martin Luther; baptism by an Anabaptist brotherhood in Strasbourg; and leadership of an Anabaptist congregation in Emden.[7] Hofmann's career embraced all the types of Reformation — state, church, and popular — and indeed they were entwined to such an extent that a sharp distinction is not necessary and might even distort our understanding of him.

However, what appear as levels of Reformation in parts of continental Europe and southeast England were experienced elsewhere as phases of Reformation. In these places the distinction between different types of Reformation is more useful. Nowhere were the phases more long drawn out than in Ireland, and here distinguishing between state, church, and popular Reformations is essential to understanding the emergence of Irish Protestantism.

State Reformations were state sponsored, of course; many initiatives were taken by the state; and it is little more than a tautology to say that state Reformations were undertaken insofar as they furthered or at least meshed with other state ambitions. The changes they sought concentrated on the point where ecclesiastical policy intersected with politics and economics. The primary method of implementation was coercion, by changing laws and by more draconian measures if necessary. If the state wanted to use other methods it had to do so indirectly, through the church.

Distinguishing between state and church Reformations is not a clean and simple matter, especially where the church was established by the state, but it can and should be done. In a church Reformation initiatives came from within the church, especially the hierarchy, and were implemented by the lower clergy and sometimes the laity. Characteristic concerns were ecclesiastical organisation, theology, lay religious practice, and clerical standards. Many of its programmes could be enacted simply on the authority of the church hierarchy. When hierarchical authority was insufficient or inappropriate as a method of implementation, all churches could call upon the various techniques of persuasion, mostly variations on teaching and preaching. An established church had the advantage of being able to call on the state for coercion in some cases instead of relying solely on persuasion, but it also bore the corresponding burden, which could be very heavy indeed, of needing to convince the state at every step of the way that reforms good for the church were also good for the state.

Popular Reformations tended to emerge from below rather than be imposed from above, and even when the seeds had been planted by a church Reformation, some wayward off-shoots were sure to go in directions the church had never intended. These Reformations, far from being encouraged, were often vehemently denounced by churches and vigorously suppressed by governments. They commonly allowed a greater role for the laity, including women, the poor, and the unlearned, than did other types of Reformation; they were vulnerable to excess and often suffered from schismatic tendencies. All popular Reformation groups demanded the whole-hearted commitment of adherents, some kind of involvement in an intense cell group or conventicle was common, and behavioural standards were often quite rigorous. Some of the classic manifestations of popular Reformation sprang up on the continent during the early 1500s and in England during the mid 1600s; in these epochs of general social upheaval, radical solutions to all sorts of problems were rife, and a few radical religious groups had correspondingly radical political ambitions or visions. Although a small number of groups resorted to violence, most had no recourse but to persuasion, which made the popular Reformation more missionary than its state and church counterparts. States feared some manifestations of popular Reformation as politically dangerous, and established churches seem to have regarded most, even the apparently benign, as a religious threat.

Applying this scheme of state, church, and popular Reformations to Ireland, it is obvious that Ireland's state Reformation took place in the sixteenth century. The state continued to support an established church after that, but from the point of view of the Church of Ireland the support was sporadic and limited, and never again did the state actively promote Reformation. Even for the sixteenth century, Bradshaw concludes that the ultimate blame for the failure of the Reformation must lie with 'the central administration in England', which was unwilling to devote the resources necessary to pursue a strategy of either coercion or persuasion.[8]

The church Reformation in Ireland is the one described by Alan Ford in his recent book *The Protestant Reformation in Ireland, 1590-1641*. Here the distinction between church and state Reformations really comes into its own, for how else can we account for a book that skips lightly over the events of the sixteenth century and yet is clearly describing a process that can only be called a Reformation? Ford is analysing a church Reformation, which he shows was not seriously attempted until the 1590s. The great burden of this Reformation was creating a clearly Protestant theology and clergy as a prerequisite for converting the Irish masses. Debates about the relative merits of coercion and persuasion remained central, but the locus of discussion and initiative had shifted from the state to the church. Church and state worked together, of course, but the state was frequently reluctant to enact what the church wanted, and laws once established were inconsistently enforced and occasionally repealed. This infuriated church leaders, as did the failure of the laity to give adequate help in enforcing the Reformation process. A rift began to open between the church, for which Reformation was the chief concern, and the state and the laity, which both wanted Reformation, but balanced that consideration with many others.[9]

Our knowledge of the Church of Ireland after the rebellion of 1641 and through the eighteenth century remains scanty, so definitive statements about this period are impossible. Events of the 1640s and 1680s made glaringly obvious Irish Protestants' absolute reliance on English support, which left the Church of Ireland virtually no bargaining power with the state. It lost the right of convocation early in the eighteenth century (as did the Church of England), and appointments to Irish bishoprics were made to service English political debts, not the needs of the Irish church. The available evidence might reasonably be interpreted as suggesting that efforts at a church Reformation continued, but less through a coordinated church strategy than by the heroic but doomed efforts of isolated bishops and parish priests. No one tried harder than William King, first as bishop of Derry and later as archbishop of Dublin, but by 1724, after more than three decades as a bishop, he was a deeply discouraged man. He believed that 'the methods which have been taken since the Reformation, and which are yet pursued by both the civil and ecclesiastical powers' could only be interpreted as meaning that 'there never was or is any design that all should be Protestants.'[10] Right through the eighteenth century the church continued to be plagued by the tension between church ideals and state and lay pragmatism which Ford observed in the period before 1641. Clergy and laity finally came together, at least in part through the influence of evangelicalism, but church frustration with state pragmatism did not end until 1871, when disestablishment severed the relationship altogether.

The final phase of the Irish Reformation was the one to which Archbishop Magee referred in his testimony before the house of lords. It was a popular Reformation, but something more as well. It was a revival of the church Reformation, as Magee's participation suggests, and perhaps a more vigorous effort at church Reformation than ever before. A quantitative study would probably find that it was more successful than the seventeenth-century Reformation in the percentage of clergy it influenced, and it was certainly a far more Irish phenomenon. Ford clearly demonstrates how much the development of a Protestant church in the seventeenth century depended on importing a Protestant clergy, but the church Reformation of the late 1700s and early 1800s was built on Irish-born and -educated clergy. For instance, of the eighty-three men who held clerical office in Ossory in 1800, only two were foreign-born, only six had not graduated from Trinity, and all of the seventeen men who in that year founded the evangelically inclined Ossory Clerical Association were Irish and Trinity graduates.[11] The simple fact that this was both a church and a popular Reformtion was noteworthy in itself, because previous Irish Reformation efforts had been quite distinct: state first, then church. But the practical effect of these simultaneous Reformations was still more important, because without the resources, the energy, and the co-operation of both church reformers and popular reformers, efforts to revitalise the church would have been hindered, and a serious attempt to convert Irish Catholics would probably not have been possible.

Evangelicals figured prominently in both church and popular Reformations. In fact a church Reformation would have been impossible had evangelicals not provided many of the dedicated ministers necessary for the work and helped to instil a new sense of religious seriousness and attention to church duty within the laity. But the evangelicals were by no means alone, and the leadership of it was not in their hands. The Dublin-based Association for Discountenancing Vice, founded in 1792, quickly became the key institution for the church Reformation. Its members included most of the bishops and hundreds of the clergy of the Church of Ireland, along with many prominent laymen, but few of the members and none of the leaders were evangelicals.[12]

But the Second Reformation was not only a church Reformation, it was Ireland's first popular Reformation, and this was an almost exclusively evangelical phenomenon. Of course, it could not be a popular Reformation in the same sense that it would have been if a similar movement had sprung up in sixteenth-century Ireland. By the eighteenth century Ireland had long been divided along religious lines, which made it most unlikely that any new religious movement could appeal equally to Catholic, Protestant, and Dissenter alike. Any popular Reformation movement was likely to have either Protestant or Catholic roots and appeal, and evangelicalism was decidedly Protestant. Even within Protestantism, until well into the nineteenth century evangelicalism had little impact on the Presbyterian church, which was a product of the Scottish Reformation, not the Irish. Evangelicalism appealed to few Catholics, and if it did they became Protestants. Ironically then, developments within the Catholic church during this same time period might fruitfully be regarded as a Catholic Reformation. The relative strength of Tridentine Catholicism as against traditional popular religiosity in eighteenth- and nineteenth-century Ireland remains a hotly debated topic among scholars. But they do seem to agree that Counter-Reformation success varied widely from one region to another, and that in any case the character of Irish Catholicism underwent some rapid and decisive changes during the first half of the nineteenth century. This suggests that perhaps the Catholic church was undergoing a Reformation experience parallel to the significance of the evangelical movement for Protestantism. If so, there are at least two reasons why these impulses would have been channelled entirely into internal reform rather than schism. First, Irish Catholics and Protestants had been shaped by a mutual antipathy at least partially defined in religious terms for so long that even radically discontented Catholics would have shared a kind of cultural immunisation against either joining a Protestant group or doing what Protestants do—that is, starting a schismatic group. Second, for those who did leave the Catholic church, they had a broad array of existing Protestant groups to choose from, including the Church of Ireland, which claimed to be the true heir of St Patrick and early Irish Christianity. These considerations made it unlikely that even in a religiously charged atmosphere, any indigenous dissenting group would emerge directly from the Catholic church.

Even within the Church of Ireland, evangelical consciousness of inheriting Reformation doctrines and of participating in an international evangelical revival meant that evangelicals could hardly have had the same sense of breaking new ground that sixteenth-century reformers must have had. Evangelicalism in

Ireland could only be simultaneously a Reformation revival, an international religious movement, *and* a first popular Reformation. But evangelicalism brought into Irish Protestantism, especially the established church, a spirit hitherto little known and bearing a marked resemblance to popular Reformations of other times and places. The cumulative evidence constitutes a strong prima facie case for describing the evangelical experience as a first popular Reformation in Ireland.

The first point must be to note the apparent lack of any strong tradition of popular piety in the Church of Ireland. In November 1742, several hundred people gathered in Spa Fields Tabernacle in London 'to celebrate the latest news of religious revival'. They sang a hymn written specially for the occasion, which went in part:

> Great things in England, Wales and Scotland wrought,
> and in America to pass are brought,
> Awaken'd souls, warn'd of the wrath to come
> In Numbers flee to Jesus as their Home.[13]

Ireland is conspicuous by its absence from this hymn and from the recent *American Historical Review* article which quoted it. 'A transatlantic community of saints: the great awakening and the first evangelical network, 1735–1755' exhaustively demonstrates a vast international correspondence and information network covering England, Scotland, Wales, and North America, but without a single Irish participant. In an essay on the origins of English evangelicalism, John Walsh has demonstrated how essential for evangelical success were the efforts and institutions of immediately previous church reform movements. These in turn can be traced back to Puritanism and even, perhaps, to the Lollards, the point being that evangelicalism in England was only a modern manifestation of a centuries-old, continuous movement.[14] In Ireland, any similar search for evangelical foundations discovers mists and vapours, but few solid objects. One writer mentions 'religious societies' of 'serious seekers' in the early eighteenth century, but gives no numbers or sources.[15] Another book cites what must be the same societies, but links them specifically to English-based movements, the Societies for Reformation and Propagation of Christian Knowledge, and their successor, the Society for the Promotion of Christian Knowledge. These involved members in meetings for worship and mutual edification, and as many as ten groups were established in Dublin and some elsewhere in Ireland, all supported by bishops or other clergy.[16] The world of Irish Protestant popular piety was not a complete void, and given the abysmal state of our knowledge about early eighteenth-century Irish Protestantism perhaps much more remains to be discovered. But the evidence available now would not justify describing popular piety in this period as anything more than a pale reflection of an essentially English phenomenon.

A second observation must be the derivative character of Irish Protestantism. The sixteenth-century Reformation, whatever about the extent of its appeal in Ireland, was an English initiative. Alan Ford has demonstrated how in the seventeenth century the development of a strongly Protestant Church of Ireland depended upon importing English and Scottish clergy. Not until well into the nineteenth century did Presbyterians cease to rely almost exclusively on Scotland for training their clergy — in fact Irish Presbyterianism frequently functioned as a kind of ecclesiastical province of Scotland. Some strands of Protestantism were introduced to Ireland through plantation. By the end of the eighteenth century Protestant groups in Ireland included Quakers, Huguenots, Baptists, Independents, Methodists, Lady Huntingdon's Connexion, Kilhamites, Moravians, Lutherans, several varieties of Presbyterians, and — insofar as it was Protestant and reformed — the Church of Ireland. Every one of them had originated outside Ireland, even the small splinter groups. The Kilhamites broke away from the Methodists in the 1790s, and soon Kilhamite groups appeared in Ireland. But the most striking example was the split between the Burgher and Anti-Burgher Secession synods, which was faithfully carried over into Ireland even though it had resulted from exclusively and peculiarly Scottish disagreements.

Although evangelicalism in all its varieties was originally no less derivative than other Protestantism, the extent to which it became indigenous is striking and noteworthy. One of the several achievements of Irene Whelan's fine M.A. thesis on Irish evangelicalism from 1800 to 1835 is to demonstrate how thoroughly *Irish* evangelicalism became, in personnel, purposes, and programmes.[17] Her primary focus was on Church of Ireland evangelicalism, but the same point could be made no less emphatically for Methodism. When the Irish Methodist Conference first met in 1752, it was dominated by English preachers. Twenty conferences later, in 1789, nearly all of the fifty preachers were Irish,[18] and from the early nineteenth century onward, Irish Methodism became a net exporter of preachers on a massive scale, influencing the growth of Methodism around the world.[19] The extent of Church of Ireland exports is less certain, but W. R. Ward has highlighted the importance of Irish preachers in nineteenth-century Britain.[20] Evangelicalism may have been transplanted from abroad, but it sank deep Irish roots that nourished a vigorous local growth.

Popular Reformations were generally marked by a relatively greater role for the laity, including women. Certainly Irish evangelicalism, especially in its early stages, included a prominent role for laypeople. A. C. H. Seymour's richly detailed account of early Irish evangelicalism is littered with references to women, mostly wealthy women, who were among the prime movers in the world of Irish evangelicalism.[21] This was especially true of Methodism. C. H. Crookshank selected eighteen eighteenth-century *Memorable women of Irish Methodism* primarily on the basis of their piety and courageous commitment, and some of them never had any formal responsibility: but their number also included class leaders, missionaries, evangelists, organisers, preachers, and even a blind itinerant. These were not aberrations from Methodist ideals, but expressions of them, for John Wesley himself approved of including women among Methodism's lay preachers.[22] Probably the most striking of many examples of lay self-confidence and power was the interdenominational York Street chapel in Dublin, founded in the early 1800s. The nine evangelical businessmen from several denominations who founded the chapel not only bought a site with their own money, made themselves trustees, and assumed complete control of every aspect of the chapel's affairs, they also wrote into the chapel's charter a clause forbidding any clergyman to become a trustee—and if any sitting trustee was ever ordained, or even became a lay preacher, he was required to resign.[23] Except for the Society of Friends, surely no religious movement in Irish history had ever come close to providing as much scope for lay involvement and initiative as did evangelicalism.

Irish evangelicalism was in no way more clearly marked as a popular Reformation movement than by its missionary emphasis. 'It is the indispensable duty of Gospel ministers,' said evangelical preacher George Hamilton in 1798, 'to go out after poor sinners into the remotest parts of the country; and to compel them to come in, that Christ's house, the Church, may be filled.'[24] Hamilton was addressing Irish preachers, but all evangelicals knew they had a similar mandate to exercise in their own settings, however exalted or however humble. Evangelical mission work had three strands to it: preaching to nominal Protestants, proselytising Catholics, and evangelising foreign pagans. These distinctions are perhaps somewhat academic, because from an evangelical viewpoint, all three constituencies—Protestant, Catholic, and pagan—were equally hellbound so long as they remained outside the gospel pale as understood by evangelicals. The variously directed missionary efforts reinforced one another, and the evangelicals' sense of responsibility and basic message to each group was the same. Nonetheless, it is worth noting that Irish evangelicalism, usually analysed in the context of its efforts to convert Catholics, was first and foremost a movement for Protestant renewal.[25]

If popular Reformations frequently coincided with great social turmoil, Irish evangelicalism coincided with a period of upheaval second to none. Late eighteenth-century revolution in France, war between France and Great Britain, extension of some political rights to Catholics, and finally, rebellion in 1798 created a climate of comprehensive uncertainty which inspired both anxiety and exhilaration among Irish Protestants. In the course of an eighty-five lecture survey of western history from the fifth century through the French Revolution, George Miller, a fellow of Trinity College Dublin, confidently reduced the events of thirteen centuries to 'one great system' of providential action. But in 1811, at the close of his lectures, he could only say of his own era that 'a new order of ages has begun.'[26] The post-revolution 'new order of ages' certainly did not create evangelicalism, nor was it even the context of evangelical origins—by then evangelicalism had been established for several decades, internationally and in Ireland. But in Ireland these foundation-rattling events were definitely an important catalyst for evangelical activity and influence. In such times the initiative lay with those who had energy and vision, and evangelicalism had both in abundance.[27]

Popular Reformations were frequently judged to be subversive of church, state, or both, but this would seem to be a case in which the popular Reformation shoe does not fit the evangelical foot. After all, evangelicals became fierce denominational loyalists, and they showed only the faintest traces of political radicalism. However, beneath these apparently straightforward exceptions to the typical standards of popular Reformations lie some more complicated truths. This is especially so in the case of evangelicalism's tempestuous relationships with the established denominations. Through the eighteenth century and well into the nineteenth, evangelicals were widely feared as subversive of the settled religious order, and with good reason. Evangelicals' eventual intense loyalty to their denominations must not overshadow the fact that they were not always or necessarily so, for hostility between evangelicals and church hierarchies was intense, and it took a long time to go away. In 1809 a Church of Ireland clergyman, after describing the indignities and injustices his church suffered at the hands of Catholics and their sympathisers, went on to complain about evangelicals:

> Another host of enemies, equally inveterate, and implacable, has risen against us in these self-appointed teachers, who claim to themselves the distinction of belonging to the reformed Church, but with restless and indefatigable zeal, spread their poisonous doctrines among our people, and labour to debauch them from all confidence in their lawful ministers, all reverence for their preaching, all respect for their characters.[28]

His was a widely shared and stated assessment of evangelicalism, and as late as 1821 John George Beresford, Church of Ireland archbishop of Dublin and soon to be primate of all Ireland, said much the same thing.[29] Evangelicalism was genuinely a threat to the ecclesiastical established order, a fact that is now partially obscured because the evangelical cause was partially triumphant.

The lack of political radicalism among Irish evangelicals is as real as it is apparent, but some qualifications do need to be made. First, of the various popular Reformation traits discussed here, political radicalism was probably the least important. While popular Reformations were rife with levelling implications, these were rarely acted upon in any directly political way, and in fact in the history of popular Reformations, radical or visionary politics was usually the exception to a general rule of political indifference, or at least inactivity. The high visibility of a few exceptional cases — chief among them the sixteenth-century Anabaptist kingdom of Munster, which for centuries provided theologians of the main denominations with all they wanted to know about Anabaptism — has made radical politics seem more important than it actually was. Second, evangelicalism did have some levelling instincts. As John Walsh has observed, 'Evangelical theology, having first put all men on par as equal sinners in the eyes of God, thereafter taught that the meanest in the Kingdom of God was greater than the richest among the unregenerate.'[30] This was why the duchess of Buckingham was so repelled by evangelicalism: she thought it was 'monstrous to be told that you have a heart as sinful as the common wretches that crawl on the earth. This is highly offensive and insulting.'[31] That evangelicals rarely drew direct social or political consequences from such teachings can be accounted for by several reasons. Until well into the nineteenth century, most Irish evangelicals were members of the Church of Ireland; their position as members of the established church was always likely to incline them towards protecting their privileges, not extending them to others, an attitude which was powerfully reinforced by the defensiveness and anxiety that accompanied being a minority. Furthermore, in the eighteenth century political radicalism and infidelity were conventionally understood to be linked — which became a rigid equation after the experience of the French Revolution and the writings of Thomas Paine — and evangelicals were certainly not infidels. And when radical politics in Ireland heated up in the 1790s, many of the central issues involved concessions to Catholics, a platform which was never going to hold great appeal for many evangelicals.

A final characteristic of popular Reformations was a tendency to generate schism and a radical fringe. Commenting on the history of radical Christianity, John Bossy has said that no one who turns from 'the Germany of the 1520s and 1530s to the England of the 1640s and 1650s can fail to get the feeling that he has been there before'. He might have added that if this same person would then turn to Ireland at any time through the eighteenth century, the feeling would immediately go away. Bossy mused on how such ideas were transmitted, but suggested that this is the wrong question: 'Perhaps we should think of them as spores secreted in a Christian culture, guaranteed to produce mushrooms at a certain temperature.'[32] He is probably right, and his metaphor could be extended to include not only the growth of radical Christianity but of schism generally— schism is, among other things, a mark of a religious environment heated to a critical temperature. The significance for Ireland is this: the early 1800s witnessed the emergence of the first indigenous dissent, the first indigenous religious radicalism. This new departure in Irish Christianity is strong evidence that a popular Reformation was generating religious heat which had finally reached a temperature unprecedented in Ireland.

These years produced two indigenous dissenting groups, the most important being the Church of God, founded in 1804.[33] Bossy's spores-and-mushrooms metaphor is satisfactory for describing the genesis of the Church of God out of evangelical soil, but once in existence the new church required a different metaphor, for it went on producing heat by continual friction with just about every other Christian group in Ireland, especially its former evangelical compatriots. Its founder was John Walker, a Trinity College Dublin graduate in 1790, a Trinity Fellow from 1791 to 1804, a Church of Ireland minister, a chaplain of Bethesda chapel (then the spiritual centre of Church of Ireland evangelicalism) from 1794 to 1805, and until his departure from the established church in 1804, the most important figure in Irish evangelicalism. Walker was a most complex character. The Church of God's contentious character and conflict-ridden career was a faithful reflection of Walker's public role as a hard-driving, caustic, and uncompromising preacher, and yet he was also a shy and sensitive scholar, in fact the finest classical scholar of his generation in Ireland. And although Walker did have a set of political and cultural ideas, he was remarkable for being about as purely religious a person as can be imagined. Religion was his ultimate and consuming concern, and he allowed nothing to keep his religious ideas from being realised. Up to 1804 that religion was firmly evangelical—in fact it was almost a caricature. In him any soft edges of ambiguity were cut away, and the characteristic tendencies of evangelicalism appeared in sharp relief. Two of Walker's evangelical beliefs, about the nature of the church and about pastoral duty, are especially significant for understanding the emergence and the nature of the Church of God.

Evangelicals believed that the true church was an invisible communion of the regenerate, who were to be found in many denominations, a belief that had no more fervent proponent than John Walker. This ecclesiastical orientation normally left evangelicals rather indifferent to the usual denominational boundaries and structures, but Walker, true to form, took it further, in some instances to a point very near to actual hostility. He preached whenever and wherever he could, without regard for formal permission from church leaders. More fundamentally, he firmly opposed the claims of any one denomination, including his own, to a greater than usual grasp of religious truth. When preaching on the glories of the church, he hastened to add, 'let not any particular department in the visible and professing Church arrogate to itself the privileges which belong only to the true spiritual and universal church of God.' This had been the sin of the Jews, and now the 'Roman Communion' shared it. 'Where it prevails in any body of Christians, they have fallen from the simplicity of evangelical truth; they have lost sight of the real nature of Christ's Kingdom.'[34] True Christians were scattered far and wide, and 'nothing but blind bigotry suggests that they are to be found only under one denomination.'[35] He tended to disapprove of activity organised on a denominational basis, even when he approved of the intent. In 1799 he observed with pleasure the 'appearances of a great work in our church', but when a close and respected friend wrote to him about a group meeting to pray for the revival of vital religion in the Church of Ireland, Walker judged the scheme 'too contracted'. He wanted prayers for 'the general church'—'I can bring promises with me to the throne of grace for that, which I cannot use for any particular church with certainty.'[36] Such convictions led him to place great faith and hope in the Dublin-based and interdenominational General Evangelical Society, founded in 1787. Here 'lively Christians of all denominations', who were 'all one body, having one Lord, one faith, one hope', discovered 'themselves to be *Brethren*' and worked together 'for the advancement of that one cause, which alone will certainly prevail. That is not the cause of any human party, or outward denomination in the Church of Christ. It is the cause of Christ's kingdom.'[37] True Christians may have been one body, but up to 1804 he did not wish to see evangelicals withdrawing from their denominations. The beauty of the General Evangelical Society was that it united evangelicals in fellowship, and even allowed them to work together, without severing their denominational ties. In 1799 he wrote to a fellow evangelical minister, 'I hope it will long continue the standard of union, which no new party can be.'[38]

Walker was also an extremist on another typically evangelical emphasis—the understanding of pastoral duty. According to him, 'it is at *all* times the incumbent duty of Christ's ministers to deal *plainly* with sinners', without flattering or soothing.[39] Any minister who would try to make Christianity appear pleasing 'by concealing its offensive truths' was guilty of treachery. 'Our business is, not to sing a lullaby to the sleeping conscience; not to assist in attiring the proud worm with the fancied plumes of his own wisdom, strength and virtue; not to smooth the sinner's way to eternal death.' The preacher's task was to speak boldly against sin, leaving the results to God.[40] By this standard he judged contemporary ministers as miserable failures. For so many of them the ministry was nothing more than a human profession. Absenteeism was a tremendous problem among the clergy, but their presence was not necessarily an improvement on their absence as they trudged indifferently through the course of their duties, ministering to equally indifferent congregations.[41]

Walker was certainly unexceptional in his contempt for his nonevangelical ministerial peers and his conception of ministry as the straightforward denunciation of sin. These were evangelical staples, and many an evangelical preacher subjected his audiences to verbal pummellings. But Walker seemed to throw an exceptional number of punches, sometimes loaded with an extra sting. In 1794, his final sermon before being silenced by the archbishop (on charges that amounted to being an evangelical) might have seemed the occasion for a discreet and conciliatory address. But he chose instead to speak 'with boldness', a hopelessly inadequate euphemism for what amounted to a sustained attack on his congregation. In seeking charity for the poor, he accused his audience of listening,'cold and insensible, contracted into the narrow sphere of their selfish principles and selfish views', leaving him 'to wring a poor mite from the unwilling hand of avarice'.[42] If he spoke of faith, he said, he would be considered a Methodist, an enthusiast, an antinomian. 'Considered so by whom? By men who call themselves believers.—Believers! no; they are baptized infidels.'[43] Simon Magus had a certain kind of faith, as did devils, 'and you are unbelievers while you have no other faith than that which is common to devils and hypocrites'. 'Stout-hearted rebels!', he called them. 'Dissipated triflers!', 'self-deceiving, self-righteous hypocrites!', 'miserable souls!'[44] Hypocrisy was probably his greatest hate. On the occasion of a national day of fasting he assailed the multitude of hypocrites 'who have assembled in the house of God—formal, and hypocritical, and inconsiderate, to add *insult* to *rebellion*' by offering 'before the majesty of heaven a solemn mockery of external service'. 'You *pray*,' he accused them, 'that is, you *say* prayers with your lips: but are they anything else than a mockery of God?' Such hypocrites would leave worship 'as thoughtless as they came'.[45] Tales of Walker's ferocity circulated among the devout. A representative (and verifiable) story had Walker accepting an invitation to read prayers in a Church of Ireland congregation, but later that week writing to the minister and accusing him of 'sending his flock to the Devil'.[46]

In 1804 John Walker, for all his evangelicalism, became the founder of a new denomination. He now became an enemy of the established order in church affairs and church-state relations, while most evangelicals, even those who did not support the ecclesiastical status quo, did nothing directly to subvert it and stayed within their denominations, however precariously in some cases. To the casual observer, Walker's departure from the established church must have seemed a dramatic turnabout for an evangelical leader. But it was no sudden whim. Even though the seeds of dissent did not bear publicly visible fruit until 1804, they had been germinating in many areas of his life and thought since at least the early 1790s.

What must have terrified Walker's former evangelical allies, and strengthened the resolve of their opponents, was that his formation of a new church followed, at least in part, from his evangelical convictions. Evangelicalism's enemies in the main denominations had always contended that it was innately subversive of the ecclesiastical established order, and now the leading Dublin evangelical had made the point more eloquently and forcefully than they could ever have hoped to do. In order to stretch established ecclesiastical boundaries without actually breaking them, evangelicals relied more on self-restraint and pragmatism than they did on principled arguments. This ambiguity lay at the very heart of evangelical convictions. As mentioned above, evangelicals believed that the true church was an invisible church, composed of many true Christians scattered among the masses of unbelievers and half-believers who made up the traditional denominations. Evangelicals chose, for the most part, to organise themselves in ways that fell short of being a church, but why they should exercise this restraint was never entirely clear, and in fact their reasoning was far more pragmatic than principled. They were, therefore, always vulnerable to the objections of someone who would argue on principle, as Walker now did, that evangelicals should come out from among their several denominations. The mental shift necessary for an evangelical to move from staying within the established denominations to joining a new one was not very great.

Although Walker's reasons for leaving the established church were all compatible with his evangelicalism, some were not so directly derived from evangelical emphases. For example, his biblicism had a restitutionist edge to it that not all evangelicals shared. From very early on, he measured the church of his day against apostolic standards and found it wanting. For him the early church as described in the book of Acts was a living model for what the church must once again become. 'Are we to hear of these days without looking for their return? God forbid! . . . [I]t is no vain or groundless expectation that primitive Christianity shall yet be revived.'[47] In 1796 Walker regretted that if 'someone dare to exhibit apostolic conduct, and declare apostolic truth,

he is opposed as needlessly singular or derided as a wild
enthusiast.' His ministerial standards were those of the early
church, when ministers were 'fervent in spirit, devoted in life,
indefatigable in labour, disinterestedly forsaking all earthly
comfort to serve a Saviour whom they loved, and joyfully
encountering trials, reproach and persecution'.[48] By the time he
left the Church of Ireland his views were uncompromising: the
principles on which he withdrew from the establishment 'call
the attention of *all believers* of the Gospel to the Apostolic rules,
delivered to the first Churches of Christ, as those by which we
are still bound to walk'.[49] In 1804 he no longer believed this
principle could be faithfully fulfilled within the existing
denominations.

Beneath the turbulent waves of theological ideas ran a quiet,
difficult to discern undercurrent of personal crisis that may have
been just as important in pulling Walker out of the established
church and evangelical circles. Walker the hard-driving dogma-
tist was so formidable and oppressive a presence that one can
easily neglect Walker the gentle aesthete and forget how this
aspect of his character may have touched his religion. However,
a handful of clues and a rumour suggest that he was looking for
something more than pure doctrine in a church and that he left
the establishment for more than doctrinal reasons. Already in
1794, when discussing the primitive Christianity he hoped to
see revived, Walker identified as its 'distinguishing mark', not
pristine apostolic structures or uncorrupted doctrine, but
'mutual love'.[50] Ten years later, when he left the established
church, a failure of love among evangelicals was one of the
reasons. He lamented various evils in the evangelical world,
'evils especially, which stand opposed to the law of brotherly
kindness and sympathy with the afflicted . . . I began encreas-
ingly [sic] to remark how the disciples, in the apostolic
Churches, *walked together* as brethren, closely united with each
other, and separated from them that believed not.'[51] Apparently
Walker was as much concerned with quality of relationships as
with purity of doctrine in his search for an Apostolic standard of
church life.

The engine that finally moved Walker to act on his long
developing ideas seems to have been a coterie of like-minded
Dublin Christians. Here, for once, he was not entirely in the

lead—he acknowledged lagging behind 'some dear brethren, who were much suprised and pained at my continuance in the Establishment'.[52] They may have been meeting as a semi-fellowship from as early as 1802,[53] and two of their recurring topics were the extent to which true believers had been tainted by being 'awfully scattered among the heathen', and the necessity that they 'be collected together as of old, and called back—both for their own profit and for the glory of the Lord—to walk together according to the Apostolic rule'.[54] By the beginning of 1804 he was ready to go public with these ideas by publishing *Hints on Christian fellowship*, an interesting pamphlet that revealed his thinking at a point midway between his earlier full-blown evangelicalism and his imminent sectarianism. For instance, although he wanted all Dublin believers to join in a fellowship that fulfilled all the functions of a church, he did not think they needed to leave the congregations to which they already belonged.[55] But Walker's basic instincts demanded all or nothing, and he did not rest long at this halfway point.

After *Hints*, events leading to his departure from the established church began rapidly to gain momentum. In about February 1804 Walker was rumoured to have offended Bethesda chapel members by comparing their spiritual condition unfavourably with the reformed or reforming prostitutes who worshipped with them.[56] Shortly thereafter, around March 1804, the first indigenous Irish dissenting church came into being. In Walker's words, written near the end of the year,

> a very small number (nine persons), who were of one mind, commenced the attempt; and united together to walk as one body—in the one character of believers of the Gospel of Christ—with the one object of following Him, and serving one another by love—and desiring to be regulated in all their course by one rule, the rule of his word; being persuaded that, in whatever way Christians were called to walk in the days of the Apostles, they must at all times be called to walk in the same way.[57]

The rupture with his old connections was not complete, however, for Walker remained a Church of Ireland clergyman, a Fellow of Trinity College, the chaplain of Bethesda chapel, and a member of several church-related societies. Over the course of

the next year these connections were severed one by one—
slowly, publicly, and with great pain for all concerned.

No more than a brief sketch of Walker's new church and
theology is possible here. The Church of God's combination of
Calvinist theology and anti-establishment principles sometimes
elicited comparison with the Sandemanians—followers of the
eighteenth-century Scottish reformer, Robert Sandeman—and
yet the two groups had significant differences. An early account
of Walker's church described it as 'formed or forming on a
different plan to perhaps any other in the world',[58] and so it
was.

For the purposes of this study, however, the most important
fact about Walker's new theology is how little it had changed. In
order to maintain pan-evangelical unity, evangelicals distilled
from the bible, the Westminster Confession of the Presbyterians, and the Thirty-Nine Articles of the Anglicans, a general,
informal orthodoxy they sometimes called 'the doctrines of
grace'.[59] By these standards, Walker continued to be impeccably
orthodox: he was as firm a biblicist as ever, conversion remained
absolutely essential, and his doctrine of salvation was not
altered even an iota. When asked in 1804 if he stood by his two
earliest theological productions, from 1792 and 1794, Walker
was somewhat reluctant to affirm them in their entirety, not
having read them for many years, but he did say, 'I believe they
both contain, and am sure that one of them contains, all the
essence of that truth which I am now so much more offensively,
because more clearly witnessing.'[60] Walker had always been
and would always be an advocate of what he called the apostolic
gospel or apostolic faith. Now he had added to that the
necessity of walking by the apostolic rule of life, by which he
meant primarily a certain pattern of church government.[61] Only
his ecclesiology had changed, and even then his new doctrine
built logically on evangelical theology.

But what had changed, had changed radically. His new
understanding of the church made Walker, formerly the leading
champion of evangelicalism in Dublin, its most bitter enemy,
which powerfully demonstrates the importance to evangelicals
of their doctrine of an invisible church whose members were
scattered among the denominations. Perhaps the most significant change was Walker's revised assessment of the importance

of church structures. In their efforts to maintain unity among themselves, evangelicals relied heavily on the assumption that they could distinguish between Christian essentials — chief among them a shared doctrine and experience of salvation — and non-essentials, which certainly included the varieties of church structures they worked within. This was the evangelical understanding of their favourite text, 'I am determined not to know anything among you save Jesus Christ, and him crucified.' But implicit in everything Walker did from 1804 onwards was the assumption that the whole concept of non-essentials or 'subordinate matters' was at best questionable — and certainly the organisation of the church did not belong in this category. An evangelical non-essential now became a Walkerite essential, and the evangelical basis of unity was exploded.

Everything else changed as well. Evangelicals emphasised the universal and invisible church, Walker the local and visible church. With this shift came a rigorous emphasis on the distinction between church and world. Although always implicit in a relatively mild form in evangelical theology, it became an obsession with Walker. In the summer of 1804, after his new church had started, Walker boldly exploited the anomaly of his continuing status as a Church of Ireland minister to preach from many pulpits a sermon urging members to leave the established church. This sermon was choked with language suggesting the church/world distinction: 'not of the world', 'strangers and pilgrims', 'unequally yoked together with unbelievers', '*come out*', 'be *separate*', '*peculiar people*', 'a nation *holy* to the Lord'.[62] In his final months at Bethesda chapel he considered eliminating pews, arguing 'that as long as they remained, the *true* church were not sufficiently *outwardly* separated as a body, in one place, from unbelievers.'[63] An outsider observed that in Walkerite worship services, 'those not in connexion are allowed to look on but no more — a standing principle is not to have religious communion with any other party whatever, but to come out from among them and be separate.'[64] An evangelical who tried to dispute their church/world distinction was sharply rebuked. 'They lectured me at full length on my making light of outward distinctions, and said, that if *even a coat* would mark a believer as distinct from the world, it became a point of importance, and they would wear it.'[65] Walker's position came to be known as 'marked separation', which was soon the subject of fierce and anguished disagreement in evangelical circles.[66] The categories of essentials and non-essentials were under siege.[67]

Three illustrations of Walker's new ecclesiological priorities sum up how radically he had changed. In 1802 he was still willing to address Methodists as his fellow Christians, however misguided they might be; after quitting the established church he would stigmatise such loose talk as 'my sin' and 'wicked nonsense'.[68] In 1800 he had been convinced that no church could be identified with the one true church, and any church that was so deluded had 'lost sight of the real nature of Christ's Kingdom: and they may expect to have their mistake corrected, by having their candlestick removed'; but in 1804 he asserted that his was the only true Christian church in Ireland.[69] In 1799 he had praised the General Evangelical Society for allowing evangelicals to work together without leaving their denomina-tions—he hoped it would 'long continue the standard of union, which no new party can be'; but in 1804 Walker said, 'from my soul I hope, that the day is not far distant, when there will not be a single disciple of Christ remaining in the Established Church, nor in any similarly corrupt communion'.[70]

Walker's innovations had a devastating effect on vital religion in Dublin and farther afield. He had attacked Methodists in 1802, and throughout 1803 he published a series of seven pamphlets savaging Alexander Knox, a widely known and excellent lay theologian in the Church of Ireland, for his defence of Methodism. Now Walker and his 'pert and petulant boys', as Knox called them,[71] afforded the same treatment to everyone else in sight. Bethesda chapel, which Walker no longer con-sidered a Christian congregation, must have been dealt a drubbing every Sunday until Walker left in January 1805. Even after he left, a small group of his followers would occasionally attend sermons, waiting to hear any reference to good works or other hints of Arminianism, at which they would march out, 'declaring this was legal doctrine, and not such as a Christian could listen to'.[72] His former evangelical allies he dismissed as hypocrites and compromisers.[73] In 1804 a Walkerite publication, the *Advocate of Revealed Truth, and Inspector of the Religious World*, attacked Trinity Fellow George Miller, the evangelical London Missionary Society, English evangelical leader Charles Simeon,

Church of Ireland priest John Jebb, and almost everyone else in sight;[74] in 1805 another Dublin publication, *The Messenger of Truth*, was using the same style and themes, whether or not it was formally connected with Walker.[75] After a dispute about baptism, Walker himself attacked the Baptists in print, arguing that there was no New Testament warrant for adult baptism of a person raised in a Christian home, that Baptists could not consistently even teach their children, that child baptism was the rule in the early church by around AD 150.[76] He never missed the chance to express his disagreement with dissenters generally, lest his grounds for dissent be confused with theirs.[77] While Walker was still at Bethesda, he and his friends held an open Friday evening meeting for discussion, which was described by a participant as 'conducted in a very irreverent manner; and the object seems to be to triumph over, and laugh at a fallen objector, overcome by superior reasoning and subtle argument'.[78] A few years later his Stafford Street congregation was using similar public disputes, presumably as a means of witnessing.[79] According to one evangelical, for two years after Walker's departure, evangelical cooperation and activity were stymied by a 'fierce warfare . . . carried on by opposing parties on the subject of church government, which was very inimical to the real interests of vital godliness'.[80] A survey of contemporary pamphlets suggests that 'fierce warfare' was no exaggeration.

Walker's opponents responded in a variety of ways. Some people could ignore him or take him lightly, others were hurt or angry, some fought back. At least one Dublin magistrate thought that 'Government ought to *exterminate from society* such principles'.[81] Some just sneered. An anonymous pamphleteer thought the best remedy for Walker's ideas would have been 'a strait jacket—a shaven head—some clean straw—and a dark room in Swift's-Hospital', but with this opportunity lost, 'all that remain, (for let us never think of dignifying their nonsense by persecution,) are refutation and ridicule'.[82]

But another common response, often mingled with others, was fear. Already in 1802 John Jebb had been among those who sneered at Walker: 'poor Walker. . . . Is it certain that his brain is sound?'[83] But even while dismissing Walker as mentally unstable, Jebb admitted to his friend Alexander Knox that he almost feared to examine Walker's vehement yet limpid exposition of the doctrine of salvation. Knox, having mistaken his fear for misunderstanding, sent back a blithe and simple summary of Walker's doctrine. But this was not the problem—Jebb was not at all sure that he wanted to understand. Jeer as his opponents might, Walker's energy, clarity, and single-mindedness formed a whirlpool that many feared to approach too closely, lest they too be sucked in by at least the illusion of truth.

Walker's church was always tiny, probably never numbering more than a dozen small congregations. However, several of those congregations were in Scotland and England—a small but significant reversal of the usual flow of Protestant influence from Great Britain to Ireland—and the church's impact was out of all proportion to its size. Walker was an outstanding spokesman for the understanding of the Christianity he represented; his ideas were influential long after his death.[84] Although the Church of Ireland was well used to challenges directed against the principle of religious establishment, so vigorous an attack had never been mounted from within its own ranks. Walker's departure must also have caused some anxiety within Trinity. If he had long been harbouring anti-establishment ideas, then perhaps he had infected some of the young men he taught. His close friendship with Benjamin Mathias, one of Walker's former students and by 1804 an evangelical minister, was well known, and even though Mathias always remained faithful to the established church, guilt by association may have been the reason that the Trinity provost forbade students to attend Bethesda chapel after Mathias succeeded Walker as chaplain in 1805.

But his former evangelical allies undoubtedly suffered most. Alfred Blest, who was by 1804 already a veteran evangelical, later wrote, 'when Mr. Walker withdrew from the Established church, I looked on all that was done in conveying the leaven of divine truth into the college and the Church, as blasted for ever.'[85] A delegation from the London Hibernian Society, which visited Ireland in 1807, described in greater detail the potential damage threatened by the Walkerites and their 'repulsive peculiarities'.

> The broaching of their system in Ireland, a country where, if in any other, the union of Christians should be carried, with a holy vehemence, to its last lawful limit, is calculated to do

unspeakable mischief. Should it be suffered by Divine Providence to flow in a more copious stream, the eager propagators of Christianity will feel themselves proportionally thwarted in their noblest endeavours. Papists will declaim with renewed advantage on the divisions of Protestants, and the sons of infidelity and vice will approach the majesty of pure and undefiled religion with augmented violence and scorn.[86]

These dire prophecies were not fulfilled in their entirety. But the threat was genuine, Walker definitely did damage and alter evangelicalism, and evangelicals spent much time and energy in combat with him and his followers. By one account, 'the Separatists [a common designation for Walker and his followers] pursued the leading evangelical clergy everywhere; poaching upon their congregations, robbing them of their most devout adherents, and representing themselves as specially and exclusively spiritual.'[87] Families formerly united in evangelical faith were devastated when a few newly Walkerite family members, putting into scrupulous practice the principle of marked separation, would refuse to worship with them.[88] In 1812 Henry Maturin, an evangelical Church of Ireland minister in Raphoe, observed some progress for the evangelical cause there, but he was still complaining that 'the secession of Mr. Walker and others and the prevalence of their principles weakens our hands.'[89] In that same year Walker still had 'a great following amongst the students of Trinity College'.[90] As late as 1815, Peter Roe's *Evil of separation from the Church of England* was little more than a collection of letters and articles responding to Walker's attacks on establishments in general and the Church of Ireland in particular.[91]

In fact Walker's departure from the established church to form a new church did much to shape the subsequent course of Irish evangelicalism. The interdenominational approach to Christianity they so favoured looked much less plausible after Walker had attacked it in principle and denied it in practice with his new sectarian approach to church life. In addition to sparking self-doubt within the evangelical community, Walker's well-publicised new initiatives put Church of Ireland evangelicals, whose denominational loyalty had always been considered doubtful by the hierarchy, under still more suspicion and pressure from outside their ranks. But even though trapped between a crumbling interdenominationalism and a growling hierarchy, few evangelicals were interested in following Walker on to new ground. The post-Walker evangelical was a chastened and more wary creature, and if the interdenominationalism which had been so essential to their identity was gradually dropped or curtailed, the vast majority were not ready to replace interdenominationalism with a new denomination. They gradually found their way on to safer terrain, a new synthesis of churchmanship and evangelical doctrine, a kind of evangelicalism within one denomination. This reduced the difference between evangelicals and the other members of their own denominations, especially in the case of the Church of Ireland, so that evangelicals became less and less a reform group with a distinctive vision and programme, and more and more simply Protestants with energy. The shifting emphasis from evangelical interdenominationalism in the period up to 1800 to evangelical churchmanship by mid century cannot be explained by any single factor (contemporary British evangelicalism experienced much the same thing, with no influence from Walker), but in Ireland surely no cause was more important than the direct challenge posed by John Walker and the Church of God. Regardless of the exact relationship of various causes, evangelical withdrawal from interdenominationalism made church leadership less suspicious of evangelicals, and this made some cooperation possible, which in turn made possible the Second Reformation as a church *and* popular Reformation. Without these new species of cooperation between evangelicals and churchmen a serious effort to convert Irish Catholics to Protestantism might not have been possible at all, and if the task had been attempted under the old circumstances, the result probably would not have been vigorous enough or coordinated enough to warrant the title 'Protestant crusade'.

The story of John Walker and the Church of God is just one example — although certainly one of the more striking — of the way in which the characteristics and the career of Irish evangelicalism closely matched the typical features of popular Reformation movements. In this it did not differ from evangelicalism in other countries, but Irish evangelicalism was set apart by its unique status as a *first* experience of popular Reformation. By the time other European Protestants got around to evangelicalism, they built on a long-standing tradition of popular piety developed out of medieval heresies, the classical Reformation, Anabaptism, Puritanism, and Pietism. Even American evangelicals worked with essentially the same tradition, for many of these religious impulses had flourished when transplanted to American soil. But in Ireland such movements of popular piety had made a lighter impression, if any at all, so Irish Protestants had less precedent to build upon. If nineteenth-century Irish evangelicalism sometimes seemed shriller than other varieties, if the social conflict it touched off seemed fiercer than elsewhere, perhaps we should look for explanations not only to Irish irascibility or to Ireland's admittedly peculiar and explosive social and political circumstances, but also to the fact that Ireland was only then experiencing its popular Reformation. If John Bossy's time-travelling student of radical Christianity was ever going to recognise in Ireland the patterns of Germany in the 1520s and 1530s and England in the 1640s and 1650s it would not be until the first half of the nineteenth century, when a variety of forces, evangelicalism prominent among them, had pushed Ireland's religious temperature higher than ever before. Nicholas Canny has argued that the Reformation in Ireland cannot finally be said to have failed until the close of the Second Reformation.[92] In at least one sense he is right, for only then had Ireland experienced a full Reformation, state, church, and popular.

9. *Popular religion and clerical influence in pre-famine Meath*

CONSIDERABLE attention has focused in recent years on the evolution of the Catholic community, and the influences which shaped it in the social, economic and political turmoil of the late eighteenth and nineteenth centuries. One of the most interesting and neglected fields of study related to the Catholic community is the area of folk practices and beliefs. There was a rich cloak of early Christian and even pre-Christian practices, which survived right through the Middle Ages, around the body of purely Catholic beliefs. This was an integral part of the cultural religious consciousness of the poorer sections of the community, and it was in the nineteenth century that they largely faded and died.

In recent studies of this period, a clearer picture has emerged as to the place of folk practices in the community and the forces which were to crush them. Not all studies agree on the importance of these beliefs. Desmond J. Keenan sees them as having little importance in the community. Although he recognises that a mixture of non-Christian beliefs persisted, he claims they were essentially harmless. He goes so far as to state that it is difficult to say Catholics in those days were more superstitious than in our own. There was, however, a successful effort to purge any elements directly contradictory to official formulations, so that popular beliefs of any kind did not contradict official beliefs at any point except perhaps on purgatory.[1]

Considerably more weight is attached to these popular beliefs by Patrick J. Corish. In the seventeenth and eighteenth centuries he sees an amalgam of paganism and Christianity running through the life of the poor. Both were real to them, and while reliance on superstition, miracle and prophecy might have obscured orthodox Catholic teaching, it did not blot out the

Christian quest for salvation.[2] Superstition always haunts the human consciousness, the basically pagan notion of a divinity waiting to strike if the rites are not duly observed. Yet, by the closing decades of the eighteenth century, Corish notes that the Catholic bishops had set themselves against many of these observances, notably patterns, pilgrimages and wakes, although it may well be that individual priests did try to keep religious observances alive at the pilgrimages denounced by their bishops. In their opposition, the bishops and clergy were hampered by the general social structures of the nineteenth century, which were still looking back to the past. Their opposition was based on the fact that it was felt that traditional patterns and pilgrimages had lost much of their religious significance and had tended to become rowdy social occasions. However, many traditional usages such as wakes, funerals and patterns kept their grip despite clerical opposition, and in the case of patterns and pilgrimages the degeneration which was observed was partly caused by the clergy turning their backs on them. As the nineteenth century progressed, the ancient traditions and usages of the countryside were in full retreat, not just because of ecclesiastical pressures but also because of the changing values of society. A monetary economy was spreading to replace the old subsistence, communal economy, and practices such as wakes became socially unacceptable as the general values of society became more 'respectable'.

A whole world of cultural values also decayed with the decay of the Irish language. Religious values were at the heart of this culture, some of them superstitious. However, much of this decline can be traced to the increased prestige and power of the Catholic church, symbolised by the priest. It is not too much, argues Corish, to see him as inheriting some of the powers of the taoiseach from Gaelic Ireland. This power increased in some respects as he made his way to political power, through emancipation, tithe war and repeal agitation. In peasant Ireland, the priest was a father figure, not to be lightly crossed. Orthodox Catholicism increased as the influence of Catholic schools came to the fore. This was augmented considerably by Catholic book societies, confraternities and the patronage of wealthy Catholic merchants and land holders. The essential point, Corish claims, was that as the Irish lost one identity, they found another and the new identity was Catholic.[3]

Perhaps the most detailed examination of the position of folk practices in the life of the Catholic community has been that of Sean Connolly in *Priests and people in pre-famine Ireland 1780–1845* (Dublin, 1982). In this he traces the changes which took place in the structures and position of the Catholic church during this period, and their ramifications in popular religion. He sees this as a time when the Catholic church was moving from being a technically illegal organisation to being an accepted part of the structures of power and influence within Irish society, and a time when new connections were established between religious affiliation and political allegiance. It saw the installation of religion at the heart of the new forms of popular political activity which emerged during this period, in the shape of emancipation, tithe and repeal agitation. He also emphasises the new-found political and social power of the priest, and the different factors which buttressed his position—the social origins and lifestyle of the clergy, their lack of connections with the political and social establishment, their education and the absence of alternative social leaders, and the atmosphere of an authoritarian culture. The influence of the church was greatly aided by the reforming bishops of the early nineteenth century (including Bishop Plunkett of Meath), who tried to ensure that their clergy paid proper attention to preaching, catechising and other routine pastoral duties and that they maintained a reasonable standard of outward display in their religious services. This provided the laity with a knowledge of the doctrine of their religion, and was supplemented by the measure of formal instruction given to the young in Catholic schools. These measures were to have a considerable impact on informal, popular practices by mid century.

However, in the early nineteenth century, churches were the centre of the religious life of the parish to a much lesser extent than later in the century. They were little more than mass houses, with private homes often providing the venue for stations, communion, baptisms and marriages. Furthermore, the religious practice of the great majority of Irish Catholics remained severely limited in frequency of attendance, in the range of devotional observances and in the degree of ceremony and external display with which public worship was conducted. Formal religion was something which intruded into their lives with considerably less frequency than was the case in later decades. Connolly maintains that for a real understanding of Irish Catholicism in this period it is necessary to look beyond these doctrines and rituals to another set of beliefs and practices, some of them identifiable as survivals from earlier religious traditions, others examples of the type of magical and supernatural belief which can be found at any time in societies below a certain threshold of economic and social development. Rituals of this kind permitted people to feel that they exercised some control over the mysterious forces which governed the uncertain fortunes of life and farming life in particular—thus arose such beliefs as those in fairies, practitioners of white magic, calendar customs, traditional crosses and bonfires. The relationship between the two sets of beliefs was rarely one of conflict. Where they did not coexist peacefully, they overlapped and provided mutual reinforcement, as when pilgrims visiting a holy well combined the sympathetic magic of a piece of cloth tied to a nearby bush or tree with prayers learned from the Catholic church. The only traditional observances which might become the object of an all-out attack were the wake and the pattern, both of which were opposed partly as examples of popular magic, but primarily as threats to popular morals.

Yet by the 1830s, Connolly sees the first signs of decline in these beliefs. Part of the reason for this, he claims, was the growing power and hostility of the Catholic clergy. This hostility was prompted partly by their superior education and relatively favoured social background, and partly by the new-found strength of the Catholic church with its better internal ecclesiastical discipline, its prominence in public affairs and its desire to live up to its new social status and prestige. However, even by the 1830s, suppression of such observances and the beliefs out of which they grew never became a major element in their programme of social control (except in the case of wakes and patterns). Nevertheless, Connolly argues that by catering for psychological and emotional needs which would otherwise have been met by formal religion, the beliefs and observances of popular tradition inevitably reduced the extent of people's dependence on the Catholic church and its rituals. The prestige of the church and the place it occupied in the lives of its members can only have been diminished by the fact that it did not have a monopoly either of the interpretation of the supernatural world or of the manipulation of the forces it contained.

It was against the social aspect of these gatherings that the main thrust of clerical disapproval was directed. Where patterns were not suppressed entirely, the clergy succeeded in exercising a more effective supervision over the conduct of those who attended. Yet in the 1840s, patterns, even if somewhat diminished in popularity, remained a familiar part of Irish life. It can be suggested, according to Connolly, that the opposition of the clergy to patterns and similar assemblies achieved a real, but limited, success. The successes they achieved, furthermore, must be seen in the context of a broader change which was taking place in popular attitudes and behaviour as a whole range of traditional beliefs and practices began to be abandonded. Like the political economists and moral reformers of the same period in England, the clergy were attempting to impose orderly habits on a population whose living conditions and whose work itself encouraged irregularity and disorder. But their efforts were not supplemented by the massive economic and social changes which were taking place in Britain, which replaced the rhythm of nature by the turning of the clock. The passing of the irregular rhythms which had characterised the social life of pre-famine Ireland was a long slow process, yet the efforts of the priests (and others) were not entirely without effect.

It can be said then, that to condemn wakes and patterns and other practices was not just to regulate disorderly gatherings for amusement but also to oppose the manifestations of an alternative supernaturalism which continued to play an important role in the lives of large sections of the Catholic population. It was also to set oneself up against a whole rhythm of work and leisure, extravagance and deprivation which, however at variance with the standards and outlook of Catholic churchmen, remained ultimately related to the conditions of rural Irish life and to its level of economic development. Connolly goes so far as to maintain that to some extent one can talk of a popular culture diverging in important respects from that represented by the Catholic church and its clergy. The manifestations of this included not only folk beliefs, but also faction fights, secret societies and clandestine marriages. It would also be wrong to think that all sections of the Catholic clergy were equally opposed to popular beliefs and practices. Yet the overall influence of the Catholic clergy was a limited one.[4]

Folk customs were highly practical measures concerned with human life and its welfare. They were in the main attempts to protect vital human interests. They provided cathartic extravagance in a life immersed in deprivation and hardship, repression and economic tension. They answered a need. Folk practices were based on emotion rather than reason. The poor regarded nature as something subject to laws, but their explanation followed a type of mysticism, a belief in the powers of magic to control those of nature.[5] It is through these practices and beliefs that we begin to get a flavour of the lives of a hard pressed people; a people who, long living wretchedly, needed all the comfort and colour, solace and spectacle, which religion in all its forms could bring to them. This existed side by side with, or overlapped with, the practices of orthodox Catholicism, and this accommodation was a condition, as Corish puts it, of the survival of Christianity in a living community. This 'civic religion allowed the average sensual man, not perhaps the full implication of the gospel, but at least to identify with the pieties of his kind, and to cultivate an essentially religious sense of identity and loyalty that traditionally has brought the political bonus of providing the moral justification for the sacrifices that often have to be asked for if society is to hold together, and for which it would be hard to find a viable alternative'.[6] Little work has been done by way of case studies of folk practices in local areas. The present essay aims at illustrating the range and extent of these customs in Co. Meath, and outlining the changes which were becoming obvious in the decades leading down to the famine.

Two particular folk practices which were impressive both in terms of attendance and the range of activities attached to them in Co. Meath, were the holy well and the patron or pattern, the latter of which Estyn Evans calls 'a holy fair'. The pattern was a gathering to celebrate the feast day of a local patron saint, although it has been claimed that Christianity merely transformed many traditional gatherings at already sacred sites into patterns.[7] These patterns most often, though not always, occurred at holy wells. Wells were made all the more significant, according to Barry Cunliffe, by Celtic belief in ritual shafts, by which contact could be made with the underworld.[8]

Many of the holy wells are found near old monastery and church ruins, and the holding of patterns at them is possibly indicative of one of three things. The first is a fusion of custom, when people were persuaded to celebrate the old festival days at new Christian sites.[9] Conversely, it may be because of a new belief in the power of the well growing up, in consequence of the well being used by the monks and saints of the early Church. It was within this context that the holy well became linked with the splendour of Christian symbolism about water. Pouchin Mould sees in this the natural step being taken from a belief in the cleansing power of water. Furthermore, she sees the 'rounds' which took place there and elsewhere, like their counterpart the earlier stone circle, as being linked with the track of the sun. Therefore, she sees the Celtic church as not just giving a redirection to the cult of the well but probably giving it new life and energy.[10] This ties in with the third possible reason for the proximity of early churches to wells—that the churches sought out these sites and made them their own, thus further strengthening their hold on the beliefs of the people.

In all, by the 1830s, there were eighty-three identifiable holy wells in Co. Meath (see p. 196) recorded in O'Donovan, *Letters of the Ordnance Survey*, travellers accounts and the Ordnance Survey field name books. When these are mapped, together with other major pilgrimage sites, a clear spatial pattern emerges. Folk customs are generally strongest in north Meath, with its arable economy, and weakest in pastoral south Meath. It is noticeable that with the exception of Kells, folk customs tended not to be pronounced near the major urban centres. Note the patterns near Trim and Navan and in the Boyne estuary nearing Drogheda Co. Louth. They also tend to fall off near the borders of Dublin and Kildare. The main centres for all types of customs were Kells, Nobber and Slane in north Meath, while Skreen in south Meath was important for holy wells and Ratoath was the centre of funeral customs in the county. All of these were either tillage areas or areas of mixed tillage and pasture farming. It is probable that the clearances in the late eighteenth and early nineteenth centuries which created the pasture land of south Meath did much to end folk customs there and that many of the dispossessed populations from these areas carried on the same practices in new homes in the tillage areas where they could. The difference that the economy of the area made for customs can most clearly be seen when the concentration of sites near the rivers Boyne and Blackwater is studied.

In north and central Meath, folk sites cluster densely around the river banks, while as you travel further south fewer and fewer sites appear on the banks of the Boyne.

Holy wells were by far the most common of the venerated sites in the county. Despite Cunliffe's contention that wells were invariably associated with female patrons, only eighteen of the eighty-three claimed female saints as their patrons. Perhaps even more significant were the twenty-four wells which claimed no patron saint at all, a clear indication that this transition from pre-Christian to Christian worship was not always as clear cut as it might have been. The fact that there was no patron saint did not seem to disturb the faithful, and the stations went ahead regardless. Such wells were generally known by the name of the area (e.g. Tailteann well); by their medicinal powers (e.g. Tobarnasool in Killallon which was reputed to cure sore eyes) or by their physical location (e.g. Tobar Alta an Easa in Kilmainhamwood, the well at the precipice of the waterfall). Some had more colourful and obviously pagan associations. Near Ratoath was Goban's Well, where the legendary Goban Saor, being thirsty as he passed this way, struck the ground and caused the spring to flow (an almost biblical reference). At Loughan, the venerated well was known as Tobar na Caillige, the well of the hag, while at Castletown there was a well called Tobarnaneenog, the well of the ravens.[11] Tailteann pattern, which occurred on the Celtic festival of Lammas Day near Lughnasa, had no saint associated with it, but it had still vestiges, according to Wilde, of the great Celtic sports occurring there each year.[12]

Nevertheless, it is true that most of the important wells had been Christianised long before the nineteenth century. The most common patron saints for these wells were those who were most closely linked with Irish affection—St Patrick had fifteen wells associated with him, St Brigid had ten, St Columcille had four, seven bore the name Lady Well, while the favourite local saint was St Ultan with three. Therefore, it is uncertain whether these wells came into veneration due to their association with these saints, or whether the early church took them over as its own by using the power and prestige of the names of the saints concerned. It is interesting to note that out of this total of eighty-three, only ten wells were noted for their ability to cure disease or disability. Obviously, this property was secondary in the minds of the people to the concept of the well

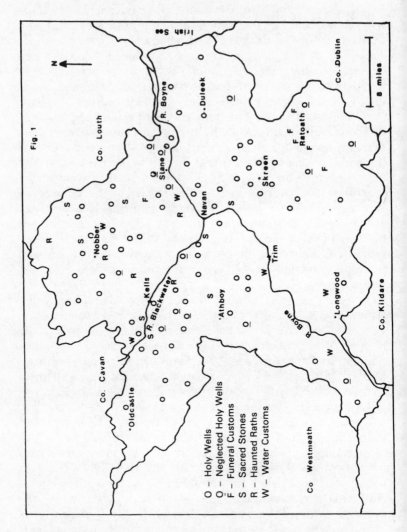

Pilgrimage and other Holy sites in Meath *c.* 1830.
    Source: OSNB; Wilde, *Beauties;* O'Donovan, *Letters;* Outrage Reports.

as a place of worship, when such a great number survived without any miraculous properties.

Not all patterns were held at holy wells, and indeed it is impossible to trace the date of many patterns that did occur at them. Nevertheless, it is possible to trace the dates of ninety-four patterns in Meath, whether at holy wells or elsewhere in the parish. Therefore it is possible to get an indication of how closely these now Christian festivals followed the dates of older, pre-Christian ceremonies. By far the highest concentrations of patterns took place at the harvest period, and often carried names such as Great Lady Day in Harvest. This period, roughly from the first Sunday in August, through the fifteenth of August and up to the last Lady Day celebrations on the eighth of September, accounted for thirty-six of the total (38 per cent). These dates, of course, fall near the period of the great Celtic harvest festival of Lughnasa. This same echo of the past can be found in the thirteen patterns which occur on St Brigid's day, 1 February, the beginning of spring and also the time of the Celtic festival of Imbolc. However, it is dangerous to overstress this point, as the other two great Celtic festivals of Bealtaine (1 May) and Samhain (1 November) were largely ignored as a time for patterns. However, mid-summer, near the solstice, did feature prominently in patterns, with fifteen of the total occurring near this great turning point of the year, or days such as the festivals of St John, St Peter and Paul, and St Columcille. But again the winter solstice was largely ignored for patterns, possibly due to its proximity to Christmas. The most important solely Christian feast day was St Patrick's day, with nineteen patterns.

By the late eighteenth and early nineteenth centuries, a fruitful symbiosis had developed between many of the Celtic feasts and centres of veneration, and the Christian saints and days of worship. The functions of these wells for the people were many and varied. There was an obvious connection between having a well on your land, and the fertility of the land, and such wells were usually jealously guarded. Of course their most famous use was for healing and cures. In Sydden, St Birran's well was said to have cured a cripple, and his litter took root and a tree grew from it over the well. Two wells near Kells without Christian patrons were renowned for curing many diseases, including jaundice.[13] Lady well in Slane cured toothache, and was used as a charm when sprinkled on new-born children and new-bought cows.[14] It was not just people they cured—at Kilmainhamwood, St Patrick's well was famous for curing cattle 'with a swelling in the head' which was very prevalent in Cavan and Meath in the early nineteenth century.[15] These wells had to be treated with respect, or they could take on a life of their own. When a woman washed dirty clothes in St Senachen's well in Dowth, the well removed itself a distance of about three quarters of a mile from its original position.[16]

Patterns were not just religious centres, however. Together with the fair they were also the great centres of social life and entertainment for the community. At Martry pattern, for instance (another without a Christian patron saint), boxing, wrestling and 'other athletic exercises' were carried on, as was the case at Tailteann pattern.[17] In many ways, these were cathartic extravagances, with violence and drunkenness an accepted part of the loosening of the rules of society for the day. Cole Hamilton, a magistrate from Kingsfort in north Meath, displayed in 1815 both his opinion of these festivities and his desire to stop them, when he wrote in his manuscript diary: 'A very thronged pattern at Loyd (Kells) in honour of St Peter's. . . . Broken heads and bloody noses in abundance from the pattern, but was deaf to every complaint'.[18] The police reports for this period are littered with evidence of the extent of violence and disturbances at patterns. At Bective pattern near Trim, in 1822, several riots occurred, to which the military had to be called, with reading of the riot act. At Mornington, near Drogheda, in 1836, the pattern led to a fierce faction fight. At Rossan pattern, near Slane, in 1837 police had to be sent in to prevent the usual rioting. This violence was encouraged by the amount of whiskey available at most of the patterns.[19]

The two most famous patterns and holy wells in Meath were probably St John's well in Warrenstown, and St Kieran's well at Castlekeeran, though for totally different reasons. St John's pattern displayed all the anarchic features of the 'holy fair' with little of its religious qualtities in evidence. When the bishops of Armagh province resolved in 1781 to suppress all pilgrimages, they singled out St John's well for special attention, as being 'attended with such scandalous enormities as to require immediate redress'. Within the next two years, the bishop of Meath and archbishop of Dublin had prohibited attendance at this well

on pain of incurring the most severe ecclesiastical penalties.[20]
As many of the activities at the well had nothing to do with
religion, this seems to have had little effect. When Wakefield
visited it in 1810, he found that 'the Catholic bishop of the
diocese, Dr Plunkett, has done everything in his power to
suppress this meeting, but the superstition and inveterate habits
of the people are not easily overcome. It is attended on by
itinerant friars, as he never authorises any of the clergy of his
diocese to officiate there. . . . It is an annual source of confusion, drunkenness and debauchery, bearing a greater resemblance to a fair than an assembly for the purpose of devotion.'
Violence was no stranger to this pattern, with a young girl being
killed here in a faction fight at the start of the century.[21]

The power of the Catholic church was not easily denied
during these decades, however, and a remarkable transformation occurred in popular attitudes to the well, presumably
because of the influence of the clergy allied to stricter civil
controls. By 1836, no comment was being made on the disrepu-
table nature of the well, instead 'hundreds of Roman Catholics
from the surrounding country meet on the eve of St John to
drink the water and perform stations. Some affirm the lame, the
blind and those who are annoyed with pains get completely
cured'.[22] In its new, respectable and religious form it continued
in existence, with the blessing of the church, until well after the
famine. It was still being visited, and many people were making
the stations in 1886.[23] In fact, the clergy in the form of the
Salesian order, rescued the well from neglect in 1944, and
pilgrims continued to come here at least into the 1970s.[24]

St Kieran's well, near Kells, rivalled the fame of St John's well,
but in this case without any taint of violence or debauchery. St
Kieran's pattern fell on the first Sunday in August, and was
attended by a vast number of pilgrims. Near the well stood an
ogham stone, a ruined monastery and a church, showing the
full gamut of influences there. A special watch was kept for
sacred trout which were supposed to appear in the well near
midnight. These trout were held in such esteem by the people
that when they cleaned the well annually, they removed the fish
and put them back as soon as possible. The well is close to the
river Blackwater, and at midnight before the pattern, men on
horseback would ride across it from one bank to the other, to
keep their horses immune from all danger for the next twelve

months. Two pools of water were near the well, and one was said to cure headache, the other toothache. If both feet were placed in the stream which flowed from the well, it was claimed that it prevented sore feet for the next twelve months. St Kieran's seat itself, a large hollow stone, was known as a cure for backache. Football and athletics were held in a nearby field, while vendors and publicans also did a big trade, but there is no record of any of the abuses associated with St John's well. About 1838, a report spread around Meath and surrounding counties that St Kieran's ash tree, which sheltered the well, was bleeding, and thousands flocked to see it, and to carry away some of the fluid for cures.[25] Again, this well not only retained its reverence through the nineteenth century, but was being visited at least up to the 1970s, although the custom of swimming horses had by now faded away.[26]

This particular folk practice of swimming horses and cattle across rivers to preserve them from harm for the coming year, was, according to Maire MacNeill, almost unique to Meath. It occurred not only at St Kieran's well at Carnaross, but also at the Bridge of the Blackwater near Rathcore, at Broad Boyne Bridge near Stackallen (cattle), and at Kilbride near Nobber, usually on the first Sunday in August. Perhaps the most famous of these rituals occurred at Newtown near Trim, where two thousand people turned out to watch and participate in 1842.[27] One unusual variation on this property of well and river water to cure diseases occurred at Clonard. There a square trough, thought to be the washing place of the ancient monastery, was said to contain water at all times, and this water was believed to cure the illness and prevent the death of geese and all other animals which drank it. It was also an infallible remedy for warts.[28]

Needless to say, superstition and belief in mystical power were not confined to wells and rivers. One of the most obvious remnants of veneration from a pagan past can be seen in the sanctity of some ancient marked stones in the county. Many of these had also been Christianised. The belief in the power of a large hollow stone, called St Kieran's seat, has already been mentioned. Perhaps the most interesting example of this was 'The Stuck Stone' at Killary near Slane, a place which also had its own pattern (without a Christian patron), where Christian ceremonies were held under an upright, standing stone on the top of a small rath or moat.[29] Probably in the minds of the faithful, there was little difference between this and the religious worship which went on at Dunsany, near the remains of an ancient cross.[30] A similar phenomen could be seen at Rathcore where there was a rath, with a stone with two natural holes in the lower part of it. This was called St Laurence's stone, and tradition stated that St Laurence carried it for some distance and laid it down where it then stood. Those with pains in their backs were said to be relieved by laying themselves down on it.[31] The most common explanation given for the veneration of these ancient stones was that they bore the imprint of one of the early Irish saints. One such stone was at Carrick, on the Cavan border, and the indentations on it, which resembled a hand, were said to have been left there by St Columcille when he lifted it.[32] At a holy well near Lismullen, the marks on a flag were said to be caused by St Patrick's knees.[33] Two stones at Muff near Nobber, had an even more elaborate explanation. They bore the marks of the knees and elbows of St Patrick.[34]

These ancient stones could also play a part in the funeral customs of the day. One of these was the equally ancient custom of doing the rounds, or taking a circular path with the corpse. At Slane, there was a very old, probably either Christian or prehistoric tomb, described as consisting of 'two large gable shaped flags, about three foot of which rise above the ground, and separated by an interval of six feet. Each of these stones is grooved, exactly like the gables of a house, the grooves appearing to be intended for the reception of the ends of horizontally inclined flags which formed the roof'.[35] It was close to a holy well, and when funerals were entering the graveyard, they invariably laid the coffin down for a short time at this spot.[36] The Ratoath and Dunshaughlin areas were rich in such funeral customs. At Cookstown, near Ratoath, there was a lone bush banked up with a mound of earth, around which they carried the bodies on the way to the graveyard.[37] In the village of Ratoath, funerals did the rounds at an old cross called the Market Cross. On the Dunshaughlin road outside the village, the coffins were brought around the White Cross, even though the cross had fallen. Further on the Dunshaughlin road stood a tree called the Red Cross tree, although there was no memory of a cross ever having been there. Funerals likewise went around this. These were not the only trees and bushes thus honoured. At Monument Bush at Lismalion and the Big Tree of Rathregan, funerals also did the rounds.[38]

Many superstitions also touched the raths, mottes and other mounds which studded the Meath countryside. Wilde claimed that in Meath 'superstitious reverence attaches. to them in the minds of the peasantry, by whom they are often styled "fairy raths" and fairy circles, and are believed to be now inhabited by, if not the original handiwork of, the "gentry" or "good people", whose music is said to be often heard within their enchanted precincts in the calm summer evenings'.[39] One such haunted rath was at Rahoon, near Castletown, where local people claimed to hear music frequently at night, and that men dressed in military uniform and mounted on horses could also be seen there.[40] At Lisgimmell there was a fort where the locals said lights could be seen frequently at night.[41] People feared to tamper with these mounds. At Connell's Cross, near Emlagh, where a Mr Connell had a public house, he refused to level a fort contiguous to his house to make a good kitchen garden, because of the superstitious observations of his neighbours.[42] At Tierworker, near the Cavan border, lights were often seen on a fort, and music and singing could be heard from it. Local farmers left bits of oats uncut, as food for the fairies in this fort.[43] O'Donovan discovered that 'there is a tradition in this county that all these moats [sic] have caves within them, in which bars of gold are laid up, but it would be dangerous to open them as evil spirits are watching the treasures'.[44] This idea of hollow, treasure-laden mounds, often connected by underground passages is confirmed by the Folklore Commission.[45]

Some people were more fortunate than others in their dealings with the fairies. At Oristown a man called Martin was carried into its 'subterranean abodes' by the 'good people' but returned to tell the tale, and the rath became known as Rath Martinraw.[46] One particularly interesting story, showing the cross fertilisation of pagan and christian comes from Donaghpatrick. Here the underground passage leading to unlimited wealth was not into a rath, but instead under the local Catholic church. The story is the traditional one associated with ill-advised entry of raths:

Not many score years ago, a number of young men and women entered the abode of gold and fairies for the purpose of searching every hole and corner of it for the treasure, and in order to inspire themselves with Irish courage, they took with them a piper and some whiskey. . . . The piper was heard playing (by those outside) until he had come under the church, after which the animating tones of his instrument were hushed to silence. Not one of the party ever returned.[47]

Many calendar customs can be traced in Co. Meath, celebrations on days that had a special potency particularly at the changing of the seasons. These are faithfully recorded by the Folklore Commission, and although they were documented in the twentieth century, they were practices firmly rooted in the past, and were certainly unlikely to have commenced in the post-famine period. Already by the 1920s and 1930s, they were mere memories belonging to the old. One of the periods of the year which had many calendar customs was early November, from Hallowe'en to St Martin's day (11 November), and this may help account for the paucity of patterns at this great turning point of the year, the beginning of winter and the Celtic festival of Samhain. On Hallowe'en night there was a strong belief that the deceased relatives and friends of a family were at liberty to come back, a fire was left burning for them, and an unlit candle was left for them with a box of matches. The family would go to bed early so as not to disturb this return of the dead.[48] The people would start blowing horns on the first of November.[49] At Dunboyne, on St Martin's day, all neighbours were good friends, and there was not a cross word between the bitterest of enemies. No work was done except in the case of extreme necessity. A cock's blood was shed, the oldest cock of the oldest clutch of the year, preferably black. It was to be done by the man of the house, the oldest male member of the family, dressed in his 'best Sunday rig out'. It was believed the man who honoured St Martin most would have the best stock.[50] In Dunshaughlin, on the other hand, the finest and youngest cock in the yard was killed. Its blood was then sprinkled on every door, inside and out.[51] This was a time for 'revels and sports' not only in the human world but also in the fairy world. Singing could be heard in raths on the eve of All Saints' day, and also on May Eve.[52]

May Eve and May Day, signalling the imminent arrival of summer, were also very significant dates for the people. On May Eve, farmers took steps to ensure that their milk and butter would not be stolen by witches during the year, by gathering herbs and flowers by the river banks, boiling them, and smearing them on every cow.[53] This was, of course, the ancient Celtic feast of Bealtaine, and appropriately many bonfires were lit on hills as the sun went down.[54] 'Round berry rings' were shoved onto cows' tails to stop witches stealing the milk.[55] The connection of Bealtaine or May Day with renewed fertility is most obvious at St Kieran's well at Carnaross, even as late as the 1920s and 1930s. The first person to the well on that morning would have plenty of luck, and of butter, for that year. People would tie a green string to the horns of a cow for luck when putting the cows out to grass on May first, which was the day cattle were moved to new grass there.[56] The May bush was decorated and put in front of doors at least into the 1930s at Kilmainhamwood, Bohermeen and Cortown.[57]

Another important period for calendar customs was the end of June, near to the summer solstice and the Christian feasts of St John and Saints Peter and Paul. In north Meath on 23 and 28 June a great many farmers and labourers lit bonfires on the hills nearest to their homes. The night of the 28th had the principal bonfire, with dancing, music and cheering going on late into the night. This was done to bring good luck to the crops and to keep evil spirits or people with the 'evil eye' from doing any injury to them.[58] Bonfires were also lit around Kells,[59] and near Skreen in south Meath, where a piece of the remains of the bonfire was brought home and put into the hearth for luck.[60]

Other customs were also common. St Brigid and St Patrick's crosses were made, and hung inside or over doors for luck, and to keep the 'evil eye' from cattle and the household.[61] At a harvest celebration at the house of Mr Cole Hamilton in September 1811 he remarked that 'in the evening, the labourers, by way of celebrating harvest home, exhibited a rural masquerade under the parlour window, two stiff old fools, cover'd entirely in straw, pretended to dance'.[62] Another custom, though not a calendar custom, shows how the power of the priests had again got intertwined with the popular superstition. Near the aforementioned indented stone at Carrick, on the Cavan borders, the people would carry away portions of clay from a priest's grave, using it as a cure for several diseases.[63]

The Folklore Commission lists literally hundreds of superstitions and beliefs which played an intrinsic part in the lives of the people, in Meath as in other counties. In many cases these beliefs were as solid to the people as their Christian belief. Estyn Evans and Maire MacNeill have claimed that such beliefs are often much older than Christianity, reaching back even as far as the megalithic era during the second millenium BC, and certainly as far as the Celtic roots of the country.[64] A few of these practices, such as St John's well and St Kieran's well, showed remarkable tenacity and lasted into the modern era. These are the exceptions, however, and by the beginning of the nineteenth century a change was taking place in a religious life which was centuries if not millenia old. At least eighteen recorded holy wells (22 per cent) had already been abandoned, wells such as Monknewtown, Drumcondra, Ballyboggan, Dunshaughlin, Balrathboyne,[65] Donaghpatrick, Kells and Kilbeg.[66] These wells were scattered in every part of the county. Many factors contributed to a general decline in patterns. At Nobber, a pattern was ended by magistrates, concerned because of its annual violence.[67] Indeed by the 1830s, the authorities were beginning to take a much more serious view of these centres of possible violence. Police were then sent to those patterns which had a tradition of lawlessness to keep the peace, and undoubtedly that would have caused patterns to lose much of their appeal for a section of the community. The police were sent to patterns at Clonabry, Wilkinstown, Rossan, Sydden, Martry, Stackallen, Trim and Kilbride between 1830 and 1844, often with the military to back them up.[68] Allied to this was the campaign against alcohol, and the success of Fr Mathew, which would have robbed the patterns of some of their boisterousness. Some patterns had been banned by local magistrates or police because of the drunkenness and violence which took place at them (e.g. Tailteann pattern).

However, it was not the action of magistrates which had the ultimate effect on folk practices, but rather a change in attitude on the part of the people, possibly sponsored by an increasing awareness of modern economic and religious realities. It is obvious from the sources of the period that this had begun well before the crackdown in the 1830s.[69] Already by the 1830s, the stations which had been performed at St Seachlain's well could not be recalled in living memory. At Kilmoon, the local people could remember there had been a pattern in the past, but not the date or the saint associated with it.[70] The well at Monknewtown was closed down because a mill was built beside it. The well at Tailteann was finally destroyed by the draining of the boggy field in which it rose. These same stories of neglected and overgrown wells came from all over the country and the change in attitude they illustrated was summed up by the wry comment of O'Donovan about St Patrick's well at Kilbeg: 'when used with proper faith, it possessed miraculous power of curing diseases about a century ago, but (it) is now used only for curing drought'.[71]

This decline in traditional practices affected much more than patterns and holy wells. The funeral customs associated with the Market Cross in Ratoath were talked about in the past tense by O'Donovan.[72] In 1844 the ancient washing place at Clonard, which was said always to contain miraculous water, had to be dug out of the soil of the graveyard, where it lay completely buried.[73] The swimming of horses at Kilbride Bridge, near Nobber, had, because of the interference of a magistrate, been discontinued three years before Wilde visited the spot in the late 1840s.[74] He noted that 'until very lately' none of the people would interfere with raths and, indeed, he knew of 'blood spilled in attempting to force people to demolish an ancient rath'.[75] At Killyon, near the Westmeath borders, all the traditions were extinct by the 1830s.[76] Wakefield commented on the decline by 1812 of the 'Irish howl' or keening at funerals in Meath.[77] The Halls, in 1842, remarked on the decline of the custom which prevented people from cutting down anything which grows on holy ground, 'but this with other superstitions, is wearing away'.[78] The hallowed 'house' of St Columcille at Kells, his ancient oratory, was taken over by a poor family who used it as a base for sheep stealing in the 1830s.[79] Newtown Abbey in Trim, which had stood since 1206, was now feeling the ravages of man. 'Scarcely a day passes but several of the carved stones and portions of doors and windows are rudely torn from their situations, (some) to be used as headstones. . . . Even the ancient tombstones, many of which contain valuable Irish inscriptions, have been removed, defaced or broken'.[80] The Halls were shocked to see this desecration as they believed the peasantry venerated 'every stone connected with ancient places'.[81]

All over the county, elements of the folk practice of the people were dying; sometimes a reason was offered, more often it was not. At Drumcondra, a pattern was held at St Columcille's well, which was ended because of the difficulty of the pilgrimage. Those taking part were obliged to go on their knees from the well to Drumbride Church, a distance of several miles. It was reputed that only one person had ever performed this station.[82] It was not just what the people did in folk practices that was changing, but their general attitudes as well: 'The fine old custom of scolding and calling names is, like the more pernicious one of fighting, banished from society in the present artificial age of hypocrisy'.[83] This new attitude meant nothing was safe. Even the raths on the most famous site in Meath, Royal Tara, were not immune—'(one) was removed the year before last by an inhabitant of Navan, for manure, and we understand a similar act of desecration is meditated towards another during the present season'.[84]

Sir William Wilde, eminent surgeon and antiquarian, and father of Oscar Wilde, was one of the most perceptive and intelligent observers of this change. He tried to explain it: 'Sometimes this spoilation arises from mere curiosity or in order to manure or level the land, and frequently to our knowledge, for the purpose of 'breaking down prejudices' and showing the person no ill luck or misfortune could possibly occur from their destruction'.[85]

The increase in education for the Catholic population is often regarded as central to this idea of 'breaking down prejudice', especially as these Catholic schools were usually stongly supported by the priests and carried the orthodox Christian message, often to the exclusion of all else. Already in 1788 Bishop Plunkett was proud of having over one hundred such schools in Co. Meath. As most of these were fee paying, the majority of students would have been from the medium to strong farmer families, and would be destined to become the most influential in the Catholic community in the years to come. It was usually these men who employed labourers and rented conacre, so their opinions would have mattered. Wilde, writing in 1848, maintained that the dilapidation around Clonard occurred within the preceding twenty-five years, at the time when these early scholars would have been farmers in their own right, and raising their own families.[86] The pace at which folk practices fell into decay matched the pace of mass education, with practices strong up to the end of the eighteenth century in most areas, and then slowly falling away as the nineteenth century progressed.

This growth in mass education began well before the national education system of 1831. In fact, by 1826 there were already 272 schools in the county, a massive increase from the 1780s, catering for 10,722 scholars. Of these, only twenty-eight were free. There were 206 pay schools, with 7,239 scholars, and it was these, together with the Catholic schools maintained with the aid of local subscriptions (twelve schools with 812 scholars) and the Kildare Place schools (twenty-one schools with 899 scholars), which provided the backbone of Catholic education. Many of the other schools were tainted by allegations of proselytising owing to their adherence to scripture readings especially. These were run by organisations such as the Association for Discountenancing Vice (eight schools) and the Erasmus Smith society (two schools). In all there were 211 Catholic schoolmasters working in Meath by 1826.[87] Intimately related to this increase in educational institutions, was the increase in interest in religious education sponsored by the Catholic church itself. By 1780, Dr Plunkett stressed the need for the pastor personally to give at least a short instruction every Sunday. He also made it clear to his priests that it was their duty to teach the catechism personally, even though they might allow a clerk or schoolmaster, who could sometimes be the same person, to teach it.[88] To mobilise the lay believer in this campaign, he also set up the Confraternity of Christian Doctrine in 1796.[89]

Coupled with the growth of education for the peasantry in both temporal and spiritual matters, was a decline in the vernacular tongue of folk beliefs and practices, the Irish language. William Wilde was one of the first to point out that the 'decay of the Irish language is one of the means by which our legends and superstitions have become obliterated'.[90] Garret Fitzgerald, in his work on the minimum numbers of Irish speakers in the early nineteenth century, uses the language returns principally of the 1881 Census to build up a picture of the percentage of children raised as Irish speakers in the pre-famine decades. The figures this furnishes for Meath are especially striking.

Percentage of children raised as Irish speakers in Co. Meath

Decades of Birth:	1771–81	1801–11	1831–41	1861–71
	41%	28%	3%	0%

The decline of the language here was rapid and total. As would be expected, it was the arable areas of north Meath, and the villages and towns in them, which retained Irish the longest, and it was here that folk practices were slowest to die — areas such as Morgallion (20 per cent raised as Irish speakers in 1821–31), Fore (22 per cent), Kells Lower (20 per cent) and Slane Lower (20 per cent). Yet by the traumatic decade which contained the campaign for repeal, and the famine, the eighteen forties, the young even in these areas were no longer getting instruction in Irish. Kells Lower and Fore had fallen to 4 per cent, Morgallion to 2 per cent and Slane Lower to 1 per cent. The Irish language, like folk practices, was entering its twilight years in Co. Meath.[91]

Fitzgerald's analysis is borne out by the other primary sources for the period. By the 1830s, at Donaghmore near Ratoath, only one old man could speak Irish.[92] At Dunshaughlin, little Irish was spoken.[93] At Kilbrew, Crickstown and Cookstown, Irish had almost disappeared.[94] The manuscript census for Navan in Co. Meath in 1821 records the occupation of Charles Byrne as 'farmer, weaver and Irish interpreter', showing the degree to which mastery of the language had become a novelty.[95] Samuel Lewis in 1837 reported that English was spoken throughout every part of Meath. Richard Thompon, in his statistical survey of Co. Meath for the RDS in 1802, recorded the county in the twilight years of the language:

> The English language is pretty generally in use throughout the county, and we seldom meet with any person who is not capable of speaking it with some degree of fluency; yet, when together the peasants all converse, and if they have a story to tell, or a complaint to make, they still wish to be heard in Irish; understanding the idioms of the language better than they possibly can those of English, their story can be conveyed with more expressiveness and of course, work more upon the feelings of their auditors.[96]

The Irish language had been the repository of the concepts, stories and beliefs which were an integral part of folk practices. Maire MacNeill said of these practices that they 'were such an integral part of people's lives, so involved with their notions of welfare, that the church had to adopt them or permit them to survive'.[97] However, the decline of the Irish language did not by itself make the decline in popular superstitions inevitable. Folk practices, the active face of superstition, lasted beyond the life of the language. If they were declining by the middle of the nineteenth century, some having survived Christianisation, Reformation, penal laws and civil wars, this suggests that they were becoming less essential as a part of the people's notion of religious welfare than heretofore. Since the growing power of the Catholic church and clergy is seen as one of the major contributors to this development, the next section of this essay will turn to an examination of the evidence for the position of the Catholic church in Co. Meath by mid-century.

Juxtaposed with the decay of folk practices was the rise to prominence of the Catholic clergy in the social and political structures of this period. This rise in influence and prestige of a group who were opposed to popular superstitions can only have damaged the latter, especially when the former allied with other forces in an authoritarian society, the magistrates and police. Bishop Plunkett consistently preached against wakes and patterns, but there was never an all-out attack on folk practices. Over a period from the 1780s to the 1820s ten per cent of all the sermons recorded in his notebook were directed againt wakes and patterns, which was less than those about drunkenness (17 per cent), cursing (11 per cent) and neglect of religious duties (11 per cent).[98] His object was to make the Catholic community socially, and therefore politically, acceptable. He made this clear in 1803, when he declared:

Since I began my annual inspection of the parishes of Meath . . . a principal object of my humble endeavours has been to enforce the great duty of allegiance we owe to the government under which divine providence has placed us. I have not ceased to represent in the most earnest manner to our own people how closely this duty was connected with honour, their own interest, and above all with the sacred principles which no real Catholic could disclaim; the violation of it by seditious or disloyal practices I have held up to them as a complication of base treachery, of madness, and folly rendered unexcusable by late experience of a kind of apostasy from the religion they profess.[99]

In this fight for acceptance, he saw that the church would have to strive all the harder because of the common prejudice felt by many of the establishment after the upheavals of the 1790s, when defenders and croppies both saw action in Meath:

I have, however, to lament the inveterate prejudice and unrelenting injustice of a certain part of the public here who in defiance of common sense and common policy will not be persuaded that we clergy were not secret abettors of the mad and wicked system which threatened to bury religion under the ruins of the civil power.[100]

It is possible to see how seriously the clergy took their responsibility as peacemakers, and how effective their efforts were, in the police records of this period. These clearly show the priest as one of the major architects of whatever fragile peace existed. Many of the clergy acted promptly to try to keep the peace in their own parishes. In Agher in 1822 Fr Burke prevented his parishioners from joining a raiding mob from Kildare in their quest for arms and money, and kept them 'in most admirable good order' according to Sub-Inspector Despard.[101] In 1824, at Robertstown near Navan, the local priest was so fearful for the safety of a farmer named Bolton, on whom a threatening notice had been served, that he travelled to Dublin to plead with the authorities to send six men to protect him. In the same year, the priest in Duleek constantly denounced from the pulpit 'vagabonds on the bog of Garristown'.[102] In 1829 two priests in Navan interceded to save a man's life in a riot after he had prosecuted two men for murdering a schoolmaster.[103] At Kilmainhamwood in 1830, a major sectarian riot took place between Catholics and Protestants, and only a priest's intervention prevented serious injury.[104] In 1832 Fr Meighan of Longwood was so worried by the build-up of arms in his area that he reported confidentially to Despard, who then seized several hundred stands. In 1835, at

Laracor, Fr Dangan told his congregation that if anyone tried to seduce them into joining illegal associations, they should drag that person before the next magistrate. In 1836, Fr Draper of Longwood, hearing of plans to cut the Grand Canal bank at Blackshade, published the whole matter from the pulpit of Killyon church, thus preventing the outrage. Even Despard was forced to acknowledge the contribution of the clergy to the struggle for peace, especially against secret societies, as 'many of the Roman Catholic clergymen have denounced [Ribbonism] from the altar'.[105]

This same pattern of priests interceding to preserve civil order persisted and there is little sign that it caused them to become unpopular. That they had to preach consistently against the same activities may be taken as an indication of their lack of complete success, but it would be naive to have expected their words to have more effect than the combined powers of the military, magistrates, police, government and landlords, who were also often ineffective in curbing outrage. Their stand must be balanced against the extreme economic and social pressures that afflicted the people, which often prompted these outrages. Yet their determination could have a telling effect, even on Ribbonmen. In 1839, several Ribbonmen left the secret society and received savage beatings for doing so. They left because their parish priest had 'said he would not give the sacrament, or hear their confession, or visit any man dying who belonged to it'.[106]

While the clergy preserved the civil order as best they could, they were often equally prepared to protect the right of their own parishioners when they felt the latter had been wronged. In Oldcastle, when men were arrested on the evidence of herds for poaching hares to supplement their meagre income and diet, those same herds were denounced from the pulpit and pointed out as 'bad subjects in the country and they should be avoided by their neighbours when they met them'.[107] In 1839, at Moynalty, an informer was condemned from the altar and soon afterwards his house burned down. In 1841, the Catholic priest of Ardagh and Drumcondra, Fr McCormack, approached a Mr Fitzpatrick and advised him against taking consolidated land, after he had already exhorted people 'not to work for anyone who would take the poor people's land'. Another unnamed priest followed his example in 1842, denouncing from the pulpit people taking land over other people's heads' and telling his flock not to give their manure for land so taken.[108] Some priests went even further. In 1836, Fr Kennedy was accused of inciting a mob to attack two process servers in his area,[109] while in 1832, the bishop was forced to apologise to the authorities because the curate of Athboy, Fr Birmingham, had organised the rescue of a prisoner.[110]

It appears, then, that on the whole the clergy tried to act as arbiters and peacemakers in their local communities whenever possible, using their considerable influence first against the violence of secret societies and then against those economic abuses which had aroused the anger of their community. They were, as Corish points out, what their society wanted them to be: '"men of power" rather than good men, men of the Christian God'.[111] This power transferred from civil matters into politics, especially where Catholic interests were involved, and that the people often expected the transference is shown by an incident at Trim in 1830. When the parish priest, Fr Clark, and his curate did not turn up for a repeal meeting, threatening notices were sent out to his parishioners not to pay their parish dues, and warnings were also sent to others who did not attend.

The reluctance shown by Fr Clark was certainly not shared by many of his fellow priests in the Navan area. A petition survives which lists the occupation of over forty people who demanded repeal, and the largest single group among these were twelve priests.[112] As repeal retreated temporarily into the background during the greater part of the 1830s, another issue took its place in the minds of many of the clergy, the question of the payment of tithes to the established church. This was felt by many to be an insufferable extra burden on the already tenuous existence of the hard-pressed small arable farmers, and a tax from which they derived no benefit whatever. The clergy were often quick to come to their aid. In 1831–32, Edward Rotherham, a magistrate in Oldcastle, claimed that there 'has been a very great reverse [in social relations] and a great deal of it I attribute to the change in Roman Catholic clergy . . . some [priests] have an appearance of [encouraging] these combinations against tithe. . . . The Catholic clergy are inimical to tithe'. James Napper, a landlord and magistrate with extensive interests in north and

north-west Meath, shared his opinion: 'I certainly consider the
Roman Catholic priests . . . have exceeded what I should conceive was their duty as priests, and have taken a line in politics
which I do not think has tended to their own respectability, and
has certainly excited the minds of the people. . . . Their conduct
generally has tended to promote a very great degree of excitement and agitation'.[113]

By 1832, Catholic chapels were the main venues for anti-tithe
meetings—at Kilmessan, Ardbraccan, Painstown, Trim and
Athboy. Among the most active opponents of title were Fr
Ryan, parish priest of Kilmessan, and five priests from Slane,
Morgallion and Navan areas, and the priests from Trim.[114] In
1833, anti-tithe meetings were being held in Dunshaughlin
chapel.[115] As the fight for the abolition of tithes gained momentum, one of the chief clerical protagonists was Fr O'Reilly of
Trim. Not only was he active in his own parish, but he helped
organise resistance in Kentstown and Stackallen parishes, and
together with the Catholic magistrate, L. C. Smith, it was he
who bought the distrained goods sold at auction in Slane at the
only recorded distraint sale of the year.[116] Clerical opposition
was also fierce in the north of the county where Moynalty was
most disturbed, and collectors were warned to give up their
jobs, and those who refused were denounced from the pulpit.[117]

However, it was the return to prominence of repeal in the
1840s which saw the most organised clerical involvement in
politics. This involvement was encouraged by James Cantwell,
bishop of Meath from 1830, who is reported to have felt

inclined to censure a clergyman or bishop who would not
make a good speech in politics, because the present state of
Ireland was so mixed up with the comforts and happiness of
the people, that he conceived it was the sacred duty of every
man—prelate, priest or layman—to do everything in his
power in advocating the political interest of his country.[118]

Many priests took him at his word. Fr Halligan addressed 500
people at a repeal meeting at Trim[119] in 1841. The local clergy
were active in organising the Kells repeal meeting where over
1,000 attended.[120] In 1842, Fr Keely of Kells took the chair at the
Navan meeting, and addressed a crowd of over 600.[121]

It was in the 'year of repeal', 1843, that the clergy made their most significant contribution to this cause. At the Trim meeting, Bishop Cantwell attended the dinner, while Fr McEvoy, parish priest of Kells, and Fr Halligan, the curate from Trim, were the principal speakers at the meeting of over 5,000 people.[122] This meeting was far outstripped by the Kells meeting, where 20,000 attended. The bishop and many Catholic priests were conspicuous on the stage, and Fr McEvoy spoke once again, together with Fr Kelly, parish priest of Kilskeer. At the Drumcondra repeal meeting, seven priests were on the stage, and the chair was taken by Fr McCormack.[123] Bishop Cantwell and his clergy would also have taken considerable pride in the biggest meeting of all, at Tara, where over a quarter of a million attended.

The performance of the clergy in Meath drove Captain Despard, sub-inspector for the county, to lament that the Catholic clergy were using 'every means in their power to force their flocks to join'.[124] Some idea of the influence of these men can be gleaned from an incident reported in a letter from Fr Kealy to the Repeal Association and published in *The Pilot*. He related how the pastor at Navan happened to mention in the presence of a group of his parishioners his determination to join the Repeal Association. Within the space of a few hours, 150 of his flock had imitated his example.[125] This influence in political and civil matters was at times actively supported by politicians in the county. At a Navan tithe and repeal meeting, Henry Grattan, Protestant MP for the county, exhorted the people always to obey the clergy, and avoid their mutual enemies, the secret societies.[126] This mutual support was further illustrated when the parish priest of Longwood urged the people 'to join in one body and support the Roman Catholic members of parliament'.[127]

The role and influence which the clergy had in politics is reflected in many other aspects of the secular life of the Catholic community. By the early decades of the nineteenth century, Lecky's contention that the Catholic church had replaced the landlords as leaders of their people,[128] had to a large extent been accepted by populace and the authorities alike. The select committee on the state of drunkenness in 1834 maintained that in Meath 'the influence of the priesthood is sufficient to induce people to abstain from ardent liquor' long before Fr Mathew's campaign.[129] Numerous cases of the influence of priests in local affairs came to the attention of Dublin Castle and the authorities. The Devon Commission in 1845 was told by J. D. Balfe, a large farmer from north Meath, that when Protestant landlords set up schools for children of their Catholic tenantry 'the Catholic clergy felt bound to oppose them, and the people joined them . . . with the result that a good deal of the system has been given up in Meath. Lord Darnley has given it up, Mr Waller has given it up, Mr Disney has given it up'.[130]

Anything which militated against social equilibrium—be it secret society, land-hungry tenant, drunkenness or clandestine marriage—was severely frowned upon by the Catholic clergy. In return for this influence, the community expected a certain level of behaviour from a leader who was himself a central part of the same community. If he broke this code of behaviour himself, the attitude of the community was as stern as if he were a farmer or labourer. At Longwood, in 1832, Fr Meagher, the parish priest, took land from Sir William Somerville where tenants had been evicted. In response, Fr Meagher's outhouses were burned, his ditches levelled and a man who persisted in working for him despite warnings was shot and wounded.[131] At Culmullin in 1842, the chapel was closed against the parish priest, Fr Leonard, because he had evicted a Mr Daly and other tenants and consolidated their land.[132] Occurrences like this must be balanced against the evidence for a general harmony between priest and flock. As De Beaumont puts it 'In Ireland, the priest is the only person in perpetual relation with the people who is honoured by them . . . I found that the Catholic clergy were the only persons in Ireland who loved the lower classes and spoke of them in terms of esteem and affection'.[133]

Given the social standing and influence of the clergy in pre-famine Meath, it is little surprise that the levels of Catholic religious observance were high. The *Report of the commission of public instruction* for 1835 furnishes an indication of the frequency of attendance at mass in the area, and makes it possible to see this in relation to the national figures. In Meath, a total of 46.5 per cent of the Catholic population attended mass, conspicuously higher than Larkin's national figure of 33 per cent,[134] and higher than Millar's figure of 40 per cent which is also accepted by Connolly. The Meath figure is even more respectable if it is accepted that up to 25 per cent of the population was prevented from attending mass by being too old, too young or too infirm or ill.[135] This increases the mass attendance rate to over 70 per cent, and the resulting picture of a healthy Catholic church is confirmed by the evidence given by priests when asked by the commissioners if their congregations were falling or rising in numbers. Only two parishes admitted to a fall in numbers attending, while 45 claimed numbers were stationary, and 53 maintained their congregations were increasing. This picture of relative health is compounded if one takes into account the ratio of priests to people for the county, which can also be deduced from the commission's report. The figure for Meath is one priest to 2,475 people, as against Larkin's national figure of approximately one priest for 3,000 people.

The evidence adduced here for the role and power of the Catholic clergy in Co. Meath fits many of the points made by Corish and Connolly. The limited evidence regarding clerical attitudes to folk practices shows Bishop Plunkett's concern to have been with their possible adverse consequences for the recognition of the church as part of 'respectable' society, and so with their social rather than doctrinal implications. As for the power of the church, the priest in Co. Meath was indeed developing an authoritative leadership role in religious, social and political affairs. In line with this, orthodox Catholicism was effectively extending its hold in the county.

The evidence also supports the view that the power of the priest over his flock was far from being unconditional, and depended to a considerable extent on his leading where they were willing to be led. Where they were not willing, his power was limited and his authority did not prevent open hostility against himself if and when he was seen to act against their perceived interests.

The unevenness in the rate of decline of folk practices in Co. Meath, and the fact that they survived more tenaciously in rural than in urbanised areas, and in districts of tillage and mixed farming rather than pasture, points to a complex situation in which it would be difficult to pinpoint any one factor as bearing the main responsibility for this decline. Instead, the Co. Meath situation would appear to be more satisfactorily explained in terms of a process of adaptation by different groups in Irish society to a rapidly changing economic, social and political order. The changing role of the Catholic church and clergy, the decline of the Irish language, and the spread of education can all be seen as playing important roles in this process.

The adaptation explanation directs attention to the community istelf as the central active agent in the abandonment of folk beliefs and practices. In so far as these beliefs and practices were strategies adopted by a community to protect its own interests by exercising what powers it could muster over its environment, they can be seen to have been in growing competition with alternative strategies in the early nineteenth century. In 'modernising' Irish society, various social and economic groups might differ as to what were the most advantageous strategies to protect and advance their particular interests. For some groups 'respectability' and acceptance into the new order, including the development of new skills within the formal political framework, might be realistic aims promising substantial rewards. The goals of orthodox tridentine Catholicism were not dissimilar and an alliance might have a lot to offer, particularly since most of the clergy were themselves members of this social group and could understand and share their objectives. For other groups, lower down the social and economic scale, such an approach might appear too far beyond the bounds of practical possibility to be worth attempting. For them, continued reliance on the old strategies could retain its attraction.

The decline in the Irish language and the spread of education can also be assessed in terms of adaptation and choice of strategy. Further and more detailed local studies of folk beliefs and practices and their decline are needed to develop a fuller picture of the role they played in the lives of different communities at different periods, and of the causes which led to their decline.

10. Religion and opportunity in the Irish police forces, 1836–1914

IN recent years the police forces of nineteenth-century Ireland have attracted the attention of historians. Much of the results of their research has been in line with the findings of similar research into the police forces of nineteenth-century Britain. But the general picture that is emerging is of the essential differences between the Irish and British police forces, whether in recruitment of personnel, training or duties.[1] One of the important topics peculiar to Irish police history is that of confessional rivalry in the various police forces.

Before the reform of the County Constabulary in 1836, it was perceived by most Irish people as a sectarian force. Alexis de Tocqueville in 1835 was struck by the bitter feelings evident between people and police in many parts of the country.[2] Galen Broeker points out that the attitude of the police and peasantry towards each other before 1836 'can only be described as hatred'.[3] This can partly be explained by the role of the constabulary in unpopular duties such as tithe collection, but another important factor in much of the country was clearly the disproportionate number of Protestants in the police. In 1830 only Kerry had a police force composed mainly of Catholic policemen, although even here 60 per cent of the officers were Protestant. In one county, Down, there was not a single Catholic policeman in a force consisting of 136 men and officers. By 1832 Kilkenny, Tipperary and Galway, as well as Kerry, had more Catholics than Protestants in their force, although the officers remained predominantly Protestant.[4] The admission of Ulster police officers in 1835 that many of their men were or had been Orangemen[5] did not help to allay the impression that the County Constabulary was not free from sectarian bias. Although the proportion of Catholics in the constabulary was already slowly increasing in the early 1830s,[6] it was Thomas Drummond, under-secretary from 1835 to 1840, who made the police membership more representative of the population in general by encouraging Catholics to join following the re-organisation of the County Constabulary as the Irish Constabu-lary in 1836 (called the Royal Irish Constabulary from 1867).[7]

A general code of conduct, completed in 1837, went to some lengths to remove the taint of partiality from the new force.[8] The sixth article of the new code stipulated that 'above all, both officers and men are to avoid, in every respect, the most remote appearance of partisanship, or the expression of sectarian or political opinions'.[9] Recruits to the constabulary had to swear an oath that they were not members of secret societies, with the exception of the freemasons,[10] a requirement designed to keep out both Orangemen and Ribbon partisans. To ensure freedom from local bias policemen were not allowed to serve in their native county or in any county in which they were 'connected by marriage or otherwise'.[11] The policeman was also forbidden to serve in or near a district in which 'any relation or connexion [sic] of his keeps a shop, or is otherwise engaged in public business'.[12] The constabulary authorities were careful when allocating men to stations to see that the religious denomina-tions of a county's police force reflected as much as possible the religion of the county's civilian population. Two observers in the 1840s pointed out that most police in Ulster were Protestants, while most in the rest of the country were Catholics.[13] Accord-ing to a later source, Sir Duncan McGregor, the inspector-general of constabulary from 1838 to 1858, tried to accommodate the men in barracks in the proportion of two Catholics to three Protestants, or vice versa, to prevent the fears (or hopes) of the local population that the police were the creatures of one faction or another.[14]

It is unlikely that it was possible to follow such a precise guide-line to the letter—the 1872 constabulary code, laid down some years after McGregor's retirement, simply stated that 'The proportion between men of different religious persuasions at each station is to be as nearly as possible the same as that which exists throughout the whole force of the county'.[15] This regula-tion still shows the anxieties of the authorities that the force should not be considered obnoxious by the local population, on sectarian grounds. Although professing a neutrality in religious matters, the constabulary authorities stipulated that all men and officers (and, if they were married, their wives and children) be regular attenders at 'divine service', each sub-inspector to vouch in his monthly report for the attendance of himself and his men. They added that 'any man who is negligent of these his highest obligations cannot be regarded as trustworthy in other respects'.[16] County inspectors were told that 'no man ought, if it can be avoided . . . to be kept longer than twelve months at any post which is not within a reasonable distance of his place of worship'.[17]

It is clear, in their efforts to blend their men in with the local population and their encouragement to their subordinates to feel part of a neutral Christian rather than narrow sectarian organisation, that the constabulary authorities were determined to avoid some of the mistakes of the pre-1836 force. They were successful, to the extent that the post-1836 constabulary was accepted by the population to be non-partisan, although this was not necessarily considered an improvement by some Ulster people.[18] The proportion of Catholics in the new force was strikingly higher than in the County Constabulary, especially in the lower ranks. In 1841, slightly over 51 per cent of the rank and file were Catholics,[19] a figure which increased gradually throughout the nineteenth century. By 1851 the figure stood at 64 per cent, by 1861 it was about 69 per cent, in 1871 it was just over 70 per cent, by 1881 73 per cent; and by 1914 almost 81 per cent were Catholics.[20] Although Catholics predominated in the rank and file from the start, the higher non-commissioned ranks continued to be held by Protestants for some years, until the policy of merit-promotion in the ranks tilted the balance in favour of Catholics. It was not until 1851 that most of the constable ranks were held by Catholics, with 866 out of 1,721 positions; by 1863 Catholics predominated in the rank of second class head constable, with 152 out of 310 positions, while it was not until 1871 that Catholics held most posts in the highest non-commissioned rank, that of first class head constable, with 38 out of 67 positions.[21] In 1859 Sir Duncan McGregor explained that the discrepancy between the proportion of Catholics in the rank and file and their non-attainment of a commensurate proportion of the higher non-commissioned ranks was the result of the long service of the original 1836 head constables and constables, most of whom were Protestants, but that such discrepancy was bound in the long term to be done away with as the numerically stronger Catholic sub-constables achieved long service and became entitled to fill the higher ranks.[22]

In the post-1836 constabulary much was made of the claim that, in their dealings with each other, the policemen of various religious denominations were remarkably free from sectarian bias. Inspector-general Brownrigg claimed in 1863 that 'there is an absence in the force of any manifestation of sectarianism — Protestant and Catholic alike discharging duties at the same station with, so far as I can learn, entire harmony amongst themselves'.[23] Visitors to Ireland often echoed this claim, both as regards the constabulary and the Dublin Metropolitan Police.[24] Such claims appear an accurate enough appraisal of the behaviour of the men towards each other; there are some rare examples of ill-feeling based on religious grounds, but these are so rare that they scarcely serve as qualifications to Brownrigg's general claim. Often these exceptions to the general rule involved drink. On 11 February 1853 two Co. Clare sub-constables were dismissed for 'improper manifestation of sectarian feeling on the public road, and being under the influence of liquor'; on 14 February 1853 a Co. Meath sub-constable was dismissed for 'grossly insulting another sub-constable on account of his religion', and on the 19th of the same month a Co. Cavan sub-constable was dismissed for 'threatening and assaulting a comrade from sectarian feelings'. In June 1860 a Queen's County sub-constable was dismissed for drunkenness and 'using offensive party expressions'.[25] In June 1871 two Co. Limerick sub-constables were dismissed over a dispute they had held 'relative to the merits of their respective prayer books'.[26]

Despite the paucity of instances of open sectarian feeling in the constabulary, periodic discontent arising from perceived religious discrimination is one of the minor threads one picks up from a study of Irish police history. Their protestations of impartiality notwithstanding, the police authorities were at times partly responsible for such feelings of discontent. At the height of the repeal agitation in September 1843, when Chief Secretary Eliot complained to the home secretary, Sir James Graham, that the lord lieutenant had failed to appoint a Catholic police officer over the past 12 or 14 appointments, Graham replied to him that this was necessary to combat the 'pernicious influence' of doubtful officers, 'especially at the present moment, when the arts and power of the Roman Catholic priesthood are exerted to shake the fidelity of the armed force in Ireland, and in particular of the constabulary'.[27] Lord de Grey later denied to Graham that Catholic *officers* had ever given him grounds for alarm, and claimed that 'some of the most valuable and trustworthy [officers], and those who stand in the highest confidence of the inspector-general, are Roman Catholics', but added that,

> As regards the *men* there is a difference. We know that some of them have been tampered with; and though I as lord lieutenant have nothing to do with the enrolment of recruits, I know that Colonel Macgregor did not feel it safe to increase the number of Catholics.[28]

A year later the home secretary admitted to the Duke of Wellington that the constabulary,

> notwithstanding its military organisation and military discipline . . . are not held to be entirely trustworthy, on account of the large proportion of Roman Catholics, and the influence which daily intercourse with a disaffected population cannot fail to exercise, in a religious struggle, on members of the same communion.[29]

Given these attitudes, it is hardly surprising that from 1841 to 1847, by which time it was clear that the repeal campaign was on the wane, only 25 out of 85 officers appointed below the rank of county inspector were Catholics, and four of these were to the 'safe' position of paymaster. Nine Catholics were appointed during 1847, a 'safe' year as far as repeal was concerned; in contrast there were no Catholic officer appointments in 1842, and only one in 1843.[30]

The under-representation of Catholics in the officer ranks of the constabulary often gave rise to whispers of discontent, especially at times when there were already widespread feelings of anger over poor service conditions. In the 1850s none of the officers above the rank of county inspector were Catholics. In 1850 only three out of 37 county inspectors were Catholics, and none of these were of the first class. In 1854 there were no Catholic county inspectors, and for the other years from 1852 to

1858 there was only one Catholic county inspector, who was never of the first class.[31] In the same decade Catholics held between 23 per cent and 25 per cent of sub-inspector positions.[32] By 1892 their share of county inspectorships had risen to five out of 38, but Catholics then held only 18 per cent of district-inspectorships.[33] By 1914 Catholics held four out of 37 county inspectorships and, due partly to a rule introduced in 1895 of reserving half of the district inspectorships for the (mainly Catholic) head constables, Catholics held 45 per cent of district inspectorships.[34]

The question of the religious breakdown of the officers was of importance to the men, as there were often rumours of favouritism shown by officers to men of their own creed. A committee of enquiry into conditions of service in the Royal Irish Constabulary in 1872 was told by one policeman that the fact that most officers were Protestants, meant that Catholic officers went out of their way to be stricter on their co-religionists: 'Considering the number of officers at headquarters who are Protestants, the Roman Catholic officers are afraid to do their duty to their own co-religionists. To show their impartiality they really become partial.'[35] Another sub-constable claimed that most of the men wanted the superior officers to be 'half and half of the same religion, as it would cause them to have more confidence in the decisions they give in cases'.[36] Concerns about the imbalance between a mainly Catholic rank and file and a mainly Protestant officer group were expressed more frequently in the early 1880s. These were often combined with fears about the influence of Freemasonry in the force. For example a Constable O'Hara, serving in Co. Armagh, told the 1882 committee of enquiry into the R.I.C. that

> Freemasonry in the service is causing universal dissatisfaction. The Catholic portion of the service is prohibited by the head of their church from joining the craft, and they believe that the officers, who are nearly all Freemasons, do everything in their power to get a sub-constable who is a mason either promoted or transferred to a favourite station.[37]

A constable serving in Co. Derry told the committee that 'it is the feeling of a great many, whether rightly or wrongly, if a young man is promoted, and he happen to be a Freemason, to attribute his promotion to that fact.[38]

The theme was also taken up in anonymous letters to the newspapers. For example 'Justice' complained on 3 May 1880 that 'the officers of the force, who are almost all Protestants and Freemasons . . . recognise only the claims and consider the interests of those who are of their own creed or who are brother masons'.[39] 'A Wexford Sub' complained that the higher ranks were 'nearly monopolised by the favoured creed', and that while a Catholic policeman 'will consider himself lucky if he aspires to the rank of constable, his Protestant comrade will not be satisfied with anything less than head constable or sub-inspectorship'.[40] The complaints of the anonymous letter writers were echoed by a Presbyterian sub-constable serving in Roscommon in 1882 who complained that promotions in the R.I.C. were due to 'sectarianism, favouritism, and flunkeyism'. He added that sectarian influence 'does not go all the one way', implying that it worked to the advantage of Catholics as well, but concluded that, 'as a rule, the Protestants get far greater advantages that way than the others'.[41] The county inspector for Cork West Riding admitted that such fears were general throughout the force, regardless of their validity.[42]

It is impossible to prove that sectarian influences materially affected a man's career in the R.I.C. It *can* be shown that for almost every year from 1841 to 1914 Catholics were more likely to be punished by dismissals, fines or disratings than their Protestant fellows, but it would be misleading to assume that discrimination accounts for this fact; most of the lesser ranks were filled by Catholics in this period, and it was notoriously the younger, less-experienced sub-constable who was most likely to be guilty of breaches of discipline.[43] The charge of sectarianism seems to have more validity when we examine the Belfast Borough Police, founded 1845, who were responsible for the policing of Belfast until their abolition and replacement by the Irish Constabulary in September 1865. Of 160 men in the force in 1864, only five were Catholic, and all of the officers — two chief constables, 12 inspectors and four acting inspectors — were Protestants.[44] The chairman of the Belfast police committee, responsible for hiring Belfast's policemen, unconvincingly tried to explain this state of affairs by asserting that Protestants in counties Down and Antrim, the main sources of recruits, were 'generally stronger than the lower classes of the Roman Catholics ',[45] and therefore more suitable as recruits.

The committee did not cast its net very widely when looking for recruits: five of its force were natives of Ballinderry, eight came from Drumbo, nine from Derriaghey, 17 from Magheragall and 23 came from Glenavey, 'an Orange walking district'.[46] Interestingly, one recruit who joined the force in the 1850s, named Pope, was a Presbyterian convert from Catholicism who had left the Irish Constabulary because 'he could not get peace from the Roman Catholic sergeant who was over him'; he managed to get a transfer to Newcastle, but 'they were treated him worse there, and called him a "Souper"'. His application to join the Belfast force caused some 'jocularity' to the police committee, on account of his name, but he was accepted as he was 'a good Presbyterian' and had 'left the papists'.[47] The Belfast force was abolished because it was believed, following riots in 1857 and 1864, to be hostile to the Catholic portion of the population.[48]

In the late 1850s, at the same time that the Belfast Borough Police was coming under the close scrutiny of the Dublin Castle authorities, the Dublin Metropolitan Police (founded in 1836) was being subjected to the same treatment, and for the same reason—allegations that it was an intrinsically sectarian force. As early as 1858 the Irish executive had made a determined bid in parliament to abolish the D.M.P. and have Dublin city and its suburbs policed by what it perceived as the less partisan Irish Constabulary. At first glance it seems surprising that allegations of sectarianism should have been raised against the D.M.P. The Dublin force was modelled closely on the London Metropolitan Police, so much so that it even used the same type of books for registering recruits, in which there was no column for a candidate's religion, so the question never arose.[49] When questioned in 1839 as to the denominational make-up of his force, one of the two D.M.P. chief commissioners, John Lewis O'Ferrall, replied that 'It is very hard to state that accurately; we apprehend there are from 300 to 400 Protestants, and from 600 to 700 Roman Catholics', but he could not give more precise figures.[50] The other chief commissioner, Major George Brown, claimed that the men of different religions, whatever their numbers might be, got along quite well together: 'I never know religious dissension among them; in fact the duties of our police are so severe that they have scarcely any time to think about those things'. He added: 'I am sure any man of the force would arrest the Pope or the archbishop of Canterbury if directed, they are so free from political bias'.[51]

The first exact figures we have of the number of Dublin policemen of different religious persuasions date from February 1857, as a result of a 'private enquiry' ordered by the lord lieutenant, the earl of Carlisle. This ascertained that out of a total force of 1,092 officers and men, there were 135 Protestants and 957 Catholics. Protestants made up slightly more than 12 per cent of the D.M.P. rank and file, but filled 21 per cent of the officer ranks.[52] This over-representation in the officer ranks was partly a consequence of the early recruitment of the D.M.P., when selected men were brought in from the London Metropolitan Police to give the fledgling force a backbone of experienced officers: most of those sent over to Dublin by the commissioners of the London Metropolitan Police happened to be Protestants.[53]

Despite what appears to have been a rather favourable position for Protestants in the D.M.P., there were numerous claims in the 1850s that the Dublin force was permeated with an anti-Protestant bias. Such claims came from both inside and outside the force. The first slight indication of the existence of hostility on religious grounds towards the D.M.P. which this writer found was in the case of a drunken coppersmith from Kevin Street, who was arrested in July 1851 after emerging from a public house in Golden Lane and shouting out 'To hell with the pope and popery and the bloody papist police – I will have £5 a head for shooting them shortly.'[54] Feelings of hostility towards the mainly Catholic D.M.P. by a section of Dublin's Protestant population were probably intensified as a result of a series of incidents on the day of the arrival of a new lord lieutenant, the earl of Eglington, on 10 March 1852. As the lord lieutenant's procession was passing Trinity College one of the students tied a large orange handkerchief, bearing a representation of King William, to a lamp post at the college gates. This led to 'great excitement among the population in the street', so Constable 159 D removed the offending object. His action merely heightened the excitement, and led to a three-way affray between police, a 'large body of students', and bystanders, as a result of which four students were arrested for assault and obstruction and fined on the same day by magistrates.

On the release of the offenders from custody a large crowd of students marched to King William's statue at College Green, again to the annoyance of a crowd of onlookers, but were dispersed by a detachment of the 'B' division of police under Inspector Walpole. Later that night a crowd of nearly 200 students attempted to march around the statue but were stopped by a party of about forty police and some arrests were made; other prisoners were taken when more students came out of the college and attempted to rescue those who had been arrested. Later still an even larger gathering of students attempted to march around the statue, and came into collision with the police. The *Freeman's Journal* states that 'several of the students were provided with sticks, which they freely used', and more than twenty were lodged in College Street station as a result of the night's proceedings.[55] Resentment over the conduct of the police undoubtedly festered with some of the student body. In May 1854, when two Trinity students who were 'roaring, shouting, and creating noise and disturbance' in French Street were threatened with arrest by Constable 83 B if they did not go home quietly, they replied to him, 'Of course you will bring us up before [Magistrate] Hugh O'Callaghan and trump up a popish story against us.'[56]

These undercurrents of hostility towards a police force considered by certain Protestants to be excessively composed of Catholics came out in the open later in the 1850s. Some time around November 1856 the Jesuits of Gardiner Street chapel, aware that Catholic policemen often had difficulties in regularly attending at church, due to their hours of duty, began to invite Catholic D.M.P. men to attend at their chapel 'at hours most convenient to the police, however inconvenient to the clergy'.[57] Apparently many of the D.M.P. took up the offer of the Gardiner Street priests, because in November 1857 the *Daily Express*, the leading Conservative journal in Ireland,[58] proclaimed the following:

It is a startling fact, to which we have often thought of directing the attention of the public, that considerable detachments of the metropolitan force have been in the habit of attending the establishment of the Jesuits in Gardiner Street in this city. They have been observed going there in groups, in their uniform, regularly, so early as five o'clock in the morning—for what purpose it is not difficult to conjecture. . . . They cannot need the spiritual guidance of a foreign society, so notoriously hostile to the state, and so justly obnoxious to the great body of the Protestants of the country. To say the least, it is an extremely suspicious circumstance that the body which is armed and paid to preserve the peace—our 'National Guard' we may well call it—should be placed to any extent under the spiritual 'direction' of a society which, above all others in the Church of Rome, is sworn to labour for the subversion of every Protestant state in the world, and of England above all.[59]

Bearing in mind the recent Sepoy mutiny in India, the article went on to ask: 'Who knows at what hour of England's peril a Nana Sahib, who has been smiling blandly among the most obsequious in the gay circle of the viceregal court, may suddenly stand unmasked as the perfidious and cruel chief of the revolted constabulary of Ireland?'[60]

It is not without coincidence that George Browne, the Protestant commissioner of the D.M.P., chose this time to make a series of allegations about discrimination against Protestants in the force he jointly commanded with the Catholic commissioner John Lewis O'Ferrall. Browne claimed that 'the great evil of the force arises from the thorough conviction of the Protestants in it that they have not fair play'. He and the Protestant D.M.P. men believed that 'slight offences would be reported by Catholic officers, if committed by Protestants, when the same offences would not be reported if committed by Roman Catholics'. Citing the example of a Protestant acting-inspector whom a Catholic sergeant spotted coming out of a brothel, he said it was his belief 'and that of all the Protestants in the service, that if the acting inspector had been a Catholic, he would not have been reported'. Commissioner O'Ferrall offered a detailed refutation of Browne's general statements about the unfair treatment of the D.M.P.'s Protestant policemen, which appears to have been accepted at first by the chief secretary,[61] but the issue of sectarian bias in the D.M.P. was to be raised just three months later in March 1858, and to be used by the conservative government in the attempt to abolish the force.

The immediate spark to the controversy was another clash between the Dublin police and the students of Trinity College. On 12 March 1858, on the occasion of the entry to Dublin of the lord lieutenant, the Earl of Eglington, a group of Trinity students were engaged in a high-spirited display of noise-making accompanied by throwing oranges and 'squibs', which frightened the horses of the mounted police but amused the spectators at College Green. After commissioner Browne was struck by an orange, he ordered the police to disperse the students, which they did with some brutality, including a charge by sabre-wielding mounted policemen. Many of the students were hurt as a result of the police charge.[62] Three days later the lord lieutenant was informed that the Trinity students were convinced that the men of the 'B' division of police 'bear a decided hostility to them, to their principles and religion', and that 'if they do not go prepared to meet any attack that may be made on them (similar to the late one) either their lives may be endangered or their persons seriously injured'.[63] According to Under-Secretary Thomas Larcom it was the Trinity College fracas which convinced Lord Naas of the need to amalgamate the D.M.P. with the Irish Constabulary.[64]

When Naas, chief secretary for Ireland, introduced his bill for this purpose on 15 June 1858, most of his speech concentrated on the alleged benefits of an amalgamation of the two largest Irish police forces. However, in one minor passage of his speech he introduced a controversial religious element which was to prove fatal to the successful passage of his bill:

> Both the Belfast and Dublin police forces were open to the grave objection of containing an undue proportion of men of the same religion, which was particularly objectionable in a country like Ireland, where the population was divided between two religions, because it gave a sectarian character to the force, which it was most desirable to avoid.[65]

On 8 July he went further, by stating that 'the Dublin force is to a great extent—to an extent which I think improper—Roman Catholic'.[66] Such statements by the effective head of the administration in Ireland robbed the issue of amalgamation of whatever merits it may have possessed in the minds of most people in Dublin, and the issue became a straightforward confessional one. J. Lambert, a member of Dublin corporation, claimed on 1 July 1858 that if the bill were defeated, 'the Protestant party in Dublin may for ever hold down their heads. Mr. Commissioner O'Ferrall and the Jesuit fathers of Gardiner St. and the Dublin police may be called our governors'.[67] A song entitled 'The Popish Police' was sung in some Protestant circles, one extract from which amply illustrates its theme:

> Nay, his number, six hundred and sixty and six!
> Good heavens! when will warnings and prodigies cease?
> In bright letters of brass, we have all seen it pass,
> On the collar of one of the Popish Police.[68]

Catholic opponents of the bill were scarcely more restrained. Alderman Reynolds, formerly a critic of the D.M.P. force, considered it bad grace to dredge up their past errors 'when those men are on trial for their religion'.[69] Most Dublin city councillors, and the *Freeman's Journal*, took the same view.[70] In the face of what the *Freeman's Journal* claimed was the opposition of nine-tenths of the city of Dublin to the bill, the government withdrew the proposal as unworkable.[71]

With the failure of the bill, Naas ordered Colonel Henry Atwell Lake, who had just succeeded Browne as chief commissioner on his retirement, on a recruiting mission especially designed to attract Protestant recruits. By the end of November 1858 some 40 Protestant recruits were signed up, 37 of these coming from Ulster.[72] In 1859, the first full year of this special recruiting drive, Protestants comprised almost 31 per cent of all D.M.P. recruits.[73] This was to be the year with the highest proportion of Protestant recruits; throughout the 1860s and 1870s Protestants made up approximately 13 per cent of all recruits, in the 1880s they made up almost 21 per cent, in the 1890s around 19 per cent, and from 1900 to 1914 they made up 11 per cent of all recruits.[74] Are we to conclude, then, as Lord Naas did in July 1858, that Protestants did not join in greater numbers because they objected to joining a mainly Catholic body?[75] While this is one possible explanation, it appears to this writer to be an inadequate one: such an objection could equally have been raised against joining the Irish Constabulary, yet

Protestants continued to join it in large numbers throughout the period. It seems that until the early 1880s service conditions in the D.M.P. were simply not attractive enough to draw recruits away from mainly Protestant Ulster: D.M.P. men were much more likely to be assaulted than their Irish Constabulary counterparts, service in Dublin was much tougher than in the towns and rural areas of Ireland, and complaints over inadequate pay were frequent from the 1850s onwards. An Ulster Protestant (or Catholic) was much more likely to join the Irish Constabulary where at least he would be stationed in a county near to his home;[76] it is no coincidence that until the early 1880s, the D.M.P. was recruited overwhelmingly from Leinster, and especially the counties nearest to Dublin—most Catholic *and* Protestant recruits were Leinster men.[77] Significantly, it was only in 1883, when conditions of service in the D.M.P. had been greatly improved by the legislature, that Ulster Protestants outnumbered Protestant recruits from the rest of Ireland. This continued for most of the years until the turn of the century, by which time discontent once again increased in the D.M.P., and the number of Ulster Protestant recruits fell dramatically.[78]

As stated earlier, it was usually at times when there was widespread discontent about pay and general conditions that claims about religious discrimination in the police forces came to the fore. Often policemen accounted for what they considered to be their unhappy lot by alluding to the sinister machinations of unseen forces. This is certainly the case with the anonymous writer of the pamphlet *Promotion in the Royal Irish Constabulary* (1906), who, the internal evidence suggests, was almost certainly a policeman. He re-echoed the claims of many R.I.C. men in the early 1880s as to the advantages enjoyed by Protestants and Freemasons when it came to promotion.[79] Suspicions about favouritism in the R.I.C. were especially intense in Belfast at the turn of the century. A commission appointed to examine conditions of service which particularly affected members of the R.I.C. in Belfast, but whose findings were suppressed by Chief Secretary Birrell at the request of Inspector-General Neville Chamberlain, pointed out that owing to the large numbers of men serving in Belfast—1,065 men in 1906—and the small number of sergeants, most of whom were slow to retire, competition for promotion was particularly keen there, and the promotion rate slower than in the rest of the country.[80] The force consisted of 561 Protestants (53 per cent) and 495 Catholics (47 per cent) and, as far as the commission could see, there were no reasonable grounds for assuming a sectarian character behind the workings of Belfast's police force. The men did not see things this way, however; the commission pointed out that both Catholics and Protestants complained that their 'side' was entitled to a larger share of promotions. There was particular controversy over the allocation of the 26 station sergeantships, with 18 filled by Protestants and eight by Catholics.[81]

Regarding relations between the men, Head Constable William Cassidy told the commission: 'I do say there is a little party feeling in the force in Belfast. There are some stations it does not exist in, but there are a great many [in which] it does'.[82] Writing shortly after the Belfast police strike of 1907,[83] the Belfast R.I.C. town commissioner stated that the three great difficulties for the maintenance of discipline in the city were the hours of duty, which prevented officers from seeing the men frequently, the considerable numbers of police living together in large barracks, and 'the sectarianism which prevails locally and which, after a time, is apt to affect men living amid such surroundings'.[84] In his opinion the latter factor would prevail 'so long as sectarianism exists in Belfast', and surprisingly he suggested that the only remedy was 'the prompt transfer to another part of Ireland of any man who gives evident proof of having been tainted with sectarianism'; the regulations stated that such a man should be dismissed, but the inspector-general apparently endorsed the town commissioner's suggestion.[85] The feelings of rivalry between the denominations in the Belfast R.I.C. must have been fairly apparent at this time, because even a German observer of the British and Irish police systems noted in 1908 that only in Belfast did the men of various denominations keep a jealous eye on promotions.[86]

The R.I.C. authorities greatly reduced the standards for recruits joining their force at the turn of the century, especially the educational requirements, in an endeavour to compensate for falling numbers of applicants.[87] Such lowering of standards may account for the reports of sectarian feelings amongst some of the Belfast men. The problem does not seem to have been confined to Belfast. Constable Thomas Healy of the Ballymena

R.I.C. told the 1914 R.I.C. committee of enquiry that the recruits, especially from Ulster, were of a very poor stamp:

> They are themselves, and so are their fathers, brothers, and relations, either rabid Orangemen, or low-class Ribbonmen; call them Molly Maguires, or whatever else you wish, the terrible fact that they are totally unfit to be admitted to the service remains unaltered. In some barracks in Antrim and Derry the most melancholy exhibition of sectarian bitterness prevails, and the promoters and participants in this unseemly conduct are the men admitted in recent years to the ranks of the service. The sergeant's influence to restrain them seems in many cases unavailing. If he threatens to report one of these characters for such unseemly conduct, his own position is made intolerable. The theory that he is a tyrannical bully is disseminated broadcast, and the associates of his subordinates plan, and sometimes succeed in effecting his ruin, so that he, very often, considering his own prospects, deems it wiser to permit irregularities inside than come into conflict with violent partisan leaders outside.[88]

The members of the committee expressed their 'regret' that the constable should have raised such a topic, but it does tie in with the suppressed and secret police evidence concerning the R.I.C. in Ulster which we have already seen. It was not the first time, nor was it to be the last, that an Irish police force had to address the problem of sectarianism in its ranks.

11. *Monaghan Protestants in a time of crisis, 1919–22*

IN 1919 the Unionists of Monaghan—effectively the twenty-five per cent of the county's population that was Church of Ireland or Presbyterian—could scarcely have been less prepared to cope with the growth of lawlessness and disorder spreading throughout the country as the Republic, which was reaffirmed by Dáil Éireann in the same year, began to enforce its claim to be the legitimate government of Ireland. The Anglo-Irish War was to be the occasion of the last, but also the most bitter, manifestation of hostility to be directed against Unionists there by their Nationalist neighbours. It came at a time when local Protestants were most vulnerable to a co-ordinated attack aimed at removing the last pedestals of Unionist power within the county, for political, social and economic developments in the preceding half century had left them largely devoid of organisation and leadership.

Less than a decade previously, Unionist organisation in Monaghan had reached its zenith when five thousand men signed the Solemn League and Covenant in 1912.[1] This was essentially a symbol of their alignment with their co-religionists in the rest of Ulster bent on the resistance, by force if necessary, to Catholic aspirations to be ruled by a Nationalist government in Dublin. However, the subsequent formation of Unionist clubs and the Ulster Volunteer Force only served to antagonise local Nationalists. The latter in turn flocked to the National Volunteers which were seen as 'a protection and means of defence against the hotbloods of the North'.[2] The motivation of the National Volunteers in Monaghan had been made quite clear by the then chairman of the county council, Thomas Toal, when, at the inaugural meeting in Monaghan town in January 1914, he stated that Catholics 'would not allow them [Protestants] to trample on them as they had done in the past'.[3]

For some time before the formation of both these rival forces, political influence in the county had been placed very much in the hands of Catholics. The franchise and redistribution legislation of 1884 and 1885 left Monaghan with a northern and a southern constituency, each with a clear Catholic majority, while the Local Government Act of 1898 enabled the Catholic majority to obtain useful administrative experience, and at the same time gave Nationalists countrywide an added incentive to seek complete self-government. The new county council, which became a predominantly Roman Catholic, Nationalist body, was a great source of anxiety to local Unionists in whose opinion it was being used as a means to remove Protestants completely from the power bases in Monaghan. In 1912, a member of the gentry and a leading Unionist, J. C. Madden, pointed out that:

We who live here know the Local Government Act has been used to keep us out of every office of profit in our county. . . . Wherever a place is going to which a salary is attached then I say the principle acted upon is that no Unionist need apply.[4]

Madden's statement was not exaggerated for in the previous year Nationalists had been awarded all available clerical and professional positions, thirty-seven in all, by the county council,[5] while a study of the minutes of the same body shows a consistent trend in this direction right up to the formation of the Free State.

While the outbreak of World War I averted a situation which could have resulted in civil war, it merely postponed until 1919 the looming sectarian clash in the county. The total unpreparedness of Unionists for the forthcoming conflict was a direct consequence of events during the intervening years. The determination of Protestant leaders in Monaghan to maximise the war effort resulted in an almost total demise of Unionist organisation there. By 1915, the Unionist clubs and UVF in the county were totally inactive.[6] Equally detrimental to the Unionist cause was the cleavage which developed between the rank and file of the movement and their traditional gentry leaders. Unlike their co-religionists elsewhere in the province, the former hung back from recruitment with the result that their complacency on the subject incurred the wrath of the gentry. Largely for economic reasons, it did not suit the prospering

Protestant farmer or businessman who had backboned the UVF to respond to their leaders' recruiting calls.[7] The leaders, in turn, became totally disillusioned with Carson, Craig and the other members of the Ulster Unionist Council because of another development during the war years—the partition crisis. This crisis ultimately resulted in the Unionists of Monaghan being 'thrown to the wolves' by the members of the UUC determined to safeguard for themselves a politically reliable area in the shape of the six north-eastern counties of the province. The consequent feelings of desertion and betrayal experienced by Unionist leaders in Monaghan were unprecedented, and their attitude towards their former Ulster leaders changed from respect to disgust. Their feelings of alienation meant they no longer had either the incentive or the heart to organise Unionist activity in the county at a time when it was most needed. For local Protestants were soon to realise that they, because of their past, their politics, their religion and their large stakes in the county, had most to fear from the growth of lawlessness and intimidation which characterised the War of Independence there.

By 1919 Unionist fears of being governed by a Nationalist parliament in Dublin had been heightened by the growth of Sinn Féin. In the general election of 1918, Sinn Féin had won both parliamentary seats in Monaghan, and by 1920 it also had control of local government. In May of that year the IRA commander in the county, Eoin O'Duffy (later to become a commissioner of the Gárda Síochána), was instrumental in having a vote of allegiance to Dáil Éireann passed by Monaghan County Council by twenty votes to four, the first of its type in the country. The four who voted against it were the Unionist members.[8]

The Unionist representatives on the county council and, indeed, Protestants all over Monaghan had by then become only too aware of the extent to which outrages were being directed against them because of inadequate protection by the central government. Frequently reiterated cries by Unionist leaders for more decisive administration went unheard, much to their dismay.

At the Twelfth of July celebrations in 1920 a motion had been passed by the Orange Order in Monaghan appealing to the British government to deal resolutely with 'the cruel and treacherous warfare which is being carried out in the county involving the sacrifice of the lives of loyal men, and the senseless destruction of life and property'.[9]

At a meeting of the Royal Black Institution of Monaghan and Cavan held at Cootehill in August 1921, Rev. R. J. Little was to interpret the deeds of the IRA as 'an alarming attempt to rout Protestants out of the country', adding that he thought it a shame that the British government 'should allow good citizens to be hustled about'.[10]

Such appeals, however, fell largely on deaf ears. Even when the government did make attempts to restore law and order, their efforts did not satisfy the Unionists who viewed them as ill-conceived. This was especially true of the government's decision to close the police barracks in outlying isolated districts. This policy left many Protestant communities in the county largely unprotected. Apprehension continued to grow as the patrols sent out to defend these areas, and even the barracks in the larger towns, became the targets of IRA attacks. This type of IRA activity was greatly enhanced in the winter of 1919–20 by the visit of Ernie O'Malley to the county. O'Malley was present at the successful attack on Bellatrain barracks in February 1920, an attack which generated a great deal of enthusiasm amongst the local Volunteers as Bellatrain was only the third barracks of its type to be overrun in Ireland. As the barracks was closed afterwards, a wide area of the countryside was relieved of the authority of the police forces, and thus the IRA was allowed greater freedom of movement in an area densely inhabited by Protestants.

As the guerilla campaign intensified throughout the country, the need to strengthen the crown forces in Ireland became more obvious. During the latter months of 1920 and the first half of 1921 the Auxiliaries and the Black and Tans spearheaded the government's attempt to break the IRA. However, the arrival and subsequent conduct of these reinforcements in Monaghan both accentuated the loss of acceptability of the Irish Constabulary in nationalist eyes and brought the county's sectarian tensions to exploding point.

When the Black and Tans arrived in Castleblaney in December 1920 they immediately assumed an aggressive attitude towards the residents of the town. On Christmas Eve, they went on a rampage of violence: discharging shots at houses; breaking the windows of business premises; assaulting a number of people and shooting and wounding one man. When a reporter of the *Dundalk Democrat* arrived in the town, he found the local inhabitants in a state of terror and tension.[11] On 23 May 1921 a company of Auxiliaries arrived in Castleblaney.[12] This was the only company in any location north of Dublin with the exception of Gormanstown, Co. Meath. Such assistance was more than welcome to Unionists, suffering as they were from threats of burning, boycotting, enforced trench-digging for the IRA and threats of death for non-compliance with the orders of IRA men. But identification with the crown forces was only to make matters worse by giving local Volunteers a pretext for subsequent sectarian attacks on Unionists.

The growth of sectarian bitterness in Monaghan between 1919 and the truce of July 1921 is evident from the various monthly police reports of the County Inspector and the Inspector General. In July 1920, the Inspector General reported that 'party feeling' was running very high in the county and that in the areas where Unionists were particularly strong, there was a serious danger of reprisal if 'Sinn Féin lawlessness' continued to grow unchecked.[13] Three months later, the County Inspector reported that party feeling had continued to grow unabated and he feared that a little provocation from either side would result in a serious outbreak of hostilities at any time.[14] In February 1921 he observed that the response of Unionists towards Sinn Féiners was hardening and that Unionist patrols were now being organised to guard the local Orange halls. He reiterated his view that a time was coming 'when both parties would engage in armed attacks on each other'.[15]

Such general statements become more concrete by reference to the limited number of statistics available on the type of outrages committed in the county at this time and an analysis of whom they were directed against. In June 1920, seventeen crimes were reported, eight of which were directed against Protestants. These included the burning of Braddox Orange hall and raids for arms on Protestant houses in Clones and Carrick-macross, as well as cases of arson and intimidation also directed against Protestants.[16] In July of the same year, seventeen outrages were again reported, but this time the number directed against Protestants had risen to ten.[17] In February 1921, fifteen outrages were reported. Although this is not a very significant number in absolute terms, the extent to which sectarian animosity had grown is evident in the fact that the County Inspector reported that of the fifteen outrages one was a case of firing at a constable in Carrickmacross, while the remainder were all of 'a party nature'.[18]

Reprisal answered by reprisal eventually became a characteristic of the Anglo-Irish war in the county. On 10 March 1921, a Protestant railway worker was shot and wounded for no apparent reason at Newbliss station. Two days later, two Catholics were fired on in the same area, although neither was injured.[19] Others were not so fortunate and the callousness of some of the sectarian crimes is best illustrated by reference to two in particular.

During a raid for arms in 1920, a Protestant farming family, the Flemings, who lived outside Castleblaney, had managed to drive the raiders off. It was later rumoured that one of the IRA men involved in the raid had been shot by William Fleming, and quietly buried.[20] At the end of March 1921, between forty and fifty armed men called to the Fleming homestead threatening Fleming that his house would be burned to the ground if he did not surrender. A guarantee was given that his home would be spared if he did. Fleming subsequently surrendered, but then both he and his son were taken out to the main road where they were shot dead in the presence of another son and a young daughter.[21]

In April of the same year, a middle-aged Protestant spinster, Kate Carroll, who lived with her invalided elderly parents was similarly taken from her home by a number of armed men and murdered. She had been suspected of giving information to the RIC and thus a note warning spies to beware was pinned to her chest.[22] The brutality of this crime led the prime minister, Lloyd George, to condemn it in the Commons as one of the outrages that had a particularly bad effect on the prospects of peace.[23]

No evidence has been found to suggest that either of these crimes was ordered to be carried out by the local leaders of the IRA, nor on the other hand that the IRA members in question were reprimanded by their superiors. In the light of a general order issued in November 1920 with regard to women spies, it would seem that the Volunteer officers in the county may at times have been unable to contain the vengeance of the rank and file who were obsessed with ancestral grievances in such rural districts. This order stated that:

> Where there is evidence to suggest that a woman is a spy or is doing spy work, the Brigade Commandant whose area is involved will set up a court of enquiry to examine the evidence against her. . . . It shall be intimated to her that only consideration of her sex prevents the infliction of the statutory punishment of death.[24]

Instead, the woman, if found guilty, was to be given seven days to leave the country. As Kate Carroll was a Protestant murdered against the directions of a general order, it would seem that IRA practice in a county such as Monaghan where Protestants had traditionally held the upper hand, was dictated, to a certain extent, not by a national cause but by a desire to exact revenge at a local level.

On the other hand, a high proportion of the outrages directed against local Protestants were part of the organised campaign of warfare which enveloped the country, in that they were aimed at the acquisition of arms stored in Unionist homes. An earlier series of unco-ordinated raids of this nature by the local IRA had not had the desired effect, so in August 1920 Eoin O'Duffy got permission from General Headquarters to carry out a general raid. Nearly every Unionist home in the Churchill district was raided, as were Protestant homes in the rural districts of Monaghan town, Newbliss, Clones, and Ballybay, along with Lough Fea Castle outside Carrickmacross.[25] Many Protestant families, especially in North Monaghan, strongly resisted the raiders, and four Volunteers were reported killed.[26]

After this raid even Nationalists admitted that such attacks only helped to further incense Unionist opinion. Denis Carolan Rushe, secretary of Monaghan County Council, wrote that the general raid did 'a lot of harm'.[27] A Volunteer who was involved in the raids admitted that they 'made the Unionists more antagonistic than ever'.[28] He claimed that after this, armed Orangemen in the predominantly Unionist areas patrolled the roads at night creating an 'extra hazard' for Volunteers travelling from one place to another.[29] The raid had the further effect of mobilising Unionist organisation once again, although this time the initiative was largely taken by those who had followed rather than led in the Unionist mobilisations of previous years.

In September 1920, a large meeting representing Unionists all over the county was held in Monaghan town. Those in attendance (many of whom were members of the Protestant clergy) vehemently condemned the recent campaign of murder and outrage carried out in Ireland 'by the advocates of a republican government'.[30] They strongly criticised the Roman Catholic clergy of Monaghan and the country as a whole for not doing likewise. They furthermore condemned the recent attacks on the homes of Protestants in the county 'whereby the property of peaceful citizens had been stolen and destroyed and their wives and children terrorised'.[31] They reached the conclusion that it was now incumbent upon the Protestants of the county to take all the necessary steps to protect themselves from similar attacks in the future. A decision was made to appoint committees with the necessary authority to do this.

Shortly afterwards, the Unionists of Drum formed a 'town guard' to defend their property 'against the marauding bands of ruffians who, under the guise of political organisations, are robbing and terrorising the peaceful inhabitants in other parts of the county'.[32] Almost simultaneously a Defence Association to safeguard Unionist interests was formed at a meeting at Smithboro to work on an all-county basis. It was reported at this meeting that many local district committees had already been formed for that purpose and that the object of the new association was now to extend and consolidate the work already undertaken and to link up the various local organisations under a central authority for the whole county.[33]

As a result of these meetings the local Volunteers were now not only faced with the crown military forces, but also with a fifth column of Unionists who were as familiar with the local terrain as they were themselves. As one Volunteer mildly put it almost fifty years later, such Unionists 'scattered over the area created somewhat of a problem'.[34] Another mused on how actively opposed to the IRA Unionists became especially in the rural districts where they considered it their duty to assist the RIC. He claimed that in the Loughgall area, where there was a large Protestant population, rifle shots were frequently fired by

Unionists at motor cars travelling the roads at night.[35] Similarly, at Annyalla, the Unionist element were equally vigilant, giving information concerning the IRA to the crown forces and 'maintaining a most hostile attitude to everything republican'.[36]

Unionist resistance to IRA activities in Monaghan was further reinforced by the involvement of a large number of local Protestants in the newly formed Ulster Special Constabulary Force officially launched in November 1920. By April 1921 it was reported that there were 620 Monaghan Protestants serving in the force.[37] There were also 1,250 Specials stationed in the border towns of counties Tyrone and Fermanagh which were within the Monaghan IRA Brigade's area.[38] The fear of this new Special police force was universal among Nationalists throughout Ulster. In the words of the *Fermanagh Herald* of 27 December 1920, it was thought that the force would be composed of

nothing more and nothing less than the dregs of the Orange lodges, armed and equipped to overawe Nationalists and Catholics, and with a special object and special facilities and a special inclination to invent crimes against Nationalists and Catholics.

Although Eoin O'Duffy's assertion that 'every Unionist may be safely reckoned one of them'[39] [i.e. a Special] was exaggerated, the extent to which the force antagonised him was not. He claimed in February 1921 that in practically every company of the Monaghan brigade, republicans had received threatening letters signed 'Ulster Black Hand' and that in some cases Specials had actually visited homes in the county and threatened people.[40] The last straw for O'Duffy came when another local Special took it upon himself to hold and search Catholic boys at Rosslea, just over the Fermanagh border, to see if they were carrying IRA dispatches. It triggered off what was to be perhaps the climax of sectarian animosity in the north Monaghan area.

An antagonised O'Duffy immediately ordered the execution of this Special and deputed two Volunteers to shoot him. On the morning of 23 February 1921, the Special was shot but escaped wounded. As a reprisal, ten Catholic homes in the village of Rosslea, just across the Fermanagh border, were burned down and two Catholic men shot and wounded. One Special was accidentally shot dead during an attack on the home of the local parish priest.[41]

O'Duffy was infuriated. In a report to Michael Collins he asserted that 'we cannot let this wanton conduct go unpunished', and asked 'Am I right in assuming I have a free hand in this matter?'[42] It would seem that he got the 'free hand' for which he asked because shortly afterwards he called a meeting of the officers of the Monaghan, Clones and Scotstown battalions of the IRA at which it was decided to shoot four Special sergeants and to burn the houses belonging to sixteen Specials in Rosslea. O'Duffy had decided that 'the only way to put a stop to such work in the future was to teach them such a lesson as they would hardly forget for a while'.[43]

The attacks began at midnight on 21 March 1921 with eight Volunteers alloted to each designated house. Fourteen houses were subsequently burned and four Special officers shot, two of whom died. It was estimated that £30,000 worth of damage was done in Rosslea that night and the attack was looked upon in official circles as 'a deliberate attempt to disarm the force and paralyse its effectiveness by endeavouring to terrorise the members'.[44]

The 'Rosslea burnings', as the incident later became known, had a tremendous effect on local Protestant communities who now more than ever feared a full-scale onslaught on their lives and property. The *Northern Standard* reported that in the Smithboro area the tension was almost unbearable as Protestant inhabitants sat up every night watching and waiting for fear of attack. Then tired and sleepless, they would turn out to the fields for work the following day.[45] Their apprehensions were not helped by O'Duffy's attitude to an all-party conference held at Clones at which a joint committee of leading Unionists and Nationalists pledged to try and preserve peace in their respective districts. O'Duffy was greatly satisfied that 'this lesson [Rosslea attack] had apparently the right effect as leading Unionists have since approached some of the Catholic clergy with a view to having a truce', resulting in the Clones conference, but he informed those who attended it that 'there would be no truce until the Special constables surrendered their arms and ceased all hostility towards us'.[46]

But while attacks on Unionists were characterised by armed raids on their homes, intimidation and murder, there were other, less apparent, forces at work aimed at breaking the Protestant economic hold on the county. The catalyst in this process during the War of Independence was the cutting off of Monaghan from its economic hinterland by the imposition of the boycott on Belfast products by Dáil Éireann in September 1920. The reasons for the initiation of the boycott were twofold. Firstly, it was meant to illustrate the importance of the south as a market for northern goods and thereby to demonstrate the folly of partitioning the country as the Government of Ireland Bill now proposed to do. Secondly, the boycott was also a direct consequence of the outbreak of riots in Belfast and Derry during the course of 1920 when an estimated 11,000 Catholics were forced to leave their jobs.[47] Of 455 killed, 58 per cent were Catholics although they made up only 24 per cent of the population of Northern Ireland at this time.[48]

The industrial expansion of Belfast during the nineteenth century had consolidated Monaghan's links with the rest of Ulster. Because of its greater scale of industry, the wider range of opportunities which it offered and, not least, Monaghan's accessibility to Belfast, the city became the natural urban focus of migration from the rural areas of the county. Throughout the nineteenth century, Monaghan's trade links were predominantly with Belfast and these links were greatly consolidated in 1882 with the establishment of a railway linking Belfast with Clones and Monaghan town. Consequently, the markets in Co. Monaghan became very popular with Belfast traders; all the county's flax went to Belfast, while all the county's imported goods came via Belfast. Thus, by 1919, most of the large traders in the towns of Castleblayney, Ballybay, Monaghan, Carrickmacross, and Clones were distributors for Belfast firms and many of these traders were Protestant.[49]

Largely because of its geographical position, Monaghan became one of the few areas where the boycott was effectively enforced. Besides, the success of the boycott in Monaghan owed much to the fact that it was seen by local Nationalists as an effective weapon to break the commercial grip which Unionists had on the county. In August 1920, Monaghan County Council, many members of which were Catholic businessmen who would have welcomed a boycott of Protestant traders, adopted a resolution stating that:

> As an Dáil has decreed the imposition of religious or political tests for industrial employment illegal, we call upon the people of County Monaghan to refuse to have any dealings with firms in Belfast or any other part of Ireland which are guilty of this illegality.[50]

Later in the month a deputation of four, representing a newly formed committee of the Catholic traders, visited all the shops in Monaghan town with a request that they sign the following declaration:

> We, the undersigned traders of Monaghan town, hereby pledge ourselves not to deal directly or indirectly with Belfast Unionist firms or traders until such time as adequate reparation has been made to the Catholic victims of the recent Belfast pogrom.[51]

All Catholic traders were reported to have signed the petition, but Protestant traders did not commit themselves, their pretext being that it was economically unsound to seek alternative supplies from Dublin.[52] The following month, September 1920, a Unionist meeting condemned the action of those who were enforcing and supporting 'the boycott of Protestant traders in this county'.[53] It is significant to note that this meeting considered the boycott to be wholly directed against Protestant traders, as indeed would seem to have been the case.

Owing to their refusal to sign the petition, Protestant merchants in Monaghan town became subjected to more stringent tactics. Pickets were placed outside their premises by the local IRA units. Although 'friendly persuasion' was used by the picketers and no attempt was made to prevent people who had the definite intention of dealing with Unionist traders from doing so, the fear of being 'marked' was sufficient to keep away many of their Nationalist customers.[54]

By October 1921 a list of merchants in Castleblayney town and district allegedly still trading with Belfast firms had been published and circulated in the area. It contained the names of twenty-one traders of which only three were Catholics.[55] There was a caution included that a list of those who patronised any of these premises would be published and circulated repeatedly. The subsequent fear amongst Catholics of being 'singled out' if they traded with Unionists undoubtedly reduced the trade of the latter, as did the activity of the Sinn Féin courts in the county which came to deal primarily with cases of persons who had purchased Belfast goods in the shops of Protestants.[56] Those merchants who were 'black listed' were sent letters by the IRA informing them that if they wished to have their names removed from the 'black list' they would have to comply with the following terms: 'a signed guarantee not to offend again; all Belfast goods on hand to be returned to the Belfast consignee; payment to me [O.C. Second Brigade] of whatever fine imposed'.[57] These tactics paid dividends as Eoin O'Duffy was able to report to Collins that 'several merchants, including Unionists, have fallen in with our wishes and paid stiff fines to have their names removed from the black list'.[58]

The acquiescence by many Unionists in the demands of O'Duffy was undoubtedly also encouraged by the activities of the IRA in respect of the Belfast goods actually entering the county. When the IRA realised that picketing alone was not sufficient to prevent Unionists acquiring Belfast goods, they undertook to stop their entrance to the county by rail and road. Thus, on 4 March 1921, a train was raided by armed and disguised men at Inniskeen and a wagon containing sugar, bacon, bread and hardware was burned.[59] The following month, a mail and goods train was held up at Glaslough and several of the wagons containing large quantities of foodstuff and agricultural produce were destroyed.[60]

O'Duffy claimed that the latter incident was very important to the boycott campaign in Monaghan, as in addition to destroying several thousand pounds worth of Belfast goods, the captured railway invoices and mails gave a list of the firms still dealing with Belfast. He asserted that subsequent action against these firms had the 'desired effect on the Unionist population' leaving enforcement of the boycott much easier.[61] Previously reluctant traders gradually realised that it was neither safe nor economically feasible to order goods from Belfast 'with the result that orders to Belfast were reduced to a minimum'.[62] Furthermore,

Catholic traders in Clones town were reported to have with-drawn their accounts from Northern banks,[63] while in Monaghan town the three Northern banks suffered most from the boycott with 'thousands of pounds being withdrawn' from their branches.[64] On the other hand, the average consumer was also adversely affected. Many southern wholesalers and manufac-turers utilised the exclusion of Belfast from the southern mar-kets to raise their prices.[65] As deliveries became more uncertain, prices continued to rise and it was estimated that the working-man in Monaghan town who observed the boycott had to pay five shillings more per week for the cost of living.[66]

It is little wonder then that the Collins-Craig pact of January 1922 ending the boycott was greeted 'with jubilation' within the county by the average workman hit by the increase in the cost of living; by those made unemployed because of the embargo; by the farmers who, with the prices of all agricultural produce rapidly decreasing, were unable to afford 'to pay more for farm and household necessaries than their true value in a free and open market'; and, not least, by the Protestant traders who were worst hit of all.[67] However, it soon became apparent that the terror and counter-terror of the revolutionary years and the boycott were to have more far-reaching consequences than were envisaged at the time.

The years between the outbreak of the Anglo-Irish conflict and the establishment of the Free State gave precise shape to Protestant fears of discrimination at the hands of a Nationalist government. The boycott ultimately helped to reinforce psycho-logical partition, and the subsequent erection of an economic border in 1923 further encouraged both sides to see Ireland in terms of two mutually hostile peoples and states. This new boundary transformed Monaghan into an economic cul-de-sac as it severed the county from its Ulster hinterland. It subse-quently accentuated the rate of the migration from the county to the new state of Northern Ireland of Protestants who otherwise would have found themselves socially isolated from the heart-land of their co-religionists in Ulster.

By 1926 the Protestant population of Monaghan had declined by 22.6 per cent of what it had been in 1911, while the equivalent figure for Catholics in the county was just over 4 per cent. The extent to which Protestant decline was influenced by the events of the intervening years is clearly illustrated by a private census of Free State Protestants who had migrated to Fermanagh between 1919–25, carried out for the benefit of the Boundary Commission. Of the 2117 Protestants involved, 454 were from Monaghan.[68] The census shows that the greatest rate of migration (35 per cent of the families) took place from the Rural District Electoral Divisions adjacent to the border. These were the areas most adversely affected during the Anglo-Irish war and the boycott. Furthermore, of the 45 families who migrated from urban areas, 75 per cent of them left the border town of Clones, a further indication of the extent to which economic reasons forced many Protestants out of the Free State, as Clones was the worst hit of all the county towns by the imposition of the border.

Finally, the revolutionary years ushered in the last phase in the decline of Unionist politics in Monaghan. The terror of these years, allied to the constructive elements many Unionists saw in Free State policy, particularly the formation of an unarmed civic guard, plus the continued feelings of desertion resulting from the partition crisis, brought the majority of Protestants to the realisation that Unionism had no place in the Free State. This was particularly true of the leaders who became aware of the necessity to change their politics in order to maintain their remaining rights. Their new attitudes, reflected in their Twelfth of July speeches, greatly placated Nationalists who were now no longer aggravated by Unionist resolutions of allegiance to the crown or threats to defend Protestant rights by force. This transformation in attitudes was exemplified in a report submitted by Hugh McCartan to the Executive Council in 1923 after he had viewed the Twelfth of July celebrations in Clones that year, the only such Orange demonstration held in the Free State. While there he met an old Protestant man who had not missed a Twelfth demonstration for over thirty years and the old man's parting words were a new variant of an old and very familiar refrain: 'To hell with the devil [sic]', he said, 'and no surrender'. McCartan maintained that the substitution of the devil for the pope had a greater significance than appeared on the surface for it was a concession to the new order.[69] That evening the Orangemen of Monaghan, totally pleased by the way the unarmed civic guards had kept the streets cleared for them, went home from Clones feeling that 'the Free State was not a bad place to live in'.[70]

But while Monaghan Protestants had lost their traditional political power and were forced to surrender their Unionist principles, they did not forsake all interest in politics. Instead of fighting local government elections under the Unionist banner they now contested them as independents to 'create and build up for themselves and for those who would come after them a strong position in that county'.[71] Relations between Catholics and Protestants on the council became on the whole more amicable and it was reported that at the first meeting of the new county council after the 1925 elections there were 'loud and often angry protests' when any member tried to introduce any issue tinged with sectarianism.[72]

On an economic level, while the effects of the revolutionary years and the boycott forced many of the smaller Protestant traders to migrate north of the border from towns such as Castleblayney, Monaghan and Clones, many of the larger Protestant businessmen found it possible to stay on and cope with the evergrowing competition from Catholic traders. An examination of the Valuation Office records in conjunction with the 1911 census schedules shows that most of the larger Protestant shopkeepers were still in business in 1926. This was especially true in Monaghan town with such families as Patton, Crawford, Mills, McCaldin, Houston and Jenkins. Similarly in Clones the Diamond was enveloped by large Protestant enterprises in 1926 as in 1911. Those with the most secure economic base had weathered the storm best.

As well as businessmen, many Protestant farmers— especially, as discussed already, those in the rural district electoral divisions adjacent to the border—also migrated. However, while this contributed to the decline of the Protestant population, it did not lead to a similar decline in the amount of land owned by Protestants for it has been found in a study of Monaghan townlands for the years 1911 and 1973, that vacated Protestant farms were usually consolidated by neighbouring Protestant farmers.[73] Consequently, land ownership did not reflect the upheavals which occurred in the Protestant community, in that Protestant townlands remained so although usually with a much depleted population.

The period 1919–22 was traumatic for the Protestants of Monaghan; they came under political, physical and economic assault; they became a marooned minority set on a course of absolute and relative demographic decline in a miniature Sudetenland. Yet, ironically, in the Irish Free State they were to have more electoral influence than for a generation beforehand at local government and parliamentary level — thanks to the introduction of the transferable rate and the multi-member constituency.

12. Canon Sheehan: the conflicts of the priest-author

THE fixed conventional image of Canon Sheehan is that of a kindly, smiling, light-hearted poet-priest who knew his country well and delighted in penning happy tales for the people he loved. The real-life Sheehan presents a vastly more complicated picture. He was an anxious, isolated intellectual, uncertain of his role as a writer and far from happy with his country and his people. An examination of his career and his writing — even in the brief compass possible here — can highlight some of the conflicts and uncertainties that affected him. By extension it can provide an introduction to some of the tensions within the seemingly tranquil and triumphant Catholic community for which he has been made into a kind of mascot.

Patrick Augustine Sheehan was born on St Patrick's day 1852 in New Street (now O'Brien Street), Mallow, Co. Cork.[1] His parents had moved to Mallow from the Cloughlucas district a few miles north of the town. His mother, Joanne Regan, was of a family widely connected in Mourne Abbey and other parts of North Cork. His father, Patrick Sheehan, owned a small business. The future priest and author was the third eldest of a family of five. Hanna and Margaret, his two older sisters, entered the Order of Mercy at Mallow and died young. Denis Bernard was later to become customs officer with the civil service in Cork. John, the youngest, died at only five years. Their parents, well respected locally, were keen to have their children educated. Sheehan recounts a blissfully happy childhood in these early years in Mallow. At the local national school he first met William O'Brien, the future journalist and nationalist politician, whose friendship he maintained throughout life.

It is hardly suprising to be told that the young Sheehan was shy, dreamy and very fond of reading, though he also enjoyed cricket, handball and rambling through the fields.[2] He makes little reference to his father in his writing but attributes to his mother his enthusiasm for faith and fatherland. In the summer of 1863, when Sheehan was just 11 years old, his father died. This blow was followed, in the February of 1864, by the death of his mother. The guardianship of the young family was entrusted to Fr John McCarthy, then parish priest of Mallow. After the sale of the house and business, they were placed under the care of a lady, a trusted friend of their parents. When the girls were old enough they were sent to the Loreto Convent in Fermoy; Denis attended the Brothers' school in Mallow, while Patrick was set aside for St Colman's junior diocesan seminary in Fermoy. While not outstandingly precocious, he was usually among the first in his class in all subjects.

While still at Mallow he had come into contact with some local nationalists. He later reminisced about the idols of his youth.[3] Amongst them were ballad singers, for whom he acted as a look-out on street corners. He delighted in such ballads as 'When on Ramillies Field', 'The Battle-eve of the Brigade'. Another local rebel 'used gather us boys into a corner of that old Market-house, and pour floods of hot rebellion into our eager minds'.[4] Their 'fierce, unswerving and unselfish love for Ireland' impressed him indelibly and was to provide material for his later writing. While at St Colman's he followed anxiously the news and rumours associated with the Fenian rising.[5] It is obvious that during these early years he absorbed many of the stories and sentiments circulating around him.[6] A local priest provided a hero-figure:

> And in higher circles of society, there was that grand priest, the typical soggart of the past, Justin McCarthy, mighty in stature, and great of heart, the hero of two tithe wars, the foe of felonious landlordism, who revenged an eviction in his parish by putting a price of one shilling per head on every fox's head that was brought to his hall door.[7]

Sheehan entered Maynooth in autumn 1869. Having done well on his entrance examination, he was exempted from the preliminary course in Humanities and joined at once the Logic class. An unsettled atmosphere pervaded the college as it tried to reorganise itself in these first years after the disestablishment of the Church of Ireland and the concomitant discontinuation of the Maynooth grant. Finding Logic dry, and, with his weak grasp of Latin, cumbersome, he turned to more literary pursuits. Later in the *Irish Monthly* he commented on this period:

> Far back in the 'sixties, literature had to be studied surreptitiously, and under the uncongenial but very effective shadow of Perrone or Receveur. It was a serious thing to be detected in such clandestine studies, and I daresay our superiors were quite right in insisting that we should rigidly adhere to the system of pure Scholasticism, which was a college tradition.

He was most impressed by a young priest, Fr Wilson, a substitute lecturer who 'opened up to our wondering eyes the vast treasures of European, and, particularly, of English literature'. From him he first heard the names of Carlyle, Richter, Tennyson and Browning, and never rested until their books were in his hands. Thus was Sheehan introduced to the unofficial syllabus which, changing with each generation, was to remain a feature of intellectual life in Maynooth for the better part of another century. In 1871, he wrote for Wilson a dissertation on 'Schools of English poetry'.[8]

When asked one night during Lent for a recitation, Sheehan promptly rendered Speranza's 'The year of revolutions' one of the several poems from the *Nation* he had committed to memory. Though he later recognised his naivety in selecting such a fierce, revolutionary ode, in a house which was 'at that time distinctly conservative, if not anti-national' he was glad to note that at that very time the young Fr Wilson was writing similar material for the latter-day *Nation* under a *nom-de-plume*. His career, Sheehan evasively tells us, was 'tragical, one other instance of genius misplaced, and, therefore, hurled to prompt and inevitable ruin'.[9] The warning was not lost on the protégé.

Fr Matthew Russell S.J., Sheehan's friend and literary patron, wrote in January 1902:

> It seems a puzzle to most men who knew him in after days, . . . how a youth of such exceptional ability was able to escape distinction during his Maynooth course so completely that, since he has become famous, many who were almost his contemporaries at college have been slow to believe that he ever was a student at Maynooth.[10]

Much of Sheehan's leisure time was passed in college librar-
ies. The title characters in his novels *Geoffrey Austin* and *Luke
Delmege* suggest authorial experience of an early restlessness,
depth and introspection. In 1872, three years after entering
Maynooth, he became ill. He had been frequently upset by
periods of ill-health. Now he was obliged to remain at home for
almost a year. While he was at Maynooth, his sister Margaret,
then directress of a convent national school, died. Sheehan kept
two woven pieces of her hair together in a leather frame for the
rest of his life. As he neared the end of his studies his early
guardian, Fr John McCarthy, was appointed bishop of Cloyne.
Sheehan was ordained on 18 April 1875.

Sheehan spent the first three years after his ordination on the
mission in England, the diocese of Cloyne being sufficiently
manned at the time. His first appointment was in the diocese of
Plymouth, under Dr William Vaughan (brother of the famous
cardinal of Westminster). It is told how Dr Vaughan used to
initiate after-dinner discussions on Ireland's political claims so
as to cause Fr Sheehan to defend his country and his race. Once
when the bishop instanced certain Irish atrocities, an English
priest came to the Irish priest's assistance by reading aloud from
the daily paper a horrifying case of wife-beating in Britain, and
thus turned the tables on his bishop.[11] It is difficult to discern if
Sheehan rose to the bait, but that the discussions continued
would seem to suggest that he did. When Fr Hobson, the rector
in Exeter, fell ill Sheehan was sent to take charge of his mission
and he remained there for the last two years of his period in
England. Here he followed a hectic schedule, constantly visiting
homes, convents and schools, and meeting with various parochial organisations. As preaching of a high quality was expected
in England, the young priest was under the constant pressure of
delivering well-argued, impressive sermons. While in Exeter he
became actively involved in several associations established for
humanitarian and social purposes. These activities brought him
into contact with many Protestants so that he developed some
sympathy and toleration for their attitudes and values. Later,
when writing, he often drew on this period as a complement to
his Irish parochial experience.

Once when visiting Dartmoor prison he recognised the
Fenian prisoner Michael Davitt by the empty right sleeve of the

prison tunic. While he wasn't allowed speak to Davitt, there is no evidence that he tried.[12] In fact, Davitt had the impression that the usual Catholic chaplain avoided him as a Fenian while in both Millbank and Dartmoor prisons.[13] However the incident was later to be written into Sheehan's *The Graves at Kilmorna*.

While there is no evidence that the character of Luke Delmege is a thorough self-portrait, the many incidents in the novel of that name which parallel Sheehan's personal experiences suggest it is more of an autobiography than later Sheehan fans would allow. The haughty, ambitious self-consciousness of the early Luke Delmege are drawn with too much insight and care to pass for the warning to young priests on the English mission which some critics were content to take them for. Luke Delmege is reprimanded by his bishop for his fiery, intellectual sermons and asked to rely more closely on strictly Catholic teaching. Like Luke's early ministry, Sheehan's years in Exeter served to overhaul and readjust many of his prejudices and opinions.

Luke was grieved to discover he was being sent home to serve in Ireland. Sheehan's recall came in 1877 and from then until 1881 he served as a curate in his native town of Mallow. Perhaps it was simply that familiar surroundings would be easier on his health, or, as an early biographer suggested, that here, 'he would be amongst the associations of his youth, and this in itself would be a check on anything in the nature of Quixotic zeal with which his work in England may have inspired him'.[14]

Neither was the anxious Fr Letheby of *My New Curate* altogether a figment of Sheehan's imagination, judging by the figure he himself cut as a young priest in Mallow. It was during these years that his lifelong concerns began to surface. He lamented the backwardness of education in Ireland and worried that it would not provide protection against the dangers of the future. Much of his time was spent instructing the young in the reason behind their faith. In 1880 he established a literary and debating society in the town. By means of lectures and the distribution of good books he sought to raise the consciousness of his flock. His inaugural address explains, rather militantly, his ideals:

Catholics should take a pleasure in studying those subjects that have had such an attraction for the greatest minds. And to take a utilitarian view of the matter, we must remember that we are by compulsion a migratory race, that it is not given to all to die in sight of the fair hills of holy Ireland; but that hundreds and thousands are compelled to go amongst the stranger, and to be subjected to the critical glance of the freethinkers, who identify every Irishman with Rome and Catholicity. Is it not well that we would show them that our religion is not a superstition, and that our love for it is not founded on ignorance; that if we have been denied the blessings of education for seven centuries, we had amongst us the great civilizing agent of the world—the Catholic Church; that she supplied what our rulers denied, and that at any moment we are prepared to enter the lists even against trained controversialists, and to take our stand on the eternal principles of truth and justice to prove the teaching of the Church to be in all things consistent with the eternal verities of God?[15]

In 1881 Sheehan was appointed curate in the port of Queenstown (Cobh), Co. Cork. Here emigration was a visible flood. He often spoke to the emigrants and he worried that they and their faith would be corrupted by contact with foreign influences. At this time he began writing articles for the *Irish Ecclesiastical Record*. The importance of religious instruction in Irish schools formed the subject of his first article in September 1881.[16] 'If religious instruction', he declared, 'be practically eliminated from our public schools, by not being raised to a level of importance with secular learning, we shall not remain a high-principled race nor become a cultured one.' These ideas were later repackaged in fictional form, and the article was also transferred to the London *Tablet*. This essay was soon followed by 'A visit to a Dublin Art Gallery'[17] wherein he urged that Christianity should re-enter art. In 'The effects of emigration on the Irish church'[18] of October 1882 he rather brazenly argued that 'in the last thirty years the Catholic community spent four million pounds on ecclesiastical architecture alone'. (This figure was not wildly inaccurate judging by the findings of recent scholarship.)[19] What would the Irish church have been if the towns, now half-deserted and impoverished, were filled with Catholic populations, full of Celtic faith and generosity? He was alarmed to record that while the Catholic Irish population in America ought to be *at least* 20,000,000, in reality the total number of professing Catholics was between seven and ten million, a great many of these being German. Rather optimistically he suggested that the church decoration trade could do a lot to inspire home industry and so stem emigration.

These articles attracted little attention but no doubt gave the young priest confidence in his voice. He wrote many short and simple stories during his time in Queenstown, most of them unconcerned with Irish problems. Some were later published in *A spoiled priest and other stories* (1905) or were reprinted by the Catholic Truth Society of Ireland amongst their penny publications.

In 1888, seven years after he arrived in Queenstown and at the age of thirty-six, Patrick Sheehan's health broke. William O'Brien's wife tells us he had an 'utter breakdown', always having suffered greatly from depression and want of sleep.[20] He spent some time with Fr Daniel Keller, an old friend, improved a little and returned to Mallow again as a curate. The Mallow parish priest, Canon John Wigmore, had Sheehan and his brother Denis regularly to dine with him and entertained them with amusing anecdotes which he later delighted in claiming as the originals of Sheehan's novel, *My New Curate*.[21]

Back in Mallow Sheehan relaxed a little, spent much time talking with the local people, observing their habits and listening to their stories. It was during this period also that he began to realise that the place and power of the essay was being superseded by the novel. He saw how Dickens had succeeded in highlighting the miseries of the English poor and how George Eliot had created a wider moral world from the activities of a small English village. He began writing his first full-length work, *Geoffrey Austin*.

In 1895 when the neighbouring parish of Doneraile became vacant, Dr Browne, the new bishop of Cloyne, appointed him parish priest. Browne 'had recommended it to him as an out-of-the-way place offering abundant opportunity to a priest of literary habits to indulge his bent while serving the simple peasantry in the capacity of pastor'.[22] As for Sheehan's response, chapter two of *My New Curate* is helpful; Fr Letheby speaks:

I was a dreamer, and the dream of my life, when shut up in musty towns, where the atmosphere was redolent of drink, and you heard nothing but scandal, and saw nothing but sin—the dream of my life was a home by the sea, with its purity and freedom, and its infinite expanse, telling me of God.[23]

Doneraile, notwithstanding its inland location, proved very conducive to Sheehan's literary activities. But how did he feel as he pushed pen towards paper?

Like most fledgling writers venturing into print, he felt insecure. But his fears were compounded by his self-consciousness as a priest writer. The tradition of Irish priestly fiction writers was hardly reassuring. John Boyce (1810-64), a Donegal priest who served in America, published three novels under the pseudonym of 'Paul Peppergrass'. Richard Baptist O'Brien (1809-1885), dean of Limerick, wrote also three novels. Dr George Crolly, later archbishop of Armagh, wrote at least one story 'Mary Anne O'Halloran', and Dr Matthew Kelly, an erudite antiquarian, began writing 'The life and labours of a catholic curate' in Duffy's *Irish Catholic Magazine*, but this was a short-lived affair.[24] There were other scattered examples, but the overall total was so small that Sheehan rightly felt himself to be a pioneer, venturing where angels feared to tread. His dilemma was expressed by the older priest, Fr Dan, addressing Fr Letheby in *My New Curate*:

There are whole fields of literature yet untrodden by us, but where heretics and others are reaping rich harvests. Yet, who would dare make the attempt? Don't you know that the ablest professors in your own time in Maynooth never ventured into print? They dreaded the chance shots from behind the hedge from the barrels of those masked bandits, called 'critics'.[25]

A later Sheehan character referred to 'that dread or shyness of print which seems to be the *damnosa hereditas* of the Irish priesthood'.[26] More was involved than the recurring Christian unease about the frivolousness of fiction and the vanity of literature for its own sake. Sheehan's fellow-ministers, with a few notable exceptions, had an aversion to committing themselves to print, even on doctrinal and pastoral matters. This was enshrined in the assumptions of a collective clerical ethos which the intellectual Sheehan never understood:

> But what are the opinions of the hundreds of Irish priests who never speak in press or on platform? And what is the meaning of the attitude of silent watchfulness which they assume?[27]

On a holiday in Kilkee, after his had become a household name, he recorded sadly in his diary that the other priests he met there were distant and aloof.[28]

Sheehan's attitude to fiction reveals a sense of excitement and novelty:

> 'Truth is stranger than fiction'. No! My dear friend, for all fiction is truth — truth torn up by the roots from bleeding human hearts, and carefully bound with fillets of words to be placed there in its vases of green and gold on your reading-desk, on your breakfast table. Horrid? So it is. Irreverent? Well, a little. But you, my dear friend, and the rest of humanity will have little else.[29]

Sheehan worried himself about the future of humanity in general and Irish humanity in particular. Many of his later characters, projections of the writer, are burdened by deep, constant and insoluble puzzles. Excited by the intellectual world which he discovered in his wide, energetic reading, he felt impelled to bring it to the people:

> The desire to form even one link in the electric chain that stretches down through the ages, magnetising generation after generation with thoughts that thrill and words that burn — this, so far from being ignoble, may assume the sacredness of a vocation and an apostleship.[30]

The purpose of fiction, Sheehan held, was primarily to popularise philosophy and inculcate moral standards. M. P. Linehan, a biographer and devotee of his, attributed to him the credit of responding to the challenge of the 'uncatholic' literary revival.[31]

Though *Lorna Doone* was his favourite modern novel, Jean Paul Richter was the writer whom he most wished to emulate for his 'humour, gentleness, strength and sublimity'.[32] Tennyson, he later wrote, influenced his sentiment but Carlyle made a deeper, and more lasting impression.[33] However 'it took many years and some suffering to see that . . . this too was vanity'.[34] Goethe interested him despite his 'covert atheism and pagan voluptuousness'.[35] Sheehan liked to see himself as a self-educated Arnoldian missionary popularising 'the best that is thought in the world'.

> Let us try the effect of Christian idealism; and let us try the experiment at home. The literary instinct has died out in Ireland since '48. Our colleges and universities are dumb. The art of conversation is as dead as the art of embalming. And a certain unspeakable vulgarity has taken the place of all the grace and courtesy, all the dignity and elegance of the last century.[36]

Having been impressed, through his reading in German literature and philosophy, by the German educational system, with which he acquainted himself at first hand, it is no surprise that his first novel *Geoffrey Austin, Student* (1895) was a hard-hitting critique of the lack of adequate religious instruction in Irish Catholic schools. Published under a *nom-de-plume* it was based on Gayfield (Mayfield in the book), a secondary school near Dublin which he saw only once, on his way from England.[37] However, his brother Denis spent a while studying there and it was from him that Sheehan learned the details of the educational system. As a novel it is marred by its shallow character portrayal, loose plot and all too obvious didacticism. It had a very limited sale, remaining on the shelves for months.[38] That Sheehan had not exaggerated the detective powers of the clerical critics is evidenced by their prompt response. 'Mayfield was found to have its prototype in half a dozen Irish colleges, and some of my *dramatis personae* were supposed to be easily recognised in certain well-known professors'.[39] While some critics expressed appreciation of its literary merits, many of the author's co-religionists showed their resentment at its vigorous condemnation of the Catholic educational system. They queried why what had operated 'from time immemorial' should only now be subject to adverse comment and then by an unknown (and very possibly lay) critic.[40] It was ignored in Britain, recommended by *The Catholic Word* in New York, and translated into German though mainly because it struck a chord in the debate on German educational issues.[41] Later it was translated into French also.

Some in Maynooth never quite forgave him. Sheehan maintained that

> a secret and insidious attempt was made to wreck the sale of the book, whilst not one of its secret critics had the manliness to come forward and contradict what was palpably the main, and, indeed, the only thesis advanced.[42]

But there were oblique attacks aplenty, such as the suggestion that the name of the book's eponymous hero reflected the author's *shoneen* bent—this was made by the Rev. John F. Hogan, professor of Modern Languages at Maynooth.[43]

It is surprising that he wrote any more. But barely three years later *The Triumph of Failure* was published. Fr Matthew Russell, S.J., editor of the *Irish Monthly* and steady supporter of many literary aspirants, constantly encouraged him and guided him particularly in the direction of American Catholic magazines like *The Messenger of the Sacred Heart*, the *Catholic Word* and *Ave Maria*.[44] It was to be through these channels, rather than through Irish ones, that Sheehan's merits were recognised. Russell read the manuscript of *The Triumph of Failure* in 1898 and offered detailed suggestions.

The Triumph of Failure was written as a sequel to *Geoffrey Austin*. It is more surely written and continues the story of Geoffrey's battle with the world. He wrote a preface for it, to head off the condemnation which *Geoffrey Austin* had attracted, but in the event it was excluded from the volume. Defending its unrealism he insisted that a writer of fiction must aim at being an 'architect and framer of personalities, which may not exist just now'.[45] The second book treats of Geoffrey's intellectual pride versus the solace of religion. Life eventually beats him down so that he finds peace at last as a monk. Set in Dublin, it can be seen as a deliberate attempt on the part of Sheehan to break away from the Catholic rural peasant tradition of the earlier nineteenth century and reflect a growing interest in town life. He later commented that he had an 'ambition of writing an Irish story without peasants or policemen', believing that the best material for Irish fiction lay still untouched 'in the little dramas of our cities and towns'.[46] Sheehan was later bravely to remark that he put more effort into this, his second novel, than into any other.[47] He cannot have but been discouraged by its almost non-reception. He had great difficulty in finding a publisher for it. It was not until after the success of *My New Curate* that *The Triumph of Failure* was acknowledged and published by Burns and Oates of London (1899), American publishers having earlier refused it.

Dr Herman J. Heuser, professor of Theology in the seminary of St Charles at Overbrook, had read Sheehan's *Geoffrey Austin* and praised it in the *American Ecclesiastical Review* of which he was editor. Soon after, when travelling to Belgium, he arranged a detour to Doneraile to visit Sheehan. The well-cited description of the genesis of Sheehan's success is his own:

> During the evening he asked him to write something for the *Review* with a sparkle in it, as well as a substratum of pastoral theology, saying that American priests were hard worked, and required a flush of humour to light up the pages of a serious review. The host assured him that he had never attempted anything of a light nature. Then a thought flashed upon him. There was a small bundle of manuscript stowed away in a back drawer. He had written it partly for amusement, and cast it aside. 'The very thing I want,' said the delighted editor, when he had read it. 'Continue that.' The tied-up bundle contained the first five chapters of—*My New Curate*.[48]

Serialisation brought American acclaim and publication in book form.

My New Curate: a story gathered from the stray leaves of an old diary, explores lightheartedly the relations between an old parish priest, Fr Dan, and his new and young curate, Fr Letheby. It was the work for which Sheehan was, and still is, most popularly acclaimed. It succeeds in balancing youthful enthusiasm against knowing cynicism and in the process reveals much of Sheehan's shrewd analysis of the Irish religious scene. Set in rural Ireland, its success prompted from him a spate of similar 'clerical' stories.

Shortly after the success of *My New Curate* Sheehan reflected on his position in a letter to Heuser:

> For the years I was writing for the *Irish Ecclesiastical Record* I never received one word of encouragement. You and my dear friend Fr Russell are the only priests that have ever said a kindly word of my work hitherto. Now I am on the full swing

of the tide; and my last book has made me a thousand friends. But it was weary work; only that I felt that I was working for our Lord and he would reward me. And He has a thousand-fold. But venturing into the field of Catholic literature is a greater risk than many are aware of; and many a writer can say, as Dr. Barry says, *aquae inundaverunt animam meam.*[49]

In the same letter he shows delight about letters of praise received from priests in America and France and gripes that 'No magazine at this side of the Atlantic would have published *My New Curate*. They are all old-fashioned and conservative', but thinks that it has 'caused some searching here in Ireland'. *My New Curate* had been published anonymously at first. When it became successful Sheehan claimed it, and once his name appeared, his two earlier novels acquired value. *Geoffrey Austin* leaped into a new edition. *My New Curate* had an immense circulation and was translated into a dozen languages. It was not published in Ireland until 1928 — a reflection of the state of Irish publishing rather than of Irish demand for *My New Curate*.

It was popular because it broke new ground. It refreshed the image of the priest for both priest and laity and it gave the laity an inside view of the way they were thought of by an Irish priest. Hitherto the priest had been depicted rather than explored. As Sean O'Faolain observes, you either had a jovial, hunting, hearty priest or a rigorous unbending ascetic.[50] That a changing society was trying to make sense of an unchanging priesthood is suggested by George Birmingham, an observant outsider:

Poets and novelists insist on our thinking of priests as saints and devils. Politicians, apostles of 'causes' and reformers of every kind, insist on trying to rope priests into their enclosures, but the human priest survives.[51]

Sheehan did not consciously try to 'humanise' the priest, but by placing varying clerical personalities in familiar and unfamiliar situations he did succeed in showing the richness and diversity of clerical life. Part of the charm of the individual priests in Sheehan derives from his own dilemma as a priest writer. He must be responsible. At best he should be a missionary writer, at worst he should supply harmless amusement. The creative urge in him prompted some of the less saintly features of some of his characters and this is what gives his writing credibility and interest. It also accounts for both his popularity and his unpopularity. By displaying features of clerical minds he inevitably draws on both the secular and the spiritual. As each of his main characters is an extension of his self, they form an intriguing drama between priest and man. It is remarkable, as Peter Connolly notes, that this kind of theme, fruitful for Irish writing, is quite unknown to contemporary fiction about the priest in other countries.[52] Connolly reaches the heart of the matter by recognising that this 'bears witness to something genuine and deeply rooted in the consciousness of contemporary Ireland, a consciousness which so often comes to a point in the priest'.[53]

Sheehan watched carefully the reception of his works. In a letter, again to Heuser, he writes: 'The bishop is taking round with him the May number and reading it at the visitation dinners here in Cloyne.'[54] Before *My New Curate* was published in book form, there was a sizeable order for the *American Ecclesiastical Review* from Ireland, which goes to show the efficiency of Irish-American communications.

His next novel, *Luke Delmege*, was published by Longmans in 1901. As the author saw it, its central idea was 'the doctrine of vicarious atonement'. It tells the story of a priest's spiritual and psychological adventures from ordination, through work in England, to his experiences in a homely Irish parish. Incidentally, the author criticises the educational equipment of the Irish priesthood and the inadequacies of old-time methods. The weary, soul-searching Luke Delmege may be Sheehan's closest self-portrait. Perhaps it is because of this and because it is padded with abundant philosophy that it gives the impression of the author's absence of control: 'It is withal, a solemn history; and many, perhaps, will find in it deeper meanings than we have been able to interpret or convey.'[55]

Why should a cloud ever have rested on that sacred brow? Why are the great and the holy dishonoured in life; only honoured in death? Why are men so cruel and vindictive towards each other? What is the dread secret of man's inhumanity to man?

Poor Luke! he can never leave these turbulent questions alone.[56]

Though it enjoyed general popularity, it was received in clerical circles with hostility. The most cutting blow came from Hogan of Maynooth, in the *Irish Ecclesiastical Record*. His first point of criticism was directed at the consistently 'unIrish' names of Sheehan's characters.

> Perhaps Fr Sheehan knows best what his public likes. He may have taken his Irish readers at their own estimate, knowing the weakness of so many amongst them for the style and title of people whom they regard as their betters. But then we should not quite expect that a seer and a prophet would allow himself to be influenced by the vitiated taste of the public. Is it not his mission to educate and reform? . . . Fr Sheehan, no doubt, wrote for English and American readers, as well as for the people of Ireland. He is the very last person, we are quite sure, to whom the intention could be imputed of holding up his own countrymen to the ridicule of foreigners; and yet we can scarcely deny that some things at least in his book, whether he wished it or not, are calculated to leave the impression that he has done so on the mind.[57]

According to Hogan, Sheehan's contrast of learning and piety was to the detriment of the former and was thus opposed to the teaching of the best spiritual guides. He concluded that though it is a book full of 'stilted nonsense', it is also 'a clever, an instructive, and a good one'.

This onslaught, coming through the pages of the quasi-official organ of the church and of Maynooth, almost snuffed him out. Sheehan avoided writing a predominantly clerical novel again until 1909. During these eight years he had seven other works published. His early reputation, especially among his clerical brethren, as an erudite pedant who affected learning which he could not possibly possess (having experienced the same educational system as themselves), was revised by the appearance in 1903 of *Under the Cedars and the Stars*. Here we have a composite of the author's notes on a wide range of subjects, including religion, philosophy, art, literature and science. They revealed a mind immersed in the great question of life, and satisfied many that there was some depth to his thinking. It did not, of course, achieve the same popularity as the novels but it bolstered his reputation and confidence. The respect which it engendered is evident from a comment in the *Irish Monthly*: 'for it is a book quite out of the common run and such as London and New York do not expect to be sent to them by Dublin'.[58]

Evidence of respect from another quarter came in 1903 when the parish priest of Doneraile was made a canon of the Cloyne diocesan chapter. The official church had come to terms with Sheehan's literary role; but that did not make him any less exceptional among his fellow diocesan priests.

His next literary attempt was a play, *Lost Angel of a Ruined Paradise*, a drama, this time, about girls leaving school. Though published by Longmans it was never staged. Russell discouraged further attempts in the same direction and that seems to have ended his playwriting career.[59] Meanwhile his *Glenanaar* was being carried, not this time in the *American Ecclesiastical Review* but in the New York *Dolphin*, and with great success. Published as a book in 1905, it is, like *My New Curate*, lightly written, fast moving, and entertaining. It owes its inspiration to Sheehan's discovery in the house of an acquaintance of an old file on the *Southern Reporter* containing the trials for the Doneraile conspiracy of 1829 and O'Connell's colourful defence of the prisoners.[60] He then went to Cork and obtained permission to examine the old court records of the famous trial. He had the book completed in six weeks.[61] Everywhere it was received warmly but especially in Ireland.

In 1904 he made the first of two trips to the German Rhineland. He must have been excited at touring the country which had produced many of his favourite philosophers and writers. Here he admired the piety of the German Catholics and received warm adulation from the many German readers of his works.

A Spoiled Priest and Other Stories (1905) and *Early Essays and Lectures* (1906) were then published. They had been written much earlier and required little work to prepare them for publication. He offered the essays rather pompously as a 'record of certain phases of thought or problems of great moment during a literary novitiate extending over many years'.[62] They include his thinking on Emerson and on the writings of St Augustine, but generally they have little to say to the modern reader.

1907 saw the publication of *Lisheen: or the Test of Spirits*. It is his most socially concerned novel. The influence of Victorian English critics is evident here as he attempts to apply their vision to

Irish circumstances. Earlier, in *My New Curate*, he had revealed his awareness of the complexity of attitudes within Irish life, as Fr Letheby is warned:

> You have, as yet, no idea of how many ways, all different and mutually antagonistic, there are, of looking at things in Ireland. . . . There are a hundred mirrors concentrated on the same subject, and each catches its own shape and colour from passion and interest.[63]

Sheehan lived through and watched closely some widesweeping changes in Irish life. The local government act of 1898, followed by the Wyndham land act of 1903 both seemed to point to a new independence and comfort for his once oppressed Catholic flock. His later novels therefore are much more concerned with the quality of Irish life, with nationality, and with his reservations about how well the new Ireland would adapt to these changes, some of which were already accomplished and more of which were on the horizon. *Lisheen* was Sheehan's equivalent of Tolstoy's *The Power of Darkness* where, as Sheehan tells us, 'the author clearly wants to prove that, deep down beneath the stagnant surface of peasant life in Russia, there are hidden springs of nobility that only need a strong hand to spread abroad and sweeten all the land'.[64] Here Sheehan reveals clearly his confidence in an idyllic, feudal society as an alternative to the anarchy of democracy. From this point on, alas, his novels assume a mildly eerie, exotic complexion. The introduction of such lurid elements as Indian magic and ghosts in ruined castles was probably intended as a brightening effect but all too often tends to obtrude awkwardly on the main plot.

Lisheen was also a popular success. The response from Hogan in the *Irish Ecclesiastical Record* was as sharp as ever as he reduced the novel to a compilation of influences:

> Substitute Maxwell for Nekludoff, [of Tolstoy] and you have the skeleton of the novel. . . . Hamberton, in like manner, can be traced to George Eliot or Mrs Humphrey Ward: and people somewhat like Outram are to be met with in Haggard and Kipling. Finally, the Major's oaths and expletives are more reminiscent of Charles Lever than of present-day realities . . . but it is so much better than anyone else can do at the

present day in the same line, that it may be disposed of with almost unqualified praise.[65]

Parerga, a companion volume to *Under the Cedars and the Stars*, was published in 1908 along with another volume of short stories called simply *Canon Sheehan's Short Stories*, a sure indication of the currency of his name. The fact that he always had several works in process at any time is shown in his tendency to overspill his ideas from one into another, and in his all too tidy and fantastic manner of sewing up plots when he decided he had made his point in any particular work.

The Blindness of Dr Gray appeared in 1909. The closely detailed character study of the ageing parish priest and his image and self image are the chief merits of this novel. Owing to a very episodic structure there are perhaps too many lives here woven too loosely together. The orphaned niece of Dr Gray arrives from America much to his consternation but eventually succeeds in softening the hard edges of this stern character.

The Sunetoi, published in 1911 as *The Intellectuals: An Experiment in Club Life*, consists of a series of reports of an imaginary discussion society. The individuals involved include a university professor, a bank manager and his wife, a Catholic curate, a young English engineer, a young lady B.A. of the Royal University of Ireland, a poet, a doctor and his wife. It is a brave effort on Sheehan's part to show that 'thought, opinion and judgment is in each individual nothing but the subjective impression of objective facts'.[66] The clash of opinions fails to have the intended stimulating effect either on the characters or on the reader. It was published serially in the *Irish Rosary* but as it proved unpopular it was terminated. Sheehan told Russell of his letter from the editor, Fr Coleman, who thought its continuation would put the magazine in jeopardy. In a slightly hurt tone he wrote: 'I confess I saw all this; and that it was with much reluctance and only at his repeated solicitations I placed the manuscript in his hands.'[67] Having read the somewhat affected *Intellectuals*, Russell cautioned the writer: 'Now mind, the holier you are and the more Irish, the better literature comes from you.'[68] However, it was reprinted twice in 1911 and again in 1919 and 1921.

The Queen's Fillet, his historical romance of the French Revolution, was also published in 1911. His aim here was to prove two favourite theories of his — that injustice begets injustice, and that fear has been the cause of the world's greatest crimes. It is hardly surprising then that a novel like *Miriam Lucas*, exploring among other things the labour question and socialism, should follow in 1912. Because socialism was causing concern also in America, Heuser had since 1904 been pressing Sheehan for a story on the subject. Sheehan's lukewarm response reveals his confusion, his possible openmindedness and his intellectual isolation from current affairs:

> I have been thinking much about your socialist novel; but it is a good deal outside my sphere of thought. What should be the underlying principle? Do atheism and socialism go together? How are we to keep the golden mean between labour and capital? What of Christian socialism? These are a few of the questions that keep cropping up when I allow myself to think of the matter. . . . Books are no guide. One or two facts about socialists would guide me better.[69]

In another letter of the same period he wrote to Heuser: 'I am now labouring at the *Labour and Capital* novel, but am making no headway. The agony of the thing does not strike us; and all my sympathies are with the labouring classes.'[70] But not with socialism.

It was another eight years before *Miriam Lucas* appeared. It is a strange novel. Many of the characters never come alive owing to Sheehan's unfamiliarity with city life in Ireland. Speaking of the novel, he claimed it was the completion of the trilogy for which *My New Curate* and *Luke Delmege* were the first parts:

> It is an idea of forecasting a perfect civilization founded purely on religious lines. You will notice the refrain running through *Luke Delmege*: we must create our own civilization. I am anxious to formalise such a civilization founded on simplicity, and self-surrender: and as alien as possible to all our modern ideas of progress. You will perceive that Luke's failure sprang from his want of touch with this supernatural element.[71]

The *Irish Ecclesiastical Record* welcomed *Miriam Lucas* as a weapon against 'Godless realistic fiction' which could join forces with Fr Benson's *None Other Gods* and the work of Rene Bazin in France, but recognised the 'heavy and elaborate background' as a defect.[72]

The Graves at Kilmorna published in 1915, two years after his death, was written out of a sense of nostalgia for the idealism of the Fenian movement which he witnessed during his very early years in Mallow. Although during the writing of it Sheehan was constantly interrupted by periods of ill-health, the intensity of his feelings for the subject gives it power and cohesion. It is essentially a pathetic contrast between the Fenian leaders and what Sheehan saw as the slippery politics of the Irish parliamentary party. It is a valuable interpretation of the nature of nineteenth and twentieth century nationalism as Sheehan compares also the popular nationalism of the two eras. He blinds himself to many of the undesirable conclusions which the comparisons suggest in his determination to place his Fenians as idols before the 1912 generation.

> They did not love their motherland because she gave them a scrap of her bogs, or fields, or mountains, or because they could sell her interests at a brigand's valuation; but because she was Ireland, and she had wrongs to be avenged and sorrows to be redressed.[73]

It is difficult to pinpoint Sheehan's political sympathies. They were complex and confused. It is clear that he wanted the connection broken with England but he was not clear about what that objective meant. He feared and hated the image of English civilisation as industrialised and low-thinking and wanted nothing of it for Ireland, but beyond that he had no image of how an independent Ireland might be governed.

Neither had he any faith in democracy and least of all in socialism. He could never come to terms with any form of government based on popular rule, as this would inevitably induce a vulgar, ignorant society. In *The Graves of Kilmorna* he gives voice to disdain for the 'elephantine hooves of democracy' which since the French Revolution 'have been trampling out all the beauty and sweetness of life'.[74] Sheehan's views are a mixture of the romantic nationalism of 1848, learned at his mother's knee, the highmindedness of the Victorian social critics, and a fear of 'progress'. He was a regressive thinker rather than a visionary. Yet Sheehan involved himself before and after the Wyndham land act of 1903 in the unromantic business of ensuring that the local changes in ownership would be carried out peacefully and properly. By means of Sunday meetings he interpreted the act and gave advice and information to the would-be landowners. Afterwards he wrote in most vague terms:

> 'The League' is still a power in the parish, but it is a league for the pacification of the country by combining Irishmen of all creeds in the cause of their common native land.[75]

In 1904 William O'Brien moved to live near Skibbereen and visited Sheehan regularly. The two were fond admirers of each other. Sheehan liked O'Brien's quixotic idealism but also his sense of practicality in politics, while O'Brien marvelled at Sheehan's literary skills. Sheehan's sympathy with the conciliation policy of the Cork-based All-for-Ireland League prompted him to contribute anonymously two lengthy and strongly-worded articles to the first number of O'Brien's *Cork Free Press* in 1910. He deplored the abandonment of conciliation by the nationalist leadership:

> 'Whatever measure you can agree upon between your-selves—be it land measures, local government measures, education or even Home Rule, I, George Wyndham, promise, with the aid of my conservative government, and with the House of Lords at my back, to pass it into an act of parliament.' Was the offer accepted? Of course not. We wanted a little more fighting, a little more speech-making, a little more hunting after will-o'-the-wisps, a little more blind trusting in the promise 'To-morrow, and to-morrow, and to-morrow!' A little more blundering and plundering. 'Short, sharp and decisive!' said Mr. Parnell, twenty five years ago. Alas! And we are further than ever from national independence today. . . . A goose does not like to be plucked. But the people like to be deceived. And let them be deceived.[76]

Sheehan wavers uneasily here between his 'crack of the rifle' solution and his optimistic confidence in conference and conciliation between Nationalist and Unionist. Was *The Graves at Kilmorna* then, a political statement, indicating a U-turn to the Fenian cult of physical force? Was it a final desperate cry for attention to the old nineteenth-century values now fast disappearing? The irony in Sheehan's work is that he worshipped only the ideal of independence. Any objective move towards independence that was realisable by non-heroic means was scorned because it offered no sense of manliness or dignity. In any case, Sheehan's contributions to the *Cork Free Press* stopped abruptly. According to the memoirs of O'Brien's wife, Sheehan did not explain the reason and no more was said on the subject.[77]

The Graves at Kilmorna was first issued in 1915 but it was not until after the 1916 rebellion that it drew attention as a work of prophecy and began to sell. Later Sheehan fans delight in denting Yeats's stature as the ideologue of the period by claiming it was *Kilmorna* which sent out 'certain men the English shot'. It is more probable that Pearse and Sheehan were both simply and separately complying with their myth-filled conscience, which dictated a revulsion against a modern Ireland in a modern world.

Sheehan wrote a plethora of pious or denominational works. *Mariae Corona* is probably his best work of this type. His volume of poems *Cithara Mea* published in 1900 in Boston was justly neglected. He also managed to find time to write hymns, one of which 'O Sacred Heart', became popular, at least in Doneraile.[78] His sermons were collected by his good friend Fr M. J. Phelan and published in 1920. Some of his most revealing essays in autobiography and literary matters, *The Literary Life and Other Essays*, edited by Edward McLysaght, were also published in 1921.

Apart from two visits to Germany and occasional trips to Cork and Dublin he led a very quiet life. It may have been his lonely, monotonous life which drove him to write in such volume: 'No matter how close the ties of affection may be, the priest moves through his people, amongst them but not of them'.[79] Sheehan felt his greatest want to be intercourse with other stimulating minds. The Abbey Theatre interested him greatly but he regretted the negative attitude of some of its members towards Christianity. He felt Synge had attempted a compromise with paganism, and Yeats, while being an unquestionably fine poet, lacked a genuine faith in life. In T. C. Murray, whose *Birthright* had just been produced, he was very interested.[80] He allegedly wished to meet Daniel Corkery, the animating figure of the literary revival in Cork but 'modesty bred of restricted environment kept them apart'.[81] In Kenneth McGowan's brief sketch of Sheehan, [82] we are told that owing to his enjoyment of friends more learned than himself, he cultivated numerous friendships amongst the Jesuits, Capuchins and Dominicans. This would seem to be borne out by their many fulsome tributes to him later. Yet McGowan adds that, though the famous Fr Vincent McNabb S.J. was 'a close friend' of Sheehan's, he (Sheehan) considered it 'a great honour' to be invited to visit.[83]

Though later biographers are at pains to point out that his literary work never interfered with his pastoral activity in Doneraile, his involvement with the latter was usually in a passive, supervisory capacity. His 'keen interest in the Irish language and Irish games' amounted to a sadness at the passing of the former and regular attendance at important matches and *feiseanna*.[84] He promoted, however, many practical improvements in the town. The electric light was introduced from a plant at the local mill, the water supply was extended and a bridge was built. He was elevated by the local community to the status of hero when, one night, he smelt the smoke from the burning flour mill nearby and warned the occupants of the nearby convent and other houses.[85] He may have been instrumental in inducing Lady Castletown to build the town hall with stage, greenrooms, reading rooms and billiard room, as he was on friendly terms with her husband. No doubt, the town hall provided a venue for the St Vincent de Paul Society which he also established. A hint appears, in McGowan's biography, of tension between the priest and his flock when we are assured that the priest 'would not tolerate anything whether words or actions which tended to demean him in any way. There was no compromise for any offender who invariably suffered at least a severe reprimand.'[86] Perhaps the affected nonchalance of 'Dr Gray', born of his misunderstanding in the parish, was inspired by the pain of experience.[87]

He contributed much from his own pocket to the renovation of the church and schools and donated a handsome sum to the refurbishment of his earlier college of St Colman's. He handed over the entire proceeds of one of his works to found a cot in the children's hospital of Temple Street, Dublin, though he had no other relations with the institution.[88] In 1905 he ceded all his valuable literary work to the bishop of Cloyne for the support of the sick and aged priests of the diocese.[89]

In 1910, suffering with severe pain, he consulted Sir Charles Ball in Dublin and was told that his illness was fatal. He was advised to desist from his writing and strenuous duties. Two years later his condition grew very serious and he was removed to the South Infirmary in Cork. His correspondence during this time, however, was remarkably cheerful and even humorous. After five months and much pleading, he was eventually allowed to return home to Doneraile, where he insisted on resuming some of his parochial duties. He died on Rosary Sunday, 5 October 1913, three years after he first fell ill. During this time he had published *The Intellectuals*, *The Queen's Fillet* and was almost certainly writing *The Graves at Kilmorna*. According to the death certificate, the cause of death was cancer of the pelvis, a condition which had been diagnosed in 1911.

Shortly before he died, he burnt his memoirs, saying to his brother Denis: 'These may do harm to somebody else.' He had earlier sent them to Russell, with a note specifying that they were not at any time intended for print, and though he feared Russell would not find them 'too entertaining' he believed there were 'a few interesting episodes here and there'.[90] Though many acquaintances engaged in speculation after his death as to their content, it is unlikely that they would have contained anything very careless. Apart from *Tristram Lloyd*, an unfinished and unremarkable novel later finished by Fr Gaffney (1928), it is believed that there were other unfinished or unpublished writings left when Sheehan died. These, however, were withheld from publication, by the express desire of the writer, made known to his executors and close friends.[91]

He was buried in the churchyard of Doneraile, according to his wish, so that the schoolchildren would say a prayer on their way to and from the school building. A plain celtic cross marks his grave with an inscription of his own choosing:

'Where dwellest thou Rabbi?'
And Jesus said: 'Come and see.'

His obituaries filled the pages of both the *Cork Free Press* and the *Cork Examiner* for days after his death with tributes from far and wide.[92] His benign bishop contributed a panegyric, in which he insisted, for the benefit of those who may have harboured other suspicions, that 'Canon Sheehan was a priest, first and last'.[93]

But the priest-writer had not necessarily revealed very much about his priestly life. Fr Peter Connolly in a review of 'the priest in modern Irish fiction' was the first to point out that Sheehan's much-vaunted 'insight' into the 'inner clerical life' was in fact no insight at all:

> Though Canon Sheehan had inner access he did not choose — he probably could not in his day — to reveal more of his priests than could be observed by any member of the parish committee, namely, the priest's pastoral methods and some of his intellectual worries.[94]

Because he was a priest — and a canon at that — Sheehan's fiction was deemed to be safe for people who were deemed to be at risk from 'bad' modern (especially English) literature. In any case many readers would have appreciated a light-hearted alternative to an English fiction reflecting a culture of which Irish people had no experience. Sheehan's readers selected and cherished those images of themselves which they found flattering and were all the more grateful to him for advertising their Catholic respectability abroad. Sheehan managed to express a set of familiar Catholic and patriotic values but in a refreshingly new way. In recent times a number of scholars have assessed his significance in terms of these collective pieties.[95]

But Sheehan's popular readership missed — or conveniently ignored — his criticisms and his deeper concerns. Many read his novels, as he early suspected, purely for light amusement, oblivious to the warnings and admonishment of contemporary Irish life, the redemption of which was, ironically, the author's professed purpose in writing them. In fact the corpus of Sheehan's work is full of doubts about the people and the country. The following expression of sentiment by a landlord in *My New Curate* can be taken as an artist's dramatic presentation of an alien viewpoint:

> I have never been able to shake off a feeling of contempt for these poor, uneducated serfs. And their little cunning ways and want of manliness have always disgusted me.[96]

But a detached reading of all his works makes it abundantly clear that at least one side of the author shared these very sentiments. Benedict Kiely has gone so far as to conclude that Sheehan's denunciations of 'the people and the country' are more severe than those of the harshest of the later realists.[97]

Canon Sheehan is still seen by many as a friendly, fatherly 'Soggarth Aroon' who delighted in scribbling happy tales of, and for, the people. The worrying, lonely, wary priest who did not know quite what to make of himself or his people was from the beginning generally ignored.

13. *The historical writings of Patrick J. Corish to 1989*

An attempt has been made here to list all Patrick J. Corish's published writings in the field of history. Included are reviews of books, though not of journals.

C. J. Woods

1947

Nicholas French, bishop of Ferns, and the peace with Ormonde, 1649. In *Ir. Comm. Hist. Sc. Bull.*, no. 49.

Review of Dauphin, *Le Bienheureux Richard, abbé de Saint-Vaune de Verdun* (1946). In *I.E.R.*, 5th ser., lxix, 74–5.

Review of Cyfeillion Cymru, *Daffodils under the snow* (1946). Ibid., pp 460–61.

Review of Hughes, *A history of the church*, iii (1947). Ibid., pp 647–8.

Review of *St Mary's Cathedral, Kilkenny: centenary souvenir* (1943?). Ibid., p. 1035.

1948

Bishop Nicholas French and the second Ormond peace, 1648–9. In *I.H.S.*, vi, no. 22, pp 83–100.

Review of Luddy, *The case of Peter Abélard* (1947). In *I.E.R.*, 5th ser., lxx, 472.

Review of Masson, *Missionaires belges sous l'ancien régime*, i (1947). Ibid., p. 760.

Review of Laurent, *Le Bienheureux Innocent V* (1947). Ibid., pp 857–9.

Review of Gwynn, *O'Connell, Davis and the colleges bill* (1948). Ibid., pp 1131–2.

Review of Hughes, *A history of the church*, i-ii (1948). Ibid., pp 1143–4.

1949

The Catholic Truth Society of Ireland: the first fifty years, 1899–1949. In Catholic Truth Society of Ireland, *First fifty years: golden jubilee record, 1899–1949* (Dublin: Catholic Truth Society of Ireland, [1949]), pp 11–23, illus.

Review of O'Brien & Ryan (eds), *Devoy's postbag, 1871–1928*, vol. i (1948). In *I.E.R.*, 5th ser., lxxi, 92.

Review of Autin, *Henri Bremond* (1947). Ibid., pp 165–6.

Review of Beckett, *Protestant dissent in Ireland, 1687–1780* (1948). Ibid., pp 173–4.

Review of O'Sullivan, *Cistercian settlements in Wales and Monmouthshire, 1140–1540* (1947). Ibid., p. 188.

Review of Gwynn, *Young Ireland and 1848* (1949). Ibid., pp 469–70.

Review of Ullmann, *The origins of the Great Schism* (1948). Ibid., pp 563–4.

Review of Wingfield-Stratford, *Charles, king of England, 1600–1637* (1949) and idem, *King Charles and King Pym, 1637–1645* (1949). Ibid., pp 568–70.

Review of Dvornik, *The Photian schism* (1948). In *I.E.R.*, 5th ser., lxxii, 73–7.

Review of Mathew, *Catholicism in England* (1949). Ibid., pp 92–3.

Review of Hayes, *Biographical dictionary of Irishmen in France* (1949). Ibid., p. 185.

Review of Madariaga, *Christopher Columbus* (1949). Ibid., pp 285–6.

Review of Tierney (ed.), *Daniel O'Connell: nine centenary essays* (1949) and Landreth, *The pursuit of Robert Emmet* (1949). Ibid., pp 561–2.

1950

The restoration of the English catholic hierarchy. In *I.E.R.*, 5th ser., lxxiv, 289–307.

Review of Petrie, *Earlier diplomatic history, 1492–1713* (1949). Ibid., lxxiii, 462.

Review of Gwynn, *The history of partition* (1950). Ibid., lxxiv, 467.

Review of MacLysaght, *Irish life in the seventeenth century* (1950). Ibid., p. 468.

Review of McSorley, *An outline history of the church by centuries* (1950). Ibid., p. 477.

1951

The Fall in Greek tradition. In *Ir. Theol. Quart.*, xviii, 138–60.
  Tatian, Irenaeus, Clement of Alexandria, Origen.

Rinuccini's censure of 27 May 1648. In *Ir. Theol. Quart.*, xviii, 322–37.

Review of Hughes *The Reformation in England* (1950). In *Ir. Theol. Quart.*, xviii, 291–4.

Review of Wingfield-Stratford, *King Charles the Martyr* (1950). Ibid., pp 297–8.

Review of *Mélanges colombaniens: actes du congrès international de Luxeuil, 20–23 juillet 1950* (1951). In *Ir. Theol. Quart.*, xviii, 397–9.

Review of Jedin, *Papal legate at the Council of Trent: Cardinal Seripando* (1947). In *I.E.R.*, 5th ser., lxxvi, 88–9.

Review of Gwynn, *Cardinal Wiseman* (1950). Ibid., pp 90–91.

Review of Grisar, *Martin Luther, his life and work* (1950). Ibid., pp 171–2.

Review of Beck (ed.), *The English catholics* (1950). In *Furrow*, ii, 393–5.

1952

Review of Lynch, *Pii antistitis icon* (facsimile repr., 1951). In *I.H.S.*, viii, no. 30, pp 171–2.

Review of Jedin, *Geschichte des Konzils von Trient* (1949). In *Ir. Theol. Quart.*, xix, 91–3.

Review of Gutiérrez, *Españoles en Trento* (1951). Ibid., pp 200–1.

Review of O'Hegarty, *A history of Ireland under the union* (1952). In *I.E.R.*, 5th ser., lxxviii, 71–4.

Review of Schuster, *Saint Benedict and his times* (1951). Ibid., pp 74–5.

Review of Mooney, *Devotional writings of the Irish Franciscans, 1224–1950* (1952). Ibid., p. 156.

Review of Robertson, *The religious foundations of Leveller democracy* (1951). In *Cath. Hist. Rev.*, xxxviii, 42.

1953

Two contemporary historians of the Confederation of Kilkenny: John Lynch and Richard O'Ferrall. In *I.H.S.*, viii, no. 31, pp 217–36.

Review of Bosher, *The making of the Restoration settlement* (1951). In *Cath. Hist. Rev.*, xxxix, 419–20.

1954

John Callaghan and the controversies among the Irish in Paris, 1648–54: the end of the Confederation. In *Irish Theol. Quart.*, xxi, 32–50.

'Religio depopulata'. Ibid., pp 234–8.
> The Reformation in England.

Irish history and the papal archives. In *Ir. Theol. Quart.*, xxi, 375–81.

Ireland's first papal nuncio. In *I.E.R.*, lxxxi, 172–83.
> Rinuccini, 1645–9.

Review of Schieffer, *Winfrid-Bonifatius und die christliche Grundlegung Europas* (1954). Ibid., pp 281–2.

Review of Bieler (ed.), *The works of St Patrick* (1953). In *I.E.R.*, 5th ser., lxxxi, 155–6.

Review of Pochin Mould, *Ireland of the saints* (1953). Ibid., pp 156–7.

Review of Baird, *The tomb of St Peter* (1953). Ibid., pp 157–8.

Review of Leslie, *Cardinal Gasquet* (1953). In *Christus Rex*, viii, 303–4.

Review of Brunton and Pennington, *Members of the Long Parliament* (1954). In *Cath. Hist. Rev.*, xl, 328–9.

1955

Some problems in the history of the Reformation. In *Ir. Theol. Quart.*, xxii, 49–57.

The crisis in Ireland in 1648: the nuncio and the supreme council: conclusions. In *Ir. Theol. Quart.*, xxii, 231–57.

Review of Villoslada, *Storia del Collegio Romano* (1954). Ibid., pp 179–80.

Review of Dawson (ed.), *The Mongol mission: narratives and letters of the Franciscan missionaries in China and Mongolia in the thirteenth and fourteenth centuries* (1955). Ibid., pp 277–9.

Review of van der Wyngaert and Mensaert (eds), *Sinica Franciscana*, v (1954). In *Cath. Hist. Rev.*, xli, 163–4.

1956

The church in Ireland in the fifteenth century, v: summing up. In *Ir. Cath. Hist. Comm. Proc.*, pp 14–16.

Irish ecclesiastical history and the papal archives: introduction. In *Ir. Cath. Hist. Comm. Proc.*, pp 17–20.

The Vatican excavations. In *Ir. Theol. Quart.*, xxiii, 273–7.

Review of Pantin, *The English church in the fourteenth century* (1955). In *Ir. Theol. Quart.*, xxiii, 89–90.

Review of Gwynn (ed.), *The writings of Bishop Patrick, 1074–1084* (1955). Ibid., pp 185–7.

Review of Talbot (ed.), *The Anglo-Saxon missionaries in Germany* (1954). Ibid., pp 187–8.

Review of Lubac, *The splendour of the church* (1956). In *I.E.R.*, 5th ser., lxxxvi, 211–12.

Review of Jarrett, *The life of St Dominic* (1955), Placid Conway (trans.), *Lives of the brethren of the order of preachers* (1955) and Gumbley, *Obituary notices of the English Dominicans, 1555–1952* (1955). Ibid., pp 442–3.

1957

Father Luke Wadding and the Irish nation. In *I.E.R.*, 5th ser., lxxxviii, 377–95.

The beginnings of the Irish College, Rome. In *Father Luke Wadding commemorative volume*, ed. The Franciscan Fathers, Killiney (Dublin: Clonmore & Reynolds), pp 284–94.

The church and Irish nationalism. In *Iris Hibernia*, iii, no. 5, pp 9–22.

The reorganization of the Irish church, 1603–41. In *Ir. Cath. Hist. Comm. Proc.*, pp 9–14.

Review of Twemlow (ed.), *Calendar of entries in the papal registers: papal letters*, vol. xiii (1956). In *I.H.S.*, x, no. 39, pp 328–33.

Review of Giblin (ed.), *Liber Lovaniensis* (1956). Ibid., pp 333–4.

Review of Rahner (ed.), *Ignatius von Loyola: Briefwechsel mit Frauen* (1956). In *Ir. Theol. Quart.*, xxiv, 108.

Review of Wiltgen, *Gold Coast mission history, 1471–1880* (n.d.). Ibid., pp 366–7.

Review of Hales, *Mazzini and the secret societies* (1956). In *I.E.R.*, 5th ser., lxxxvii, 153–4.

Review of Edwards & Williams (eds), *The Great Famine* (1956). Ibid., pp 387–9.

Review of McNamara, *The American College in Rome* (1956). Ibid., pp 477–8.

Review of Speaight, *The life of Hilaire Belloc* (1957). Ibid., lxxxviii, 64–7.

Review of Randall, *Vatican assignment* (1956). In *Christus Rex*, xi, 663.

1958

An Irish counter-reformation bishop: John Roche. In *Ir. Theol. Quart.*, xxv, 14–32, 101–23.
>   John Roche, bishop of Ferns, 1624–36.

A new edition of Butler's 'Lives of the saints'. In *I.E.R.*, 5th ser., lxxxix, 195–8.

The pontificate of Pope Pius XII. In *I.E.R.*, 5th ser., xc, 299–311.

Reformation and Counter-Reformation, 1500–1700 [in Wexford]. In *Centenary record: Wexford twin churches* (Wexford), pp 25–49, illus.

Review of Martin (ed.), 'Sources for the history of the Irish Capuchins' (1956). In *I.H.S.*, xi, no. 41, p. 83.

Review of Donohue, *Tridentine seminary legislation* (1957). In *Ir. Theol. Quart.*, xxv, 200–1.

Review of Fr Colmcille, *The story of Mellifont* (1958). Ibid., pp 392–3.

Review of Schnürer, *The church and culture in the middle ages* (1956). In *I.E.R.*, 5th ser., lxxxix, 78–9.

Review of Buehrle, *Rafael Cardinal Merry del Val* (1957). In *Christus Rex*, xii, 67.

Review of Sykes, *William Wake, archbishop of Canterbury, 1657–1737* (1957). In *Cath. Hist. Rev.*, xliii, 490–91.

1959

An Irish counter-reformation bishop: John Roche. In *Ir. Theol. Quart.*, xxvi, 101–16, 313–30.
>   Contd from *Ir. Theol. Quart.*, xxv (1958).

Two reports of the catholic church in Ireland in the early seventeenth century. In *Archiv. Hib.*, xxii, 140–62.

> Reports by Bishop Roche of Ferns, 1625 and 1629.

Cardinal Cullen and Archbishop MacHale. In *I.E.R.*, 5th ser., xci, 393–408.

Review of Kearney, *Strafford in Ireland* (1959). In *Studies*, xlviii, 470–72.

Review of Jedin, *Geschichte des Konzils von Trient* (1957). In *Ir. Theol. Quart.*, xxvi, 89–90.

Review of Hales, *The catholic church in the modern world* (1958). Ibid., pp 194–5.

Review of Daniélou, *The lord of history* (1958). Ibid., pp 197–8.

Review of Todd, *John Wesley and the catholic church* (1958). Ibid., pp 204–5.

Review of Sitwell (ed.), *St Odo of Cluny* (1958). In *I.E.R.*, 5th ser., xci, 468–9.

Review of Jones, *Mountjoy* (1958). Ibid., pp 259–60.

Review of Kearney, *Strafford in Ireland* (1959). In *Studies*, xlviii, 470–72.

1960

Review of Mac Niocaill, *Na manaigh Liatha in Éirinn* (1959). In *Ir. Theol. Quart.*, xxvii, 78–9.

Review of Colum, *Arthur Griffith* (1959). In *I.E.R.*, 5th ser., xciii, 200–1.

Review of Ricciotti, *The age of martyrs [A.D. 284–337]*. Ibid., xciv, 60–61.

Review of Macken, *Seek the fair land* (1959). Ibid., pp 190–91.

Review of Dickson, *Revolt in the north: Antrim and Down in 1798* (1960). In *Christus Rex*, xiv, 297.

1961

St Patrick and Ireland. In *I.E.R.*, 5th ser., xcv, 223–8.

St Patrick and Ireland. In *Saint Patrick: a symposium held in St Patrick's Hall, Armagh, on 17 March 1961* (Dublin: Browne & Nolan, [1961]), pp 9–14.

Review of Watkin, *The church in council* (1960). In *Ir. Theol. Quart.*, xxviii, 248–9.

Review of Lecler, *Toleration and the Reformation* (1960). In *I.E.R.*, 5th ser., xcv, 61.

Review of Valtierra, *Peter Claver* (1960). Ibid., pp 70–71.
Review of Allen, *King William IV* (1960). Ibid., pp 351–2.
Review of Scott-Moncrieff, *The mirror and the cross* (1960). Ibid., p. 352.
Review of Winter, *Saint Peter and the popes* (1960). Ibid., p. 353.

1962

Cardinal Cullen and the National Association of Ireland. In *Reportorium Novum*, iii, 13–61.
The church and the councils. In *I.E.R.*, 5th ser., xcviii, 203–12.
Review of Chadwick, *The age of the saints in the early Celtic church* (1961). In *Ir. Theol. Quart.*, xxix, 163.
Review of Mac Suibhne (ed.), *Paul Cullen and his contemporaries*, i (1961). Ibid., pp 265–6.
Review of Dilthey, *Meaning in history* (1961). Ibid., pp 335–6.
Review of Eberhardt, *A summary of catholic history*, i (1960). In *I.E.R.*, 5th ser., xcvii, 66–7.
Review of Dessain (ed.), *The letters and diaries of John Henry Newman*, xi (1961). Ibid., pp 129–30.
Review of Brodrick, *Robert Bellarmine, saint and scholar* (1961). Ibid., pp 130–31.
Review of Trevor, *Newman, the pillar of the cloud* (1962). Ibid., pp 345–6.
Review of Dansette, *Religious history of modern France* (1961). Ibid., 349–50.
Review of Webster, *Christian democracy in Italy, 1860–1960* (1961). In *Christus Rex*, xvi, 71.

1963

Review of Van der Meer, *Augustine the bishop* (1962). In *Ir. Theol. Quart.*, xxx, 84–5.
Review of Blakiston (ed.), *The Roman question: extracts from the despatches of Odo Russell from Rome, 1858–1870* (1962). In *I.E.R.*, 5th ser., xcix, 63–4.
Review of Kitson Clark, *The making of Victorian England* (1962). Ibid., pp 67–8.
Review of Dessain (ed.), *The letters and diaries of John Henry Newman*, xii (1962), Althoz, *The liberal catholic movement in England* (1962) and Trevor, *Newman, light in winter* (1962). Ibid., pp 68–70.

Review of Sherry (ed.), *Holy Cross College* (1962). Ibid., p. 212.

Review of Dessain (ed.), *The letters and diaries of John Henry Newman*, vol. xiii (1963) and MacDougall, *The Acton-Newman relations* (1962). In *I.E.R.*, 5th ser., c, 133–5.

Review of Broderick, *Saint Peter Canisius* (1963). Ibid., 408.

Review of McGrath (ed.), *The consecration of learning* (1962). In *Furrow*, xiv, 468–9.

On Newman's educational writings.

1964

Trent in retrospect. In *I.E.R.*, 5th ser., ci, 217–33.

Catholic Ireland, 1864. In *I.E.R.*, 5th ser., cii, 196–205.

Ferns diocesan statutes, 1722. In *Archiv. Hib.*, xxvii, 76–84.

Correspondence of the superiors of the Jesuit mission in Ireland with John O'Brien, S.J., rector of Salamanca. In *Archiv. Hib.*, xxvii, 85–103.

Review of Jedin, *Handbuch der Kirchengeschichte*, i (1962). In *Ir. Theol. Quart.*, xxxi, 336–7.

Review of Mollat, *The popes at Avignon, 1305–1378* (1963). In *I.E.R.*, 5th ser., ci, 69–70.

Review of Giblin (ed.), *Irish Franciscan mission to Scotland, 1619–1646* (1964). Ibid., cii, 60.

Review of Bieler (ed.), *The Irish penitentials* (1963). Ibid., 60–61.

Review of Dessain & Blehl (eds), *The letters and diaries of John Henry Newman*, xiv (1963). Ibid., 61–2.

1965

Review of Lawrence (ed.), *The English church and the papacy in the middle ages* (1965). In *I.E.R.*, 5th ser., civ, 62–3.

Review of Jedin & Dolan (eds), *Handbook of church history*, i (1965). Ibid., 384–5.

Review of Dessain (ed.), *The letters and diaries of John Henry Newman*, xvi (1965). Ibid., 386–7.

1966

Bishop Caulfield's 'Relatio status', 1796. In *Archiv. Hib.*, xxviii, 103–13.

Religious liberty. In *I.E.R.*, 5th ser., cv, 1–11.

The holy see and the Second World War. In *Studies*, lv, 82–96.

Review of Friedländer (ed.), *Pius XII and the Third Reich* (1966). In *Studies*, lv, 432–4.

1967

Political problems, 1860–1878. Dublin: Gill. Pp 59 (A History of Irish Catholicism, vol. v, fasc. 3).

Thomas Furlong. In *New catholic encyclopedia*, (15 vols, New York: McGraw-Hill), vi, pp 227–8.

John Lanigan. Ibid., viii, 377–8.

Giovanni Battista Rinuccini. Ibid., xii, 507.

Sisters of St John of God. Ibid., xii, 891.

St Patrick's College, Maynooth. Ibid., xii, 928–9.

Pier Francesco Scarampi. Ibid., xii, 1117.

Review of Norman, *The catholic church and Ireland in the age of rebellion, 1859–1873* (1965). In *Stud. Hib.*, vii, 230–33.

Review of Watt, *The theory of papal monarchy in the thirteenth century* (1965). In *Ir. Theol. Quart.*, xxxiv, 87–8.

Review of Suttor, *Hierarchy and democracy in Australia, 1788–1870* (1965). Ibid., pp 88–9.

Review of Ford, *Cardinal Moran and the A.L.P.: a study in the encounter between Moran and socialism, 1890–1907* (1966). Ibid., pp 169–70.

1968

The origins of catholic nationalism. Dublin: Gill. Pp 64 (A History of Irish Catholicism, vol. iii, fasc. 8).

   Period 1534–1692.

1970

The diocese of Ferns and the penal days. In *The Past*, no. 8, pp 5–17, illus.

'Bishop Wadding's notebook'. In *Arch. Hib.*, xxix, 49–114.

Die Lage der Katholiken in Großbritannien und Irland im 17. und 18. Jahrhundert. In Wolfgang Müller *et al.* (eds), *Die Kirche im Zeitalter des Absolutismus und der Aufklärung*

(Freiburg-im-Breisgau: Herder), pp 194–205 (Handbuch der Kirchengeschichte, ed. Hubert Jedin, vol. v).

Review of Heaney, *The modernist crisis: von Hügel* (1969). In *Ir. Theol. Quart.*, xxxvii, 85–6.

Review of Anstruther, *The seminary priests*, vol. i: *Elizabethan* (1970). In *Furrow*, xxi, 602.

1971

The church under the penal code. Dublin: Gill. Pp iv, 88. Jointly with John Brady. (A History of Irish Catholicism, vol. iv, fasc. 2).

Großbritannien und Irland, 1830–1848. In Roger Aubert *et al.* (eds), *Die Kirche in der Gegenwart* (Freiburg-im-Breisgau: Herder), pp 408–14 (Handbuch der Kirchengeschichte, ed. Hubert Jedin, vi, pt 1)

Der Aufstieg des Katholizismus in der angelsächsischen Welt: Großbritannien und Irland nach 1848. Ibid., pp 551–61.

The pastoral mission in the early Irish church. In *Léachtaí Cholm Cille*, ii, 14–25.

Review of Hughes, *Stewards of the Lord: a reappraisal of Anglican orders* (1970). In *Ir. Theol. Quart.*, xxxviii, 79–80.

1972

Documents relating to the appointment of John Stafford as coadjutor to the bishop of Ferns, 1772. In *The Past*, no. 9, pp 73–9.

Irish College, Rome: Kirby papers: guide to material of public and political interest, 1862–1883. In *Archiv. Hib.*, xxx, 29–115.

The Christian mission. Dublin: Gill & Macmillan. Pp [iv], 96 (A History of Irish Catholicism, vol. i, fasc. 3).
    Early Celtic church.

History in perspective. In *Furrow*, xxiii, 327–33.

1973

Irish College, Rome: Kirby papers: guide to material of public and political interest, 1836–1861. In *Archiv. Hib.*, xxxi, 1–94.

Review of Ozment, *Mysticism and dissent: religious ideology and social protest in the sixteenth century* (1973). In *Ir. Theol. Quart.*, xl, 188–9.

Review of Bottigheimer, *English money and Irish land: the 'adventurers' in the Cromwellian settlement of Ireland* (1971). In *Studia Hib.*, xiii, 182–3.

1974

Irish College, Rome: Kirby papers: guide to material of public and political interest, 1884–94, with addenda, 1852–1878. In *Archiv. Hib.*, xxxii, 1–62.

Review of Whyte, *Church, state and nation in Ireland, 1898–1921* (1973). In *Ir. Theol. Quart.*, xli, 161–2.

Review of Daniélou, *Gospel message and Hellenistic culture* (1973). In *Furrow*, xxv, 697.

1975

Review of Fogarty, *The Vatican and the Americanist crisis: Denis J. O'Connell, American agent in Rome, 1885–1903* (1974). In *Ir. Theol. Quart.*, xlii, 159.

Review of Jedin (ed.), *Handbuch der Kirchengeschichte*, vi, pt 2 (1973). In *Ir. Theol. Quart.*, xlii, 231.

1976

The rising of 1641 and the catholic confederacy, 1641–5. In *A new history of Ireland*, iii (Oxford: Clarendon), pp 289–316.

Ormond, Rinuccini and the confederates, 1645–9. Ibid., pp 317–35.

The Cromwellian conquest, 1649–53. Ibid., pp 336–52.

The Cromwellian régime. Ibid., pp 353–85.

Review of Barnard, *Cromwellian Ireland* (1975). In *I.H.S.*, xx, no. 77, pp 66–7.

Review of Larkin, *The Roman Catholic church and the creation of the modern Irish state, 1878–1886* (1975). In *Ir. Theol. Quart.*, xliii, 296–7.

1977

Review of Delumeau, *Catholicism between Luther and Voltaire* (1977). In *Furrow*, xxviii, 721–2.

1978

Newman and Maynooth. In J. D. Bastable (ed.), *Newman and Gladstone: centennial essays* (Dublin: Veritas), pp 279–85.

Review of Tierney, *Croke of Cashel* (1976). In *Cath. Hist. Rev.*, lxiv, 702–3.

1979

The Irish church and the papacy. In *Furrow*, xxx, 612–19.

Gallicanism at Maynooth: Archbishop Cullen and the royal visitation of 1853. In Art Cosgrove and Donal McCartney (eds), *Studies in Irish history presented to R. Dudley Edwards* (Dublin: University College), pp 176–89.

Review of Hanson (ed.), *Saint Patrick: Confession et Lettre à Coroticus* (1978). In *Ir. Theol. Quart.*, xlvi, 133–4.

1980

Review of Faulkner (ed.), *Liber Dubliniensis: chapter documents of the Irish Franciscans, 1719–1875* (1978). In *Studies*, lxix, 176–7.

1981

Irish ecclesiastical history since 1500. In Joseph Lee (ed.), *Irish historiography, 1970–79* (Cork: Cork University Press), pp 154–72.

The catholic community in the seventeenth and eighteenth centuries. Dublin: Helicon. Pp vii, 156. (Helicon History of Ireland).

The condition of the catholic church in Great Britain and Ireland in the seventeenth and eighteenth centuries. In Hubert Jedin (ed.), *History of the catholic church* (10 vols, New York: Crossroads), vi, 172–83.

> Orig. pub. in German trans. (see above, 1970); trans. back into English by Gunther J. Holst.

Great Britain and Ireland, 1830–1848. Ibid., vii, 344–9.

> Orig. pub. in German trans. (see above, 1971); trans. back into English by Peter Becker.

The rise of catholicism in the Anglo-Saxon world: England, Scotland, Ireland. Ibid., viii, 121–30.

> Orig. pub. in German trans. (see above, 1971); trans. back into English by Peter Becker.

1982

Review of Cannon, *Irish episcopal meetings* (1979). In *I.H.S.*, xxiii, no. 89, pp 76–7.

Review of O'Byrne (ed.), *The convert rolls* (1981). Ibid., pp 190–91.

1983

The catholic community in the nineteenth century. In *Archiv. Hib.*, xxxviii, 26–33.

Review of Bowen, *Paul Cullen and the shaping of modern Irish catholicism* (1983). In *Furrow*, xxxiv, 791–3.

1984

Two 17th-century proclamations against the catholic clergy. In *Archiv. Hib.*, xxxix, 53–7.

David Rothe, bishop of Ossory, 1618–50. In *Butler Soc. Jn.*, ii, no. 3, pp 315–23.

The early Irish church and the western patriarchate. In Próinséas Ní Chatháin and Michael Richter (eds), *Irland und Europa; Ireland and Europe: Die Kirche im Frühmittelalter; the early church* (Stuttgart: Klett-Cotta), pp 9–15.

A contemporary account of the martyrdom of Conor O'Devaney, O.F.M., bishop of Down and Connor, and Patrick O'Loughran. In *Collect. Hib.*, xxvi, 13–19.

Review of Akenson, *A protestant in Purgatory: Richard Whately* (1981). In *I.H.S.*, xxiv, no. 94, pp 287–8.

Review of Macaulay, *Dr Russell of Maynooth* (1983). In *Furrow*, xxxv, 130–31.

Review of Keenan, *The catholic church in nineteenth-century Ireland* (1983). Ibid., pp 131–2.

1985

The Irish catholic experience: a historical survey. Dublin: Gill & Macmillan. Pp ix, 283.

Catholic marriage under the penal code. In Art Cosgrove (ed.), *Marriage in Ireland* (Dublin: College Press), pp 67–77.

The radical face of Paul Cardinal Cullen. In Patrick J. Corish (ed.), *Radicals, rebels and establishments* (Historical Studies XV, Belfast: Appletree Press), pp 171–84.

Review of Scott, *A historian and his world: a life of Christopher Dawson, 1889–1970* (1984). In *Ir. Theol. Quart.*, li, 165.

Review of Coen, *The wardenship of Galway* (1984). Ibid., p. 249.

1986

Review of Casway, *Owen Roe O'Neill and the struggle for catholic Ireland* (1984). In *Cath. Hist. Rev.*, lxxii, 277–8.

Review of Bellenger, *English and Welsh priests, 1558–1800* (1984?). In *Downside Review*, civ, 54.

1987

Irish catholics before the Famine: patterns and questions. In *Journal of the Wexford Historical Society*, no. 11 (1986–7), pp 59–66.

Two centuries of catholicism in County Wexford. In Kevin Whelan (ed.), *Wexford history and society: interdisciplinary essays on the history of an Irish county* (Dublin: Geography Publications), pp 222–47.

Looking back. In *Furrow*, xxxviii, 555–63.

Maynooth College since 1795.

Review of Moody & Vaughan (eds), *A new history of Ireland*, iv (1986). In *Cath. Hist. Rev.*, lxxiii, 632–3; also in *Jn. Eccles. Hist.*, xxxviii, 504–6.

Review of Miller, *Emigrants and exiles* (1985). In *Cath. Hist. Rev.*, lxxiii, 651–2.

1988

1989

The Irish martyrs. Dublin: Veritas. Pp 32.

Review of Larkin, *The consolidation of the Roman Catholic church in Ireland, 1860–1870* (1987), and Coldrey, *Faith and fatherland* (1988). In *Hist. Jn.*, xxxii, 504–6.

Review of Akenson, *Small differences: Irish catholics and Irish protestants, 1815–1922* (1988). In I.H.S., xxvi, no. 104.

Notes

Chapter 1, Lennon, pp 6–25.

1. For general accounts of the Reformation in Dublin, see M. V. Ronan, *The Reformation in Dublin, 1536–58* (London, 1926); in Ireland, R. D. Edwards, *Church and state in Tudor Ireland* (Dublin, 1935); and in England, A. G. Dickens, *The English Reformation* (London, 1964).
2. See J. J. Scarisbrick, *The Reformation and the English people* (Oxford, 1984), pp 21, 30n., 38, 111–16.
3. J. P. Mahaffy, *An epoch in Irish history: Trinity College, Dublin, 1591–1660* (London, 1903), p.169.
4. R.I.A., Haliday MSS, 12 E 2, ff. 26, 31–2.
5. Mahaffy, *Epoch in Irish history*, p. 169.
6. M. V. Ronan, 'Religious customs of Dublin medieval guilds' in *I.E.R.*, fifth series, xxvi (1925), pp 225–41, 364–85; 'Royal visitation of Dublin, 1615', ed. M. V. Ronan, in *Archiv. Hib.*, vii (1941), p. 13.
7. See, for example, Dickens, *English Reformation*, pp 285ff; Scarisbrick, *Reformation and English people*, pp 19–39, 65–7, 168–70; R. Hutton, 'The local impact of the Tudor Reformation' in C. Haigh (ed.), *The English Reformation revised* (Cambridge, 1987), pp 114–38.
8. See Scarisbrick, *Reformation and English people*, pp 2–12.
9. Dickens, *English Reformation*, pp 285–301.
10. Scarisbrick, *Reformation and English people*, pp 38–9, 168–9.
11. J. Bossy, *Christianity in the west, 1400–1700* (Oxford, 1985), p. 59.
12. See, for example, L. P. Murray, 'The ancient chantries of Co. Louth' in *Journal of the County Louth Archaeological Society*, ix (1939), pp 181–208.
13. R.I.A., Haliday MSS, 12/1, ff. 143, 144, 151; 12/2, ff. 26, 32–3; Ronan, 'Religious customs', pp 378–9.
14. P. J. Corish, *The Irish Catholic experience* (Dublin, 1985), p. 85.
15. The original documents are in R.I.A., Haliday MSS; 12 D 1 is the Account Book, 1584–1817; MSS 12 S 22–33 contain deeds and leases dating from the thirteenth century to the seventeenth; MS 12 O 13 is the White Book, 1655–87; and MS 12 G 10 is an abstract of deeds (nos 1–841) and a collection of miscellaneous papers. Dublin, Pearse Street, Gilbert Library (hereafter D.G.L.) has in MS 246 an abstract of deeds of the guild, fourteenth to eighteenth centuries. H. F. Berry has calendared 160 of the deeds and leases in 'History of the religious guild of St. Anne in St. Audoen's church, Dublin, 1430–1740, taken from its records in the Haliday Collection, R.I.A.' in *R.I.A. Proc.*, xxv, sect. c (1904–5), pp 21–106.

16. Ronan, 'Religious customs'; H. F. Berry (ed.), *Register of the wills and inventories of the diocese of Dublin, 1457–83*; W. Hawkes, 'The liturgy in Dublin, 1200–1500; manuscript sources' in *Reportorium novum*, ii (1958), pp 33–67; M. Murphy, 'The high cost of dying: an analysis of *pro anima* bequests in medieval Dublin' in W. J. Shiels and D. Wood (eds), *The church and wealth: Studies in church history*, xxiv (Oxford, 1987) pp 119–22.

17. Ronan, 'Religious customs', pp 25–47.

18. J. T. Gilbert, *History of the city of Dublin* (3 vols, Dublin, 1854–9), i, pp 324–5.

19. Berry (ed.), *Register of wills*, pp 58–60, 118–20.

20. Ibid., pp 13–15.

21. Ibid., pp 66–8, 109–11, 112–13, 148–9.

22. Berry, 'St. Anne's guild', p. 39.

23. See, for example, Hawkes, 'Liturgy in Dublin', p. 46 for a list of obits inserted in the antiphonarium in St John the Evangelist's church between 1547 and 1559.

24. For the progress of the Henrician Reformation in England, see Hutton, 'Local impact of Tudor Reformation', pp 114–21.

25. Ronan, *Reformation in Dublin*, pp 31–93, 112–28; B. Bradshaw, *The dissolution of the religious orders in Ireland in the reign of Henry VIII* (Cambridge, 1974), pp 103–9.

26. Ronan, 'Religious customs', pp 242–6.

27. Ibid., p. 246.

28. Ronan, *Reformation in Dublin*, pp 322–30, 340–3, 346–52, 360–4.

29. Ronan, 'Religious customs', p. 232.

30. Dublin, City Hall Archives (hereafter D.C.A.), MR/5, vii, 8 (*Anc. rec. Dub.*, ii, 30–1).

31. D.C.A., MR/5, vii, 12 (*Anc. rec. Dub.*, ii, 49).

32. Berry (ed.), *Register of wills*, pp 146–8; Ronan, *Reformation in Dublin*, pp 170–8.

33. Ronan, 'Religious customs', pp 25–47; idem, *Reformation in Dublin*, pp 162–4, 187–99.

34. *Extents Ir. mon. possessions*, pp 4–5, 84–5.

35. Berry, 'St. Anne's guild', pp 22–3; R.I.A., MS 12 D 1, ff. 1r–3r, 7r–16v.

36. Berry, 'St. Anne's guild', pp 44, 50.

37. Ibid.

38. Ibid., pp 45–7.

39. Ibid., p. 45.

40. Cf. ibid., pp 42–3, for the appointments of James More and Henry Gauran in 1535 to sing at all services and Divine Service respectively.

41. Ibid., p. 43.

42. Ibid., pp 44–5.

43. R.I.A., MS 12 D 1, ff. 1r–v.

44. Ronan, 'Religious customs', p. 232.
45. See Berry, 'St. Anne's guild', pp 94–5 for an incomplete list of masters and wardens. See R.I.A., 12 D 1 for details of office-holders from 1584 onwards. For the full list of city aldermen in the period, see C. Lennon, *The Lords of Dublin in the age of Reformation* (Dublin, 1989), appendix I.
46. Berry, 'St. Anne's guild', pp 94–5.
47. T.C.D., MS 1207, 'Will of Robert Golding', 1562.
48. R.I.A., MS 12 D 1, f. 17v.
49. Ibid., f. 18v; Berry, 'St. Anne's guild', pp 46–7.
50. Berry, 'St. Anne's guild', pp 33, 48–50.
51. R.I.A., MS 12 D 1, f. 18v.
52. Ibid., ff. 18v, 19r.
53. Ibid., f. 18v; Berry, 'St. Anne's guild', p. 29.
54. R.I.A., MS 12 D 1, f. 25v.
55. Berry, 'St. Anne's guild', pp 22, 44.
56. R.I.A., MS 12 D 1, ff. 19r–22r.
57. Ibid., ff. 3r–v; Berry, 'St. Anne's guild', pp 22–3.
58. See R.I.A., MS 12 D 1 for membership details; Lennon, *Lords of Dublin*, appendix I, for details of family relationships.
59. Berry, 'St. Anne's guild', pp 23, 40, 55, 73, 79.
60. M. V. Ronan, 'Religious life in old Dublin' in *Dublin Historical Record* (hereafter *D.H.R.*), ii (1939–40), pp 106–7.
61. R.I.A., MS 12 D 1, ff. 3v.
62. Scarisbrick, *Reformation and English people*, p. 37.
63. Lennon, *Lords of Dublin*, chapters II–IV.
64. Ibid., appendix I; R.I.A., 12 D 1, ff. 3r–v.
65. Lennon, *Lords of Dublin*, chapter IV.
66. R.I.A., 12 D 1, f. 3r.
67. Ibid., ff. 7r–11r.
68. Berry, 'St. Anne's guild', pp 28–9, 51.
69. Ibid., pp 53–4.
70. See, for example, R.I.A., MS 12 D 1, f. 14r.
71. Ibid, f. 11r.
72. Ibid., ff. 12r–16r.
73. Ibid., ff. 28r–30r.
74. See, for example, ibid., f. 20r; Berry, 'St. Anne's guild', p. 93.
75. See, for example, A. Sheehan, 'The recusancy revolt of 1603: a reinterpretation' in *Archiv. Hib.*, xxxviii (1983), pp 3–13.
76. See, for example, Berry, 'St. Anne's guild', pp 77, 86 (nos 108, 132); R.I.A., 12 D 1, ff. 19v, 28r.
77. R.I.A., MS 12 D 1, f. 22r.
78. Ibid.
79. *Fiants Ire., Eliz.*, 5834; *Cal. S.P. Ire.*, 1601–3, pp 566–9; R.I.A., MS 12 D 1, ff. 18r, 19v.
80. D.G.L., MS 246, list of miscellaneous papers (bundle N, no. 7).

81. See, H. Pawlisch, *Sir John Davies and the conquest of Ireland: a study in legal imperialism* (Cambridge, 1985).
82. R.I.A., MS 12 E 2, ff. 26, 32–3.
83. Berry, 'St. Anne's guild', pp 33–7.
84. R.I.A., MS 12 D 1, ff. 41r–v.
85. Ibid., pp 37–8; D.G.L., MS 245, 'A further consideration of the state of St. Anne's guild', 1682.
86. R.I.A., MS 12 D 1, f. 18r.
87. See ibid., f. 1r.
88. Ibid., f. 17r.
89. Ibid., f. 18v.
90. Ibid., f. 24r.
91. Ibid., ff. 14r, 19v, 24r.
92. Ibid., f. 26r.
93. Ibid., ff. 27r, 31r–33r.
94. Berry, 'St. Anne's guild', pp 33–4.
95. Ibid., p. 34.
96. Ibid., p. 37.
97. R.I.A., MS 12 D 1, f. 25v.
98. 'Archbishop Bulkeley's visitation, of Dublin, 1630', ed. M. V. Ronan, in *Archiv. Hib.*, viii (1941), p. 59.
99. Ibid.
100. Berry, 'St. Anne's guild', p. 34.
101. Ibid.
102. See Ronan, 'Religious customs', p. 381 for the text.
103. R.I.A., MS 12 D 1, ff. 12r–16r, 27r–32r; Lennon, *Lords of Dublin*, appendix I.
104. C. Lennon, 'The rise of recusancy among the Dublin patricians, 1580–1613' in W. J. Shiels and D. Wood (eds), *The churches, Ireland and the Irish: Studies in church history*, xxv (Oxford, 1989), pp 123–32.
105. P.R.O., S.P. 63/102/114, 114 (i), 103/36, 36(1)–(ii), 104/38, 38(i); H.M.C., *Salisbury*, vi, pp 431–2; *Cal. S.P. Ire.*, 1603–6, pp 348–9.
106. *H.M.C., Egmont*, i, pp 30–1.
107. D.C.A., MR/17, f. 90; D.G.L., MS 169, p. 124.
108. *Cal. S.P. Ire.*, 1611–14, p. 362.
109. *H.M.C., Egmont*, i, pp 30–1; *Cal. S.P. Ire.*, 1603–6, pp 348–9, 353–4, 391, 401–2.
110. *Cal. S.P. Ire.*, 1603–6, pp 362–3; *Cal. Carew MSS*, 1603–24, p. 271.
111. R.I.A., MS 12 D 1, ff. 18v, 22v.
112. Ibid., f. 18v.
113. Ronan, 'Religious life in Dublin', pp 106–7.
114. Ibid.,; R.I.A., 12 D 1, ff. 3r–v.
115. *Ibernia Ignat.*, p. 249.
116. Ibid., pp 228–9; *D.H.R.*, xxxvii (1984), pp 54–8.
117. Lennon, 'Recusancy among the Dublin patricians', pp 129–32.

118. See, for example, J. McErlean, *The sodality of the Blessed Virgin Mary* (Dublin, 1928); P. J. Corish, *The Irish Catholic community in the seventeenth and eighteenth centuries* (Dublin, 1981), pp 39, 85.

119. Ronan, 'Religious customs', p. 368n; *Irish builder* (1887), p. 348.

120. D.G.L., MS 246, 'A further consideration of St. Anne's guild', 1682.

Chapter 2, Walshe, pp 26–52.

1. Wallop to Walsingham, July 1582 (P.R.O., S.P. 63/94/64).

2. Note of chief offenders in the English Pale, January 1582 (P.R.O., S.P. 63/88/40iv).

3. See, for example, J. H. Elliott, *Europe divided 1559–1598* (London, 1968); also H. G. Koenigsberger and G. L. Mosse, *Europe in the sixteenth century* (London, 1968).

4. J. T. Gilbert (ed.), *Facsimiles of the National Manuscripts of Ireland*, plate xxii.

5. Anthony Wood, *Athenae Oxoniensis*, ed. Bliss. (London, 1812–14), Vol. i, p. 457.

6. Ciaran Brady, 'Conservative subversives: the community of the Pale and the Dublin administration, 1556–1586' in P. J. Corish (ed.), *Radicals, rebels and establishments. Historical Studies XV* (Belfast, 1985).

7. Wallop to Walsingham, 1 Nov. 1581 (P.R.O., S.P. 63/97/1).

8. Lord Deputy to Lords Burghley, Sussex and Leicester, 8 May 1575 (P.R.O., S.P. 63/51/8).

9. *Cal. Carew MSS.*, 1575–88, p. 103.

10. Waterhouse to Walsingham, 14 June 1574 (P.R.O., S.P. 63/46/64).

11. Patrick Collinson, *The Elizabethan puritan movement* (Oxford, 1982). See also my unpublished thesis, 'The life and career of Hugh Brady: ecclesiastical and secular roles in the life of an Irish Elizabethan bishop', pp 214–27 (M.A., N.U.I., Maynooth, 1985).

12. Matters to charge Baron Delvin with, 23 Dec. 1580 (P.R.O., S.P. 63/79/30).

13. Fenton to Walsingham (Confession of the wife of Fiach MacHugh O'Byrne), 7 Mar. 1581 (P.R.O., S.P. 63/81/10).

14. Ibid.

15. Abstract of matters against Baron Delvin, June 1582 (P.R.O., S.P. 63/93/86).

16. Ibid.

17. See, for example, Notes extracted out of the confession of J. Cusack, 14 Mar. 1582 (P.R.O., S.P. 63/90/24).

18. Matters to charge Baron Delvin with, 23 Dec. 1580 (P.R.O., S.P. 63/79/30).

19. Fenton to Walsingham, 7 Mar. 1581 (P.R.O., S.P. 63/81/10).

20. Notes extracted out of the confession of J. Cusack of Ellistonrede, 14 Mar. 1582 (P.R.O., S.P. 63/90/24). (He was also known as Walter Betagh.)

21. Lord deputy and council to queen, 23 Dec. 1580 (P.R.O., S.P. 63/79/26).
22. Ibid.
23. Ibid.
24. Wallop to Walsingham, 23 Dec. 1580 (P.R.O., S.P. 63/79/31).
25. Confession of J. Nugent, 5 Feb. 1582 (P.R.O., S.P. 63/89/18).
26. Wallop to Walsingham, 23 Dec. 1580 (P.R.O., S.P. 63/79/31).
27. Examination of James Fitzchristopher Nugent, 30 Dec. 1581 (P.R.O., S.P. 63/87/69).
28. Ibid.
29. Ibid.
30. Confession of J. Nugent, 5 Feb. 1582 (P.R.O., S.P. 63/89/18).
31. Ibid.
32. Ibid.
33. Ibid.
34. Wallop to Walsingham, 8 Mar. 1581 (P.R.O., S.P. 63/81/16).
35. Matters found in the examinations touching Lady Delvin, William Nugent and Nicholas Nugent, Mar. 1582 (P.R.O., S.P. 63/90/39); abstract of confession of J. Cusack, 14 Mar. 1582 (P.R.O., S.P. 63/90/24).
36. Confession of James Fitzchristopher Nugent, 30 Dec. 1581 (P.R.O., S.P. 63/87/69).
37. Ibid. Also Confession of J. Nugent, 5 Feb. 1582 (P.R.O., S.P. 63/89/18).
38. Confession of J. Nugent, 5 Feb. 1582 (P.R.O., S.P. 63/89/18).
39. See, for example, Brendan Bradshaw, *The Irish constitutional revolution of the sixteenth century* (Cambridge, 1979); also Nicholas Canny, *The formation of the Old English elite in Ireland* (O'Donnell Lecture, Dublin, 1975).
40. Wallop to Walsingham, 9 Oct. 1580 (P.R.O., S.P. 63/77/23).
41. Burghley to Wallop (copy), 18 Feb. 1582 (P.R.O., S.P. 63/91/2 (i)).
42. Valuation of the traitors' lands in the Pale, Apr. 1582 (P.R.O., S.P. 63/90/59).
43. Examination of James Fitzchristopher Nugent, 3 Dec. 1581 (P.R.O., S.P. 63/87/69).
44. Traitors' lands within the Pale, 26 Apr. 1581 (P.R.O., S.P. 63/82/54 (ii)).
45. Edward Cusack to Gerot Aylmer, 26 May 1582 (P.R.O., S.P. 63/88/40 (iii)).
46. Note of the lands and goods of the rebels, Jan. 1582 (P.R.O., S.P. 63/88/40 (iii).
47. N. White to Burghley, 9 Dec. 1581 (P.R.O., S.P. 63/87/22 (i)).
48. Ibid.
49. Ibid.
50. Ibid.

51. Various confessions concerning the Nugent rebellion, 9–10 Oct. 1581 (P.R.O., S.P. 63/85/19).
52. Confession of C. Bathe, 20 Oct. 1581 (P.R.O., S.P. 63/86/30 (ii)).
53. Various confessions concerning the Nugent rebellions, 24 Mar. 1582 (P.R.O., S.P. 63/90/39).
54. Confession of J. Cusack of Ellistonrede (extracts), 14 Mar. 1582 (P.R.O., S.P. 63/90/24).
55. Various confessions concerning the Nugent rebellion, 24 Mar. 1582 (P.R.O., S.P. 63/90/39).
56. Various confessions concerning the Nugent rebellion, 9–10 Oct. 1581 (P.R.O., S.P. 63/86/19).
57. Confession of C. Bathe, 20 Oct. 1581 (P.R.O., S.P. 63/86/30 (ii)).
58. Names of those apprehended since 10 Oct. 1581 (P.R.O., S.P. 63/86/30 (i)).
59. Names of those apprehended for the Nugent conspiracy and those executed for the Baltinglass conspiracy, 23 Nov. 1581 (P.R.O., S.P. 63/86/79).
60. Wallop to Walsingham, 20 Oct. 1581 (P.R.O., S.P. 63/86/27).
61. Various confessions concerning the Nugent rebellion, 9–10 Oct. 1581 (P.R.O., S.P. 63/86/19).
62. Sir L. Dillon to L. Chancellor and Sir H. Wallop, 4–5 Oct. 1581 (P.R.O., S.P. 63/86/10 (i)).
63. Wallop to Burghley, 6 July 1581 (P.R.O., S.P. 63/84/4).
64. Ibid.
65. Dillon to Walsingham, 20 Oct. 1581 (P.R.O., S.P. 63/87/27).
66. Examination of W. Clinch, 4 Oct. 1581 (P.R.O., S.P. 63/86/10 (i)); also S.P. 63/86/17).
67. Grey to Walsingham, 14 Mar. 1582 (P.R.O., S.P. 63/90/23).
68. Wallop to Burghley, 6 July 1581 (P.R.O., S.P. 63/84/4).
69. Lord Justices to Burghley, 2 Nov. 1582 (P.R.O., S.P. 63/97/1 (i)).
70. Waterhouse to Walsingham, 23 July 1581 (P.R.O., S.P. 63/84/44); privy council in Dublin to privy council in London, 31 July 1581 (P.R.O., S.P. 63/84/53).
71. Waterhouse to Walsingham, 23 July 1581 (P.R.O., S.P. 63/84/44).
72. Ibid.
73. Various confessions concerning the Nugent rebellion, 9–10 Oct. 1581 (P.R.O., S.P. 63/86/19).
74. Ibid.
75. Ibid.
76. Waterhouse to Walsingham, 10 June 1581 (P.R.O., S.P. 63/84/12 (i)).
77. Grey to Walsingham, 18 July 1581 (P.R.O., S.P. 63/84/26).
78. Confession of J. Nugent, 5 Feb. 1582 (P.R.O., S.P. 63/89/18).
79. Fenton to Burghley, 21 Sept. 1581 (P.R.O., S.P. 63/85/54).
80. Examination of William Clinch, 4 Oct. 1581 (P.R.O., S.P. 63/86/10).

81. Confession of J. Nugent, loc. cit.
82. Various confessions concerning the Nugent rebellion (P.R.O., S.P. 63/86/19).
83. Confession of J. Nugent, loc. cit.
84. Various confessions, loc. cit.
85. Ibid.
86. Abstract of matters against Baron Delvin, June 1582 (P.R.O., S.P. 63/93/86).
87. Wallop to Walsingham, July 1582 (P.R.O., S.P. 63/93/86).
88. Abstract of matters against Baron Delvin, June 1582 (P.R.O., S.P. 63/93/86).
89. L. Chancellor and Wallop to Walsingham, 24 Oct. 1581 (P.R.O., S.P. 63/86/30).
90. Fenton to Walsingham, 23 Nov. 1581 (P.R.O., S.P. 63/86/80).
91. Ibid.
92. Declaration of Lord Grey, Dec. 1583 (P.R.O., S.P. 63/106/62).
93. Report by Thomas Jones, 18 Nov. 1581 (P.R.O., S.P. 63/86/69).
94. Names of those apprehended for the Nugent conspiracy and those executed for the Baltinglass conspiracy, 23 Nov. 1581 (P.R.O., S.P. 63/86/79).
95. Lands and goods of the rebels given by the L. Deputy, 27 Jan. 1582 (P.R.O., S.P. 63/88/40).
96. The L. Deputy's disposition of traitors' goods, July 1582 (unsigned), (P.R.O., S.P. 63/94/75).
97. Chief offenders impeached by J. Cusack of Ellistonrede, Jan. 1582 (P.R.O., S.P. 63/88/40)(iv)).
98. Ibid.
99. Examination of J. McCaron, 6 Dec. 1582 (P.R.O., S.P. 63/98/18).
100. E. Cusack to G. Aylmer, 26 May 1582 (P.R.O., S.P. 63/92/69; also S.P. 63/88/40).
101. Notes from the confession of J. Cusack, 14 Mar. 1582 (P.R.O., S.P. 63/90/24).
102. Cusack to Aylmer, loc. cit.
103. Notes from the confession of J. Cusack, loc. cit.
104. Confession of James Fitzchristopher Nugent, 30 Dec. 1581 (P.R.O., S.P. 63/87/69; also S.P. 63/89/18).
105. Confession of J. Nugent, 5 Feb. 1582 (P.R.O., S.P. 63/89/18); 'Calendar of Irish council book 1581–86', in Quinn, ed., *Anal. Hib.*, no. 24 (1967), p. 121, no. 89.
106. Confession of J. Nugent, loc. cit.
107. 'Calendar of the Irish council book'.
108. Anonymous letter to Ellen Nugent, 5 July 1583 (P.R.O., S.P. 63/103/8).
109. Ibid.
110. Cusack to Aylmer, 26 May 1582 (P.R.O., S.P. 63/92/69).
111. Ibid.

112. Grey to Walsingham, 7 May 1582 (P.R.O., S.P. 63/92/11).
113. Grey to Walsingham, 12 Apr. (P.R.O., S.P. 63/91/22).
114. Fenton to Privy Council 13 Apr. 1582 (P.R.O., S.P. 63/91/31).
115. Wallop to Walsingham, 15 Apr. 1582 (P.R.O., S.P. 63/91/36).
116. Malby to Walsingham, 28 May 1582 (P.R.O., S.P. 63/92/92).
117. Burghley to Wallop, 1 Apr. 1582 (P.R.O., S.P. 63/91/2 (i)).
118 Grey to Walsingham, 22 Feb. 1582 (P.R.O., S.P. 63/89/43).
119. Names of those excepted from the general pardon, 10 July 1582 (P.R.O., S.P. 63/84/12 (i)).
120. Note written by E. Cusack, Sept. 1582 (P.R.O., S.P. 63/95/84).
121. Ibid; also Note of offenders in the English Pale, (P.R.O., S.P. 63/88/40 (iv)).
122. Note by E. Cusack, loc. cit.
123. L. Deputy's disposition of traitors' goods, July 1582 (P.R.O., S.P. 63/94/75), probably written by Wallop.
124. Note of lands and goods of the rebels given by the L. Deputy, Jan. 1582 (P.R.O., S.P. 63/88/40 (iii)).
125. *Cal. pat. rolls Ire., Eliz.*, pp 36, 73.
126. Ibid.
127. *Cal. pat. rolls Ire., Eliz.*, p. 38; Grants and restitutions from attainted lands, Apr. 1584 (P.R.O., S.P. 63/109/75).
128 *Cal. pat rolls, Ire. Eliz.*, p. 38; grants and restitutions from attainted lands, Apr. 1584 (P.R.O., S.P. 63/109/75).
129. Grants and restitutions, loc. cit.
130. Petition of St Leger for fine on W. Nugent's lands, Mar. 1584 (P.R.O., S.P. 63/108/90).
131. See, for example, Steven Ellis, *Tudor Ireland* (London 1985), pp 282–8; Ciaran Brady, 'Conservative subversives'.
132. Names of the men of Kildare and Meath executed, 3 Dec. 1581 (P.R.O., S.P. 63/87/1 (ii)).
133. Wallop to Walsingham, 24 Oct. 1581 (P.R.O., S.P. 63/86/31).
134. Examination of Delvin by Mildmay and Gerrard, 22 June 1582 (P.R.O., S.P. 63/93/50).
135. Bryskett to Walsingham, 21 Apr. 1582 (P.R.O., S.P. 63/82/45).
136. Ibid.
137. See, for example, K. Bottigheimer, 'The failure of the Reformation in Ireland', in *Jn. ecc. hist.*, xxxvi (1985); also, Sir H. Sidney to Queen, 28 Apr. 1576 (P.R.O., S.P. 63/55/38).
138 See Bottigheimer, op. cit.
139. MacGeoghegan to Walter Hope, Rome, Dec. 2 1583 (P.R.O., S.P. 63/106/2).
140. *Cal. S.P. for.*, 1582, p. 394.
141. Ibid., p. 426.
142. Examination of Nowland Tadee, 23 Jan. 1584 (P.R.O., S.P. 63/107/4).
143. Ibid.

144. Declaration of W. Nugent, 4 Dec. 1584 (P.R.O., S.P. 63/113/12).
145. 'Miscellanea Vaticano-Hibernica' ed. J. Hagan in *Archiv. Hib.*, vii (1918–22), pp 318–34.
146. *Calendar Scottish Papers*, vii, p. 200.
147. Ibid., p. 230.
148. Declaration of W. Nugent, loc. cit.
149. Ibid.
150. *Calendar Scottish Papers*, vii, p. 244; Lord Deputy and Council to Privy Council, 6 Aug. 1584 (P.R.O., S.P. 63/111/39 enclosure).
151. *Cal. Carew MSS.*, *1575–88*, p. 380.
152. Perrot to Walsingham, 4 Dec. 1584 (P.R.O., S.P. 63/113/10).
153. Declaration of W. Nugent, loc. cit.; Submission of W. Nugent, 4 Dec. 1584 (P.R.O., S.P. 63/113/11).
154. *Cal. pat. rolls Ire.*, *Eliz.*, pp 114–15; Declaration of Shane McCongowney, 5 Feb. 1591 (P.R.O., S.P. 63/163/32). This man was entertained by Nugent at this time at his house at Ross.
155. This legal battle can be easily followed through *Cal. S.P. Ire.*, *1591–2*.
156. Delvin to Mountjoy, 26 Apr. 1600 (P.R.O., S.P. 63/207(ii)/143).
157. J. H. Elliott, 'Revolution and continuity in early modern Europe' in Parker and Smith (ed.), *The general crisis of the seventeenth century*, (London, 1978).
158. A. Lloyd Moote, 'The precondition of revolutions in early modern Europe', in *Canadian Journal of History*, VIII (1973), pp 207–34.
159. I owe much information on Baltinglass's activities to Ann Egan who is working at St Patrick's College, Maynooth, on a thesis concerning the life of Baltinglass.

Chapter 3, Henry, pp 53–77.

ABBREVIATIONS

A.G.R.	— Archives Générales du Royaume, Brussels
A.G.R. E.A.	— Ibid., papiers d'état et de l'audience
A.G.R. E.G.	— Ibid., secretairerie d'état et de guerre
A.G.R. E.G.C.	— Ibid., secretairerie d'état et de guerre, correspondances des gouverneurs
A.G.S.	— Archivo General de Simancas, Spain
A.G.S. E.	— Ibid., Secretaria
Parish Records:	
A.H.V., Brussels	— Archives de l'Hôtel de Ville, Bruxelles
A.H.V., St. Michel et Gudule	— Ibid., paroisse de Saints Michel et Gudule
A.H.V., St. Catherine	— Ibid., paroisse de Saint Catherine
A.H.V., Bruges	— Archives de l'Hôtel de Ville, Bruges
A.H.V., St. Giles	— Ibid., paroisse de Saint Giles
A.H.V., Notre Dame	— Ibid., paroisse de Notre Dame
A.J.	— Archives Jesuitiques in the Archives Générales du Royaume in Brussels

1. The term 'Low Countries' has been used in this essay to denote the whole of the Netherlands while Flanders or the Spanish Netherlands has been used to refer to that part of it under Spain and later the Archdukes. It should be noted therefore that 'Flanders' does not designate the province of that name.

2. A number of sources claimed that Stanley had brought over as many as 1,500 troops to the Low Countries but this was probably the number under his command there rather than the number he actually brought from Ireland. See Dec. 1585, *Cal. S.P. Spain, 1580–6*, p. 689; Thomas Heywood, Introduction to *The copie of a letter written by M. doctor Allen; concerning the yielding up of the cities of Daventrie* . . . Chatham Society, vol. xxv (1581), pp v–vi.

3. Captains granted commissions after 1606 were also successful in recruiting their quota of 200 and these included Art O'Neill, Teig MacCarthy, Neil MacLoughlin and John Bathe. See July 1606, A.G.R. E.G., reg. 23/391–91v., ibid, reg. 23/385v–86; ibid reg. 22/95.

4. 1 June 1582, A.G.R. E.G., reg. 10/77; 1 June 1585; ibid reg. 9/274v; Brendan Jennings, *Wild Geese in Spanish Flanders, 1582–1700* (Dublin, 1964), p. 65, hereafter referred to as Jennings, *Wild Geese*.

5. *The Fugger Newsletters, 1568–1605*, ed. Victor von Klarwill, trans. L. S. K. Byrne 2nd series (London, 1926), p. 281. These letters are from the correspondence of the Fuggers of Augsburg, bankers to the Spanish government. Having connections in nearly every part of the known world, their letters formed a kind of news report on political, financial and even local events in cities such as London, Paris, Antwerp and Venice. The second series cited above related specifically to England.

6. With the reorganisation of the Army of Flanders in 1596, the Irish were grouped into two companies under John de Claramonte and Edward Fitzgerald (see 15 June 1596 A.G.R. E.G., reg. 16/113; 5 Aug. 1596; ibid reg. 16/163v) and by 1605 three other companies under Lawrence Barnwall, Alexander Eustace and William Walshe appear in the army records. See 17 Jan. 1605; ibid reg. 22/3v.; 20 Feb. 1605 ibid reg. 22/62v.; 2 April 1605, ibid reg. 22/120v.; Jennings, *Wild Geese*, pp. 77–8.

7. For Northern exiles, see particularly 4 Nov. 1607, *Cal. S.P. Ire., 1606–8*, p. 632.

8. Of Stanley's expedition in 1586, 500 were described by Deputy Perrot as 'kerne' while 600 were from 'discharged royal bands from Ireland'. Since these royal bands or English companies almost certainly contained some native Irish, the number of Irish in the expedition was probably in the region of 700. See 29 Dec. 1585, *Cal. S.P. for., 1585–6*, p. 253; 15 Sept. 1586, *Fugger Newsletters*, p. 118.

9. Apart from a handful of Scottish and English soldiers all the soldiers in Henry O'Neill's fifteen-company-strong regiment in 1609 appear to have been Irish. For reports on the size of the regiment, see note 8 above; also *H.M.C. Downshire MSS*, ii, p. 10; *Cal. S.P. Ire., 1603–6*, pp 396–8. The only names we can identify from the officer ranks between 1605 and 1610 which were obviously non-Irish were those of Nicholas Erlens (drum-major), Denis Meable (ensign), Morart Murrtog (sergeant), Thomas Goodman (ensign), John Kivett (corporal of the field), as well as possibly Captain Symond and the Scottish captain, Paul Raddock.

10. See for example *Cal. S.P. for., 1589*, pp 337–8; *Cal. S.P. Ire., 1592–6*, pp 64–7.

11. This is a very conservative estimate as the lowest ever muster roll for Stanley's regiment was 424 men in November 1591. For most years where figures are available the number was in the region of 800–900 men. A.G.S. Contaduria mayor de Cuentas, 22/6 unfol. pliegos de Asiento; Geoffrey Parker, *The army of Flanders and the Spanish road 1567–1659* (Cambridge, 1972), pp 214–15. Hereafter cited as Parker, *Spanish road*.

12. Parker, *Spanish road*, pp 208–9.

13. Ibid., pp 25–39.

14. See particularly 2 Nov. 1605, *Cal. S.P. Ire., 1603–6*, pp 345–6; 29 May 1606, ibid., pp 486–7; Mar. 1607, *Cal. S.P. Ire., 1606–8*, p. 132.

15. 16 Jan. 1606, *Cal. S.P. Ire., 1603–6*, p. 385.

16. *Cal. S.P. Ire., 1603–6*, pp 512–13.

17. Intelligence from Brussels, *Cal. S.P. Ire., 1606–8*, pp 652–3.

18. For Walter Delahide of Moyglare, Maynooth, see Jennings, *Wild Geese*, p. 484; for Thomas Stanihurst of Dublin, see Genealogical Office MS 48, p.15; Jennings, *Wild Geese*, pp 11, 13, 133–4, 529; for Thomas St Lawrence, younger brother to Christopher named above, see F.E. Ball, *Howth and its owners* (Dublin, 1917), pp 105, 108–9; Jennings, *Wild Geese*, pp 82, 87, 92, 102, 117.

19. A.G.S. E. 2744; Walsh, 'Womenfolk' in *Ir. Sword* v (1961–2), p. 100.

20. For further details on the career of Cormac Ros O'Connor in Flanders see 20 July 1589, A.G.R. E.G., reg. 12/137v. 20 Feb. 1605, ibid reg. 22/62v., 29 July 1603, ibid, reg. 21/257v. For Cornelius O'Reilly see 10 May 1606, A.G.R. E.G., reg. 23/286; Jennings, *Wild Geese*, pp 86, 135, 483.

21. 19/29 June 1591, *Cal. S.P. Ire., 1588–92*, p. 398.

22. 'Captain of the Gallowglass to Cormack MacDermot, Lord of Muskrye' 20 Mar. 1608, *Cal. S.P. Ire., 1606–8*, pp 440–1.

23. 7 Oct. 1605, *H.M.C. Salisbury MSS*, xvii, p. 449.

24. See 12 Oct. 1605, *Cal. S.P. Ire., 1603–6*, pp 336–7; James I, *H.M.C. Salisbury MSS*, xxiv, pp 254–5.

25. C.G. Cruickshank, *Elizabeth's army* (2nd edn., Oxford, 1966), p. 298.

26. H. J. C. von Grimmelhausen, *Simplicissimus — the vagabond*, trans. A.T.S. Goodrick, (London, 1924), p. 256.
27. See description of Irish women in 'Memorial Historicio Espanel', Cronica 1652–60. See Dorothy Molloy, 'In search of the Wild Geese', in *Éire–Ireland*, v (1970), p. 6.
28. See letters to Mrs Thickpenny 1586–1600, and letters of Peter Barnwall in 1608: *Cal. S.P. Ire., 1586–8*, p. 58; *A.P.C., 1586–7*, pp 178–9; *Cal. S.P. Ire., 1600*, p. 500; *Cal. S.P. Ire., 1608–10*, p. 90.
29. Of 130 leave of absences granted between 1587 and 1610 for Ireland, at least 17 were for reasons related to family and property. The term 'casa', however, in Spanish could relate as easily to the 'house' or extended kin of a soldier as to his immediate family and such a licence did not prove a soldier's wife and children were not with him in Flanders.
30. For names we have of those serving in Stanley's regiment, Independent Irish companies, and Henry O'Neill's regiment, see Appendices I–VI in Gráinne Henry, 'Wild Geese in Spanish Flanders' (M.A. thesis, N.U.I. (Maynooth), 1986).
31. *Cal. Carew MSS, 1589–1600*, p. 516.
32. A.G.R. E.A., carton 1944; Jennings, *Wild Geese*, pp 134–5.
33. A.G.R. E.G., reg. 11/45v.
34. Sept. 1607, Meehan, *Fate and fortunes*, p. 151; P.R.O., S.P. 77/11/351–2.
35. For names of captains and officers in Stanley's regiment see Ralph Sadler, *The State Papers and letters of Sir Ralph Sadler*, ed. Arthur Clifford 2 vols. (Edinburgh, 1809), pp 230–40; Heywood, *Cardinal Allen's Defence . . .*, pp xxiiiff; Valladolid documents in David Matthew, *The Celtic peoples and renaissance Europe* (London, 1933), p. 484.
36. For some Englishmen who served in Irish companies see, for example, passports to England, *Cal. pat. rolls Ire., Eliz.*, pp 255–6; *H.M.C. Salisbury MSS*, xiii, p. 398. List of English names: 19 Feb. 1605, A.G.R. E.G., reg. 22/59v.
37. There were almost certainly companies serving also under Thomas Barry and Walter Butler but I could find no trace of the actual commissions granted to them.
38. I owe a great debt to Ms Michelene Walsh under whose supervision this parish material was collected and housed in the Overseas Archives, Earlsfort Terrace, Dublin. While isolated occurrences of Irish names in parish registers may have been missed, most of the parish registers in the Low Countries, likely to yield Irish names, have been systematically searched. A similar pattern of Irish communities can be found in Spain and it should be noted that the Spanish policy of grouping Irish refugees in different parts of Spanish territory obviously accelerated the pattern of group settlement.

39. See notes above for parish records of Irish interest that have been collected from Belgium up to 1620.

40. A.H.V. (Bruxelles), St. Catherine, Baptisms Bb/3. Interestingly no Irish records have been found, at least in substantial numbers, outside Brussels or Bruges until the 1770s at Mons though many of the parish records outside the major towns were lost in the Napoleonic and world wars.

41. See Heywood, *Cardinal Allen's defence* . . ., p. xliii; P.R.O., S.P. 77/6/218.

42. Heywood, *Cardinal Allen's defence* . . ., pp xviii–xix.

43. The Prioress of the White Ladies to Luys Verreyken, 16 June 1610, A.G.R. E.A., liasse 1947 i; Jennings, *Wild Geese*, pp 125–7.

44. See Archives de l'Etat, Bruges, Inscriptions Funeraires—Notre Dame, Chapelle de Saint Marguerte, pp 328–9.

45. J. J. Silke, 'The Irish abroad, 1534–1691', in *N.H.I.*, iii p. 606; Dorothy Molloy 'In search of the Wild Geese', in *Éire–Ireland* V (1970) pp 3–14.

46. D. Molloy, 'In search of Wild Geese', p. 7.

47. See, for example, 13 Jan. 1616, A.G.R. E.G.C., reg. 179/27.

48. 3 Jan. 1635, A.G.R. A.J., carton 1973, liasse 1974; Jennings, *Wild Geese*, pp 277–80.

49. See J. J. Silke, 'The Irish abroad . . .', in *N.H.I.*, iii, p. 605; M. Walsh, *Spanish knights*, i, p. vi; A.G.R. E.G.C., reg. 182/38; ibid, E.G., reg. 25/355v; ibid, reg. 25/106v; ibid, reg. 25/324v.

50. For a good account of the Irish person's legal position in Spanish territories, see John MacErlean, 'Ireland and World Contact', in *Studies*, viii, pt. i (1919), p. 307; A. J. Loomie, 'Religion and Elizabethan Commerce with Spain', in *Cath. Hist. Review*, lx (1964), pp 46, 48. For Thomas Preston and John Kennedy, see *Cal. S.P. Ire., 1633–47*, p. 613; Jennings, *Wild Geese*, p. 333.

51. Heywood, *Cardinal Allen's Defence* . . ., p. xviii.

52. Irish were involved in at least forty-two mutinies in the Army of Flanders. For sickness in the regiment, see 19 Sept. 1610, *H.M.C. Downshire MSS*, ii, p. 363.

53. See table in Gráinne Henry, 'Wild Geese', p. 203.

54. For an excellent review in English, of Dutch and Flemish works on the Spanish Netherlands in this period, see James Tracy, 'Miscellany with and without the Counter-Reformation: The Catholic Church in the Spanish Netherlands and the Dutch Republic, 1580–1650', in *Cath. Hist. Review, lxxi* (Oct. 1985), pp 547–75. Many of these works claim that, resulting from the aggression of the Protestant north, the southern provinces developed a distinctive 'religious patriotism'.

55. A nunciature was established in Brussels in 1596 by the papacy. However, since papal decrees could not be promulgated in the

Netherlands without permission from the Council of State, initiative in religious affairs passed more and more to the Archdukes.

56. I am only examining relations with the merchant community in so far as the merchants may have formed part of the exile group as a whole. While it is certainly worth looking at this group as a separate unit which may have had specific grievances with England relating to trade, there was, unlike Spain, no large Irish merchant community in the Low Countries to merit a separate analysis.

57. Sadler, *Papers and Letters*, p. 235; John Strype, *Annals of the Reformation and Establishment of Religion . . .*, 4 vols. (Oxford, 1820–40), ii, p. 428.

58. For further information on these colleges see Helga Hammerstein, 'Aspects of the continental education of Irish students in the reign of Elizabeth I', in *Hist. Studies*, viii (1971), pp 137–54; Canice Mooney, 'The Golden Age of the Irish Franciscans, 1615–50', in S. O'Brien (ed.), *Measgra i gcuimhne Mhichil Ui Chléirigh* (Dublin, 1944).

59. See B. Jennings, 'Irish names in the Malines ordination registers, 1602–1794', in *I.E.R.*, lxxv (Jan–June 1951), pp 149–62; lxxvi (July–Dec. 1952) pp 44–48, 128–30, 222–33, 314–18, 399–408, 483–7; lxxvii (Jan.–June 1952), pp 202–7, 366–9.

60. Helen Concannon, *The Poor Clares of Ireland* (Dublin 1929), pp xxiii–xxv. The exception was Martha Cheevers.

61. 1592, *H.M.C. Salisbury MSS*, iv, p. 262.

62. See Gráinne Henry, 'Wild Geese', Appendix IX for list of all these chaplains' names.

63. A. Poncelet, *Histoire de la Compagnie de Jésus aux Pays-Bas* (Brussels, 1927–8), pp 408–11.

64. Rome, 26 June 1621, A.R.S.I. Austria 3, (l), p. 157 (Archivum Romanum Societatis Jesu). I am very grateful to Brian Jackson for allowing me to use this reference.

65. Jennings, *Wild Geese*, p. 524.

66. 14 Nov. 1607, A.G.R. E.G., reg. 24/81.

67. See Henry Fitzsimons, *Words of comfort to persecuted Catholics written in exile anno 1607. Letters from a cell in Dublin Castle and Diary of the Bohemian war of 1620*, ed. Edmund Hogan (Dublin, 1881), pp 263–4.

68. Ibid., p. 253.

69. O'Hussey, *Teasgasg Críosdaithe* (Antwerp, 1611).

70. Edmondes to Salisbury, 5 April 1606, *H.M.C. Salisbury MSS*, xviii, p. 99.

71. Note that marriage registers explored by Geoffrey Parker from the garrison church of Antwerp included the names of soldiers of many different nationalities. See G. Parker, 'New Light on an Old

Theme: Spain and the Netherlands, 1550–1650', *Eur. Hist. Quart.*, xv (1985), pp 219–37. Note also a number of statements at a later date by chaplains who testified to the validity of certain Irish marriages. See 17 Dec. 1639, A. J., carton 1962–72, liasse 1969; ibid., carton 1963–72, liasse 1968.

72. Patrick Kearns, *Down's angelic genius: Aodh Mac Aingil* (Iúr Clunn Trá, 1985), p. 24.

73. Jennings, *Wild Geese*, pp 486–8.

74. See 1 Feb. 1606, A.G.R. E.G., reg. 23/105v.–6; 30 May 1608, ibid., reg. 24/175v., reg. 24/165v. respectively.

75. 1596, A.G.S. negoc. de Flandes, E.612/125–6; For names of institutes see A.G.R. E.G.C., reg. 177/167.

76. 13 Aug. 1591, *Cal. S.P. Ire., 1588–92*, p. 410. O'Connor Sligo denied this strongly later—see Nov. 1590, ibid., p. 371.

77. A.G.S. E.2745; M. Walsh (ed.), 'The Last Years of Hugh O'Neill', in *Ir. Sword*, vii (1965–6), p. 142.

78. 16 Jan. 1606, *Cal. S.P. Ire., 1603–6*, p. 385.

79. 8 Jan. 1606, *H.M.C. Salisbury MSS*, xviii, p. 11.

80. 19 Oct. 1609, *Cal. S.P. Ire., 1608–10*, p. 300.

81. 23 Sept. 1610, ibid., p. 496.

82. See *H.M.C. Downshire MSS*, ii, pp 196, 201. Memorial of Hugh O'Neill to Philip of Spain, Walsh (ed.), 'Last years', in *Ir. Sword*, vii (1965–6), p. 336; *Cal. S.P. Ire., 1611–14*, pp 184–5.

83. For each grant see respectively A.G.R. E.G. reg. 13/121 A.G..S. negoc. de Flandes, E. 599.

84. A.G.R. E.G. reg. 12/12.

85. Ibid., reg. 12/11v.

86. For O'Connor Faly, see 23 April 1613, A.G.S. E. 999; M. Walsh (ed.), 'Last years', in *Ir. Sword*, viii (1967–8), p. 231; Last three names respectively as note 83 above and A.G.R. E.G., reg. 22/62v.

87. See Appendices cited in note 30 above.

88. See J. J. Silke, 'The Irish Abroad', *N.H.I.* iii, pp 596–7; idem, 'Spain and the invasion of Ireland, 1601–2', in *I.H.S.*, xiv, pp 300–1 for an overview of this diplomatic network.

89. See particularly 4 Apr. 1606, *Cal. S.P. Ire., 1603–6*, pp 442–3; 19 July 1606, A.G.R. E.G., reg. 23/285v, reg. 23/391; 9 Nov. 1607, ibid., reg. 24/78v.

90. 8 Oct. 1608, *Cal. S.P. Ire., 1608–10*, p. 47.

91. Jennings, *Wild Geese*, p. 135.

92. 16 May 1613, Walsh (ed.), 'Last years', in *Ir. Sword*, viii (1967–8), p. 234.

93. 26 Feb. 1613, A.G.S. negoc. de Roma, E. 999, M. Walsh (ed.), 'Last years', in *Ir. Sword*, viii (1967–8), pp 230–1.

94. Ibid.

95. Ambroise Spinola, Marques de Spinola, Commander in Chief of the Spanish troops in Flanders. 16 May 1613, as note 92 above, pp 233–4.

96. 14 Feb. 1608, *Cal. S.P. Ire., 1606–8*, p. 414.

97. 14 July 1608, A.G.S., negoc. de Roma, E. 988; M. Walsh (ed.), 'Last years', in *Ir. Sword*, v (1961–2), p. 223.

98. 12 Oct. 1610, A.G.S. negoc. de Roma, E. 1861; M. Walsh (ed.), 'Last years', in *Ir. Sword*, vii (1965–6), p. 146.

99. See accounts of Edmondes's attempts to prevent this appointment in Gerrold Casway, 'Henry O'Neill and the formation of the Irish regiment', in *I.H.S.*, xviii (1972–3), pp 485–6; also Memorial of Florence Conry to King of Spain, 9 Sept. 1610, A.G.S. E. 1751; Walsh (ed.), 'Last years', in *Ir. Sword*, vii (1965–6), p. 145.

100. He was the son of Catherine Magennis, Hugh's fourth wife.

101. 24 Jan. 1610, as above, no. 128; E. 944; p. 138.

102. The work commissioned by Sorley was *Duanaire Finn* or *The Book of the Lays of Fionn*, 3 Pts. (Louvain, 1626).

Chapter 4, Murphy, pp 78–98.

1. P. J. Corish, 'Two centuries of Catholicism in County Wexford' in Kevin Whelan (ed.), *Wexford: history and society* (Dublin, 1987), pp 222–47.

2. Wexford, Rowe Street parish archives, Church of the Immaculate Conception, uncatalogued: the register is unpaginated; Bishop Wadding's Notebook is in Killiney, Franciscan Library, MS J 5: edited by P. J. Corish, as 'Bishop Wadding's notebook' in *Archiv. Hib.*, xxix, 49–114; the Hore manuscripts are preserved in Saint Peter's College, Wexford.

3. See Kenneth Nicholls, *Gaelic and gaelicised Ireland in the middle ages* (Dublin, 1972), p. 121.

4. Benignus Millett, 'Survival and re-organisation, 1650–59' in P. J. Corish (ed.) *Hist. Ir. Catholicism*, 3, vii, p. 26.

5. See John Bossy, *The English Catholic Community 1570–1850* (London, 1975), p. 425.

6. See Hore, *Wexford town*, v, p. 363.

7. Ibid., vi, p. 324; for the recovery of the population of County Wexford after Cromwell, see M. Tóibín, 'Population trends in County Wexford' in *The Past*, vi (1950).

8. 'An account of the barony of Forth' ed. H. F. Hore in *Kilkenny and Southeast of Ireland Archaeological Journal*, iv (1862–3), pp 70ff.

9. *New Catholic Encyclopedia* (Washington, 1967), iv, 192.

10. Millet, loc. cit., p. 13.

11. *Kildare Archaeological Society Journal*, vols xv–xix.

12. There may be others of the same ilk who were never entered in the Catholic register, (which is in any case incomplete) either because

they intended to live outside the marriage laws of their Church or because they thought it unwise to have recorded evidence of a Catholic marriage.

13. This seems to have been for the purposes of secrecy. Cf., for example, the case of the Shapland baptisms in which Wadding himself and his close friend, Mary Wiseman, act as sponsors for three of the children. Later, Christine Shapland's children all have the parish priest, David Roche, as godfather.

14. Wexford, Rome Street parish archives, church of the Immaculate Conception, uncatalogued manuscript; Killiney, Franciscan Library, MS J5, 'Bishop Wadding's Notebook'; see Celestine Murphy, '"Immensity confined": Luke Wadding, bishop of Ferns' in *Journal of the Wexford Historical Society*, xii (1988–9), pp 5–22.

15. He was too closely associated with these people for this to be anything but a remote possibility.

16. 'Wadding's notebook', ed. Corish, p. 101.

17. To Mrs. Shapland his 'cittern', to Anthony Talbot his 'base viol'; 'Wadding's notebook', ed. Corish, pp 107–8.

18. Hore, *Wexford town*, v, pp 362, 370.

19. For the recovery of Irish towns commerce during these years see L. M. Cullen, *An economic history of Ireland since 1660* (London, 1972).

20. Wadding to French, quoted in Corish, 'Reformation and Counter-Reformation', *The Centenary record of Wexford's twin churches*, p. 49.

21. William P. Burke, *Irish priests in the Penal Times* (Waterford, 1914), p. 14.

22. Hore, *Wexford town*, v, p. 362.

23. 'Wadding's notebook', ed. Corish, p. 91.

24. Ibid., and also Hore, op. cit., p. 385.

25. Comparison of the names of priests referred to in the Catholic register with those listed in 'The register of popish priests' for Wexford (Grattan-Flood, *Notes towards a parochial history of Ferns, 1915*, Appendix II, p. 174) in 1704, reveals this information. Most of these clergy were educated in Spain.

26. 'Wadding's notebook', ed. Corish, p. 31.

27. Wadding often mentions the priests who performed marriage ceremonies and the districts in which they worked.

28. It will be remembered that Bishop John Roche had found such co-operation advisable. When Wadding died in 1691 he was buried in the Franciscan Friary just outside the town walls; Corish, Introduction to Wadding's notebook in *Archiv. Hib.*, xxix, p. 51, fn 9.

29. Burke, op. cit., pp 51ff.

30. Corish, op. cit. ('Wadding's notebook') p. 51. Also Thomas Wall, Introduction to *The Christmas songs of Luke Wadding* (Dublin, 1960), p. 8.

31. It is also worth mentioning in this connection that Wadding's chapel survived the 'Plot' and continued in use until 1691, completely tolerated by the Protestant element within the town. See Hore, op. cit., p. 385.
32. Wall, *Irish priests*, p. 29.
33. 'Wadding's notebook', ed. Corish, pp 54–91.
34. Wall, *Christmas songs*, p. 30.
35. Ibid., p. 11
36. Ibid.
37. Ibid., p. 14.
38. Hore, *Wexford town*, v, p. 365.
39. This decline was probably assisted by the relaxation of laws against Catholics during the reign of James II which made the use of such precautions unnecessary. Only one further case of double-registration can be discovered after 1685; the marriage of Christine Shapland to William Swiney in 1697.
40. 'Wadding's notebook', ed. Corish, pp 107–8.
41. See *The Oxford English Dictionary* under 'cousin' which confirms this point.
42. Hore, *Wexford town*, v, p. 387.
43. 'Wadding's notebook', ed. Corish, pp 105–6.
44. See Millett, 'Survival and reorganisation', pp 60ff.
45. Hore, op. cit., p. 370.
46. J. C. Beckett, *The making of modern Ireland* (London, 1966) p. 141.
47. Hore, op. cit., p. 387.
48. See his letter to Rome, *Spicil. Ossor.*, ii, pp 264–5.
49. Ibid.
50. Corish, 'Introduction to Wadding's notebook', ed. Corish, p. 51; Brady, *Episcopal succession*, i, pp 379–80.
51. Hore, *Wexford town*, p. 370; 'Wadding's notebook', ed. Corish, pp 94–5, 96.
52. 'Wadding's notebook', ed. Corish, pp 105–6.
53. Ibid., p. 99. The original text is difficult to decipher at this point but the Catholic register provides Mrs Wiseman's christian name. Wadding's 'good friend Mary Wiseman' (Notebook, p. 35) who died before 1687 (ibid) was probably Edward Wiseman's mother.
54. J. G. Simms, *The Jacobite parliament of 1689*, (Dundalk, 1974), pp 14–16.
55. Hore, *Wexford town*, v, p. 385.
56. Ibid., p. 390.
57. Maureen Wall, *The penal laws, 1691–1760*, (Dundalk, 1976) pp 11ff.
58. Hore, *Wexford town*, v, p. 394.
59. I have been unable to trace Shapland's origins successfully. The family of 'Shopland' is entered on the Speed map of the County of Leinster and the city of Dublin (1670) as owning property in north

County Wexford, slightly north-east of Ferns. This might seem to indicate that the family came to Ireland during the plantation of James I.

60. 'The impediment of cult is of divine law as long as there is a grave danger to the faith of the Catholic party and to the Catholic education of the children . . . The danger can be overcome through sincere pre-nuptial promises', after which a dispensation could be granted; *New Catholic Encyclopedia* (1967) iv, pp 904ff.

61. Hore, *Wexford town*, v, p. 370.

62. Ibid., p. 365.

63. 'Wadding's notebook', ed. Corish, pp 112–13.

64. Hore, *Wexford town*, v, p. 388.

65. T. C. Barnard, *Cromwellian Ireland* (Oxford, 1975), chapter 1.

66. Ibid.

67. Hore, *Wexford town*, v, p. 312.

68. Barnard, *Cromwellian Ireland*, pp 19ff.

69. Ibid.

70. Hore, *Wexford town*, v, pp 334–5; the list includes Edward Wiseman and John Codd who were certainly Catholic and Leonard Bolan, who in 1685 was married in a Catholic rite.

71. The Protestant traders within the town were seriously worried by the deteriorating condition of trade. In 1672 they petitioned the lord lieutenant for additional privileges to improve the situation, praying that because they are all 'protestants and sufferers for their loyalty', they should be granted such privileges as would help towards the repairing of that great decay in trade and traffic which the said late distempers have brought upon the town'; Hore, *Wexford town*, v, p. 336.

72. Wall, *Christmas Songs*, p. 17.

73. 'Wadding's notebook', ed. Corish, pp 102, 105–6.

74. Ibid., p. 24.

75. Wadding was himself extremely interested in music as his references to various musical intruments in *Notebook*, p. 67, shows. I have already made reference to his Christmas songs (see note 8 above) which are still sung in Kilmore, Co. Wexford. Cf. J. Ranson, 'The Kilmore Carols' in *The Past*, v, (1949), pp 61–102.

76. 'An account of the Barony of Forth', ed. H. F. Hore, in *Kilkenny and Southeast of Ireland Archaeological Society Journal*, 1862–3, pp 69–70.

77. Quoted in J. Delumeau, *Catholicism between Luther and Voltaire* (London, 1978), p. 227.

78. Hore, *Wexford town*, v, p. 364.

79. In the cases where old Irish parentage is not *total* it is the mother who is generally native Irish; the fathers having for the most part Cromwellian surnames.

80. Wadding indicates his pride of race clearly in the following entry in his 'Notebook', ed. Corish, pp 107–8:

'I leave the black box . . . containing a precious relicke in a small glass bottle of blood which hath been in the castle of Ballicoglie since my predecessors first came, what blood it is I know no more than that it was esteemed to be a drop of our Saviour's blood, brought by one Gilbert Waddinge who was at the taking of Jerusalem by Godfrey, duke of Lorraine . . . '

81. See Maureen Wall, 'The rise of a Catholic middle-class in eighteenth-century Ireland', in *I.H.S.*, xi (1958), pp 91–115.

82. Bossy, *The English Catholic community, 1570–1850*, p. 194.

Chapter 5, Gahan, pp 99 – 117.

1. The main works which focus specifically on the middleman are: F. S. L. Lyons, 'Vicissitudes of a middleman in County Leitrim, 1810–1827', *I.H.S.*, ix, no. 35 (1955), pp 300–18; D. Dickson, 'Middlemen' in T. J. Bartlett and D. W. Hayton (eds.) *Penal Era and Golden Age: Essays in Irish History, 1690–1800* (Belfast, 1979), pp 186–203; D. Gahan, 'The middleman tenant in southeastern Ireland, 1700–1820' (unpublished Ph.D. dissertation, University of Kansas, 1985).

2. For a comprehensive discussion of the position of the middleman in the contemporary literature see Dickson, 'Middlemen', pp 163–70. See also G. O'Brien, *An economic history of Ireland in the eighteenth century* (Dublin, 1918), pp 73–86.

3. Note: In this essay the term 'tenant' will be used to refer to those renting directly from the landowner only.

4. L. M. Cullen, *The emergence of modern Ireland, 1600–1900* (London, 1981), pp 210–33.

5. Ibid., p. 211.

6. All the rentals cited here are housed in the National Library of Ireland. The Registry of Deeds, King's Inns, Dublin, remains a largely untapped source for eighteenth-century agrarian history.

7. O'Brien, *Economic history*, pp 69–70.

8. See T. Jones Hughes, 'Landholding and settlement in County Tipperary in the nineteenth century' p. 349 and W. J. Smyth, 'Property, patronage and population: reconstructing the human geography of mid-seventeenth century County Tipperary', pp 130–1, both in William Nolan (ed.), *Tipperary: interdisciplinary essays in the history of an Irish county*, (Dublin, 1986); W. Nolan, *Fassadinin: land, settlement and society in southeast Ireland, 1600–1850*, (Dublin, 1979), p. 78; also see Cullen, *Emergence*, p. 230.

9. The management of the Rockinham/Fitzwilliam estate has been discussed at length for the period 1750–1815 by David Large. See 'The wealth of the greater Irish landowners, 1750–1815', *I.H.S.*, xv, no. 57 (1966), pp 21–47.

10. All 'acres' referred to in this paper are in Irish measure (1 Irish = 1.62 statute). See P.M.A. Bourke, 'Notes on some agricultural

measurements in use in pre-famine Ireland', *I.H.S.*, xiv, no. 55 (1965), pp 236–45.

11. Only the Kavanagh, Carew and Colclough lands were outside the general area of north Wexford/south Wicklow. The Colclough estate was unusual for south Wexford in having a large Protestant population, see Cullen, *Emergence*, p. 216.

12. Ibid., pp 211–12.

13. Gahan, 'Middleman tenant', pp 174–5.

14. Cullen calls middlemen 'progressive farmers renting roughly 300 Irish acres, working half of it and subletting the rest', see *Emergence*, p. 230.

15. Dickson, 'Middlemen', p. 170.

16. Ibid.

17. This finding agrees with an observation made by Fraser concerning the area between Oulart and Gorey in 1801, an area close to the Anglesey estate, see Cullen, *Emergence*, p. 215.

18. The complete absence of very large and small tenants from the Ram estate in 1758 suggests that many tenants on this property were comfortable farmers rather than middlemen.

19. See Cullen, *Emergence*, p. 216.

20. This finding contrasts somewhat with Dickson's view of absenteeism. See Dickson, 'Middlemen', pp 174–5.

21. See Cullen, *Emergence*, p. 214.

22. This is in agreement with one of Dickson's findings. See Dickson, 'Middlemen', pp 170–71.

23. Cullen has estimated the Protestant population of some Shillelagh parishes in the 1830s as being as high as 45 per cent. See Cullen, *Emergence*, p. 213.

24. Some of these Catholic tenants may have been among the 'ex-freeholders' of whom Dickson has written. See Dickson, 'Middlemen', pp 171–2.

25. Miles Byrne, *Memoirs* (Paris, 1861), p. 111.

26. This term is used by Dickson to describe such long leases. See 'Middlemen', p. 174.

27. Note: On the Rockingham estate few leases exceeded 21 years or two lives in 1745. Evidence from Co. Wexford generally indicates that at most 10 per cent of the land of the county was leased for 'lives renewable forever'. Gahan, 'Middleman tenant', pp 141–2, 386.

28. Registry of Deeds: 119–401–82986; 119–491–83343; 119–491–83344; 119–553–83914; 128–295–86936; 133–122–89838; 134–300–91058; 136–468–92116; 138–002–91689; 139–123–93371; 141–089–94507; 141–341–95724; 142–330–95723; 144–512–985343; 145–124–97208; 145–125–97209; 146–085–6776; 151–347–101709; 153–100–101807; 153–101–101808; 155–373–105098; 158–306–106027; 158–581–107341; 162–404–110250; 163–036–107342; 166–487–112336; 174–366–116623; 175–281–

117049; 178–247–118774; 184–564–124311; 188–102–124728; 189–321–
125598; 190–469–127703; 190–469–127704; 206–114–135373/4; 206–
113–135372; 206–127–135458; 207–043–135207; 207–056–135294; 206–
389–137494; 212–194–138974; 212–504–140178; 212–505–140179; 212–
506–140180; 213–608–143644; 214–078–140144; 219–107–142771; 219–
217–143376; 220–032–143563; 230–492–152452; 230–492–152453; 232–
331–152550; 241–432–160245; 254–170–163438; 255–554–167051.

29. Cullen has used indicators of status such as tree-lined avenues to
identify gentry in north Wexford, see his *Emergence*, pp 227, 231.

30. Ibid., p. 211.

31. Ibid., p.212.

32. Miles Byrne's embittered view of Protestant fellow-gentry probably
had its counterpart among poorer Catholics also, see note 24 above.

33. For a discussion of Protestant/middleman emigration during this
period see W. A. Maguire, *The Downshire estates in Ireland, 1809–
1845*, (Oxford, 1972), p. 230; W. F. Adams, *Ireland and the Irish
emigration to the New World*, (New Haven, 1932), pp 108–9; D. H.
Akenson, *The Orangeman: The life and times of Ogle Robert Gowan*,
(Toronto, 1986).

Chapter 6, Cummins, pp 118–34

1. On Dublin politics in the 1740s, see Sean Murphy, 'Charles Lucas
and the Dublin election of 1748–9' in *Parliamentary History*, ii (1983),
pp 93–111.

2. Thomas Bartlett, 'The Townshend viceroyalty 1767–72' in Thomas
Bartlett and David Hayton (eds), *Penal era and golden age* (Belfast,
1979), pp 88–112.

3. See L. M. Cullen, *Princes & pirates: the Dublin chamber of commerce
1783–1983* (Dublin, 1983), pp 13–21.

4. Sean Murphy,'Municipal politics and popular disturbances: 1660–
1800' in Art Cosgrove (ed.), *Dublin through the ages* (Dublin, 1988),
pp 77–92 (p. 89).

5. Charles Lucas, *The liberties and customs of Dublin asserted and
demonstrated* (Dublin, 1768), p. 57.

6. John Hely Hutchinson to . . . O'Hara [1768] (*Historical Manuscripts
Commission* (hereafter H.M.C), Twelfth report (London, 1891),
Appendix part ix, p. 264).

7. *Freeman's Journal* (hereafter *F.J.*), 14–18 Jan. 1766.

8. Cullen, *Princes & pirates* pp 20–21.

9. Duke of Bedford to Mr Pitt, 2 Sept. 1758 (Lord John Russell, ed.,
Correspondence of John, fourth duke of Bedford (hereafter *Bedford corr.*)
(3 vols, London, 1842–6) ii, 369).

10. On sectarian affrays, see Murphy, 'Municipal politics', pp 81–5.

11. Bedford to Primate Stone, 22 May 1759 (*Bedford corr.*, ii, 377).

12. *The Gentleman's Magazine and Historical Chronicle* (hereafter *Gents
Mag.*) (London, 1759), xxix, 638–9.

13. Sean Murphy, 'The Dublin anti-union riot of 3 December 1759' in Gerard O'Brien (ed.), *Parliament, politics and people* (Dublin, 1989) pp 49–68 (pp 53–4).
14. *Gents Mag.* (London, 1759), xxix, 639.
15. Lord Chancellor Bowes to George Dodington [end of Dec. 1759] (*Report on manuscripts in various collections*, vi (H.M.C., London, 1909), p. 71).
16. John Fisher to Lord Rawdon, 4 Dec. 1759 (*Hastings manuscripts* (H.M.C., London, 1934), iii, 139).
17. Bowes to Dodington [end of Dec. 1759] (*H.M.C. rep. var. coll.*, vi, 71–2).
18. Sir John and Lady Gilbert (eds.), *Calendar of ancient records of the city of Dublin* (hereafter *Cal. anc. rec.*) (19 vols, Dublin, 1889–1944) x, 393.
19. Rigby to Sir Robert Wilmot, 10 Dec. 1759 (*Bedford corr.*, ii, p. xxvii).
20. Dodington to Bowes, 19 Jan. 1760 (*H.M.C. rep. var. coll.*, vi, 72–3).
21. As J. C. Beckett has pointed out, 'It was . . . the protestants as a body, and not just the landlords, who dominated Ireland in the eighteenth century'. (*The Anglo-Irish tradition* (London, 1976), p. 65).
22. Rigby to Wilmot, 23 Dec. 1759 (*Bedford corr.*, ii, p. xxviii).
23. Same to same, 1 Jan. 1760 (ibid., p. xxix).
24. *The journals of the house of commons of the kingdom of Ireland* (hereafter *J.C.I.*), 11 Oct. 1757 to 29 Apr. 1758 (Dublin, 1796), vi, 154.
25. Murphy, 'The Dublin anti-union riot', p. 67.
26. R. B. McDowell, 'Colonial nationalism and the winning of parliamentary independence, 1760–82' in T. W. Moody and W. E. Vaughan (eds), *A new history of Ireland* (Oxford, 1986), iv, 196–235 (pp 197–9).
27. Pearse Street Library, Dublin, Gilbert collection, Charters and manuscripts of the guild of the Holy Trinity or merchants' guild of Dublin, A.D. 1438–1824 (2 vols, transcribed in 1867 for J. T. Gilbert), ii, MS 79, pp 219, 222–3.
28. *Gents Mag.* (London, 1764), xxxiv, 44.
29. *F.J.*, 14–18 Jan. 1766.
30. Earl of Halifax to earl of Egremont, 29 Nov. 1761 (Joseph Redington (ed.), *Calendar of home office papers of the reign of George III* (hereafter *C.H.O.P.*), *1760–65* (London, 1888), p. 82).
31. Charles Lucas, *To the right honourable the lord mayor . . . the address of C. Lucas . . . upon the proposed augmentation* (Dublin, 1768), pp 14ff.
32. *Gents Mag.* (London, 1765), xxxv, 441.
33. *F.J.* 14–17 Sept. 1765, from a letter signed 'A citizen'.
34. Ibid.
35. *J.C.I.*, 22 Oct. 1765 to 2 June 1772, viii, 53.
36. Charles Lucas, *A second address to the lord mayor . . .* (Dublin, 1766), p. 37.

37. Charles Lucas, *A third address to the lord mayor* . . . (Dublin, 1766), p. 12.
38. *F.J.*, 9–13 Feb. 1768.
39. Lord Townshend to earl of Shelburne, 11 Jan 1768 (Joseph Redington (ed.), *C.H.O.P., 1766–69* (London, 1879), p. 292).
40. Charles Lucas, *A mirror for courts-martial: in which the complaints, trial, sentence and punishment of David Blakeney, are represented and examined with candour* (3rd edn Dublin, 1768).
41. Ibid., p. 38.
42. Ibid., p. 5.
43. Ibid., pp iii–iv, 13.
44. J. C. [John Courteney], *Remarks on a pamphlet entitled A mirror for courts-martial* . . . (Dublin, 1768), p. iv.
45. Townshend to marquess of Granby, 5 Apr. 1768 (H.M.C., rep. 12, app. v, *Rutland MSS*, ii, p. 303).
46. George Rudé, *Wilkes and liberty* (Oxford, 1962), pp 37–56.
47. Townshend to Granby, 30 Apr. 1768 (H.M.C., rep. 12, app, v., *Rutland MSS*, ii, p. 304).
48. Same to same, 7 May 1768 (ibid., p. 305).
49. Townshend to Shelburne, 17 Oct. 1768, *C.H.O.P., 1766–9* (London, 1879), p. 379.
50. Townshend to Lord Viscount Weymouth, 5 Mar. 1769 (ibid., p. 454).
51. Same to same, 17 Aug. 1769 (ibid, pp 489–90).
52. Same to same, 5 Mar. 1769 (ibid., p. 454).
53. Weymouth to Townshend, 21 Mar. 1769 (ibid., p. 459). The sentences on the soldiers were remitted.
54. Bartlett, 'The Townshend viceroyalty', pp 96–9.
55. Townshend to Weymouth, 31 Dec. 1769 (*C.H.O.P., 1766–9*, p. 553).
56. Same to same, 15 Jan. 1770 (Richard Arthur Roberts (ed.), *C.H.O.P., 1770–72* (London, 1881), pp 4–5.
57. Charles Lucas, *The rights and privileges of parlements asserted upon constitutional principles* . . . (Dublin, 1770).
58. Bartlett, 'The Townshend viceroyalty', pp 98–101.
59. Townshend to Weymouth, 2 Mar. 1770 (*C.H.O.P., 1770–72*, p. 15).
60. Weymouth to Townshend, 9 Dec. 1770 (ibid., p. 97); Cullen, *Princes & pirates*, p. 21.
61. *Cal. anc. rec.*, xii, 103–4.
62. Townshend to Weymouth, 23 Nov. 1770 (*C.H.O.P., 1770–72*, pp 90–1).
63. *F.J.*, 19–21 Feb. 1771 (letter signed 'Patricius'); ibid., 21–3 Feb. 1771.
64. *Gents Mag.* (London, 1771), xli, 137.
65. Townshend to earl of Rochford, 28 Feb. 1771 (*C.H.O.P., 1770–72*, p. 211).
66. Ibid.
67. *J.C.I.*, 22 Oct. 1765 to 2 June 1772, viii, 365–6.

68. Townshend to Lord Frederick Campbell, 24 Apr. 1771 (quoted in Bartlett, 'The Townshend viceroyalty', p. 105).
69. Lord North was on his way to a parliamentary debate on the right of the house of commons to prevent the publication of its debates, see *D.N.B.*
70. Stanley H. Palmer, *Police and protest in England and Ireland 1780–1850* (Cambridge, 1988) pp xviii, 82–9.

Chapter 7, Leighton, pp 135–58.
1. D. Kerr, *Peel, priests and politics: Sir Robert Peel's administration and the Roman Catholic church in Ireland, 1841–1846* (Oxford, 1982) pp 4–5, 24–5, 94–5.
2. The term 'veto controversy' is not a particularly satisfactory one by which to refer to the series of debates of the late eighteenth and early nineteenth century generated by the belief that some substantial change in the polity of the Catholic church in Ireland was required if further concessions to the Catholics were to be obtained from the country's rulers. Before 1810 debate centred on a number of proposals designed to allow government a degree of institutionalised influence in ecclesiastical affairs. One of these proposals was for a ministerial right of veto on episcopal appointments. After 1810, though this circumstance has been rarely adverted to, attention was chiefly directed, in Ireland if not in England, to proposals to diminish Roman influence. These debates obtained their conventional designation, which is retained here, largely since it was the veto which was under discussion in 1808, the point at which public opinion became an important factor in them. No doubt a more comprehensive designation, such as 'securities controversy', might be adopted.
3. Bernard Ward's work, *The eve of Catholic emancipation* (3 vols London, 1911–12), despite its age and concentration on English events, is still relied upon to give convenient access to an understanding of Irish ecclesiastical affairs in the period dealt with here. Much additional information can be found in the latter parts of Vincent McNally's lengthy and somewhat unmanageable study, 'Archbishop John Thomas Troy and the Catholic church in Ireland' (Ph. D. thesis, Trinity College, Dublin, 1976). The beginnings of the public phase of the dispute are dealt with by Michael Roberts in *The Whig party, 1807–1812* (2nd edn London, 1965), chap. 1 and by Gerard O'Brien in 'The beginning of the veto controversy in Ireland', *Journal of Ecclesiastical History*, xxxviii, no. 1 (Jan. 1987) pp 80–94.
4. See, for example, D. Bowen, *Paul Cardinal Cullen and the shaping of modern Irish Catholicism* (Dublin, 1983), passim. In this work, which appears to mark the re-emergence of a distinctively Protestant historiography in Ireland, Bowen refers to a third party within the mid nineteenth-century ecclesiastical body, to which he gives the

name 'neo-Gallican'. This seems merely to refer to those ecclesiastics most influenced by nationalist sentiment.

5. R. B. McDowell, *Irish public opinion 1750–1800* (London, 1944), p. 14.

6. For an understanding of the place of Gallicanism in the argumentation against the penal laws see Edward Synge, *A vindication of a sermon . . . in which the question concerning toleration, particularly of Popery under certain conditions and limitations is further consider'd . . .* (Dublin, 1726), pp 66–71.

7. Charles O'Conor, *The principles of the Roman Catholics exhibited . . .* (Dublin, 1756), pp 67–72, 20–22.

8. Francis Plowden, *The history of Ireland, from its union with Great Britain in January 1801 to October 1810* (Dublin, 1811), iii, p. 695.

9. Ibid., iii, pp 695–700, 790–92, and Thomas Wyse, *Historical sketch of the late Catholic Association of Ireland* (London, 1829) i, pp 165–73.

10. E. O'Flaherty, 'The Catholic question in Ireland 1774–1793' (M.A. thesis, University College, Dublin, 1981), pp 60–70, and P. O'Donoghue, 'The Catholic church in Ireland in the age of revolution and rebellion, 1782–1803' (Ph. D. thesis, University College, Dublin, 1976), chap. 9.

11. The understanding of the events of 1808 and the preceding years offered here is based chiefly on the writer's own research in 'Theobald McKenna and the Catholic question', (N.U.I., Maynooth M.A. thesis 1985) pp 24–41, but also on the works listed in note 3 above.

12. J. J. Sack, 'The Grenvilles' eminence grise: the Reverend Charles O'Conor and the latter days of Anglo-Gallicanism', *Harvard Theological Review*, lxxii (1979), pp 123–42 (p. 123).

13. For a convenient survey of Gallican controversies in late eighteenth- and early nineteenth-century England, see E. Duffy, 'Ecclesiastical democracy detected', *Recusant History*, x, no. 4 (Jan. 1970), pp 193–209; x, no. 6 (Oct. 1970), pp 309–31; xvii, no. 2 (Oct. 1975), pp 123–48. A more detailed narrative, though now dated and reflecting a distinctively Catholic historiographical approach, is to be found in B. Ward, *The dawn of the Catholic revival in England* (2 vols., London 1909). The intellectual content of Cisalpinism is well discussed in J. P. Chinnici, *The English Catholic enlightenment: John Lingard and the Cisalpine movement* (Shepherdstown, W.Va., 1980).

14. The approach to the study of Irish Gallicanism adopted for this article, relating the phenomenon to its political origins rather than tracing its intellectual origins, is justified by the circumstance mentioned here and elaborated on throughout. When reference is made in this study to the Gallicanism of other countries and of earlier periods, it is made, generally, only for the purpose of comparison.

15. Duffy, loc. cit., i, pp 194–5.

16. McKenna's growing understanding of the difficulty involved in providing a policy to deal with the Catholic question can be traced from his early pamphlets, for the most part conveniently collected in his *Political essays relative to the affairs of Ireland,* . . . (London, 1794), through his pamphlets in support of the Union, *A memoire of some questions respecting the projected union of Great Britain and Ireland* (Dublin 1799), and *Constitutional objections to the government of Ireland by a separate legislature* . . . (2nd edn Dublin, 1799), to his post-union pamphlets, such as *An abstract of the arguments on the Catholic question* [published anonymously] (London, 1805). The development of his thought is discussed in Leighton, op. cit., pp 78–104.

17. Theobald McKenna, *Thoughts on the civil condition and relations of the Roman Catholic clergy, religion and people in Ireland* (Dublin, 1805), pp 112–16.

18. Ibid., p. 127.

19. Ibid., p. 131.

20. See, for example, his references to the sacramental system or to the priesthood, ibid., pp 57–60.

21. Duffy, loc. cit., i, p. 199.

22. McKenna, *Thoughts on the civil constitution*, pp 79–83.

23. Ibid., p. 35

24. Ibid., pp 142–52.

25. See the proposals to institutionalise such a disposition of power in Cornelius Keogh, *The veto: A commentary on the Grenville manifesto* (London 1810), particularly pp 76–7. Keogh's proposal to establish a representative body to regulate Catholic affairs, including those of the church, though it may appear to have been quite unrealistic, came close to realisation in O'Connell's 'popish parliament' of the 1820s.

26. See J. Blum, *The end of the Old Order in rural Europe* (Princeton, N.J., 1978), chap. 14. See also J.Q.C. Mackrell, *The attack on 'feudalism' in eighteenth-century France* (London 1973), chap. 6.

27. Quoted in J. Brady, 'Proposals to register Irish priests 1756–7', *Irish Ecclesiastical Record*, xcvii (5th series) (Apr. 1962), pp 209–222 (p. 219).

28. [Robert Clayton], *A few plain matters of fact, humbly recommended to the consideration of the Roman Catholics of Ireland* (Dublin, 1756), p. 88.

29. *Letters of Charles O'Conor of Belanagare*, ed. C.C. and R.E. Ward (Ann Arbor, Mich., 1980), i, nos 33, 34 and 35.

30. Keogh, op. cit., p. 78.

31. For an example of such rhetoric see ibid., pp i–vii.

32. N. Davies, *God's playground: a history of Poland* (2 vols, Oxford, 1981–3), i, chap. 7. See especially pp 202 and 221. See also B. K. Király, *Hungary in the late eighteenth century: the decline of enlightened despotism* (New York and London, 1969), pp 34–38, 219 et seq.

33. [Theobald McKenna under the *nom de plume*] 'A Catholic and Burkist', *An argument against extermination occasioned by Doctor Duigenan's representation of the present political state of Ireland* (Dublin, 1800), p. 27. The attribution of this pamphlet is disputed. However, the contents render the attribution to McKenna plausible and he certainly did work on a reply to the pamphlet of Patrick Duigenan mentioned in the title. See Archbishop Troy to James Clinch, 7 Jan. 1800 (Dublin Diocesan Archive, Clonliffe College, Dublin, Troy Papers (hereafter Troy Papers), 28/8/1).

34. Even within the British dominions, in Canada, government exercised, with Roman approval, a degree of authority over the affairs of the Catholic church exceeding that recommended by proponents of the veto. See I. Caron, 'La nomination des évêques catholiques de Quebec sous le régime anglais', *Mémoires de la Société Royale du Canada*, sect. i, 3rd ser., xxvi (May, 1932), pp 1–44. Such arrangements between the church and non-Catholic governments were known about by Irish Catholics and frequently referred to in the literature relating to the veto.

35. C.O., *A letter to the Roman Catholic priests of Ireland* . . . (Dublin, 1814), p. vii. The *D.N.B.* (1st edn, xlii, 345) attributes this work, quite incredibly in view of his anti-Catholic sentiments, to the evangelical Protestant clergyman, Caesar Otway. The ascription made by Vincent McNally to the English Gallican writer, Charles O'Conor of Stowe, is, in view of the pamphlet's strident anti-vetoism, equally unacceptable.

36. *Substance of the speech of John Cox Hippesley, Bart . . . on Friday 18th May 1810* (2nd edn London, 1810), app. v, pp v-xiv.

37. The bishops, of course, would have possessed excellent motives for displaying hostility to the veto, even had they considered that the influence which it would place in lay hands would lie only with the government and be exercised only when episcopal appointments were being made. Under the existing arrangements they had by far the greatest influence on those occasions, although it was already partly shared with the government which was, at least sometimes, quite capable of influencing the selection of bishops for Irish sees by dealing directly with the court of Rome. See M. Buschkühl, *Great Britain and the Holy See, 1746–1870* (Dublin, 1982), pp 36, 62–3. However, the bishops had always been anxious about the influence Irish Protestants were capable of exercising at a local level in the affairs of the Catholic church. See, for example, a letter of the Irish bishops to Cardinal Antonelli, 5 December 1793, Troy Papers, 116/5/131). Such anxieties were certainly in the minds of the bishops when they considered the veto. See [John Power, R.C. bishop of Waterford and Lismore under the *nom de plume*] Fidelis, *Letters on the royal veto* (Dublin, 1809), pp 3–9.

38. S. J. Connolly, *Priests and people in pre-famine Ireland 1780–1845* (Dublin and New York, 1982), pp 67ff.

39. See, for example, S. Ó Dufaigh, 'Notes relating to Patrick Maguire, Coadjutor Bishop of Kilmore (1819–1826)', *Breifne: Journal of Cumann Seanchais Bhreifne*, iv, no. 13 (1970), pp 94–5.

40. Connolly, *op. cit.*, pp 61ff. Further illustration of the activities of factions, both clerical and lay, in the period dealt with here, can be found in S. Ó Dufaigh, 'James Murphy, Bishop of Clogher', *Clogher Record*, iv, no. 3 (1968), pp 419–92.

41. M. Coen, *The wardenship of Galway* (Galway, 1984). One cannot help remarking that the curious history of the Galway wardenship in its latter days, with its struggle for influence in ecclesiastical affairs between an 'aristocratic', and a 'democratic' faction (the Tribes and the non-Tribes), seems to present us with something like a miniature of the contemporary veto controversy. Regrettably, Fr Coen fails to put events in Galway into a national context.

42. See, for example, J. Glynn, 'The Catholic church in Wexford town 1800–1858', *Past: The Organ of the Uí Cinsealaigh Historical Society*, no. 15 (1984), pp 5–53.

43. Bernard Ward, for example, appears to have been quite unaware of the existence of the domestic nomination issue. Thus when he encountered a speech of January 1815, in which O'Connell asserted the freedom of the Irish church to reject disciplinary decisions of the Holy See, and indeed of general councils, a view often advanced by apologists for domestic nomination, he regarded this as an isolated statement and attributed it to the fact that O'Connell was a Freemason. See Ward, *Eve*, ii, pp 142ff. McNally gives useful information about the domestic nomination debate, but fails to make clear its content, its widespread nature or its impact on the events of the period. See McNally, 'John Thomas Troy', pp 415, 457–67 and chap. 9.

44. C. Giblin, 'The Stuart nomination of Irish bishops', *Irish Ecclesiastical Record*, cv (5th ser.), no. 1 (Jan. 1966), pp 35–47.

45. It should be recalled that the distinction between nomination and canonical institution was very well understood at the time. For it was the question of the Holy See's right of canonical institution that lay at the centre of the dispute—resulting in the pope's continuing imprisonment—between Napoleon and Pius VII. See J. D. Holmes, *The triumph of the Holy See: a short history of the papacy in the nineteenth century* (London and Shepherdstown, W. Va., 1978), pp 54ff.

46. Strictly speaking, 'canonical institution' is not the correct term to use here. In canon law the use of the term 'canonical institution' indicates that nomination is made by someone other than the proper authority, which is, in the case of episcopal appointments, the Holy See. When the Holy See itself nominates the term 'free conferral' should be used. See R. Naz (ed.), *Dictionnaire de droit*

canonique (Paris, 1935–65), vi. cols 1078–9. See also F. della Rocca, *Manual of canon law* (Milwaukee, Wis., 1957), pp 167ff. This distinction is not found in the primary sources used for this study and is consequently disregarded.

47. *Dublin Political Review* (hereafter cited as *D.P.R.*), 13 Mar. 1813.
48. See, for example, *Dublin Evening Post* (hereafter cited as *D.E.P.*), 22 Feb. 1810.
49. See the open letter of Thomas Dromgoole to Archbishop Troy, written at this time and reproduced on a number of occasions in the course of the domestic nomination controversy, for example in the *D.P.R.*, 27 Mar. 1813. For Dromgoole's authorship of it, see *D.E.P.*, 17 May 1814.
50. For a text of the resolutions see *D.P.R.*, 3 April 1813.
51. For a text of these resolutions see *D.E.P.*, 17 May 1814.
52. *Proceedings of the Catholic Committee as taken from their accredited papers* (Dublin, 1811), unpaginated. See the reports of the meetings of 13 July 1810 and 12 Jan. 1811.
53. *Report on the manuscripts of J. B. Fortescue Esq., preserved at Dropmore*, (Historical Manuscripts Commission, London, 1892–1927), x, p. 50. See Roberts, *Whig party*, chap. 1.
54. McNally, 'John Thomas Troy', pp 458 and 477ff.
55. The life and writings of Charles O'Conor of Stowe, grandson of the more famous Charles O'Conor of Belanagare mentioned above, are discussed by Sack in his article already cited. See note 12. For this reason and since the best context for an understanding of O'Conor's views, despite his interest in Irish history and politics, is clearly the English Gallican tradition, extensive reference to this interesting figure has been avoided in this study.
56. James Bernard Clinch, *Letters on church government* (Dublin, 1812).
57. *D.P.R.*, 6 Mar. 1813, *D.E.P.*, 17 May 1814.
58. *D.P.R.*, 6 Feb. 1813, 20 Feb. 1813.
59. Ibid., 6 Mar. 1813.
60. Ibid., 13 Mar. 1813.
61. For an account of the Quarantotti rescript affair see Ward, *Eve*, ii, chaps. 20 and 21.
62. McNally, 'John Thomas Troy', pp 500ff.
63. The number of priests who came forward should not be exaggerated. Many, especially among the more senior, chose to remain aloof. The unsympathetic observer of the gathering of Dublin clergy hostile to the rescript reported, though not quite accurately, that it consisted of only 'a few of the parish priests . . . not more than five in number, with about sixty clergymen of inferior station'. See *D.E.P.*, 24 May 1814. See also W. J. FitzPatrick, *Irish wits and worthies: including Dr. Lanigan . . .* (Dublin, 1873), p. 166. However, that such a gathering took place at all was remarkable enough, particularly since it was being suggested in the press that the

archbishop positively supported the rescript. See *D.E.P.*, 12 May 1814.

64. *D.E.P.*, 14 May 1814.
65. Ibid., 17 May 1814.
66. Ibid., 21 May 1814.
67. McNally op. cit., p. 505.
68. This much may be said. It was never likely that the Holy See, except under the most severe pressure, which was never applied, would have consented to surrender the right of nomination. However, in the period since the cessation of Stuart nominations in 1766, the Roman authorities had neglected to devise any systematised means of obtaining recommendations to assist the Holy See in making nominations and thus there certainly were grounds for requesting some change. Taking heed of what the Roman authorities would and would not countenance, the Irish bishops, over the course of the next fifteen years, put forward schemes under which candidates for episcopal office would be selected and recommended in a formal way (but not nominated) in Ireland. Eventually, in 1829, a scheme was found which was acceptable to Rome by virtue of the fact that it paid due regard to both the claims of the bishops and those of their clergy. See J. H. Whyte, 'The appointment of Catholic bishops in nineteenth-century Ireland', *Catholic Historical Review*, xlviii, no. 1 (Apr. 1962), pp 12–32 (pp 14–17).

Chapter 8, Liechty, pp 159–87.

1. *The evidence of his grace the archbishop of Dublin, before the select committee of the house of lords, on the state of Ireland* (Dublin, 1825), pp 9–10.
2. Brendan Bradshaw, 'Sword, word and strategy in the Reformation in Ireland', *Historical Journal*, xxi, no. 3 (1978), pp 475–7.
3. Irvin B. Horst, *The radical brethren: Anabaptism and the English Reformation to 1558* (Nieuwkoop, 1972).
4. Nicholas Canny, 'Why the Reformation failed in Ireland: *une question mal posée*', *Journal of Ecclesiastical History*, xxx, no. 4 (Oct. 1979), pp 425–6.
5. Bradshaw, 'Sword, word and strategy', p. 477.
6. Stephen Ellis, 'John Bale, bishop of Ossory, 1552–3', *Journal of the Butler Society*, ii (1984), p. 292.
7. 'Melchior Hofmann', in *Mennonite Encyclopedia* (4 vols, Scottdale, Pa., 1956).
8. Bradshaw, 'Sword, word and strategy', p. 501.
9. Alan Ford, *The Protestant Reformation in Ireland, 1590–1641* (Frankfurt am Main, Bern, New York, Nancy, 1985).
10. Quoted in Patrick Corish, *The Irish Catholic experience: a historical survey* (Dublin, 1985), p. 125.

11. Joseph Liechty, 'Irish evangelicalism, Trinity College Dublin, and the mission of the Church of Ireland at the end of the eighteenth century' (Ph.D. thesis, N.U.I., Maynooth, 1987), pp 126–34.

12. The relationship of evangelicalism to other church reform organisations, including the Association for Discountenancing Vice, is discussed in Liechty, 'Irish evangelicalism'. See especially pp 95–108 and 479–82.

13. *Weekly History*, no. 84 (London, 13 Nov. 1742), quoted in Susan O'Brien, 'A transatlantic community of saints: the great awakening and the first evangelical network, 1735–1755', *American Historical Review*, xci, no. 4 (Oct. 1986), p. 811.

14. John Walsh, 'Origins of the evangelical revival', in G. V. Bennett and J. D. Walsh (eds), *Essays in modern English church history* (London, 1966).

15. R. Lee Cole, *A history of Methodism in Dublin* (Dublin, 1932), p. 9.

16. D. A. Chart, 'The broadening of the church', in Walter Alison Phillips (ed.), *History of the Church of Ireland from the earliest times to the present day* (3 vols, London, 1933–1934), iii, pp 259–60.

17. Irene Whelan, 'New lights and old enemies: the "Second Reformation" and the Catholics of Ireland, 1800–35' (M.A. thesis, University of Wisconsin, 1983).

18. Cole, *Methodism in Dublin*, p. 74.

19. Richard Carwardine, *Transatlantic revivalism: popular evangelicalism in Britain and America, 1790–1865* (Westport, Connecticut, 1978); David Hempton, 'Methodism in Irish society, 1770–1830', *Transactions of the Royal Historical Society*, 5th series, xxxvi (1986), pp 117–42 (p. 139).

20. W. R. Ward, *Religion and society in England, 1790–1850* (London, 1972), p. 211.

21. [A. C. H. Seymour], *The life and times of Selina, countess of Huntington* (2 vols, London, 1839–1840), ii.

22. C. H. Crookshank, *Memorable women of Irish Methodism in the last century* (London, 1882).
Although the laity continued to play a vital role in Irish evangelicalism during the nineteenth century, they were more prominent in the first phase of evangelicalism, during the 1700s. A shift in emphasis seems to have begun around the turn of the century. For example, in 1802 the post-Wesley Irish Methodist Conference forbade women preachers, and David Hempton sees a decisive change from the more rural, decentralised, and home-based Methodism of the eighteenth century, to the comparatively urban, bureaucratic, and chapel-based phenomenon of the nineteenth, 'when the growth of chapel building, ecclesiastical bureaucracy and formal theological training thrust Methodism into the male world of financial and denominational management' (Hempton,

'Methodism in Irish society', p. 121).

23. Liechty, 'Irish evangelicalism', pp 328–31.
24. George Hamilton, 'A sermon preached at the formation of the Evangelical Society of Ulster in Armagh, 10th October 1798', p. 6. Manuscript held by the Presbyterian Historical Society, Belfast.
25. The nature of Irish evangelical missionary interest is discussed in Liechty, 'Irish evangelicalism', pp 64–7.
26. George Miller, *A lecture on the origin and general influences of the wars of the French Revolution, being the conclusion of a course of lectures on modern history, delivered in the University of Dublin* (Dublin, 1811), pp 62, 60.
27. Although Irene Whelan surely goes too far in describing the 'swing towards political conservatism' after the French Revolution as 'the real driving force behind the evangelical impulse' ('New lights and old enemies', p. 334), she more than adequately documents the profound influence of the revolutionary aftermath; David Hempton, 'Methodism in Irish society', conducts a balanced and appropriately complex analysis of the interaction of social turmoil with other factors in the development of Irish Methodism; Liechty, 'Irish evangelicalism', pp 66, 142–65, 268–305, and 489–503, develops in more detail the broad themes of this paragraph.
28. 'An aged minister of the gospel', *An address to the United Church in Ireland, on the present crisis* (Dublin, 1809), p. 19.
29. Beresford quoted in Whelan, 'New lights and old enemies', p. 142.
30. Walsh quoted in Nancy Uhlar Murray, 'The influence of the French Revolution on the Church of England and its rivals, 1789–1802' (D.Phil. thesis, Oxford University, 1975), p. 176.
31. Quoted in Norman Hampson, *The Enlightenment* (Penguin edn, 1982), p. 154.
32. John Bossy, *Christianity in the West, 1400–1700* (Oxford, New York, 1985), p. 110.
33. The other newly-formed indigenous dissenting group may actually have a legitimate claim to be the first one. Kelly's Connexion was a group of preachers and chapels under the leadership of Thomas Kelly, one of five young evangelical preachers (including John Walker) suppressed by the archbishop of Dublin in 1794. As late as July 1800 Kelly had probably not left the established church since he was preaching in St Mary's church in Kilkenny (Peter Roe's diary, 20 and 21 July 1800, quoted in Samuel Madden, *Memoir of the life of the late Rev. Peter Roe, A.M. . . . .* (Dublin, 1842), p. 57). But by 1802 'Kelly's Connexion' was contributing preachers to the General Evangelical Society's new itinerancy scheme, if A. C. H. Seymour's account of nearly four decades later is correct ([Seymour], *Selina, countess of Huntingdon*, ii, p. 223).
The available evidence suggests that Kelly's group was less influential and less radical than Walker's, and perhaps Kelly's Connexion

was not even a 'church' in the full-blown sense of the Church of God. Kelly rejected religious establishments and stressed the need to revive the doctrines and practices of the primitive church, which made him a radical. But he seems to have been an amiable and mild person, a splendid hymn writer (whose work is still widely used), and a man little inclined to engage in controversy; he was quite happy to work with other evangelicals, even though he disagreed with them. Kelly's congregations seem less like a church than a network of slightly radical proprietary chapels. However, Kelly still awaits the thorough investigation he deserves. Meanwhile, it seems appropriate to refer to John Walker's Church of God as the first indigenous Irish dissenting church.

Important sources for Kelly are: John Hall, *The memory of the just: a tribute to the memory of the late Rev. Thomas Kelly* (Dublin, 1855); Thomas Kelly, *A letter to the Roman Catholics of Athy, occasioned by Mr. Hayes's seven sermons* (Dublin, 1823); Thomas Kelly, *A plea for primitive Christianity: in answer to a pamphlet by the Rev. Peter Roe, entitled, 'The evil of separation from the Church of England'* (Dublin, 1815); Thomas Kelly, *Some account of James Byrne, of Kilberry, in the county of Kildare, addressed principally to the Roman Catholic inhabitants of Athy, and its neighbourhood* (Dublin, 1809). He also published some other pamphlets and many collections of hymns.

34. John Walker, 'A sermon preached on Wednesday, the 12th of March, 1800, being the day appointed for a general fast', in John Walker, *Three sermons preached in the chapel of Trinity–College, Dublin* (Dublin, 1801), p. 14.

35. John Walker, *An expostulatory address to the members of the Methodist Society in Ireland*, 3rd edn (Dublin, 1804), p. 10.

36. Walker to Benjamin Mathias, Nov. 1799, quoted in [Joseph Singer], *Brief memorials of the Rev. B. W. Mathias, late chaplain of Bethesda chapel* (Dublin, 1842), pp 38–9.

37. Walker, *Expostulatory address*, p. 10.

38. Walker to Benjamin Mathias, n. d. [ca. 1799], quoted in [Singer], *B. W. Mathias*, p. 36.

39. John Walker, *Substance of a sermon preached at the Lock-chapel, on Wednesday, February 25th, 1795, being the day appointed for a general fast* (Dublin, 1795), p. 9.

40. John Walker, *Substance of a charity sermon preached in the parish church of St. John's, Dublin, on Sunday the 25th of May, 1794; for the support of the charity schools of that parish, with a prefatory address to his grace the archbishop of Dublin, and an appendix tending to prove that the doctrines asserted by the author are conformable with the tenets of the established church in these kingdoms* (Dublin, 1796), p. 16.

41. [John Walker], *The church in danger; or, a word in season, on the present alarming crisis, addressed to the clergy of the established church, by one of their brethren* (Dublin, 1796), p. 7.

42. Walker, *Substance of a charity sermon, 1794*, p. 14.
43. Ibid., p. 20.
44. Ibid., pp 22, 38, 39, 52.
45. Walker, *Substance of a sermon, 1795*, pp 5–6, 21.
46. Unidentified handwriting (probably John Barrett's) on a letter, Gerald Fitzgerald to John Barrett, 14 September 1802, TCD MS 2373, Trinity College Dublin Library.
47. Walker, *Substance of a charity sermon, 1794*, p. 15.
48. [Walker], *Church in danger*, p. 6.
49. John Walker, *An address to believers of the gospel of Christ on that conversation which becometh it, with an appendix, containing an account of the late change in the author's sentiments, concerning the lawfulness of his former connection with the religious establishment of this country, and his letter to the provost, which occasioned his expulsion from the College of Dublin* (Dublin, 1804), p. 29.
50. Walker, *Substance of a charity sermon, 1794*, p. 15.
51. Walker, *Address to believers*, p. 37.
52. Ibid., p. 42.
53. In 1821 Walker remembered that while he was writing his *Expostulatory address* in 1802 he 'was latterly attempting, with a few others, to meet on the first day of the week in Christian fellowship' (Walker to Mr. Howe, 1821, in John Walker, *Essays and correspondence, chiefly on scriptural subjects*, ed. William Burton (2 vols, London, 1838), i, p. 5). But his earlier accounts of his departure never said exactly when the group began to meet.
54. Walker, *Address to believers*, p. 38.
55. [John Walker], *Hints on Christian fellowship: addressed to the serious consideration of all believers, especially in Dublin* (Dublin, 1804), pp 12–13.
56. Unidentified handwriting (probably John Barrett's) on a letter, Gerald Fitzgerald to John Barrett, 14 September 1802 (TCD MS 2373).
57. Walker, *Address to believers*, p. 38.
58. George Carr to Church Missionary Society secretary [Josiah Pratt], 7 Jan. 1808 (Church Missionary Society Archives, G/AC 3/3, no. 84).
59. In July 1802 the editors of a new *Hibernian Evangelical Magazine* included in their prefatory 'Address to the reader' a typical expression of this pan-evangelical stance. 'While we mean to support the cause of truth, we are resolved to exclude controversy from our collection, as it frequently tends to excite animosities and divisions among those who experience the doctrines of free grace; firmly persuaded, that controversy among *friends*, will rather injure, than promote the cause of Christ.' Their magazine would be directed to those who supported the work of the interdenominational General Evangelical Society 'and maintain the fundamental doctrines of the Gospel, as pressed in the Thirty-Nine Articles of

the established Church of England, and the Westminister Confession of Faith; . . . while the names of *sects* and *parties* will be
studiously avoided, and all who love our Lord Jesus Christ, in
sincerity, embraced as members of the same body.' (*Hibernian
Evangelical Magazine*, i (July 1802), pp 2–3). Walker would soon blast
this logic.

60. Walker to Mr. P. N., 4 May 1804, in Walker, *Essays and correspondence*, ii, pp 161–3.
61. For an especially clear statement of the ecclesiologoical implications
of this 'apostolic rule of life', see John Walker, *An essay on the divine
authority of the apostolic traditions; the nature and limits of scriptural
forbearance; and other subjects, connected with the walk of Christian
churches* (Dublin, 1807). Walker also found some ethical implications in the apostolic rule of life, but in a less clear cut and
definite way.
62. Walker, *Address to believers*, pp 18–20.
63. Walker quoted in a letter from an anonymous Bethesda member to
Benjamin Mathias, 24 Nov. 1804, quoted in [Singer], *B. W. Mathias*,
p. 118.
64. George Carr to Church Missionary Society secretary [Josiah Pratt],
7 Jan. 1808. (Church Missionary Society Archives, G/AC 3/3, no.
84).
65. Anonymous Bethesda member to Benjamin Mathias, 24 Nov. 1804,
quoted in [Singer], *B. W. Mathias*, p. 128.
66. Some of the key pamphlets in the 'marked separation' debate were:
William Cooper, *An address to the church assembling in Plunket-street,
Dublin: occasioned by the late debate on separation* (Dublin, 1805); *A
letter to Mr. John Walker, late Fellow of Trinity-College, Dublin, with
notes on his 'Essay,' & c.* (Dublin, 1808); 'A member of the church of
Christ in Sligo', *Marked separation in all religious meetings (a novel
regulation, lately adopted by some of the newly formed churches in this
country,) considered* (Dublin 1805); Thomas Phillips, *A plea for the
necessity of outward purity in the social worship of Christians, intended as
a reply to the objections advanced against it in a late publication
. . .* (Dublin, 1808).
67. The ecclesiology described in this paragraph is obviously similar to
that of the Brethren (or Plymouth Brethren), another church of
Irish origin, which got underway in the 1820s and 1830s. However,
a connection between Walker and the Brethren has yet to be
established. One tantalising hint is that as late as 1877 an English
'Believer in primitive Christianity' and admirer of Walker published in London and *Plymouth* a collection of Walker's essays, and
he had also published a series of tracts by Walker in French,
German, and English (John Walker, *An address to believers of the
gospel of Christ, on that conversation which becometh it; with other essays*
(London and Plymouth, [1877])).

68. Walker, *Essays and correspondence*, i, pp 5–6.
69. Walker, 'A sermon, general fast, 1800', p. 14; anonymous Bethesda member to Benjamin Mathias, 24 Nov. 1804, quoted in [Singer], *B. W. Mathias*, pp 126–7.
70. Walker to Benjamin Mathias, n. d. [ca. 1800], quoted ibid., p. 36; Walker, *Address to believers*, p. 56.
71. Knox to John Jebb, 26 Mar. 1804, in Charles Forster (ed.), *Thirty years' correspondence, between John Jebb, D. D., F.R.S., bishop of Limerick, Ardfert, and Aghadoe, and Alexander Knox, Esq., M.R.I.A.* (2 vols, London, 1834), i, p. 113.
72. [Singer], *B. W. Mathias*, p. 149.
73. Walker, *Address to believers*, pp 37, 53–5. For later pamphlets written in the same spirit, see John Walker, *A letter to a friend in Glasgow, containing brief remarks on Dr. Chalmer's late address to the inhabitants of the parish of Kilmany* (Glasgow, 1816), and John Walker, *A sufficient reply to Mr. Haldane's late strictures upon the author's letters on primitive Christianity* (London, 1821).
74. *Advocate of Revealed Truth, and Inspector of the Religious World* (Jan. and Feb. 1804). See also, Knox to Jebb, 13 Mar. 1804, in Forster, *Correspondence*, i., p. 106.
75. *The Messenger of Truth*, no. 7 (Sept. 1805).
76. John Walker, *Thoughts on baptism: in which the principles of the people calling themselves Baptists are shown to be inconsistent with the nature of the rite, and contradicted by the apostolic practice and precepts* (Dublin, 1805).
77. Walker, *Address to believers*, pp iii, 31; Walker to Benjamin Mathias, 20 Oct. 1804, quoted in [Singer], *B. W. Mathias*, p. 102; Walker, *Essay on the prize-question*, pp iii–iv.
78. Anonymous Bethesda member to Benjamin Mathias, 24 Nov. 1804, quoted in [Singer], *B. W. Mathias*, p. 125.
79. *A letter to Mr. John Walker, late Fellow of Trinity-College, Dublin, with notes on his essay, & c.* (Dublin, 1808), pp 19–20; 'A curate of the Church of England', *The monstrosities of Methodism, being an impartial examination into the pretensions of our modern sectaries, to prophetic inspiration, providential interferences, and spiritual impulse, with a preliminary notice of Dr. Walker's new sect, and the disputing society in Stafford Street* (Dublin, 1808), preface.
80. Maiben C. Motherwell, *A memoir of the late Albert Blest, for many years agent and secretary for Ireland of the London Hibernian Society* (Dublin, London, Edinburgh, 1843), p. 181.
81. Quoted in 'The petition . . . for relief in the matter of oaths', in Walker, *Essays and correspondence*, ii, p. 13.
82. *Monstrosities of Methodism*, p. 2.
83. Jebb to Knox, 21 Dec. 1802, in Forster, *Correspondence*, i, p. 85.

84. For his influence, see [John Walker], *The duty and extent of separation from an unscriptural church . . .* (Dublin, Edinburgh, Glasgow, Aberdeen, 1843), pp 2, 36, and the introduction to John Walker, *An address to believers of the gospel of Christ, on that conversation which becometh it; with other essays* (London and Plymouth, [1877]).
85. Blest to Henry Maturin, 31 May 1817, quoted in Motherwell, *Albert Blest*, p. 168.
86. London Hibernian Society, quoted ibid., pp 191–2.
87. C. H. Crookshank, *History of Methodism in Ireland* (3 vols, Belfast and London, 1885–1886), ii, p. 236.
88. George Carr to Church Missionary Society secretary [Joseph Pratt], 7 Jan. 1808. (Church Missionary Society Archives, G/AC 3/3, no. 84); *Marked separation*, pp 21–2.
89. Maturin to Josiah Pratt; 2 Dec. 1812. (Church Missionary Society Archives, G/AC 3, no. 134).
90. Charles A. Cameron, *History of the Royal College of Surgeons* (Dublin, London, Edinburgh, 1886), p. 486.
91. Peter Roe (ed.), *The evil of separation from the Church of England, considered in a series of letters, addressed chiefly to the Rev. Peter Roe* (Kilkenny, 1815).
92. Canny, 'Why the Reformation failed', p. 450.

Chapter 9, Mooney, pp 188–218.
1. Desmond J. Keenan, *The Catholic Church in nineteenth century Ireland*, (Dublin, 1983).
2. Patrick J. Corish, *The Catholic community in the seventeenth and eighteenth centuries*, (Dublin, 1981).
3. Patrick J. Corish, *The Irish Catholic experience*, (Dublin, 1985).
4. S. J. Connolly, *Priests and people in pre-famine Ireland, 1780–1845*, (Dublin, 1982).
5. Seán Ó Súilleabháin, *Irish folk customs and beliefs*, (Cork, 1967), pp 12–19.
6. Corish, *Catholic community*, p. 5.
7. E. E. Evans, *Irish folk ways*, (London, 1957), p. 153.
8. Barry Cunliffe, *The Celtic world*, (London, 1979) p. 89.
9. Maire MacNeill, *The festival of Lughnasa*, (Oxford, 1962), p. 422.
10. Daphne D. C. Pochin Mould, *Irish pilgrimage*, (Dublin, 1955).
11. John O'Donovan, *Letters of the ordnance survey of Meath*, (Bray, 1928) pp 5, 40, 144 and Ordnance survey name books, Co. Meath, 1835–36 (TS in National Library of Ireland), ii, 177; iii, 182 (henceforth referred to as OSNB).
12. William Wilde, *The beauties of the Boyne and Blackwater*, (Dublin, 1849), p. 152.
13. J. M. Thunder, 'The holy wells of Meath' in *JRSAI*, 17, 1886, p. 657.
14. Records of the Irish Folklore Commission, MS 468, p. 226.

15. OSNB, iii, 44.
16. O'Donovan, *Letters*, p. 43.
17. Thunder, 'Holy wells' and Wilde, *Beauties*, p. 152.
18. 'Memorabilia or remarkable occurrences happening in the family (of Cole–Hamilton) of Kingsfort and its neighbourhood in the years 1810–17' (Meath County Library MS) pp 124, 154.
19. State Paper Office, state of the country papers, 1822, 2366/21 (henceforth referred to as SPO, SOC); State Paper Office, outrage reports, 1836, 22/76 (henceforth referred to as SPO, OR); SPO, OR, 1837, 22/217; SPO, SOC, 1816, 1764/26.
20. Connolly, *Priests and people*, p. 144.
21. Edward Wakefield, *An account of Ireland statistical and political* (London, 1912), p. 76.
22. OSNB, iii, 126.
23. Thunder, 'Holy wells', p. 658.
24. Patrick Logan, *The Holy wells of Ireland* (Buckinghamshire, 1980), pp 33–4.
25. Folklore Commission, MS 890, pp 61–3 and Wilde, *Beauties*, pp 141–2.
26. Logan, *Holy wells*, pp 44–5, 151.
27. Wilde, *Beauties*, p. 183; O'Donovan, *Letters*, p. 29; SPO, OR, 1842 22/102–103; McNeill, *Lughnasa*, p. 259.
28. Wilde, *Beauties*, p. 65.
29. O'Donovan, *Letters*, p. 116.
30. OSNB, iii, p. 26.
31. OSNB, iv, 149.
32. Wilde, *Beauties*, p. 45.
33. O'Donovan, *Letters*, p. 145.
34. Ibid.
35. Wilde, *Beauties*, pp 182–3.
36. Ibid.
37. O'Donovan, *Letters*, p. 104.
38. Ibid, pp 113–115.
39. Wilde, *Beauties*, p. 70.
40. OSNB, ii, 317.
41. OSNB, iv, 24.
42. OSNB, v, 88–90.
43. Folklore Commission, MS 758, pp 102–6.
44. O'Donovan, *Letters*, p. 60.
45. Folklore Commission, MS 924, p. 154.
46. O'Donovan, *Letters*, p. 21.
47. Ibid.
48. Folklore Commission, MS 758, p. 5.
49. Ibid., MS 792, p. 19.
50. Ibid., MS 681, pp 48–59.
51. Ibid, pp 118–119].

52. Ibid., MS 832, p. 382.
53. Ibid., MS 792, p. 17.
54. Rev. J. Hall, *A tour through Ireland 1813* (London, 1813).
55. Folklore Commission, MS 830, p. 8.
56. Ibid., MS 1097, p. 60.
57. Ibid., MS 1097, p. 43.
58. Ibid., MS 792, pp 41–44.
59. Ibid., MS 1097, p. 42.
60. Ibid., MS 959, p. 16.
61. Ibid., MS 1117, p. 263; MS 906, pp 42, 59; MS 792, p. 17.
62. Cole-Hamilton, Memorabilia, p. 96.
63. Wilde, *Beauties*, p. 45.
64. Evans, *Folk ways*, p. 17 and McNeill, *Lughnasa*.
65. O'Donovan, *Letters*, pp 42, 47, 84, 104, 14.
66. OSNB, i, 103; ii, 262, 307.
67. OSNB, iv, 15–16.
68. SPO, OR, 1837, 22/193; 22/205; 22/217
    SPO, OR, 1833, 615; SPO, OR, 1840, 22/14697.
69. See O'Donovan, *Letters*; OSFNB; Wilde, *Beauties*.
70. O'Donovan, *Letters*, pp 103, 63.
71. Ibid., pp 40, 110; OSNB, ii, 306–7.
72. O'Donovan, *Letters*, p. 114.
73. Wilde, *Beauties*, p. 65.
74. Ibid., p. 13.
75. Ibid., p. 70.
76. O'Donovan, *Letters*, p. 216.
77. Wakefield, *Ireland 1812*, p.76.
78. Hall, *Ireland*, ii, 380.
79. O'Donovan, *Letters*, p. 16.
80. Hall, *Ireland*, ii, 380.
81. Hall, *Ireland*, ii, p. 380.
82. O'Donovan, *Letters*, p. 47.
83. Ibid., pp 70, 82, 103, 112.
84. Wilde, *Beauties*, p. 125.
85. Ibid., p. 70.
86. Ibid., p. 65.
87. *Second report of the commissioners of Irish education inquiry*, H.C. 1826–7, (12), xii.
88. Keenan, *The Catholic church*, p. 91.
89. Corish, *Catholic experience*, p. 177.
90. William Wilde, *Irish popular superstitions*, (Dublin, 1852), p. 26.
91. Garret Fitzgerald, 'Estimates for baronies of minimum levels of Irish speaking amongst successive decennial cohorts; 1771–1781 to 1861–1871' in *Royal Irish Academy Proceedings*, ser. C, 84 (1984), p. 127.
92. OSNB, i, 317.

93. Ibid., ii, 178.
94. Ibid., ii, 112.
95. Manuscript census for the baronies of Navan Upper and Lower, P.R.O., 1A–45–8, p. 596.
96. R. Thompson, *Statistical survey of County Meath*, (Dublin, 1802), p. 94.
97. MacNeill, *Lughnasa*, p. 422.
98. 'The visitation books of Bishop Plunkett', in A. Cogan, *The diocese of Meath*, 3 vols, (Dublin, 1864), (henceforth referred to as Cogan, *Meath*).
99. J. Brady, 'Documents concerning the diocese of Meath' in *Archiv. Hib.*, viii (1941), p. 228.
100. *Second report of the commissioners of Irish education inquiry*, H.C. 1826–7, (12), xii, p. 30.
101. SPO, SOC, 1822, 2366/11.
102. SPO, SOC, 1824, 2608/2; 2608/23.
103. SPO, SOC, 1829, H22.
104. SPO, SOC, 1830, H34/4.
105. SPO, OR, 1832, 385; 1835, 22/80; 1836, 22/4, 22/23.
106. SPO, OR, 1839, 22/222.
107. *Reports from Committees, 1831–2, State of Ireland* (677), xvi, p. 285.
108. SPO, OR, 1836, 22/41; 1839, 22/4014; 1841, 22/3327; 1842, 22/4871.
109. SPO, OR, 1836, 22/41.
110. SPO, OR, 1832, 275.
111. Corish, *Catholic community*, p. 6.
112. SPO, OR, 1830, H104/4.
113. *Reports from Committees, 1831–2, State of Ireland*, (677), xvi, pp 282, 322.
114. SPO, OR, 1832, 1160, 38.
115. SPO, OR, 1833, 773.
116. SPO, OR, 1834, 522.
117. SPO, OR, 1834, 247.
118. *The Pilot*, 29 December, 1841.
119. SPO, OR, 1841. 22/19215.
120. SPO, OR, 1841, 22/19115.
121. SPO, OR, 1842, 22/19233.
122. SPO, OR, 1843, 22/5272.
123. SPO, OR, 1843, 22/7727.
124. SPO, OR, 1843, 22/7727.
125. *The Pilot*, 21 August 1840, quoted in Peter Connell, 'Politics of repeal in Meath' (unpublished B.A. thesis, Maynooth 1978), p. 4.
126. SPO, OR, 1834, 122/1–17.
127. SPO, OR, 1839, 2633.
128. W.E.H. Lecky, *Leaders of public opinion in Ireland*, (London, 1871), p. 249.
129. *Reports from Committees, Drunkenness, 1834*, (12) viii, p. 260.

130. *Report of Her Majesty's commissioners of inquiry into the state of the law and practice in respect to the occupation of land in Ireland* H.C. 1845, (605), xix, witness no. 42, p. 266.
131. SPO, OR, 1832, 817; 1842, 22.
132. SPO, OR, 1842, 22/5295.
133. T. P. O'Neill, 'The state, poverty, and distress in Ireland, 1815–45' (unpublished Ph.D. thesis, UCD, 1971), p. 263.
134. Emmet Larkin, 'The devotional revolution in Ireland, 1850–75' in *The American History Review*, 77, 1972, p. 632.
135. Connolly, *Priests and people*, p. 89.

Chapter 10, Griffin, pp 219–34.
1. For works which make apparent the different nature of the Irish police experience see Galen Broeker, *Rural disorder and police reform in Ireland, 1812–36* (London, 1970), J. J. Tobias, 'Police and public in the United Kingdom', in *Journal of Contemporary History*, 7, nos. 1–2 (Jan.–Apr. 1972), pp 201–19, Gregory J. Fulham, 'James Shaw Kennedy and the reformation of the Irish Constabulary, 1836–38' in *Éire–Ireland*, vi, no. 2 (summer 1981), pp 93–106 and Stanley H. Palmer, *Police and protest in England and Ireland 1780–1850* (Cambridge, 1988).
2. Alexis de Tocqueville, *Journeys to England and Ireland*, edited by J. P. Mayer (London, 1957), pp 151, 185, 191n.
3. Broeker, *Rural disorder*, p. 193.
4. *A return of the constabulary police in Ireland, during each of the last three years . . . and, also, a return of the number of Roman Catholics in each county, distinguishing those who have been appointed or promoted, during the same periods*, H.C. 1833, xxxii, p. 415.
5. *Report from the select committee appointed to inquire into the nature, character, extent and tendency of orange lodges, associations or societies in Ireland; with the minutes of evidence, and appendix*, H.C. 1835, xvi, p. 337; *Third report from the select committee appointed to inquire into the nature, character, extent and tendency of orange lodges, associations or societies in Ireland; with the minutes of evidence, appendix, and index*, H.C. 1835, xvii, pp 142–3.
6. Palmer, *Police and protest*, pp 345, 347–8.
7. R. Barry O'Brien, *Thomas Drummond, under-secretary in Ireland 1834–40: life and letters* (London, 1889), p. 340; Palmer, *Police and protest*, p. 362.
8. For the thinking behind the formulation of the constabulary code, see Fulham, 'James Shaw Kennedy'.
9. *Standing rules and regulations for the government and guidance of the constabulary force in Ireland; as approved by his excellency the Earl of Mulgrave, lord lieutenant general and general governor of Ireland* (Dublin, 1837), p. 6.
10. *Times*, 7 May 1836.
11. *Standing rules and regulations, 1837*, p. 30. This regulation was

probably influenced by the rule introduced for the Munster constabulary in the 1820s by Inspector-general Richard Willcocks. It forbade a constable from serving in his native barony: Michael Beames, *Peasants and power: the Whiteboy movements and their control in pre-famine Ireland* (New York, 1983), p. 160.

12. *Standing rules and regulations, 1837*, p. 30.

13. Samuel Carter and Anne Marie Hall, *Ireland, its scenery and character etc.* (3 vols, London, 1841–43), iii, pp 422n, 423n.

14. Samuel M. Hussey, *The reminiscences of an Irish land agent* (London, 1904), p. 128.

15. *Standing rules and regulations for the government and guidance of the Royal Irish Constabulary* (3rd edn, Dublin, 1872), p. 27.

16. Ibid., pp 141–2.

17. Ibid., p. 27. The Dublin Metropolitan Police did not make it compulsory for its men to attend religious services. The closest it came to such a rule was in the 1879 instruction book, where it states 'The police are as much as possible to be encouraged to attend divine service both by precept and example of the superior officers'. See *Instruction book for the government and guidance of the Dublin Metropolitan Police*, (Dublin, 1879), p. 132.

18. Resident Magistrate Goold, of Antrim, wrote to Chief Secretary Lord Naas on 17 Apr. 1852 that the constabulary of that town, who were of mixed religions, were called 'papist police' on account of their stopping illegal orange marches. H. Stanley McClintock, of Randalstown, claimed on 18 Apr. 1852 to Naas that whenever a vacancy occurred in the local police 'the place is always filled up by a papist — which will account for the opposite party feeling sore — as Antrim furnishes many recruits to the force, all Protestants of an excellent class' (N.L.I., Naas correspondence, MS 11019 (7)). In 1878 a prosperous farmer from Carnmoney was clearly upset with the very fact of Catholic policemen patrolling his district, as shown by his complaint of paying a £2.10s. fine after 'a popish vagabond of a policeman' had caught his son poaching on a neighbour's lands. See Brian M. Walker, *Sentry Hill: an Ulster farm and family* (Belfast, 1983), p. 41.

19. HO 184/54, p. 1, Numerical returns of Irish constabulary personnel, 1841–19 (P.R.O., Kew).

20. Ibid., pp 10, 20, 30, 40, 73.

21. Ibid., pp 10, 22, 30.

22. *Daily Express*, 15 Sept. 1859.

23. Sir Henry John Brownrigg, 'Report on the state of Ireland in the year 1863' (N.L.I., MS 915, p. 43).

24. See for example S.C. and A.M. Hall, *Ireland*, iii, p. 423n; Francis B. Head, *Fortnight in Ireland* (London, 1862), pp 46, 104, 106.

25. Lists of men rewarded and disciplined were published by the constabulary mostly at quarterly intervals. Practically all of these

have been lost. There is a partial list extant in the Garda Síochána archives, in a bound volume entitled 'Constabulary of Ireland. Return of men rewarded, dismissed, disrated or fined, 1848–72' from which these examples have been taken.

26. *Times*, 29 July 1871.
27. Charles Stuart Parker, *Life and letters of Sir James Graham, second baronet of Netherby, P.C., G.C.B., 1792–1861* (2 vols, London, 1907), i, p. 365. For a similar opinion from the Longford county inspector, see Donal Kerr, 'Peel and the political involvement of the priests', in *Archivium Hibernicum*, xxxvi (1981), p. 21.
28. Parker, *Sir James Graham*, i, p. 367. Letter dated 5 Sept. 1843.
29. Ibid., p. 412. Letter dated 9 Oct. 1844.
30. HO 184/45. Officers' register, volume 1 (P.R.O., Kew).
31. *Evening Post*, 11 Aug. 1859. County inspectors were divided into three classes.
32. Ibid.
33. HO 184/45, p. 51 (P.R.O., Kew). In 1883 the designation 'sub-inspector' was changed to 'district inspector'.
34. HO 184/54, p. 73 (P.R.O., Kew).
35. *Report of the commissioners appointed by the lords commissioners of her majesty's treasury to enquire into the condition of the civil service in Ireland on the Royal Irish Constabulary: together with the minutes of evidence and appendices*, H.C. 1873, xxii, p. 44.
36. Ibid., p. 36.
37. *Report of the committee of enquiry into the Royal Irish Constabulary; with evidence and appendix*, H.C. 1883, xxxii, p. 197.
38. Ibid., p. 159. The constable did not feel this himself, but was merely passing on the opinions of other R.I.C. men.
39. *Freeman's Journal*, 5 May 1880.
40. Ibid., 14 June 1880.
41. H.C 1883, xxxii, p. 216.
42. Ibid., p. 358
43. HO 184/54, passim (P.R.O., Kew).
44. *Minutes of evidence and appendix to the report of the commissioners of inquiry, 1864, respecting the magisterial and police jurisdiction of the borough of Belfast*, H.C. 1865, xxviii, pp 359–61.
45. Ibid., p. 121.
46. Ibid., pp 216, 359–61.
47. Ibid., pp 59, 208; *Report of the commissioners of inquiry into the origins and character of the riots in Belfast in July and September 1857; together with the minutes of evidence and appendix*, H.C. 1857–8, xlvii, p. 240.
48. The Londonderry local police force, which was also almost entirely made up of Protestants, was abolished in 1870 following allegations of inefficiency and partisanship, in the wake of riots in 1869. See *Report of the commissioners of inquiry, 1869, into the riots and disturbances in the city of Londonderry, with minutes of evidence and appendix*, H.C. 1870, xi, p. 411.

49. *Return of the income and expenditure of the Dublin Metropolitan Police, for the two financial years 1856–57 and 1857–58* (etc.), H.C., 1857–8, xlvii, p. 7.

50. *Minutes of evidence taken before the select committee of the House of Lords appointed to enquire into the state of Ireland since the year 1835, in respect of crime and outrage, which have rendered life and property insecure in that part of the empire, and to report to the House*, H.L. 1839, xi, p. 399.

51. Ibid., pp 434, 435.

52. *Return . . . of D.M.P., for the two financial years 1856–57 and 1857–58*, H.C. 1857–8, xlvii, p. 7.

53. *Select committee . . . to enquire into the state of Ireland since 1835*, H.L. 1839, xi, p. 119.

54. *Freeman's Journal*, 22 July 1851.

55. All these details from ibid., 11 Mar. 1852.

56. Ibid., 9 May 1854

57. Ibid., 19 Nov. 1857.

58. It was owned by a brother of one of the law advisors at Dublin Castle and a cousin of the attorney-general's. See ibid., 30 June 1858.

59. *Daily Express*, 14 Nov. 1857. Such hysteria is clearly, in part, a reaction to the strong Catholic church of the devotional revolution. Significantly the Redemptorist Fathers were also singled out for attack in the article.

60. *Daily Express*, 14 Nov. 1857.

61. Chief secretary's office, registered papers, 1858/11753. A large collection of reports from Dec. 1857 and Jan. 1858 (S.P.O.).

62. *Freeman's Journal*, 13 Mar. 1858.

63. William Monk Gibbon, LLD, to Earl of Eglington, 15 Mar. 1858 (N.L.I., Larcom papers, 7621).

64. See his account of the college riots in N.L.I., Larcom papers, MS 7621.

65. *Hansard*, 3, CL, c.2152.

66. Ibid., CLI, c.1129.

67. Lambert to Naas, 1 July 1858 (N.L.I., Mayo papers, MS 11023 (23)).

68. N.L.I., Larcom papers, MS 7621.

69. B.D. Brady to Naas, 8 July 1858 (N.L.I., Mayo papers, MS 11021 (15)).

70. *Freeman's Journal*, 23, 29, 30 June, 2, 3, 7, 8, 9, 12, 14, 17, 20 July 1858.

71. Ibid., 8, 20 July 1858.

72. Atwell Lake to Naas, 30 Nov. 1858 (N.L.I., Mayo papers, 11023 (27)); Dublin Metropolitan Police: general register, 1838–1924 (Garda Síochána Archives, Phoenix Park depot). The register records the religion of recruits from 29 Oct. 1858 onwards. I would like to place on record my grateful thanks to Sergeant GregoryAllen, Garda Museum archivist, for very kindly allowing me access to the register of D.M.P. recruits.

73. D.M.P. general register (Garda Síochána Archives).
74. Ibid.
75. *Hansard 3*, CLI, c.1130.
76. Although recruits to the Irish Constabulary were liable to be posted to any county, Ulster recruits tended to be posted to Ulster counties.
77. *Report of the commissioners appointed by the lords commissioners of her majesty's treasury to enquire into the condition of the civil service in Ireland on the Dublin Metropolitan Police: together with the minutes of evidence, and appendices*, H.C. 1873, xxii, p. 43; D.M.P. general register (Garda Síochána Archives).
78. D.M.P. general register (Garda Síochána Archives).
79. 'One who knows', *Promotion in the Royal Irish Constabulary* (Dublin, 1906), pp 8–9, 19.
80. *Belfast police commission, 1906 Report* (Dublin, 1907), pp 5–6 (S.P.O., Miscellaneous and official papers, 1876–1922, parcel no. 6).
81. Ibid., p. 7; *Belfast police commission, 1906. Appendix to report of the commissioners. Minutes of evidence, appendices, and index* (Dublin, 1907), p. 6 (S.P.O., Miscellaneous and official papers, 1876–1922, parcel no. 6).
82. *Belfast police commission, 1906. Appendix . . . and index*, p. 115.
83. The best account of this is in John Gray, *City in revolt: James Larkin and the Belfast dock strike of 1907* (Belfast, 1985).
84. N. Chamberlain, 'The recent indiscipline of certain members of the Royal Irish Constabulary in Belfast', 14 Sept. 1907 (S.P.O., C.S.O.R.P., 1908/20333).
85. Ibid.
86. C. Budding, *Die Polizei in Stadt und Land in Grossbritannien und Irland* (Berlin, 1908), p. 192.
87. See for example *Royal Irish Constabulary and Dublin Metropolitan Police, Report of the committee of inquiry, 1914*, H.C. 1914, xliv, p. 2; *Royal Irish Constabulary and Dublin Metropolitan Police. Appendix to the report of the committee of inquiry, 1914. Containing minutes of evidence and appendices*, H.C. 1914–16, xxxii, pp 9, 17–18, 73, 105, 147, 165.
88. *R.I.C. 1914 inquiry. Minutes of evidence etc.*, H.C. 1914, xliv, p. 136.

Chapter 11, Dooley, pp 235–51.
1. *The Northern Standard* (hereafter cited as *N.S.*), 9 Aug. 1913.
2. Speech by Fr. Maguire at a meeting to establish a branch of the Irish National Volunteers in Magheracloone, reported in *Dundalk Democrat* (hereafter cited as *D.D.*), 9 May 1914.
3. *D.D.*, 24 Jan. 1914
4. *N.S.*, 20 July 1912.
5. *N.S.*, 4 Feb. 1911.
6. County Inspector's Confidential Monthly Report, Sept. 1915 (P.R.O., CO904 part 3) (Hereafter cited as C.I.C.M.R.)

7. Dooley, T. 'Protestant politics and society in County Monaghan, 1911–26' (M.A. thesis, Maynooth, 1986), pp 87–130.
8. *D.D.*, 15 May 1920.
9. *N.S.*, 19 Aug. 1921.
10. *N.S.*, 17 July 1920.
11. *D.D.*, 3 Jan. 1920.
12. Dublin Castle statement: 'Breaking Fresh Ground: the work of an Auxiliary Division in a new area', n.d. (P.R.O., CO 904 pt 6).
13. I.G.C.M.R., July 1920.
14. C.I.C.M.R., Oct. 1920.
15. C.I.C.M.R., Feb. 1921.
16. C.I.C.M.R., June 1920.
17. C.I.C.M.R., July 1920.
18. C.I.C.M.R., Feb. 1921.
19. C.I.C.M.R., Mar. 1921.
20. *D.D.*, 2 Apr. 1921.
21. Statement of Dublin Castle, Apr. 1921. (P.R.O., CO 904, pt 5).
22. *N.S.*, 21 Apr. 1921.
23. Ibid.
24. General orders, new series, 1920, no. 12, 9 Nov. 1920 (U.C.D. Archives, Mulcahy Papers, P7/A/45).
25. *D.D.*, 4 Sept. 1920
26. Statement of Vol. James Sullivan, n.d., c.1966 (Monaghan County Museum, Marron Papers).
27. D.C. Rushe to Shane Leslie, 14 Sept. 1920 (N.L.I., Leslie Papers, MS 22, 837).
28. Statement of Vol. Patrick McDonnell, 1967 (M.C.M., Marron Papers).
29. Ibid.
30. *N.S.*, 24 Sept. 1920.
31. Ibid.
32. Letter signed 'Drum Town Guard' to editor of *Northern Standard*, 20 Sept. 1920, *N.S.*, 24 Sept. 1920.
33. *N.S.*, 1 Oct. 1920.
34. Statement of Vol. Brian McMahon, 1966 (M.C.M., Marron Papers).
35. Statement of Vol. Paddy McMahon, 1966 (M.C.M., Marron Papers).
36. Ibid.
37. Report of Mongahan Brig. I.R.A. to G.H.Q. 30 Apr. 1921 (U.C.D. Archives, Collins Papers, P7/A/19).
38. Ibid.
39. Ibid., Feb. 1921 (U.C.D., Collins Papers, P7/A/39).
40. Ibid.
41. Statement of Vol. Seamus McKenna, 1966 (M.C.M., Marron Papers).
42. Report Monaghan Brig. I.R.A. to G.H.Q., Feb. 1921. (U.C.D. Archives, Collins Papers, P7/A/39).

43. Ibid.
44. *Belfast Telegraph*, 23 Mar. 1921.
45. *N.S.*, 8 Apr. 1921.
46. Report of Monaghan Brig. I.R.A. to G.H.Q. March 1921 (U.C.D. Archives, Collins Papers, P7/A/39).
47. Farrell, M., *Northern Ireland: the Orange State* (London, 1976), p. 29.
48. Laffan, Michael, *The Partition of Ireland 1911–25* (Dublin, 1983), p. 76.
49. For example, the Diamond, the commercial heart of Monaghan town, was completely enveloped by Protestant businesses and enterprises. The only newspaper in the county was printed here and it was the Unionist controlled *Northern Standard*. Using the *County Monaghan Year Book and Directory, 1912*, it was found that all the hotels were Protestant owned, as were the vast majority of commercial businesses in the town, with Protestant hardware merchants outnumbering their Catholic counterparts by three to one.
50. *D.D.*, 14 Aug. 1920.
51. *N.S.*, 21 Aug. 1920.
52. Ibid.
53. Ibid., 24 Sept. 1920.
54. Ibid.
55. Report of Head Constable of Castleblaney to District Inspector, 31 Oct. 1921 (P.R.O., CO 904, pt 6).
56. Article entitled 'Sinn Fein Courts' 20 Oct. 1921 (P.R.O., CO 904, part 6).
57. 'Black list' of traders dealing with Belfast firms, 1921. Compiled by O.C. No. 2 Brig. 5th N. Div. I.R.A. (M.C.M., Marron Papers).
58. Report of Monaghan Brig. I.R.A. to G.H.Q. April 1921 (U.C.D. Archives, Collins Papers, P7/A/39).
59. Statement of Dublin Castle 10 May 1921 (P.R.O., CO 904, pt 5).
60. Ibid.
61. Report Monaghan Brig. I.R.A. to G.H.Q. Apr. 1921.
62. Statement of Vol. Seamus McKenna, 1966 (M.C.M., Marron Papers).
63. *N.S.*, 4 Sept. 1920.
64. Letter from D. C. Rushe to Shane Leslie, 14 Sept. 1920 (N.L.I., Leslie Papers, MS 22, 837).
65. *D.D.*, 28 Jan. 1922.
66. *N.S.*, 27 Jan. 1922.
67. *N.S.*, 27 Jan. 1922.
68. Letter from J. Cooper to F. Bourdillon enclosing a list of 2117 Protestants from the Free State living in Fermanagh since 1919, 15 May 1925 (N.L.I., Boundary Commission Papers, Pos 6515).
69. Report on 12 July Celebrations 1923 at Clones by H. McCartan for Executive Council 17 July 1923 (S.P.O., Gov. and Cab. files, S1955).

70. Ibid.
71. M.E. Knight at 12 July celebrations 1923, *N.S.*, 20 July 1923.
72. *N.S.*, 10 July 1925.
73. P. J. Duffy, 'Population and landholding in Co. Monaghan: a study in change and continuity', Ph.D. thesis (U.C.D., 1976), p. 421.

Chapter 12, Candy, 252–77.
1. Published studies of Sheehan include: Francis Boyle, *Canon Sheehan: a sketch of his life and works* (Dublin, 1927); H. J. Heuser, *Canon Sheehan of Doneraile* (Dublin, 1918); M. P. Linehan, *Canon Sheehan: priest, novelist, man of letters* (Dublin, 1952); Kenneth McGowan, *Canon Sheehan of Doneraile* (Dublin, 1963).
2. Linehan, *Sheehan*, p. 14.
3. P. A. Sheehan, 'The moonlight of memory', *Literary Life and other essays* (Dublin, 1921 edn), pp 170–80 (hereafter *Lit. Life*).
4. Ibid., pp 170–3.
5. Ibid., p. 180.
6. Ibid., pp 114–20.
7. Ibid., p. 185.
8. *Maynooth College Kalendarium 1871*, p. 63.
9. *Lit. Life*, pp 114–20.
10. Matthew Russell, S. J., 'Luke Delmege' in *Irish Ecclesiastical Record*, xi (Jan. 1902), p. 212; (hereafter *IER*).
11. Linehan, *Sheehan*, p. 33.
12. Heuser, *Sheehan*, p. 39.
13. T. W. Moody, *Davitt and the Irish Revolution, 1846–82* (Oxford, 1981), p. 267.
14. Boyle, *Sheehan*, p. 25.
15. Sheehan, 'Inaugural address to Literary and Debating Society of Mallow' (Nov. 1880) in Boyle, *Sheehan*, pp 28–9.
16. *IER*, ii (Sept. 1881), pp 521–31.
17. 'A visit to a Dublin Art Gallery', *IER*, ii (Dec. 1881), pp 726–7.
18. 'The effects of emigration on the Irish church' in *IER*, iii (Oct. 1882).
19. Emmet Larkin, 'Economic growth, capital investment, and the Roman Catholic Church in nineteenth-century Ireland' in *The Historical Dimensions of Irish Catholicism* (Washington D.C., 1984).
20. Mrs William O'Brien [Sophie O'Brien] 'Canon Sheehan' in *Studies*, xix (Sept. 1930), pp 492–8.
21. Ibid., p. 492.
22. Heuser, *Sheehan*, p. 14.
23. *My New Curate* (1928 ed.), p. 10; (hereafter *M.N.C.*).
24. M. Russell, S. J. 'Concerning the author of *Luke Delmege*' in *Irish Monthly*, xxx (Dec. 1902), p. 661.
25. *M.N.C.*, p. 187.
26. *The blindness of Dr Gray* (Phoenix edn), p. 35.
27. 'The Irish priesthood and politics' in *Lit. Life*, p. 114.
28. Pádraig Ó Dargáin in *Capuchin Annual* (1952), pp 404–12. The diary was then 'held by a dear friend'. I have not succeeded in tracing it

but the reflections referred to by Ó Dargáin are not in the Commonplace book. (Mc Lysaght Papers, N.L.I. MS 24, 950).

29. *Luke Delmege* (London, 1919 edn), p. 91 (hereafter *L.D.*).
30. *Lit. Life*, p. 9.
31. *Linehan*, p. 55.
32. M. Russell S. J., 'Concerning the author of *Luke Delmege*' in *Irish Monthly*, xxx (Dec. 1902), pp 661–9 cites an article entitled 'Books that influenced me' in the *Weekly Register* to which Sheehan contributed.
33. Canon Sheehan 'Unpublished preface' to *The Triumph of Failure* in *Lit. Life*, p. 64.
34. Ibid., p. 64.
35. Ibid., p. 64.
36. Ibid., p. 65.
37. P.E.K., 'An Interview with Brother Mulhall' in *Capuchin Annual*, xxx (1952), p. 386.
38. M. H. Gaffney, 'Herman J. Heuser and Canon Sheehan' in *IER*, liv (Oct. 1939), p. 370.
39. 'Unpublished preface' in *Lit. Life*, p. 60.
40. 'Unpublished preface' in *Lit. Life*, p. 69.
41. Heuser, p. 199.
42. *Lit. Life*, p. 61
43. J. F. Hogan, '*Luke Delmege*' in *IER*, xi (Feb. 1902), p. 150.
44. Russell letters to Sheehan (McLysaght papers, N.L.I., MS 24, 950).
45. *Lit. Life*, p. 63.
46. Ibid., p. 65.
47. Boyle, *Sheehan*, p. 67.
48. M. J. Phelan, 'Canon Sheehan' in *IER*, ix (Jan. 1917), p. 35.
49. Gaffney, 'Dr Herman J. Heuser and Canon Sheehan' in *IER*, liv (Oct. 1939), pp 367–374, cites a letter of Sheehan's to Heuser dated 1899.
50. Sean O'Faolain, *The Irish* (London, 1947), pp 108–10.
51. George Birmingham, *Irish Men All* (London, 1913), p. 49.
52. Peter Connolly, 'The priest in modern Irish fiction' in *Furrow*, ix (Dec. 1958), p. 793.
53. Ibid., p. 793.
54. Heuser, loc. cit. p. 141.
55. *L.D.*, p. 15.
56. Ibid., p. 19.
57. J. F. Hogan, op. cit., p. 152.
58. Review of *Under the Cedars and the Stars* (probably by Matthew Russell) in *Irish Monthly*, xxi (Mar. 1903), p. 702.
59. Heuser, loc. cit., p. 237.
60. Barry was the uncle of M. P. Linehan, author of a biography of Canon Sheehan (see note 1 above).
61. Heuser, loc. cit. p. 191.
62. Preface to Sheehan, *Early essays and lectures* (London, 1906).

63. *M.N.C.* pp 50–51.
64. *Lisheen, or the test of spirits,* (Phoenix edn), p. 6; (hereafter *Lisheen*).
65. J. F. Hogan, *IER*, xxi (Feb. 1907), pp 640–2.
66. *Intellectuals* (London, 1921 edn), p. 228.
67. Gaffney, 'Dr Herman J. Heuser and Canon Sheehan', p. 371.
68. Rev. S. Rigby, 'Jottings on Canon Sheehan' in *IER*, lxxviii (Nov. 1952), pp 321–9.
69. Heuser, op. cit., p. 189, citing letter from Sheehan (13 June 1904).
70. Ibid., p. 190.
71. Fr Michael, 'Canon Sheehan's Letters to Heuser and Russell' in *Capuchin Annual 1942*, p. 276.
72. *IER*, I (Feb. 1913), pp 220–2.
73. *Lit. Life*, p. 173.
74. *The graves of Kilmorna*, p. 258.
75. *Lit. Life*, p. 189.
76. *Cork Free Press.*
77. Mrs William O'Brien, 'My earliest Irish friends' (1949), pp 99–104.
78. *Cork Free Press*, Oct. 1913.
79. *Triumph of failure* (London, 1899; reprint, Dublin 1906), p. 17.
80. D. C. Kelleher, 'Canon Sheehan philosopher and friend' in *Capuchin Annual* (1952), pp 350–52.
81. Ibid.
82. Kenneth McGowan in *Capuchin Annual, 1952.*
83. Ibid.
84. John J. Morgan, 'Canon Sheehan: a memory and an appreciation' in *Irish Monthly*, xlii (Jan. 1914), pp 1–12.
85. Kenneth McGowan in *Capuchin Annual* (1952).
86. McGowan, *Sheehan.*
87. *The Blindness of Dr Gray*, (Phoenix edn), p. 316.
88. Michael J. Phelan, 'Canon Sheehan' in *IER*, lx, (Jan. 1917), p. 43.
89. Gaffney, op. cit., p. 371.
90. Heuser, op. cit., p. 291.
91. Ó Dargáin in *Capuchin Annual*, 1952, p. 406.
92. *Cork Examiner*, 9 Oct. 1913; *Cork Free Press*, 9 Oct. 1913.
93. Ibid.
94. Peter Connolly, 'The priest in modern Irish fiction' in *Furrow*, ix (Dec. 1958), pp 782–97.
95. For example: Patrick O'Farrell, *Ireland's English question: Ireland and England since 1800* (London, 1975), Chapter 10; Tom Garvin, 'Priests and patriots: Irish separatism and fear of the modern, 1890–1914' in *Irish Historical Studies*, xxv (May 1986), pp 67–81,; Jeremiah Lovett, 'Vision and technique in the novels of P. A. Canon Sheehan' (M.A. thesis, Maynooth, 1974).
96. *M.N.C.* (Talbot Press edn 1958), pp 79–80.
97. Benedict Kiely, 'Canon Sheehan, the reluctant novelist' in *Irish Writing*, xxxvii (Autumn 1957), pp 35–45.

Index